Society, Spirituality, and the Sacred

Society, Spirituality, and the Sacred

A SOCIAL SCIENTIFIC INTRODUCTION

by Don Swenson

broadview
press

CANADIAN CATALOGUING IN PUBLICATION DATA

Main entry under title:

Society, sprirituality, and the sacred: a social scientific introduction

ISBN 1-55111-242-6

1. Religion and sociology.   2. Psychology and religion.
I. Title.

BL60.S94 1999   306.6   C99-930707-X

BROADVIEW PRESS, LTD.
is an independent, international publishing house, incorporated in 1985.

North America
Post Office Box 1243, Peterborough, Ontario, Canada K9J 7H5
3576 California Road, Orchard Park, New York, USA 14127
TEL (705) 743-8990; FAX (705) 743-8353; E-MAIL 75322.44@compuserve.com

United Kingdom and Europe
Turpin Distribution Services, Ltd., Blackhorse Rd.,
Letchworth, Hertfordshire, SG6 1HN
TEL (1462) 672555; FAX (1462) 480947; E-MAIL turpin@rsc.org

Australia
St. Clair Press, Post Office Box 287, Rozelle, NSW 2039
TEL (612) 818-1942; FAX (612) 418-1923

www.broadviewpress.com

Canadä

Broadview Press gratefully acknowledges the support of the Ministry of Canadian Heritage through the Book Publishing Industry Development Program.

Cover design by Marc Bélanger and Zack Taylor, Black Eye Design.
Typeset by Zack Taylor, Black Eye Design.

Printed in Canada

10 9 8 7 6 5 4 3 2 1

Contents

ACKNOWLEDGEMENTS

This book has been a long time in creation. I first thought of the importance of the concept of "the sacred" as being central to the social scientific study of religion twenty-five years ago when I taught at St. Thomas Moore College in Saskatoon, Saskatchewan. Since then, the individuals who have helped me in this project are fellow academics: Bill Zwerman, John Thompson, David Klein, and Keith Brownsey. Staff of Broadview Press in general and Michael Harrison in particular have walked with me through the last stages of the book. Angela, who has stood by me for the last six years, has encouraged me significantly in many ways.

This book is dedicated to my wife, Angela Swenson, and our common children: Niall O'Dwyer; Tim and Stephanie Pearce with their son, Michael; Catherine; Rachel, with her son Brennan; David; Jared; and Joel Swenson.

PART ONE

World Views, Social Boundaries, Religious Experiences and Institutions

CHAPTER ONE

Introduction: Perspectives on Social Science and Theory

Religion and politics, according to common lore, are two topics of conversation to be assiduously avoided if harmony is to prevail in social gatherings. Allegedly, people cling to beliefs and opinions in both areas that often defy rational discussion. A Jewish man's testimony at a family gathering that he has "found Jesus" or a well-liked businesswoman's announcement at a promotion meeting that she is leaving her job to join a religious commune would be certain to produce stress at either function. Comments about the Pope might offend some Catholics, analyses of religious television might offend some evangelicals, and discussing homosexual ministers might annoy some in historic churches. The best way to reduce tension is to maintain a polite silence about religious tenets in secular gatherings. Religion, etiquette decrees, is deemed to be a private matter best kept to oneself.

Yet there is a bit of the voyeur in each of us. We are curious about the religious beliefs and behaviour of others, particularly if we sense they are different from our own. Despite the taboo on discussing religious issues in religiously mixed company, many of us want to learn more about how and why others believe as they do. The perspective of social science taken in this text allows us to approach the study of religion in a civil manner; but, as we shall see, tensions between divergent perspectives still remain. Social science, I believe, can be used as a medium of civil discourse to bridge understanding among divergent beliefs about religion.

It is vital to recognize that in engaging in a social scientific study of religion, we become vulnerable to enlisting rationalistic perspectives that tend to erode or to eliminate the awe, the wonder, the reverence, the veneration, the fascination of the subject of religion. The phenomenological and comparative religion scholar van der Leeuw (1938:23) points out that the object of religious experience — and I would add, the object of the social scientific research of religion — is represented with adjectives such as powerful, influential, strong, majestic, and plenteous. It is important that this object should never be lost sight of as we proceed to study religion in a social scientific way.

The approach that I take in the text, by relying on the concept of the *numen* or the *sacred* as the heart of religion (outlined in Chapter Four), acknowledges the fact that the sacred is mysterious and cannot be wholly understood, yet can, at least in part, be subjected to social scientific scrutiny so that a student of religion matures in comprehending the manifested effects of the sacred.

PERSPECTIVES ON RELIGION: COMMON WORLD VIEWS, HUMANITIES, AND SOCIAL SCIENCE

Religion can be viewed from different perspectives, with social science being but one point of view, albeit the most important one for this text. Two other approaches that I would like to compare are the *common world view* which people use but often do not reflect upon, and more systematized and formal *humanistic world views*. Common world views are less formal than either the social scientific or humanistic approaches. They represent a fundamental level of consciousness that includes all our perceptions and determines how we actually experience "reality." They are "taken-for-granted" perspectives that are generally not seriously questioned. On the most basic level, most of us do not question that time proceeds in one direction only (we cannot go back in time) or that the sun (not the moon) reigns over our days. Common world views are "common sense" realities, the *essence* of which is proverbial lore or folk wisdom. They are less dependent on formal reasoning and scientific analysis than are the other two major perspectives. Religious beliefs are clearly an important part of these kinds of world view, particularly those of pre-modern societies. It is taken for granted in folk societies that the deities bring rain, ensure good health, promote fertility, and provide in a myriad of other ways for human needs.

As societies become more modern, their world views become increasingly more rational. People demand the proof of rational arguments and scientific evidence. Theological explanations give way to scientific ones. Meteorologists explain and attempt to alter weather patterns; medical researchers explore the causes of and cures for diseases; and social biogeneticists may use their technical knowledge to change social demographics. In the minds of many modern men and women, God the creator is replaced with science as a creative process with powers to alter the world.

Not surprisingly, tension often develops between beliefs anchored in a folk culture and those produced by the forces of modernity. Religion and science coexist but as increasingly unequal partners. Some individuals tend to align more with one perspective (often uncritically) than with the other.

An uncritical acceptance of a particular religious world view may be reflected in the once-popular bumper sticker: "The Bible says it; I believe it; that settles it." Such an acceptance of unproven and taken-for-granted assumptions is not limited, however, to Christian fundamentalists. Religious skeptics may demonstrate a similar naivete in asserting that belief in a deity is a useless artifact of unenlightened earlier periods in the history of humankind.

The reader may wish to reflect on the way different points of view may function in his or her thinking about religion by using the simple model for the social construction of religious reality found in Table 1.1. Table 1.1 incorporates multiple perspectives in its illustration of the construction of religious reality. It assumes the influence of what the philosopher Immanuel Kant (1724-1804) referred to as *noumena*, a world that is beyond the reach of scientific proof and empirical observation. This world includes spirits, deities, and the human soul, none of which, according to Kant, can be approached through science or defended by reason (Charon 1992). *Noumena* contrasts with what Kant called *phenomena*, the world of physical and material objects. Natural and human-made artifacts surround us and are readily observable. In contrast to *noumena*, the world of *phenomena* is open to scientific and rational investigation.

PERSPECTIVES ON RELIGION

COMMON WORLD VIEWS	HUMANISTIC WORLD VIEWS
Taken-for-granted; common sense	SOCIAL SCIENCE (Psychology, sociology, anthropology, and economics)
	HUMANITIES (theology, philosophy, history, religious studies, and comparative religious studies)

TABLE 1.1

Social Science and the Noumena-Phenomena Dilemma

Caution must be taken neither to reduce *noumena* to *phenomena* when discussing religion nor to assume a pneumatological approach that ignores material and social reality. Social scientists are prone to one horn of the dilemma that assumes that religion does not possess a "really real" quality (Segel 1989). Often they inadvertently "explain away" religion by reducing spiritual noumena to material causes (phenomena). Early examples can be found in the classic works of sociologist Emile Durkheim and psychologist Sigmund Freud. For Durkheim (1915), God was nothing more than society made divine; i.e., when people worshipped God or gods, they in fact were paying homage to their social order. For Freud (1914), religion was a misguided "illusion" — simply "fulfillment of the oldest, strongest and most urgent wishes of mankind."

Social scientists, whose approach demands proof in the form of empirical evidence, tend to accept uncritically a Durkheimian or Freudian tradition which reduces the spiritual to social or psychological forces. Although there is much merit in stressing empirical factors over spiritual ones, there is also an inherent danger. Social scientists correctly emphasize that issues such as the existence of God or the truth or falsity of a particular religious tenet (since neither can be empirically proven) are outside the realm of social science. The focus of study, insist social scientists, must be on the investigation of the origin and development of religion and particularly on religion's effects upon the individual and society. For example, social science can neither prove nor disprove the existence of God, but it can determine whether a belief in God has some effect on the lives of people. The danger, as already noted, is one of reducing spiritual phenomena totally to empirical observations. In the process of study, the religious view that motivates religious actors often fades from analysis. On the other hand, social science cannot accept uncritically descriptions of the pneumatic,[1] offered by any particular religion.

Although we can separate noumena and phenomena for heuristic purposes, the two forms of reality cannot be totally divorced from one another when studying human beings. Kant (1929) contended that people are both phenomena (thus subject to laws of nature and open to scientific investigation) and noumena (in that men and women are at least partially "free" agents whose behaviour cannot be reduced to scientific laws). A course in the social science of religion may be said to employ the methods used to investigate phenomena for the study of noumena (uniquely human experience). Such a paradoxical approach has social scientists walking a tightrope between the total reduction of religion to the laws of science on the one hand, and the abandonment of a scientific study of seemingly unapproachable religious issues on the other. The challenge facing social science is to balance its investigation of religion between the horns of the noumena-phenomena dilemma, that is, by using the scientific method to study a topic which in its final essence may be beyond the realm of science.

16

_____

1   Of or pertaining to the spirit.

Insights from "Common Sense" and Caveats from Humanism

As discussed above, common world views are "common sense" realities, the essence of which is found in the proverbial lore or folk wisdom of pre-modern societies. In folk societies world views are less dependent on formal reasoning and scientific analysis than are the other two major perspectives. In modern western societies, assumptions about the superiority of formal reasoning and the supremacy of scientific thought are untested (and untestable) assumptions which are built into our cultural world views. This may be illustrated in the anthropomorphism of science and technology, giving them nearly human qualities. Phrases like "scientific evidence demonstrates," "computers tell," and "medical science shows" all can be used to demonstrate the importance of science and technology in constructing the modern world view.

As societies become more modern, their world views tend to become increasingly more rational and materialistic. Demands are made for both logical proof and scientific evidence, as simple explanations give way to more complex ones.[2] Meteorologists, physicists, biologists, and chemists have all brought into question the way people of pre-modern societies understood the natural world. In the minds of many modern men and women, a personal creator is often replaced with impersonal science in any thought about the material world.

In pluralistic modern societies, taken-for-granted realities can cause tensions among different groups. The world views of an evangelical Christian believer and those of an agnostic humanist, for example, may conflict on unexamined assumptions each makes about the nature of person and society, leading to overt conflict over tangible issues such as school prayer, homosexuality, abortion rights, and the teaching of evolution. Underlying the tension are unexamined assumptions causing each side to lament about the other: "why can't they think like we do?" All of us bring assumptions, including whether we accept or do not accept some religious reality, to our personal world view — assumptions that in turn will affect our interpretations of other more formal fields of study.

Thus there are inevitable tensions between common world views and the empirical rationality of social science. One tension may be illustrated by a

---

2   Some social philosophers have questioned the pre-eminent place given to science as a knowledge system. Michael Polanyi (1949), for example, asserted that both science and religion are in fact faith systems: science is simply the one which western society tends to regard as superior. Without going into a long discussion of the merits of Polanyi's argument, I wish simply to emphasize that there are different ways of knowing, with science being but one vantage point.

common posture found among students who enrol for a sociology or psychology of religion course. Each student brings his or her taken-for-granted reality to the learning process (be it skepticism or faith) and may find this common-sense reality disturbed by the scientific approach. Sometimes students enrol in a course with hopes of resolving a personal religious quest or in strengthening a particular faith position. Studying religion from a social scientific perspective is no more able to provide answers to faith questions than family sociology is able to teach students how to fall in love or medical sociology is able to provide a secret key to health. What social science can do is to offer insights that are helpful in examining issues for those who are interested in understanding religion — whether they are believers or non-believers.

Differences among commonly held, often unexamined ways of knowing are thus further compounded by differing assumptions underlying more formal ways of studying religion. The humanistic disciplines, the social sciences, and theological studies all rest on different assumptions that guide the respective disciplines. There can be major disagreements, for example, between scholars who approach the study of religion from a humanistic perspective and those who employ a social scientific perspective. Humanistic scholars include many historians, philosophers, theologians, and others in the field of religious studies. At the base of the tension is an unprovable assumption about the nature of religion. Religious studies, for example, an inclusive discipline that utilizes history, theology, and philosophy, tends to assume that there is a genuine substance to religion — in other words, religion is a unique reality that cannot be reduced to something else. In some ways, those in religious studies do a better job of straddling the noumena-phenomena dilemma than do many social scientists. By limiting their work to descriptions rather than explanations, humanistic scholars are sometimes less prone to distort their subject matter.

Having acknowledged some of the weaknesses and limitations of social science, I wish to emphasize that it is an invaluable tool for a better understanding of religion. It is important to remember, however, that the social sciences represent a perspective that makes certain assumptions, namely, that religion can be studied empirically and that this empirical evidence can be scrutinized according to scientific canons. The reader must keep in mind that this is not the only way of approaching religion — nor should it be claimed as the "best" way to describe religious phenomena. What social scientific approaches do is to provide different lenses through which religion may be viewed.

| SOCIAL SCIENTIFIC APPROACHES IN THIS TEXT

This text represents a social scientific introduction to the study of religion, but I recognize that this perspective often has its own limitations. As I have already suggested, often the social scientific study of religion proceeds as if "religion is not really real." This liability is coupled with a failure to recognize that there can be no thing as a "presupposition-less science." In the words of sociologist William Swatos (1987:ix): "All human life depends upon trust or faith, upon statements 'taken-for-true,' an important criterion for which is experience. Differences in experiences lead us to accept different criteria for 'truth'...." In other words, we bring our world views with us when we approach the more formal analysis of religion. (Students may wish to reflect on their personal world views on the spiritual or non-material world and how these views may affect their approaches to a formal study of religion.)

Although I am a sociologist, I am convinced that an interdisciplinary social scientific perspective provides an invaluable key to understanding religious behaviour. In other words, a systematic study needs to be informed not only by research findings from sociology but also by related disciplines, including psychology, social psychology, anthropology, history, political science, and economics.

19

THE SACRED AND RELIGION

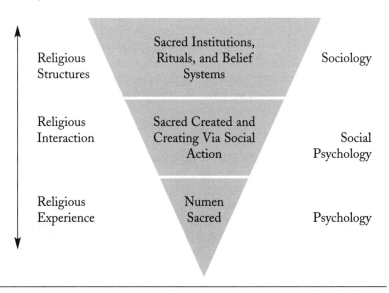

Religious Structures	Sacred Institutions, Rituals, and Belief Systems	Sociology
Religious Interaction	Sacred Created and Creating Via Social Action	Social Psychology
Religious Experience	Numen Sacred	Psychology

FIGURE I.I

The model I propose to guide my presentation is illustrated in Figure 1.1. It begins with *numen* or the *sacred* — in Durkheimian terms "that which is set apart and forbidden." The essence of the sacred cannot in its purest form be measured by science. Science cannot determine whether God exists, whether human beings in fact have souls, or whether the spirit world communicates with humans. One can assume, however, that the sacred, whether it be expressed in terms of God or gods, impersonal spiritual forces, or material things that are rendered a set-apart status, can have an impact on individuals. Experiences of the sacred have been an important part of common world views, and they should be included in social scientific investigations.

In Figure 1.1 we see that some experience of the sacred can touch individuals, who in turn collectively create a common world view. This "collective conscience" (to use a Durkheimian phrase) acts back on individuals living in a particular culture. Modern men and women also create more formal ways of knowing, represented by social science and humanistic scholarship. Individuals trained in the humanities have produced philosophies, theologies, and histories of religion. Other individuals oriented toward empirical study have produced social sciences of religion, including psychology, sociology, and anthropology. These approaches to knowledge also act back on the larger society.

One of the most inclusive and fruitful approaches to the social scientific study of religion has merged sociology and psychology, allowing for a study of how religious reality is socially constructed by individuals. Using a social psychological approach that describes a social construction of reality, one can trace the impact that religious experiences may have in the origin and maintenance of religious social structures. Although social scientists cannot determine the authenticity or inauthenticity of a person's encounter with the sacred, many scholars have regarded such experiences as the foundation of institutional religion. Founders of major religions have reportedly encountered the sacred in some real and personal way. Their experiences (and those of their immediate disciples) have been at the heart of religious ideologies and rituals. Psychologists have sought to describe such experiences and to interpret them within the framework of social science. They are often joined by other social scientists, especially anthropologists and sociologists, who seek to combine the psychological approach with their own focus on religious institutions.

Religious experiences are not strictly personal in nature; they also have a social dimension. Personal experiences of the sacred may be regarded as the matter from which cultural and institutional forms of religion originate and are renewed. In other words, the institutional elements of religion are often by-products of religious experiences. Put yet another way, human beings, with varying experiences of the sacred, collectively create their social world. This creative enterprise takes form in religious institutions, rituals, and belief systems, as diagrammed in Figure 1.1. The work of social psychologists (whose mother disciplines represent psychology, sociology, and anthropology) focuses on the process through which religious reality is socially constructed. These scholars seek to understand the two-way link between the individual and religious institutions. Some social psychologists emphasize the role that social actors play in creating the religious order; others take a somewhat broader perspective to study the impact the institutionalized product has upon individuals.

The dialectical relationship between the individual and society may be best described by the phenomenological sociologist Peter Berger (1963). He sums it up in three succinct statements: society is a human product; society is an objective reality; and human beings are social products. In other words, men and women throughout time have created the social world in which they live. I would suggest further that religious reality has come about, at least in part, as a result of encounters of human beings with the sacred. Such encounters or religious experiences are an important part of any study of religion. Religious experiences are the catalysts that have led to the development of dogma, ritual, and religious institutions that are part of the real social world. Institutional religion, in turn, acts back on people to socialize them into its norms and values.

There are thus two approaches to social psychology. One approach focuses on how human beings perceive and encounter the sacred as they "create" religious reality. The other approach focuses on how individuals are "shaped by" the religion they and their ancestors have fashioned. One perspective sees human beings as active creators of religion; the other regards people as passive products of institutional forces. A dialectical strategy (such as the one taken by Peter Berger) acknowledges that we are both products of and makers of our social world.

Berger's model readily moves out of the realm of social psychology into sociological studies of religious organizations and anthropological studies of religious cultures. Here the descriptions move away from the individual or micro-level to the organizational or macro-level analysis. The processes by which the social institutions are shaped as well as the processes by which human beings are formed by them are left behind to focus on the institutions themselves. From Figure 1.1 it may be seen that there is an interdependence of religious and non-religious institutions in contemporary society. (Students may consider the controversy in topics such as school prayer, tax exemptions for religious organizations or the political campaigns of conservative religious groups to illustrate such interdependence.) The research questions guided by a more macro-level approach to religion in society centre on the study of religious institutions and the interplay between religious and secular institutions in contemporary society. Here sociologists and anthropologists are often joined by political scientists, social historians, and economists in researching macro-level religious issues.

Peter Berger's own work in the sociology of religion tends to focus on a more macro-level of social reality. Although he acknowledges that men and women help to create the social world in which they live, his scholarship often shifts to larger questions about the modern world. In the tradition of Max Weber, Berger has directed much of his attention to the tension that exists between religion and the modern secular world. Although Berger's theoretical model seems to transcend the micro-macro gap in social science, his work in the sociology of religion has tended toward the macro tradition that is indebted to social history.

In summarizing the different ways we can study religion, we might consider how we link the sacred with different dimensions of our humanity and the social sciences. When we examine the sacred *within* the person, psychology comes to mind; with the sacred *between* persons, social psychology; and, lastly, the sacred *among* people or a characteristic of the social group, sociology and anthropology.

The more objective social facts inherent in society may be illustrated by the canons of science put forth to guide modern scholars. Science is an institution in the modern world, and it has its own norms and values to which its practitioners must adhere. At the same time, social scientists (including textbook writers) are human agents with values and norms reflecting personal world views. Scientific canons dictate that these norms must be bracketed (held in one's consciousness but not allowing them to bias or predefine social reality) when "doing" science, but such a compartmentalization is never complete. Regardless of how scholars strive to separate personal value positions from factual observations, personal bias is subtly but inevitably interwoven with the presentation of scientific facts (Weber 1978; Giddens 1977).

WORLD VIEW:
AN AUTOBIOGRAPHICAL ACCOUNT

Despite all attempts to be "objective," the author of this text comes with certain assumptions and a "common world view" reality that in some ways shape the presentation. This unintentional blending of formal and informal perspectives is not to be interpreted as a weakness for which apologies must be offered. Even social scientific perspectives which claim "objectivity" rest on unverified assumptions about the nature of person (are men and women free actors or determined by circumstances?) and about the nature of society (is it based on consensus among humans or conflict of interests?). Any social scientist who studies religion has, within his or her toolbox, not only different theories and research skills but also "common sense" knowledge that comes from a personal spiritual odyssey. I am no exception. For this reason I feel it is important to briefly sketch my religious journey. I am joined in this impression with another sociologist of religion, David Lyon, of Queen's University, who writes: "If, as has been argued, religious background influences theory formation and modes of analysis, then clear acknowledgment of faith orientation would make for more honest, open scholarship" (1996:26).

Having been raised in a small, traditional village in Alberta, Canada, and having attended a Catholic separate school, I readily embraced the changes brought into the Church by the Second Vatican Council (1962-1965). I have always been and remain a practising Roman Catholic. I enrolled in a seminary where I received degrees in philosophy and theology. I was ordained a Catholic priest and served briefly as a missionary in Guyana and the Philippines. Upon my return from the Philippines I began to study sociology — an endeavour I continued after leaving the active priesthood, first as a student and then as a college instructor. Eventually I left the academy to serve as a lay administrator of a Catholic parish, a position I held for five years. In the mid-1980s I returned to graduate school to complete my Ph.D. and now teach in a two-year college in Calgary.

My personal history represents resolutions of tensions between my own faith commitment and my academic scholarship. For a time, I sought to integrate my academic training as a sociologist with parish ministry, reflecting a tension between the so-called "ivory tower" of research and the "real world" of applying sociological principles. As someone who has been actively involved in the charismatic movement in the Roman Catholic Church, I have endeavoured to balance both my experiential faith and my theological training with the sociological approach. As a professional social scientist, I continue to seek harmony between the differing assumptions offered by theology, religious studies, and sociology, exploring possibilities of a more holistic and integrated approach among these seemingly irreconcilable perspectives. My life-long commitment to Catholicism, training in theology, experiences with the charismatic renewal (including living in covenant communities), and, currently, being part of the construction of Small Church Communities in a local parish have inevitably coloured my approach to the sociology of religion.

Although I attempt to bracket our respective world views in doing sociology, I also know that this text will (despite my best efforts) bear the imprint of its author. I feel the reader has the right to know something about my background — a background containing experiences which simultaneously provide greater insight into some arenas of religion but which may limit us in other ways.

| OVERVIEW OF THE TEXT

Society, Spirituality, and the Sacred: A Social Scientific Introduction reflects my sensitivity to remaining true to the canons of scientific scholarship without compromising the essence of religion. It is the German sociologist Max Weber's (1864-1920) theories on religion (together with the contemporary theorists who have built on Weber) that have provided the basic framework for much of this book. Weber's distinctive theoretical approach anchors sociology in the study of the mutual orientation of social actors and on "understandable" motives of their actions. Such a focus eschews the temptation to reduce sociology to economic, political or psychological factors that are detached from the "meaning" religion has for social actors.

The title of the text is illustrative of the contents. The term *society* indicates the focus on the sociology and anthropology of religion. *Spirituality* refers to the subjective aspect of religion that is studied by psychology. The concept of the *sacred* invites us into scholarship emerging from the comparative and historical study of religion and religious studies.

This text is divided into three major parts. The first part focuses on the creation and maintenance of religious world views and on how boundaries are established to differentiate religious perspectives from other world views. These two chapters will introduce the reader to some of the significant differences and similarities among religions, both among major world religions and diverse religious traditions found in North America. Any such comparative endeavour quickly uncovers tensions that exist between religions as well as within religious traditions. One of the most commonly recognized points of tension is the clash between the pre-modern world, for which religion was a major source of legitimation, and the modern world, in which religion has lost its position of pre-eminence to science.

Tension exists not only between religion and other potentially competitive world views but also within the very process of creating and maintaining religious reality. One example of such tension may be found on the individual level where there is both an attraction to the sacred and a simultaneous self-distancing from the holy. This will be the focus of Chapter Four, with an extension to look more closely at spirituality through psychological lenses.

Chapter Five concludes Part One with an explanation of the relationship between religious experience and institutions. This relationship is framed by Thomas O'Dea in the form of the dilemmas of the institutionalization of religion. It is O'Dea's theses that serve as the structure for the second section of the text.

Chapter Six focuses on the dilemma of "mixed motivation," which struggles to maintain the single-mindedness of the original vision. Discussions of religious leadership are outlined in this chapter. Chapter Seven analyzes the importance of viable symbols in maintaining a religious world view, covering significant theoretical and empirical findings on religious rituals. The need for an administrative order often threatens the free-flow of charisma. Chapter Eight discusses the rise of different types of religious organizations and church government. The "dilemma of delimitation" is the framework used to consider the function of ethos within religious organizations. This dilemma is used to frame Chapter Nine. The final chapter of this section focuses on the "dilemma of power" and the twin functions of religion as a source of social support as well as an agent of social control. This chapter outlines the relationship between religion and politics. O'Dea's dilemmas serve as the sociological form into which research findings on religion are poured, thus blending theory with empirical evidence. Through the constant interplay of theory and research, the reader is provided with a social scientific framework to organize the diverse and colourful pieces of the religious mosaic.

The discussion of O'Dea's dilemmas of institutionalization begins with a micro-analysis, but it quickly moves toward a more macro-level presentation. Although its focus is on religion as a social institution, no social institution exists in isolation. Religion is but one component of a larger societal system that includes other institutions such as economics, the family, the polity, medicine, and education. There is a dialectical relationship between religion and the larger society, with religion being impacted by other major institutions and other institutions serving to shape religion. Part Three takes an inter-institutional approach by considering the linkages between religion and the family, economy and stratification, and finally between religion and culture. The text concludes with a discussion of secularization, the postmodern world, and the New Age Movement that has recently appeared in the American and Canadian religious mosaic.

| THE THEORETICAL APPROACH TO THE TEXT

Before the theoretical approach to this text is presented, it is important to the reader that she or he is aware that there are many theoretical approaches to the study of religion. For example, the classical theorists who inform much of the social scientific study of religion include Karl Marx, Emile Durkheim, Max Weber, Georg Simmel, and Sigmund Freud. Marx's theory of religion will be presented when religion and economy are linked in Chapter Twelve, and Durkheim's important insights will be presented when looking at societal boundaries in Chapter Three, in the study of ritual (Chapter Seven), and ethos (Chapter Nine). Both Simmel and Freud are important historically to the study of religion, but their heritage is not used frequently in current research. As already indicated, Max Weber's work is central to the theoretical basis of this text.

More current theoretical perspectives include structural functionalism, conflict theory, symbolic interactionism, phenomenology,[3] and rational choice theory. Of all of these current perspectives, the one that has received most attention and has informed a wide range of research is the rational choice theory. Because of its vitality and importance, I shall outline this perspective first.

A Rational Choice Theory of Religion

The sociological theorists Wallace and Wolf (1995) note that the theory assumes that people are rational and that they base their decisions on actions that will yield the most effective results. Its roots go back to nineteenth-century utilitarian philosophy and classical economics. Utilitarians argued that people are "self-interested" and that morality was measured on the amount of utility it gave to individuals. Adam Smith added that the national economy was a result of individuals' numerous economic choices.

The theory has further roots in the work of the anthropologist Malinowski, behaviourist psychology, and the theory of games. It is best represented, however, by the sociologists George Homans, Peter Blau, and James Coleman. All three have been significant contributors not only to the theory but also to sociology in general. Using the model, they look at a wide range of sociological topics and issues: power, aggression, the need for approval, social conformity, the creation of social norms, trust, legitimacy, collective action, and consequences of choice. I will attempt to outline how sociologists of religion have used assumptions and basic tenets of the theory in explaining religion.

RELIGION AS A REWARD AND A COMPENSATOR

Stark and Bainbridge (1985) are among the first sociologists of religion to introduce a rational choice model into the social scientific interpretation of religion. They assume that religious behaviour is similar to all other kinds

---

3 Bruce (1995b:1-354) edited an extensive outline of theory and religion, and Chafant, Beckley and Palmer (1994:30-60) offer a short summary of current perspectives other than the rational choice theory.

of social action: that the individual chooses means to achieve a goal that maximizes returns. Religious behaviour results in a different kind of reward that they call a "compensator." They write: "A compensator is the belief that a reward will be obtained in the distant future or in some other context which cannot be immediately verified" (1985:6). With this in mind, they define religious organizations as "human organizations primarily engaged in providing general compensators based upon supernatural assumptions" (1985:8).

They go on to use this definition to explain various issues and topics normally discussed in the sociology of religion. In addition to the term compensator, they use the central term in rational choice theory called "rewards." In this way they build on what Homans (1961:4) calls "elementary social action": "...social behaviour is elementary in the sense that the two social actors are in face-to-face contact, and each is rewarding the other directly and immediately: each is able to do his/her work better here and now." The central feature of Homans that Stark and Bainbridge use here is reward. They, however, define it in sociology of religion terms: religious activity that results in tangible rewards such as social status, earning a living, leisure, and human companionship. They argue that the wealthy and privileged religionists are more likely to receive rewards whereas the marginalized and poor are more likely to receive compensators. In their theory of sect and cult formation that I shall look at in Chapter Eight, sects are likely to emerge when churches become too secularized (receiving rewards). Some participants become dissatisfied with this and seek compensators or supernatural rewards. They form sects, in part, to receive these compensators.

Bibby (1987), in his research on religion in Canada, uses a similar model called the "market model." He notes that Canadians tend not to disaffiliate from their churches but they do choose elements from the churches or "fragments" which serve their own desires. Examples of this include the desire and the action to have access to "rites of passage": baptism, marriage, and a funeral. From the vantage of the organizations, the denominations compete for consumers just as economic institutions do. Churches offer a wide range of ministries and services to attract members, such as bible study and prayer groups, day-care services, and numerous interest groups.

Why is this the case, Bibby asks? Congruous with Stark and Bainbridge, fragments are chosen because they work and because they lead to such rewards as role consistency,[4] well-being, and success. Compensators are selected because they provide for people a sense of meaning that goes beyond the temporal. The problem with religion being seen as a market

---

4 A sense a person has that his or her many roles have consistency among them because of what is selected from the religious commodity.

commodity or a reward and compensator is that if it becomes nothing more than a consumer item, the consumer is in charge, and religion is relegated to an *à la carte* role about everyday life (Bibby 1987:149).

A NEW PARADIGM: RELIGION AS A COMPETITOR AMONG
COMPETITORS IN A CULTURAL OPEN MARKET

In an article that presents a new paradigm in the social scientific study of religion, R. Stephen Warner (1993) bases it on a rational choice theory of religion. It is his impression that the old paradigm, whose focus is on religion as providing meaning to life, has led to many inclusive results, particularly in understanding secularization (see Chapter Thirteen). This old paradigm seems workable only in a society that has one major religious organization, such as in medieval Europe or present-day Iran. In a country like the United States (and, I would argue, Canada), where religious pluralism is the mode, this paradigm is not adequate in explaining religious organizations, participation, world views, and ethics.

In his article, Warner reviews a wide range of research that lends credibility to the new paradigm. The baseline for the paradigm is an historical one: the disestablishment of religion in the United States with the founding of the state in the late eighteenth century. The American society is an economically free market that is also integrated with a religious free market: no one denomination or church has dominance or a privileged position as it did historically in Europe. In this free market, there has been a long history of mobilization of religious human capital[5] to compete for scarce resources, one of which is organizational membership. Warner (1993:1055) indicates that the "Christianization of the United States was neither a residue of Puritan hegemony nor a transplantation of a European sacred canopy but an accomplishment of nineteenth-century activists."

Warner continues in the article to provide further evidence for the model. He notes, for example, that it is useful in explaining conversion and secularization. I shall refer to this in Chapter Four in the discussion on conversion and in Chapter Thirteen in investigating secularization.

This new paradigm is definitely a challenge to the overall thesis of this textbook: that the sacred is a unique phenomenon, that world views are critical in analyzing religion, and that religious experience (and attending routinization processes) makes a difference in peoples' lives. One may argue that my model, to be presented in the next section of this chapter (fitting much more closely to the old paradigm), takes more of a global view and tries to understand religion from a more cross-cultural perspective. In addition,

---

5   The term refers to all the skills and talents that a person has to be used for the production of commodities.

this new paradigm is reductionist in nature in that only the manifestations of the sacred inform the model. Lastly, the theory in general, and particularly with regard to religion, is unidimensional. Social action is defined only in rational terms and not in nonrational ones such as affective or charismatic (see below under Weberian theory). I would argue that the new paradigm's credit is that it can explain many of the manifestations of religion linked to other social and psychological phenomena. However, it does not go far in explicating the experiential dimension of religion and the focus on the sacred element of religion. In other words, this new paradigm's strength is in measuring the external manifestations of the sacred and of mythologies, but does not attempt to consider the sacred and mythologies as factors in social change.

The paradigm is further criticized by Bruce (1995a), who challenges the empirical findings of many researchers devoted to the paradigm. His position is similar to mine in that the model does not take seriously the question of culture and that it is reductionistic in nature. He writes: "the validity of the rational choice models is not a small methodological quarrel but goes to the heart of the nature of religious belief. If one considers what sort of society it would be in which economic models of religious behaviour worked well, the answer would be one in which religion no longer matters at all" (1995a:354).

| THE DEBT TO WEBERIAN THEORY

As I have already noted, Weberian sociological theory is used as a foundation for much of the discussion in this text. The social scientific basis of the text relies on the classical sociological meaning of scientific research. The theorist Jeffrey Alexander (1987) argues that sociology is indebted to the classical founders in a fundamental way. Contrary to Giddens (1976a), who believes that Durkheim and Weber are obstacles to the sociological enterprise, Alexander contends that they, as well as Marx, are central to this enterprise.

I concur with Alexander and take a position in this text similar to Durkheim (1938), Weber (1978), and Marx (1967). They agree that the study of social phenomena (of which religion is one) necessarily follows, in part, the path of natural science in that ideology and preconceived ideas are not to precede and potentially bias the description and explanation of social phenomena. Weber (1978) calls this "value-free sociology." Durkheim (1938) refers to it as the task of considering social facts as things and the eradication of preconceived ideas, and Marx (1967) argues for the necessity of searching for the basic fact of the economy: the "commodity" that is, in his terms, "an object outside of us, a thing that by its properties satisfies human wants of some sort or another" (1967:35).

Weber's sociology in general, and his sociology of religion in particular, structures this text. Weber defines sociology as "a science concerning itself with the interpretative understanding of social action and thereby with a causal explanation of its course and consequences" (1978:4). There are two key terms in this definition which warrant discussion and explanation: interpretative understanding and social action. I shall add two concepts vital to this text: the ideal type, and charisma and the routinization of charisma.

Interpretative Understanding

Both formal and informal approaches to describe the social world include objective description and subjective interpretation. Subjective interpretation emerges from a person's world view. An example from a teacher in management skills, Stephen Cory (1989), may help us. He recalls that on a Sunday afternoon in New York, he was taking the subway when a man and his children entered the car. While the man, seated next to him, was self-absorbed, his children were behaving in the most inappropriate manner according to the decorum of subway travel. Cory asked him to take some control of his children. The man apologized and explained that he and his children were just returning from a hospital where the children's mother had just died. Cory said that he immediately changed his world view from one of "children should behave well in public" to compassion and understanding to the father and his children. Two world views interpreted the same phenomenon in quite different ways.

Weberian *interpretative sociology* focuses on such differing interpretations of reality rather than merely on the objective conditions. Weber's own writings in the sociology of religion provide a model for blending the study of objective facts with subjective interpretations given to these facts by social actors. In one of his major works, *The Protestant Ethic and the Spirit of Capitalism*, Weber (1958a) discussed at length how the religious beliefs of the English Puritans and Methodists were an important factor in the rise of the western capitalistic system. In other words, the subjective interpretations of reality presented by Protestantism had an objective impact on the economic system. These interpretations are what are referred to as sacred world views, or the term that will be used in Chapter Two, mythologies.

Through the use of *verstehen* or interpretative understanding, sociology can be used to explain the development of social phenomena (as Weber used *verstehen* to interpret the Protestant world view to explain the rise of capitalism). Weber did not believe that the social scientists (acting as social scientists) had a right to make value judgments, but rather that social scientists must take into account the values of those under study. The social scientist is interested in human action, the particular qualities of human actors, and the meaning they ascribe to their actions.

Social Action

Weber (1978:4) speaks of *social action* insofar as individuals attach subjective meanings to their behaviour. I have already demonstrated how specific acts may be framed with either a secular or religious world view. Such world views are not developed in isolation; they are social in that they are developed and maintained in concert with others. Weber maintains that there are three primary types of social action that are reflected in human behaviour: traditional, rational, and affective.

Traditional social action is guided by set patterns that have developed over time together with a sense that things must "always be that way." It is a commitment to believing and acting in ways that seem to have always been there. Backers of tradition often use religious myth to support preferred behaviour and to resist change. Vestiges of the patriarchal family form and sexual taboos provide examples of traditional social action. Those who insist, for example, that the husband must have authority over his wife — that the husband is the "head" of the family — often use select biblical texts to "prove" that God ordained this social arrangement. Other examples of traditional action may be seen in many religious people's opposition to homosexual behaviour, abortion, birth control, and extra-marital sex. Preference is given to long-established codes embedded in religious history over the recent changes in gender roles and sexual behaviour.

Although tradition guided human action for much of history, Weber felt it had lost ground to what he called *rational social action*.[6] *Legal or instrumental rational action* is determined by the expected responses of others as "'conditions' or 'means' for the actor's own rationally pursued and calculated

---

6 Weber identified two forms of rational action, legal rational and value rational, although most of his writings on rationality refer to legal rational action. *Value rational action* is characterized by its adherence to some ethical, aesthetic, religious or other principles, independent of its prospects of success. Weber (1978:25) provides as examples of value rational action those persons who act according to their convictions, whether they be duty, honour, the pursuit of beauty, a religious call, personal loyalty, or some sense of calling. The successful engineer who leaves her profession to become a missionary to Africa is acting value rationally. She is behaving on the basis of conviction, probably sensing a religious call to spread her religious faith.

    Although this distinction has some heuristic value and seems very relevant for the sociology of religion, Weber made little use of it. Whimster and Lash (1987:17) suggest that Weber did not identify any authority type as stemming from value rational action because it is of little sociological consequence in the modern world. I would further suggest that action that may be initially classified as "value rational" may, on closer analysis, be reclassified as "instrumental rational" or "affective."

ends" (Weber 1978:25). In other words, actors anticipate potential responses to their behaviour and act in such ways as to bring about things they desire. Such action may be demonstrated by changes that have occurred in the practice of birth control and in attitudes toward it. Early in the twentieth century, Margaret Sanger, the family planning activist who coined the term "birth control," was arrested for speaking on the topic; and it was not until 1965 that the Supreme Court finally struck down laws prohibiting the sale of birth control devices to married couples in Connecticut on the grounds that these laws infringed on an individual's right to privacy (Collins and Coltrane 1991:502). Tradition, undergirded with religious myth, played an important role in the opposition to birth control. (The account in Genesis 38:9-10 of Onan being struck dead after practising coitus interruptus was a frequently cited story to support the proscription.) Tradition, however, has clearly given way to rational action as the century comes to a close. The vast majority of couples use birth control (the "means") to limit family size (the "calculated end"), despite the strong religious taboo that once existed against this practice.

Affective social action is emotional rather than means-end oriented. Its driving force is specific affects or feeling states. Weber (1978:25) notes that action is affective if it satisfies a need for revenge, sensual gratification, devotion, contemplative bliss, or for working off emotional tensions. Weber (1995) continues by saying that religious states, to some degree, have been sought for the sake of an emotional value they offer to the devout. As I shall demonstrate throughout this text, affective action, having this emotional component, is at the core of religion. It is also at the heart of many religious myths which express a range of feelings, including love, hate, fear, and awe. As the late humanistic psychologist Abraham Maslow (1970) has noted, myth often embodies the intense experiences (peak experiences) of the founders of great religions. From Abraham's calling, through Moses' experience on Sinai, from Jesus' baptism, through Paul's conversion, Judeo-Christian religious myth is rife with accounts of affective action.[7]

Weberian sociology recognizes that shifts have occurred in these three types of social action. Human behaviour was once largely traditional in nature, guided by beliefs and values that seemed ingrained and by patterns of social action that were stable and repetitive. People followed traditions

---

7 Although this form of action is important for an interpretative understanding of religious behaviour, Weber saw it as a residual category and did not explore it in any great detail. Later social scientists, following Weber, have also tended to downplay the importance of affective social action in modern society. It is only within the past ten years that some social psychologists working in the newly developed field of "sociology of emotions" have begun to demonstrate how important affective action is for understanding human behaviour.

and were very resistant to changing their long established ways of living. These traditions were often sanctified with religious myths. In contemporary societies, men and women are now more likely to behave in accord with legal rational behaviour, guided particularly by scientific knowledge.

The Weberian model of societal transition depicts a move from traditional societies, in which religious thought is the pre-eminent world view, to modern legal rational societies, in which scientific knowledge is a dominant theme. In the process, religion has lost the prominent place it once held in the public sphere, being relegated largely to a private world. In modern societies, individuals make personal choices about whether or not to be religious and about their respective religious paths. The writings of Max Weber have been utilized by members of diverse schools of thought, including functionalism, structuralism, interactionism, and conflict theory, thus providing a social scientific perspective of much depth and breadth.

Ideal Types

The methodology I employ is Weberian in that it uses ideal types whenever possible. An *ideal type* may be described as an analytical construct that serves as a measuring rod to determine similarities and differences in concrete cases. It usually does not exist in its pure form, but it is of heuristic value for discussing the real world. For example, Weber created an ideal type of authority that is basic to his theory. Traditional authority rests in long-standing practices and institutions (e.g., a monarchy). Legal-rational authority is rooted in rules and procedures (such as the possession of necessary qualifications by leaders to carry out well-defined responsibilities). Charismatic leaders appeal to people's emotions and lead on the basis of personality. It is evident that, although most leaders in modern society are examples of legal-rational authority, tradition (e.g., a well-known name) and especially charisma (e.g., television appeal) also enter the picture.

The use of ideal types permits comparisons between and among different types of religious leaders as well as between and among different religions. The focus of this text is on American religions, but I will compare religious beliefs, practices, and organizations of American society with those in earlier eras as well as in other parts of the world. Even the United States and Canada provide excellent data for comparative purposes. Although the two countries share many cultural similarities, there are significant religious differences which will challenge readers from both countries to consider the religious alternatives available to contemporary societies. While this text cannot provide details about the development of different religious traditions found in North America, I will utilize historical and ethnographic accounts to put flesh on the theoretical concepts and theories — accounts that provide basic information about the wide array of religions found on this continent.

Finally, the Weberian approach to sociology — especially in the hands of modern sociologists of religion like Peter Berger and Thomas O'Dea — is a dynamic one that includes social change. It allows for the tensions that arise when old meanings are confronted with new interpretations, when modern rational thought clashes with traditional values and beliefs, when old priests struggle against new prophets. The tensions between individuals and the collectivity, between older and newer religious perspectives, and between religious and secular institutions are sources of energy that propel social change.

Charisma and the Routinization of Charisma

34

It is in the context of religion being a source of social change that another set of Weberian concepts will be used in a central way in this text: *charisma* and the *routinization of charisma* (Weber 1978:1111-1148). Weber restricts their usage to religious leaders who are initiators (as in founders of religion like Abraham or Zoroaster), innovators (like Joseph Smith of Mormonism), renewers (as in the case of Benedict of Nursia, the founder of the Benedictines), or reformers (like Martin Luther or Gautama Buddha). He situates the charismatic stage to the era of these kinds of leaders, and routinization to successors (and followers) who, in many cases, effectively lose the charisma and routinize the sacred. I shall extend this, in light of other data on religion, to include communities and organizations which encase charisma, the routinization of it or combinations thereof. O'Dea's work on the institutionalization of religion will provide the framework for this extension.

Weberian theory makes room for a multidimensional view of society[8] that includes social agency and social order, the social actor and the institution, subjective and objective facets of society, social stability and social change, and micro and macro levels of analyses.

It is from its genius and the contributions of contemporary theorists who have built upon it that I draw my sociological inspiration. I have attempted to avoid many of the "dualisms" (to use a concept of British theorist Anthony Giddens) inherent in sociology. Two primary sources of dualism

---

8   Alexander (1983) cites such sociologists as Talcott Parsons and Robert Bellah who share this view of multidimensionality. However, Alexander disagrees with them. He considers Weber's later work to have moved away from social action and interpretive sociology to emphasize rational-legal authority in the modern world that increasingly held men and women in an "iron cage" that left little room for charisma, change, and innovation. I side with this earlier interpretation of multidimensionality.

have been the debates over, first, whether sociology should focus on human actors or the "micro" level of analysis or whether the prime concern should be over social structures representing a "macro" level of analysis and, second, whether the subject matter of sociology is subjective reality as perceived by the actors in society or objective reality described in terms of social norms, institutions, and structures. Inspired by two sociological theorists, Anthony Giddens (1976) and Jeffrey Alexander (1982), I prefer to adhere to a multidimensional approach to sociology that acknowledges that both social action and social structure are necessary presuppositional concepts in interpreting the various dimensions of human society. Social action assists us in understanding that people are active in shaping their social world while simultaneously being shaped by, but not passively determined by, social institutions, norms, and history. The symbolic interactionist Herbert Blumer says it well:

35

> Social organization is a framework inside of which acting units develop their actions. Structural features, such as 'culture,' 'social systems,' 'social stratification,' or 'social roles,' set conditions for their action but do not determine their action. (1996 [1962]: 365)

Alexander (1982) provides insights from which this diagram (Figure 1.2) was constructed to further illustrate multidimensionality. The figure attempts to capture the fact that social life and institutions are understood both to be created by individuals (from the individualist end of the social structure) and to be a result of social structure (the collectivist pole). The figure also intends to convey that social action is both rational and non-rational. Religion, both in its social action and structural dimensions, consists both of rational and non-rational elements as well as being created by individuals and a source of constraint (and enablement) to individuals.

SUMMARY AND CONCLUSIONS

In this chapter I have explored the nature of world views ("points of view") and how they have an impact upon our thinking about religion. I have noted some of the differences between common world views

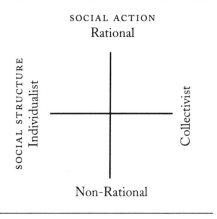

SOCIAL STRUCTURE AND SOCIAL ACTION

SOCIAL ACTION
Rational

SOCIAL STRUCTURE
Individualist

Collectivist

Non-Rational

FIGURE 1.2

that are usually unexamined in modern western society and the more formal ways of knowing through *humanistic* and *scientific* scholarship. The *noumena-phenomena dilemma* was used to illustrate some of the basic differences between humanistic and scientific analyses of religion. The Weberian perspective which informs the text was also delineated and was contrasted with the rational choice theory of religion.

One way to become even more aware of assumptions and perspectives that we all bring to our construction of social reality is to engage in some cross-cultural comparison. The comparative study of religion and the anthropology of religion will form, in part, data useful for generalizations and syntheses. In the next chapter I will explore sacred world views or the mythologies of folk and oriental societies in order to compare and contrast them with world views of the modern western world.

■ CHAPTER TWO ■

Religion as a World View

There are, as we saw in the last chapter, several vantage points from which religion may be viewed. Our everyday, taken-for-granted reality may be constructed in a secular mode that negates or downplays the religious, or in a sacred mode that elevates the supernatural. Either of the informal approaches (secular and sacred) may be supplemented with more formal investigation, including humanistic approaches and various social scientific perspectives as noted in the last chapter. Religion itself may be regarded as a particular *perspective* through which other facets of reality may be interpreted or as an *object* that may be formally studied using different academic approaches. Although most of this text treats religion as an object of social scientific study, the discussion in this chapter approaches religion from the first position. Our focus in this chapter is on how general religious beliefs or *myths* function as lenses for interpreting the social world.

This chapter is a natural progression of the Weberian perspective as presented in the introductory chapter. Religious world views, which will be defined shortly as mythologies, are central to Weber's sociology of religion. In his work on the social psychology of the world religions, Weber (1995) argues that even though it is true that material and ideal interests do affect social action, world views frame and act like "switchmen" in determining which type of religious social action one will choose:

> … very frequently, the world images [*read* world views] that have been
> created by ideas have, like switchmen, determined the tracks along
> which action has been pushed by the dynamic of interest. 'From what'
> and 'for what' one wished to be redeemed and, let us not forget, 'could
> be' redeemed, depended upon one's image of the world. (1995:26)

The importance that Weber applies to world views is substantiated by recent scholarship summarized by Whimster and Lash (1987). They argue

37

SOCIETY, SPIRITUALITY, AND THE SACRED

that the Protestant world view, which was especially rationalistic and that Weber considered to be necessary to the development of modernity, was preceded by his extensive analyses of the world views of Confucianism, Buddhism, Hinduism, Islam, Judaism, and Christianity. Weber uses changes in world views to understand the changes in Western Europe from feudalism to modern social institutions of capitalist economies and state democracies. Bendix (1962), in his important portrait of Weber, notes that he saw the study of religious ideas (i.e., sacred world views) in terms of how relevant they were for collective actions. In addition, Bendix writes, Weber considers how and if these world views were concentrated in the inspirations of a few that eventually became the convictions of many.

| MYTH, RELIGION, AND WORLD VIEW

Religion is not only an object for social scientific study; it is also a medium through which many people interpret their daily world. Accounts provided for the survival of two passengers in a potentially fatal plane crash can be used to illustrate how religious ideology may function as part of the everyday world. One survivor, an agnostic, attributes her being spared from an untimely death to having been seated next to an exit and to being in excellent physical condition. Both natural factors, coupled with some "good luck," she feels, allowed her to exit the plane only seconds before it caught fire. The other survivor is a devoutly religious man who credits his escape to divine providence. The second survivor may have a story to tell about how he felt a strong sense of God's presence as the plane was losing altitude and how he, groping through the smoke-filled plane toward the exit, felt unexplainably "led" by this presence. Neither explanation can be proved (or disproved) readily by social science. What can be observed is how each account is rooted in a different interpretation of reality, one "natural" or "secular" and the other "supernatural" or "sacred."

Human experiences (even those much less dramatic than surviving a plane crash) framed by religious ideology are the material out of which religious world views are constructed and through which they are maintained. Myths, explanations whose factuality usually cannot be determined, traditionally have been basic elements in a more general world view. They are the stories that help people to account for the origins, history, and purpose of life. They serve to interpret the cosmos, to explain suffering and death, and to provide meaning for daily life events. Social science can neither prove nor disprove myths; rather, its task is to study the impact they have on people and society.

It is important to emphasize that when we are using the term "myth," we do not wish to imply that such beliefs are false or fictitious. Nor is myth intended as a synonym for fairy tales or folk narratives (Roberts 1990:77). Myths are accounts or stories that undergird different religious world views. Their truth or falsity is not the concern of social science. All are essentially treated as being "true" in a sense because they are defined as being so by believers. In the words of the famous Thomas theorem, *the definition of the situation,* "If men define a situation as real, it is real in its consequences" (Thomas 1923:41-43). Even false definitions of a situation have psychological as well as social implications. The social scientist's task is to determine the effects of myth on believers and their society.

Religious myths once provided *the* paramount definition of reality for people in pre-modern societies. Although different cultures may have had very divergent ideas about the non-empirical world of their mythical figures, all shared the conviction that the spirits had an impact on life. As we shall see later in this chapter, it was mythology of varying shades and hues that provided a framework for interpreting civilization.

39

The primacy of this mythical world view was challenged first by philosophers and later by scientists. Although religious world views continue to occupy an important place in some parts of the world, they have lost their position of dominance in the public life of modern industrial and post-industrial countries. Rulers in modern nations do not invoke the gods as the source of their right to rule, judges do not claim to make legal decisions based on divine law, and meteorologists do not use spiritual forces to account for the weather. The myth or "story of the gods" has given way to the tenets of science in parts of Asia, in much of Australia, Europe, and North America, and among the educated in other parts of the world as well.

This erosion of the power of religious myth is most evident in the public sphere, but myth continues to function in private lives. We see this in the United States where 95 per cent of the population believe in the existence of God, with 84 per cent believing that God is a "heavenly father who can be reached by prayers" (Gallup and Jones 1989:4). The vast

---

GOD IS ALIVE: CANADA IS A NATION OF BELIEVERS.

Anywhere from two-thirds to three-quarters of the adult population describe themselves as Christians, depending on how the question was phrased: 78 per cent affiliate themselves with a Christian denomination; 74 per cent disagree with the statement "I am not a Christian"; 67 per cent believe that Jesus Christ was crucified, died and was buried but was resurrected to eternal life; 66 per cent believe that Christ was the divine son of God; and 62 per cent believe that the life, death and resurrection of Jesus Christ provided a way for their forgiveness.

SOURCE: *Macleans,* April 12, 1993:34. Data are from a national random sample entitled the Religion Poll, based on the results of 4,510 telephone interviews in 1993.

BOX 2.1

majority of Americans accept accounts that God did play an active role in creating human beings, with 44 per cent subscribing to a creationist mythology that depicts God as having "created man pretty much in his present form at one time within the last 10,000 years."[1] A plurality of survey respondents accepted accounts of biblical miracles and either completely agreed (51 per cent) or mostly agreed (29 per cent) with the statement, "Even today miracles are performed by the power of God" (Gallup and Jones 1989:10).[2]

One of the primary functions of myth is to provide a sense of meaning and purpose, even in the face of tragedy. Medical science can furnish a detailed and technical account of how and why a young child died of cancer, but such an explanation does little to comfort the bereaved parents. The importance of religion in accounting for a sense of "existential well-being," believing that life has a specific purpose, has been documented in research conducted by Poloma and Pendleton (1990). In a survey of 585 randomly selected respondents in Akron, Ohio, they found religion to be the leading predictor of high scores in having a sense of meaning and purpose in life. Religion was more important than good health, family, and friends, or a high standard of living in explaining differences in existential well-being scores. Religious accounts appear to be widely and successfully used in constructing a sense of life's meaning and purpose by millions of North Americans. Although religious myths appear to be used less in modern public life than they once were, they continue to function widely in the private sphere.

RELIGIOUS MYTHS: SUBSTANTIVE AND FUNCTIONAL VIEWS

The study of religious myths may be approached using two perspectives: substantive and functional. The *substantive approach* attempts to define the

---

1   Another 38 per cent professed to believe in an evolutionary development of humankind with God guiding creation (Gallup and Jones 1989:100). (Of the remaining 18 per cent, 9 per cent had no opinion and 9 per cent claimed to believe in a godless evolution.)

2   The United States, it should be noted, is the most religious of the world's industrialized nations (Warner 1993). Figures for all European countries (with the exception of Ireland and Poland), Japan, and Australia all show a much lower level of religious belief than do U.S. figures. Canadians are more religious than residents of most other industrialized countries, but are significantly less religious than are Americans. For example, 83 per cent of Canadians say they believe in God (in contrast to 95 per cent of Americans). These figures range from a high of 93 per cent for the Atlantic provinces to a low of 73 per cent in British Columbia (Bibby 1987:73).

essence of a myth. It seeks to clarify and illuminate, much as we have been doing in our present discussion of myth in this chapter. The *functional approach*, on the other hand, seeks to determine what effects myths have in the lives of people and the larger society. In other words, an important task of the functional perspective is to determine the purpose myth serves in maintaining the social order. While these two approaches may appear to be distinct, in actuality there is overlap. What may begin as a substantive approach may end in a discussion of the functions of myth; what is intended to be a discussion of the functions of myth may produce a tentative definition. Despite the fact that these two approaches are not mutually exclusive, discussing them separately does enable us to provide a comprehensive discussion of the nature and purpose of myth. This discussion will also serve as a base for a better understanding of accepted definitions of religion offered by sociologists and anthropologists — definitions that will be offered at the close of the chapter. In addition, the substantive and functional categories will be used frequently throughout the text to offer both substantive and functional definitions of ritual, ethos, and religious organizations.

41

A SUBSTANTIVE FOCUS: DESCRIPTION AND ORIGINS

Mircea Eliade, an anthropologist who wrote extensively about religion, has provided us with a concise description of the nature of myth:

> In short, myths describe breakthroughs of the sacred (or the supernatural) into the world. It is this sudden breakthrough of the sacred that really *establishes* [italics in the original] the world and makes it what it is today. Furthermore, it is a result of the intervention of supernatural beings that man himself is what he is today, a mortal, sexed, and cultural being. (Eliade 1973:70)

Eliade contends that myth presents a sacred history, a story of what took place in primordial time. It informs the believer of how, through the deeds of supernatural beings, the cosmos came into being. It represents a breakthrough — or more accurately, a "break into" the mundane world of the common place by non-terrestrial beings. In constructing his theory of myths, Eliade built on the work of theologian Rudolf Otto (1923), whose scholarly writings depicted the sacred as having its origins in unique and extraordinary experiences that contrasted with the routine and the mundane of daily life.

The essence of much religious myth is rooted in a polarity between "this world" and "another world," between the *profane* that is everyday and mundane and the *sacred* that is "set aside" and "forbidden." There is a tension between these two perspectives on reality. The mystery that surrounds the religious phenomena manifests itself as something that evokes a sense in the believer of the unknown, the awesome, the fearful (Otto 1958; Eliade 1959). The mysterious contrasts with the everyday world of reality, simultaneously drawing and repelling. The message of the sacred is paradoxically mixed — it invites the believer to come closer while at the same time warning against familiarity.

This desire to approach the unknown mystery, while simultaneously being repelled by it, may be illustrated in the book of Exodus, the Hebraic scripture that tells the story of the Jewish people leaving Egypt in search of

the promised land. In Exodus 19:23 we read that the people are commanded not to come close to the mountain of revelation (Mount Sinai). On the other hand, there is an invocation to come close to the deity who is described as "Yahweh, Yahweh, a God of tenderness and compassion, slow to anger, rich in kindness and faithfulness" (Exodus 34:7). The dilemma about whether to approach or to keep distant from the sacred is a specific form of a more common dilemma, namely whether and how to integrate the sacred and the profane.

The late scholar of world myths, Joseph Campbell (1964, 1987), described this dilemma in depth through what he called the "mystical function" of myth. (In fact this "function" probes deeper into describing the experience recounted in myth.) According to Campbell (1964), the mystical — standing in awe of the sacred — is at the heart of myth. It is an experience that defies definition. In folk mythology, it is expressed as demonic dread; in oriental and occidental religions, as mystical rapture. Those who have such encounters are the seers, the poets, or the religious leaders. They are the ones who are able to formulate the story that captures the religious imagination of others. Campbell contends that all those who wish to live a full life must be willing to go on spiritual journeys not unlike those of the great mystics. For Campbell, these journeys represent going inward to explore the unconscious — a venture that is both inviting and simultaneously fearsome.

Two other examples of the dilemma or dialectic between the "sacred" and the "secular" that are common to the mystical may be provided from the myths of ancient China and India (Campbell 1962). In China, the *Tao* is considered to be the way or path. Its natural tendency is towards peace, prosperity, and health (Noss and Noss 1984). Despite its being seen as a way of harmony, or integration, and cooperation, within it we find the *Yang* and the *Yin*. Campbell makes it clear that the characteristics of neither Yang nor Yin (see Table 2.1) are to be judged morally as either good or evil. Yang and Yin are present in all things and are in perpetual interaction. The sun is an example of having a dominance of Yang whereas the earth is primarily Yin in nature, yet both work together in harmony.

THE TAO

Yang	Yin
Light	Dark
Masculine	Feminine
Hot	Cold
Active	Passive
Positive	Negative
Procreative	Fertile

43

TABLE 2.1

   In India, the comparable concept is *Yoga*, "the intentional stopping of the spontaneous activity of the mind itself" (Campbell 1962:27). It is the striving for the experience of the stilled water. It is regarded as a movement from the world of nature, which is illusion, to the quietness of contemplation, the experience of utter and complete freedom of self from earthly bonds (Noss and Noss 1984). A dialectical tension is common to both the Chinese and Indian forms of mysticism, just as it is to western mysticism. In the case of China, the dialectic is understood to be within the Tao or the sacred. Unlike many religious perspectives, Taoism accepted multiple realities (including the human or so-called profane) as being valid. There was no conflict between the world and the Tao, but rather the contrasts were within the Tao itself. In Hinduism, the dominant religion of India, the dialectic is one of interaction with the world. In contrast to Taoism, Hinduism, the ancient religion from which Buddhism is derived, is monistic. The core or heart of all reality is spiritual; everything that is material is a diluted form of the spirit. In other words, anything that is *really real* is spiritual. The ascetic practices of Hinduism are aimed at freeing the person from the world of delusion. If this is not accomplished during the present lifetime, a person will return again and again (reincarnation) until freed from illusion.
   This dialectic within Taoism and Hinduism is similar to what the anthropologist Lévi-Strauss (1978) calls a *binary structure* within myths (see below). It differs somewhat from Christianity. The dualistic Christian tradition recognizes the reality of both the spiritual world and the world of

nature, but these two worlds are often in conflict. The tension that is emphasized is not one *within* a single world (as with Taoism and Hinduism) but rather between the heavenly realm of spirit and the mundane realm of nature. According to Christian mythology, the natural realm is fractured and must be brought under God's complete control for reintegration.

SOME UNIVERSAL MYTHS

The dialectic, a tension between opposites out of which wholeness is believed to come, appears to be a universal theme in religious myths. This tension has produced similar mythical stories found throughout the world (Campbell 1987). Themes such as the deluge or flood, the land of the dead, a virgin birth, and a resurrected hero have recurred in religious myths among peoples of very different cultures. These themes are rehearsed in liturgies and are interpreted by seers, poets, theologians, and philosophers; they are presented in art, magnified in song, and ecstatically experienced in visions. Campbell writes:

> Indeed, the chronicle of our species, from its earliest page, has been not simply an account of the progress of man the tool-maker, but — more tragically — a history of the pouring of blazing visions into the minds of seers and the efforts of earthly communities to incarnate unearthly covenants (1987:3).

What is striking is that these themes have a universal chord, a common thread that is not restricted to particular cultures or times.

Campbell first described some of the universal features of myth in his earliest work *Hero With A Thousand Faces* (1949). In a sense, Campbell maintains, there is but one hero and one heroic deed performed again and again by many, many people. A most common theme in heroic deeds is that of death and rebirth, with the hero either physically sacrificing himself to save others or experiencing a spiritual death and rebirth that he returns to share with others. Campbell compares the spiritual experiences of Jesus and the Buddha before each selected his disciples. Buddha went into the forest, past the gurus, to sit alone under the Bo-tree where he received the enlightenment. Immediately he was subject to three temptations. Similarly, after his baptism by John, Jesus went off into the desert where he too was tempted three times. The time in solitude and the temptations represented a time of spiritual death and rebirth.

It is common for heroes go off into darkness (which for Campbell represents the unconscious), as Jonah descended into the belly of the whale and Jesus descended into the grave. Heroes conquer the darkness much like Christians believe Jesus conquered death through his death and resurrection. Not only is the death and resurrection motif a universal one in the journeys of heroes, but it is present in initiation rites, where a young person dies to childhood and rises into adult life.

From a substantive perspective, myth is rooted in Weberian affective action. It depicts accounts of encounters with something that is non-empirical. Through the narrative, the non-empirical takes on empirical form. Myth attempts to describe experiences that are not describable, to tell about feelings that are not easily put into words, to narrate encounters with the spiritual that defy ordinary conversation. The paradoxical language that is used reflects struggle and tension, as illustrated by the common death and resurrection motif found in accounts of mythical heroes.

45

Functions of Myth

Although Campbell (1964, 1987) identifies four functions of myth, the *mystical function* just described is in fact a substantive description. The remaining three broad functions — the cosmological, sociological, and psychological — categorize some of the most important effects of myth. It is only as these purposes are fulfilled that myths remain viable in a culture.

One function of myth is to render a cosmology. In other words, it offers an account to "make sense" of the universe. The prophet or seer has received some illumination, but the understanding of the seer must be translated into cultural images, symbols, rites, and texts for it to become viable. Unless this is done, the vision will die with the visionary. There is a tension, however, between making the mystery available to the culture while at the same time retaining the awe of the mystery. This tension may be briefly demonstrated by what happened over time to the accounts of creation presented in Genesis. Most religions, including the Judeo-Christian tradition, have cosmological accounts of creation that attempt to capture its mystery. The stories are intended to help "make sense" of the origins of the world. At the same time they must capture the sense of mystery and awe reflected by the rhythm of life's polarities — birth and death, light and darkness, sowing and reaping, peace and war. When a creation story is twisted into the mould of history and science (as the book of Genesis has been countless times), a sense of mystery and awe is often lost. Paradoxically, when the myth becomes rigid doctrine, its power to serve as an effective source of cosmology is weakened.

A subset of the cosmological function of myth is a *theodicy*. Berger (1969:55) describes it as a religious legitimation of anomic phenomena. Examples of anomic phenomena may include suffering, death, or tragedy.

There is a frequent human quest of trying to understand why these adversities occur in the human condition. Religious myths attempt to give some rationale for them.

Weber (1995:19) expands on this theme. He argues that under the pressure of ever-recurrent distress, the myth of the redeemer evolved. In this distress, suffering became the most important topic. An answer to this suffering is a saviour or a redeemer who comes to free people from these tragedies, to return the good fortune of this world or offer the security of the world beyond. He presents several examples: Krishna in Hinduism, Gideon in ancient Israel, and Zoroaster of the Middle East. One could add Jesus of Christianity.

A second purpose of myth identified by Campbell is sociological, including social control, social support, and socialization. Myth functions as an agent of social control in that it reinforces the existing social order. The ten commandments given to Moses on Mount Sinai warn people against such socially divisive practices as lying, stealing, and murder. Although generally functional for society in their power to bind people together, myths may also become dysfunctional (i.e., work against the good of the social system). Myth has been used to uphold anti-social practices, including slavery, the burning of women thought to be witches, spouse and child abuse, and unfair labour practices. Myth may function to support legitimate order in society, and it may be used to bolster illegitimate power. Emile Durkheim, a founding father of sociology, tended to emphasize the positive functions of myth for upholding the social order. Durkheim believed that religion had provided an essential moral base for all societies (Bellah 1973). Karl Marx, another important early social theorist, stressed the negative functions of religion. For Marx, religion was a form of "false consciousness" which had been used throughout history to keep men and women in bondage (Marx and Engels 1964).

The sociological function of myth is built into a classic definition of religion advanced by Emile Durkheim. Durkheim (1965:62) defined *religion* as "a unified system of beliefs and practices relative to sacred things, that is to say, things set apart and forbidden — beliefs and practices that unite into a single moral community called a Church, all those who adhere to them." In this definition we see that religion includes both myth and the rituals that reflect mythical beliefs. These beliefs and corresponding rituals are of a particular kind — they pertain to the sacred (not the mundane or the secular). They function to unite believers into a single moral community or a socially cohesive group. This community is both a source of support and an agent of control.

In a sociohistorical study, Guy Swanson (1960) adopted Durkheim's basic position on the interrelationship between religious mythology and social structure. For Swanson, as for Durkheim, it is society that serves as a model for religion. In his monumental study of data drawn from preliterate and early historical societies, Swanson traces the relationship between certain kinds of belief (such as monotheism, polytheism, and the beliefs in ancestral spirits, in reincarnation, in the immanence of the soul) and various social conditions. Swanson reported, for example, that belief in reincarnation was related to the community size. In communities where the pattern of settlement is dominated by "small hamlets, compounds of extended families, small nomadic bands, scattered rural neighborhoods, or other units smaller than a village" (Swanson 1960:113), the memories of those who die are especially likely to persist after their death. These memories apparently support the belief that the dead live on and will eventually return to the community. The social relationships and structures, according to Swanson, provide a model for the development of a belief in personal reincarnation. Similarly, Swanson (1960:112) demonstrates a strong relationship between the belief in monotheism (one "high god" responsible for creating the world) and the presence of three or more "sovereign groups" (groups having ultimate decision-making authority over specific areas of life).[3]

47

Some more recent research gives credibility to the thesis that mythologies do have an impact on social actors. One way to operationalize myth is to look at who religious actors imagine God to be. Swenson (1989), in a dissertation on linking family and religion from an American data base of Roman Catholic believers, found that those who viewed God as a judge were more likely to have traditional familial attitudes than those who did not have that view. In another study using divine images, Piazza and Glock (1979), in a sample of people in San Francisco, discovered that those who saw God as influential in their own lives are consistently the most likely to accept traditional religious beliefs, to engage in traditional religious practices, to be pro-feminist, and to possess liberal racial attitudes. In addition, those who saw God as "in charge of the social order" (a Durkheimian theme) were likely to be politically conservative. In a study of Canadian evangelical ministers, Swenson (1997) saw links between divine images and

---

3   Swanson's study implies, but cannot prove, a causal relationship between social factors and religious mythology. In other words, statistical findings alone cannot determine whether religious beliefs are a result of social conditions or whether social conditions have "caused" religious beliefs. Swanson himself admits that even strong positive correlations do not establish cause-and-effect relationships, but his model suggests that the social structure is the model for religious beliefs (not vice versa). Swanson's most important contribution, as Johnstone (1988:32) has noted, "lies in having shown that certain beliefs are extremely unlikely to occur and be accepted unless certain social factors, conditions, or relationships are present."

marital quality. He found that ministers who viewed God in intimate terms had higher levels of marital quality than did those who did not.

Myth not only functions on the social level; it also functions on the individual level. Campbell (1964) terms this the psychological function of myth. Myth may initiate the individual into the reality of his or her own psyche, guiding a person toward spiritual enrichment. Campbell asserts that in folk and traditional forms of myth, the principle of personal development was often downplayed or even suppressed. In the modern world with its emphasis on individuality, myths are more likely to accent the development of full personal potential (Campbell 1968a).

The psychological function of myth, however, is not restricted to Christianity or to modernity. Eastern mythology traditionally has accented the growth of the individual person into the divine. The ultimate goal of Hinduism, for example, is for the soul (Atman) to become one with the universal soul (Brahman). A similar goal is held in Buddhism, where the follower is to become like the Buddha and to rest in *nirvana*, a state of quiescence. Perhaps what differs for the modern world is the increased primacy given to psychological functions (individual benefits) over sociological ones (collective needs).

Campbell (1987) concludes his analysis of the functions of myth in asserting that the primary benefits of myth have been cosmological and sociological. Myths provide meaning and purpose in life, and they offer a source of social control and support. Campbell (1987:471) adds that, despite the increased talk about the personal benefits of a spiritual world view, few are disciplined enough to use myth in such a way to bring about a psychological metamorphosis.

| PRIMARY MYTHIC WORLD VIEWS

Religious world views or myths may be categorized according to three general types: simple or folk,[4] oriental or eastern, and occidental or western. Given the centrality of myth for religion, noting the primary differences among these three forms will alert us to the diversity of religious beliefs. These basic differences, variations that are not easily reconciled, reflect the difficulty scholars have in defining religion.

---

4   Many anthropologists used to call ancient societies "primitive." Current usage considers this term to be offensive and alternative names are used. Some of them include "traditional," "folk," or "simple." "Traditional" is too extensive and is used, typically, in classical sociology as premodern. "Simple" may also be offensive. The term used here will be "folk," referring to hunting-gathering and agrarian-pastoral societies.

Folk Mythology

Folk mythology may be illustrated by the beliefs of elementary supernaturalism and animism. Elementary supernaturalism does not recognize specific gods or spirits, but does assume that supernatural forces have an impact on human life. Commonly found in pre-industrial societies, there are vestiges of folk mythology in the modern world. The gambler's belief in "luck," the use of horoscope predictions to guide one's decisions, or the reliance on protective charms or crystals are examples.[5] Animism, on the other hand, recognizes active, animate spirits operating in the world. Although these spirits are not gods and are not worshipped, they are regarded as forces that might be benevolent or evil. People must take these spirits into account and might try to influence them. Animistic religions have been common among tribes of Africa and the Americas. Some forms of animism persist in the modern world in rituals associated with spiritualism, exorcism, and in some forms of the occult.

Although vestiges of magic exist in other forms of religion, magic is more characteristic of animism and elementary supernaturalism than of eastern or western religions. Magic shares with animism the belief that the world is controlled by supernatural forces that determine a person's destiny. The object of magical practices is to get those forces working for you instead of against you. Magic thus involves the use of rituals to harness supernatural power for human ends (Malinowski 1954).

Most scholars regard magic as a phenomenon that is closely related to religion but not identical to it. The primary difference between religion and magic involves the attitude of the believer toward the transcendent. The religious perspective emphasizes the intrinsic need for worship, recognizing the object of worship as being worthy of such homage. Magic, on the other hand, involves attempts to manipulate the supernatural forces that are believed to control human destiny. These supernatural forces are not necessarily something with which a relationship is established, but rather are more likely to represent laws of the universe which must not be violated. The religious way leads to adoration; magic sets the road to conquer and to manipulate (Wach 1967). Durkheim (1915:44) suggests a further distinction. He argues that magic does not have a religious collective but a clientele. He

49

---

5   Significant numbers of both Americans and Canadians were found to use astrological predictions to guide decision-making. Bibby (1987:74) reports that 9 per cent of Canadians believe in the power of astrology. Poloma and Pendleton (1991), using a somewhat different question, found that 8 per cent of their sample of Americans either "sometimes" or "often" used a horoscope to guide decision-making. (Another 9 per cent admitted to having done so "once or twice.")

writes that "There is no Church of magic" (1915:44), and reasons that the social dimension of religion is essential in distinguishing it from magic, which has no collective consciousness and is only for the individual.

Sociologist Robert Bellah has observed how folk myths, whether they be religious or magical, provide a unified common world view specific to the tribal group. This world view is all-encompassing, touching nearly every practical area of life. Bellah describes the unidimensional perspective of folk religions as follows:

> Primitive religions are, on the whole, oriented to a single cosmos; they know nothing of a wholly different world relative to which the actual world is utterly devoid of value. They are concerned with the mainte- nances of personal, social, and cosmic harmony and with attaining specific goods — rain, harvest, children, health — as men have always been. (1970:23)

Eastern Mythology

A major difference in tolerance exists between religions of the East and the West that has affected their respective relations to folk religions. Western religions (Judaism, Christianity, and Islam) are much more likely to regard themselves as "the only true religion" than are Eastern religions (including Hinduism and Buddhism). While exclusivity prevailed in the West, in much of the East it was widely held that the more religion there was the better. Bryan Wilson has described this contrast in tolerance:

> The Gautama Buddha did not condemn the worship of deities, even though he was pointing to a higher path, and the majority of Theravadin Buddhists worship deities and placate spirits in practice, even though the teachings of their religion counsel quite different activities. The symbiosis of Taoism, Buddhism and Confucianism in China, and of Shinto and Buddhism in Japan, are no less social reali- ties, whatever vicissitudes occurred in governmental sponsorship of one faith or another. In contrast, Jews and Christians were taught to anathematize alien gods, and to regard their worship as false and even demonic. The Jewish god was, of course, originally a tribal deity, but eventually he came to be conceived as a universal spirit: initially supe- rior to other deities, subsequently he was proclaimed as the only true god. Christians (and in considerable measure, Muslims) inherited this orientation, and there can be no doubt of its powerful influence on western culture. (1982:56)

Aspects of folk mythologies were more likely to be absorbed into the more tolerant eastern religions while attempts were made to purge elementary supernatural and animistic beliefs from the more exclusive western religions.

The greater tolerance of eastern religions for divergent myths is readily apparent when they are contrasted with Christianity. Wilson (1982:62-66) has provided four interrelated points of contrast, summarized below, that help to describe the differences in social context between oriental and occidental myths:

1 RELIGION AND CIVILIZATION. Christianity was the primary agency of civilization for most of western Europe outside the confines of the Greek and Roman cities; Buddhism generally was accepted into societies that already had sophisticated civilization. The new religion (Buddhism) was intruded into older patterns of faith and philosophy to which it necessarily accommodated itself.

2 RELIGIOUS TOLERANCE. Eastern religion has not been marked by an emphasis on exclusivity. For example, Buddhism did not seek to eliminate local deities or local magic. In eastern cultures, diverse conceptions of the superempirical have been able to co-exist over very long periods of time. Not only was there religious pluralism, in the sense that different cosmologies, different theodicies, and different belief systems all acquired institutional expression and existed side by side, but the individual himself did not feel the need definitively to decide among them. Christianity, on the other hand, sought to take over all other religious influences, and to bring them all into systematic and coordinated relationship.

3 IMPORTANCE OF DOCTRINE. Christianity is a religion in which belief — sometimes presented as knowledge, and sometimes required as faith — constitutes the core concern. Jesus demanded faith; the Church came to require intellectual adherence to a number of propositions about God, Jesus, and by extension, humanity and the physical universe. Creed, in its minutely prescribed formulations, became the touchstone of Christianity. When we compare the religions of the East we see — even when, as in Buddhism, a profound philosophical system exists — how much more emphasis is placed on ritual performance and moral injunctions. Of course, these elements are important in Christianity, too, and the Catholic Church increasingly intensified its ritualistic preoccupations in the early centuries, while Protestantism vigorously reiterated man's obligation to obey God's

moral law. Yet in both Catholicism and Protestantism the final test was what a man *believed* — his intellectual commitment to a set of doctrinal propositions.

4 EMOTIONAL EXPRESSION. Eastern cultures of the Indian sub-continent appear to manifest a much more powerful emotional orientation than those of the West. Whereas western religion sought to discipline and regulate all forms of emotional expression, rejecting dance, eroticism, stimulants, and other ecstasy-inducing substances and procedures as unsuited to religious liturgy, these things have persisted in some branches of Hinduism and in Indian folk religion. Like western religion, Buddhism, too, sought to regulate emotional expression, but the very tolerance of Buddhist religion permitted the continuance at the level of folk culture, of emotive expression cast in a broadly religious guise.

52

Weber adds to this contrast in explaining differences between Christianity and Indian religions (Hinduism and Buddhism). He argues that whereas Christianity buttressed an attitude of the growth of the self and the world by dominating them through social action, the Indian religions encouraged an attitude of self-deification and world rejection through contemplation (see Schluchter 1987).

Despite the tolerance and the diversity, oriental mythologies do possess some central elements. Joseph Campbell (1968a) identifies five commonalities. First, the ultimate mystery, the sacred, is transcendent, or above all of the cosmos. At the same time it is mysteriously immanent — it dwells within all things. Second, the purpose of the eastern mythologies is to bring people into an awareness of their own identity. Paradoxically, this identity is actually non-identity, for it is grounded in the spiritual, which alone is real; self and the cosmos are one. Third, eastern mythologies give pre-eminence to the order of natural law that is everlasting, wondrous, blissful, and divine. There is no special revelation and no special theology. According to Campbell, this natural law is manifested in the universe (the "macrocosm"), the individual heart (the "microcosm"), and the hieratic order of the state with its symbolic arts and rites (the "mesocosm"). Fourth, there is more use of the feminine image in the mythologies of the East, particularly in Hinduism. For example, *maya*, non-empirical reality which alone is "really real," is personified as a woman within the Hindu world view. Finally, unlike Judaism, Christianity, and Islam, there is no one unique divine manifestation. All personifications, forms, acts, and experiences make manifest in some way the transcendent universal mystery.

In sum, eastern religions tend to be monistic. The heart of their world view is spiritual, with all that is material being regarded, ultimately, as illusion. The function of religion is to move people beyond illusion into ultimate reality. Although the sacred texts of oriental religions tend to include both transcendentalist and immanentist teaching, the everyday lived oriental religions tend to emphasize immanentist religiosity. A profane world separated from a distant holy god is embodied more in transcendental Christian, Jewish, and Islamic teachings than in immanent oriental thought.

Western Mythology

The dominant religious myths that emerged in the West are contained in what is known as the *Levantine* tradition, represented by Judaism, Christianity, and Islam. These three monotheistic world religions replaced the early polytheistic mythology of ancient Greece and Rome, with Christianity coming to dominate civilization for centuries. As I have already noted, Christianity is much less tolerant of religious diversity than are most oriental religions. In the words of Wilson: "Exclusivity and the demand that religious dogmas should be logically set out without internal contradictions gave rise in Christianity to a system of theology that was highly logical" (1982:38). Local beliefs and local magic gave way little by little to the gradual acceptance of a Christian world view dominated by a strong Roman Church.

Christianity is but one of the major world religions in the Levantine tradition. Levantine refers to the cultures bordering the eastern Mediterranean that gave rise to Judaism, Islam, and Christianity. Several general characteristics may be found in all three mythological systems that contrast with oriental mythologies (Campbell 1968a; Bellah 1970). First, all three religions tend toward dualism. God is transcendent and separate from the world in a fundamental way. Second, all are based on special revelations that go beyond nature. The giving of the decalogue to Moses in Judaism, the incarnation of God in Jesus taught in Christianity, and the role of Mohammed as the Prophet of Islam are all illustrations of supernatural manifestations of God. Third, in contrast to the acceptance and tolerance of eastern religions, all three Levantine religious mythologies hold a stance of exclusivity. Each believes itself to be the sole carrier of special revelations. Fourth, the dualism of the Levantine traditions is manifest in their focus on the need for people to be saved from the secular, from evil, from that in the world which binds them. Fifth, unlike folk or oriental mythologies that exist without a time reference, Levantine mythologies are historic. These myths focus, not upon a time beyond history, but on specific historic events. For Judaism, a focus is on the Exodus, marking the flight from the slavery of Egypt; for Christianity, the nucleus is Jesus' crucifixion and resurrection; the heart of Islam is the revelation of the Koran to Mohammed. Sixth, all three Levantine mythologies depict a masculine-like deity. Women do not have as special a role in the functioning of myths as they do in oriental thought.

Although I have presented a number of points of contrast between eastern and western mythologies, the basic difference is found in their respective perceptions of what is real. The world view of the spiritualistic eastern tradition stands at the opposite pole of the western materialistic tradition. In many oriental religions, the physical world, including human emotions such as love, hate, pity, anxiety, compassion, jealousy, and envy, is illusion. The eternal alone is real; the individual personality is *maya* and must be transcended. The western world view, in contrast, regards the physical and spiritual realms as being interrelated. Both are regarded as real and valuable. Since emotions, if properly understood, can push us toward the centre of meaning, love (which may be regarded as illusion in Buddhist traditions) is often esteemed in western religions as the motivating and creative core of the universe. This may be illustrated through mystical traditions of Christianity, Sufism (Islam), and Hasidism (Judaism), where a primary goal is becoming one with Divine Love or a Divine Lover (Kelsey 1983:23).

These contrasts are summarized in Table 2.2.

A Further Dichotomy

Before we leave this section, an additional dichotomy will assist us in understanding various mythologies. One set of myths is called "human ascent and divine response," in contrast to "divine descent and human response."

"Human ascent and divine response" refers to a myth which presents a sacred world view that sees the human condition as one of struggle and hard work or of the human quest as being one of ascending to the divine realm by one's own efforts (be they good works, proper sacrifices, well performed rituals, or moral codes). The hope is that the divine figure would look with kindness on these efforts and reward the seeker with eternal life, riches, blessings, and good things. The human subject may be called the "seeker." Empirical credibility to this kind of myth is given to us from Weber's summary of Asiatic religion (Hinduism, Buddhism, Confucianism, and Taoism). He argues that all the philosophies and soteriologies of Asia had a common presupposition which was that knowledge, *gnosis* (having the right knowledge), was the absolute path to holiness (1958b:330).

OCCIDENTAL AND ORIENTAL MYTHS

OCCIDENTAL	ORIENTAL
the creator is distinct from the creation	creator is not distinct from the creation and Self=Cosmos=Divine
prominence given to revelation	prominence to nature
eternal life consists in continued, personal existence	eternal life consists in the absorption into the divine
masculine images of the divine are common	both masculine and feminine images of the divine are common
there is a unique revelation beyond nature	there is no unique revelation beyond nature
tend to exclusivity	tend to inclusivity
Levantine	non-Levantine
historical	non-historical (Buddhism and Sikhism are exceptions)
tend to begin civilizations	tend to be absorbed into already existent civilizations
tend to control the environment	tend to submit to the environment

TABLE 2.2

Two images capture this kind of myth: a seeker on the bottom of a mountain begins a long ascent to the top where the sacred dwells. The hope is that once the top is reached, justice and rewards will be forthcoming. Another image comes from a common theme in myths: light and darkness. Most myths see people living in darkness and groping for the light. However, there is, typically, a large chasm that separates the two eternal regions, and the seeker needs to build a bridge to cross over through his or her own effort.

The second set of myths, "divine descent and human response," refers to the divine descending down to the human condition and inviting a response from the human subject (here called the "one who trusts"). In the mountain image, the sacred, manifested as a conscious person, descends down from the mountain and offers to take the one who trusts up to the top. All the human subject has to do is to respond in trust (expressed also in behaviours that reflect the sacred) and be carried. In the second image of darkness and light, the divine constructs a bridge from the realm of light, walks across it to the region of darkness, and carries the one who trusts back to the light.

All mythologies that express the first option are the mythologies of the East, folk societies, and Islam.[6] Only Judaism and Christianity reflect the second option. The divine descent myth is at the core of Judaism in that the deity loves people and creates a group so that salvation can be given to all humankind.

Several texts from the Hebrew bible illustrate this kind of mythology. The God of Israel is described as one who is "a God of tenderness and compassion, slow to anger, rich in graciousness, relenting from evil" (Jonah 4:2). This deity was seen to act on behalf of the people as is illustrated in a dialogue between Yahweh and Moses, the deliverer and law giver: "I have seen the miserable state of my people in Egypt, I have heard their appeal to be free of their slave drivers. Yes, I am well aware of their sufferings. I mean to deliver them out of the hands of the Egyptians and bring them up out of that land to a land rich and broad, a land where milk and honey flow" (Exodus 3:8). Another text explicates the sacred descent: "He let you hear his voice out of heaven for your instruction; on earth he let you see his great fire, and from the heart of the fire you heard his word. Because he loved your fathers and chose their descendants after them, he brought you out of Egypt, openly showing his presence and his great power... and brought you into their land to give it to you for your heritage" (Deuteronomy 4:35-38). After the rescue, the people were required to be obedient to a covenant established by God in the Sinai desert (Exodus 20) and thus continue to experience this intimate care.

Christianity goes a step further in its mythology that the sacred actually becomes human in the person of Jesus and bids people to come to him and thus enter into a divine life. It is in this latter mythology that God is defined as love and is intimately involved in the human condition. An early Christian writer says it in this way:

---

6 Weber substantiates this impression in noting "But Islam was never really a religion of salvation; the ethical concept of salvation was actually alien to Islam. The god it taught was a lord of unlimited power, although merciful, the fulfillment of whose commandments was not beyond human power" (1978:625).

Out of his loving-kindness for us he came to us, and we see this in the way he revealed himself openly to us. Taking pity on mankind's weakness, and moved by our corruption, he could not stand aside and see death have the mastery over us; he did not want creation to perish and his Father's work in fashioning man to be in vain. He therefore took to himself a body, no different from our own, for he did not wish simply to be in a body or only to be seen.... In death the Word made a spotless sacrifice and oblation of the body he had taken. By dying for others, he immediately banished death for all mankind. (St. Athanasius 1976:1808)

However, the response was not only trust but also to take on the character of Jesus, who forgave those who hurt him, loved the marginalized, and showed mercy to the forsaken. Morality becomes a goal not of reaching the sacred but living out the myth in everyday life (see Chapter Nine).

| ANTHROPOLOGICAL STUDIES OF MYTHS

Additional insights about mythology come from some anthropologists of religion, particularly Claude Lévi-Strauss. He is especially known for being a representative of structuralism and is even called the "father of structuralism" (Ritzer 1996). The term "structuralism" has a different meaning, however, than that found, for example, in Marx and Parsons. In a simple way the term tries to capture the "grammar of social life," the order present in what appears to be chaos, and the common features of social organization that is quite variant. I shall rely on three of Lévi-Strauss' works (1978, 1987 and 1993) to present his theory of structure in myths.

Consistent with a theme in this text that the sacred is not reduced to another phenomenon, Lévi-Strauss considers myth to be non-reductive. He claims that on the surface, the vast range of variation in myths may indicate that they are nothing but social products of their own cultures. If this is the case, he writes, "how are we going to explain the fact that myths throughout the world are so similar?" (1993:335). He finds that there is a remarkable order among this variation. Myth is considered be a kind of metalanguage that can be understood only if one considers the myth as a whole, as a unitary system. In this light, he presents three ways that a common structure underlies this variation. His data consist of North and South American aboriginal myths and one famous myth from Greece, Oedipus, upon which Freud constructed his "Oedipus Complex."

Found not only within these myths but in culture in general is a "binary structure" which patterns relationship in a binary fashion such as good/bad, male/female, yes/no, black/white, human/nonhuman, and raw food/cooked food. In his review of the American aboriginal mythologies, this pattern is evident. A second structure is that of a dynamism between *chaos* and *nomos*, of disorder and order. Very frequently, especially in the creation myths, the universe in general and the earth in particular was seen to be "without form," or "void." To provide order, the deity (or deities) put order into that chaos. A special feature of this structure is that the earth continues to move toward chaos, thus endangering the survival of humankind. The mythical figures are present to make a safe and ordered place for the human subject.

Another feature of myths is that they are like stories, dramas that have a beginning, a middle, and an end. In Lévi-Strauss' (1993) analysis of the Greek myth of Oedipus, he claims that there are four structures within the myth that capture common human experience. One structure (he places the myth in four columns) focuses on the closeness of people to their families, another, the struggles and distance found within families. A third structure depicts the common human experience of battle, fighting against forces that would destroy individuals and threaten human society. A final one depicts humans as being made from the earth, of being connected to nature.

Many have been the critiques of Lévi-Strauss. What has been termed as "post-structuralism," a denial of structure, has been the most potent. Yet if one considers his work with Campbell, there does seem to be some evidence of common features of myth that are universal and timeless. Another consistency between his work and the many anthropologists, sociologists, and comparative religion scholars reviewed in this text is a fundamental binary: the sacred and the profane.

| THE CONTEMPORARY CRISIS IN WESTERN MYTH

Even a cursory review of major mythological systems underlying different religions demonstrates a great deal of diversity that is not easily reconciled. Is the world "real" or is it an illusion? Is the sacred transcendent or is it immanent? Are all myths frail human attempts to talk about the sacred or does the sacred reveal itself to humankind in special ways? As we have seen, there are significant differences between eastern and western religious world views. Despite these differences, both religious perspectives have suffered with the advent of modernity.

In pre-modern societies, religion played an important role in propagating meaningful interpretations of the world, in regulating personal feelings and actions, and in contributing, directly and indirectly, toward unifying people. Levantine religions, primarily because of their exclusive mythologies, have been effective in exerting social control. Who could dare risk the wrath of Israel's Yahweh or Islam's Allah? Although he invited people to approach him, God also warned Jews, Christians, and Muslims to remember that he is an all-powerful God who punishes those who stray from his revelations. There has been a decided weakening of the power of religious world views in contemporary societies. Modernization, notes Robert Bellah (1970:74), "inevitably disturbs the pre-existing structure of meaning and motivation in any society where it gets under way." What we see is competition between different ways of framing the social world, with religion having lost ground to other secular perspectives.

The tension between religion and modernity has its roots in earlier developments within Christianity, the religion that dominated the western world for centuries. As we have already noted, Christianity placed much emphasis on an exclusive and logical belief system, but paradoxically this logical system also sowed the seeds for a rational and materialistic world view that became inimical to religion. Morton Kelsey summarizes the process well:

> Simply stated, the story is this: The classical Christian view of reality (which has never been lost in the Greek Orthodox tradition) was supplanted in Europe during late medieval times by the philosophy of Aristotle. Within that philosophical system, human beings have no direct contact with a spiritual world. We are limited to experiences of the five senses, with which to explore the knowable world, and reason, with which to make logical deductions and inferences about the world we do not experience through the senses. Aristotle cast grave doubts upon the existence of any world not discovered by reason and sense experience.
>
> The beliefs of Aristotle came to be the foundation for both Protestant and Catholic scholasticism. In the eighteenth century the Enlightenment, following the lead of Thomas Hobbes, went even further, denying the existence of any spiritual world. Then, in the nineteenth century, chemistry, physics, medicine and other sciences produced dramatic successes without taking any spiritual dimension into consideration. Many thinkers concluded that science had final truth and the spiritual world was illusion. (1983:13)

Peter Berger (1967), a contemporary sociologist of religion, provides additional insight about this crisis of myth caused by religion's confrontation with modernity.[7] The primary reason for the predicament is the weak-

---

7 As indicated before, Weber uses the term "world views" to discuss what historians of religion call "mythologies." Berger employs the concept "symbolic universes" to discuss a similar phenomenon. *Symbolic universes* are those "bodies of theoretical tradition that integrate different provinces of meaning and encompass the institutional order in a symbolic totality" (Berger and Luckmann 1966:95). In the discussion of Berger, I will continue to use the terms "world view" and "myth."

CHANGES IN MYTH THROUGH THE INTERNET

"It seems as though the Net itself has become conscious," says William Gibson, the science-fiction writer who coined the term cyberspace. "It may regard itself as God. And it may be God on its own terms." These radical notions dovetail with a spiritual movement known as process theology, whose propagandists argue that God evolves along with man. "If God doesn't change, we are in danger of losing God," says William Grassie, a Quaker professor of religion at Temple University, "There is a shift to the idea of God as a process evolving with us. If you believe in an eternal, unchanging God, you'll be in trouble."

In fact, as much as the Net is changing our ideas of God, it may be changing us ever more. For many, signing on to the Internet is a transformative act. In their eyes the Web is more than just a global tapestry of personal computers and fibre-optic cable. It is a vast cathedral of the mind, a place where ideas about God and religion can resonate, where faith can be shaped and defined by a collective spirit. Interconnected, we may begin to find God in places we never imagined.

SOURCE: "Finding God on the Web: Across the Internet, believers are reexamining their ideas of faith, religion and spirituality." *Time*, December 16, 1996: 52-58.

BOX 2.2

60

ening of what Berger terms "plausibility structures." Plausibility structures are social interactions within a group which serve to sacralize the shared meanings of the group. In other words, they make the religious world view "plausible" or believable. Given the secular nature of modern society, fewer and fewer plausibility structures are available to support religious myth. Where they are available, however, myths are viable. For example, persons who identify strongly with and associate regularly with a particular religious group are able to accept the group's tenets, regardless of how strange the beliefs may appear to those outside the group.

For myths to survive, they must be rooted in a social base that creates a sense of sacredness about the beliefs; in other words, they must be grounded in plausibility structures. In pre-modern societies, religious myths provided an important foundation for interpreting the world. Social interaction within these pre-modern groups reinforced religious myths, and these myths in turn provided people with a believable meaning system. In modern pluralistic societies, several different meaning systems compete for adherents, making it difficult to regard any one as having absolute truth. One of the major lines of cleavage is between the traditionalism of religious world views and the rationality of the modern scientific world.

There is no doubt that rationalization,[8] a process that has affected modernized peoples of East and West, has been an important factor in the weakening of religious world views. What had been overlooked by some scholars of religion a few decades ago, however, is that this process is not linear. (Those who wrote obituaries for the Judeo-Christian God in the 1960s learned that they had exaggerated his death!) Despite the limited influence of religious mythology in the public sphere, it still plays, as shall be demonstrated throughout this text, a significant role in private lives. Since people collectively create and modify any world view, the private effects of religion may also spill over into the public arena, making religion a force to be dealt with beyond the private sphere.

THE POWER OF MYTH AS AN AGENT OF SOCIAL CHANGE

The approach I have taken to our discussion is but one way of looking at myth. Underlying the dominant sociological perspective used in this chapter is the assumption that myth is an indispensable part of social reality and that it functions in positive ways to support the existing social order. The mythical world view may be regarded as a "hidden structure," having certain similarities across cultures but being manifested in different cultural forms. Although there are noteworthy differences in the lives of the Buddha, Abraham, Jesus, and Mohammed, all share certain characteristics of religious heroes who have animated different religious traditions. These religious traditions have enabled millions of people to "make sense" of the universe (the cosmological function of myth). They have provided mechanisms for social control, social support, and socialization (sociological functions). Furthermore, they have guided people toward spiritual enrichment (psychological function).

My approach to myth has focused primarily on its ability to maintain stability in society, but myth also has the power to bring about change. African American religions bestow many illustrations of the way in which religious world views may challenge the existing conditions by providing mythologies that confront the world view of the dominant culture rather than simply comforting their followers. One special African American religion is the Nation of Islam. Because of its unique and special place in

---

8 The specific sociological meaning of the term comes from Weber. Ritzer (1996:136) considers it to be a process that is both personal and social that endeavours to capture human life under categories of the mind in order, eventually to control life by knowing more and more about the physical, organic, and social world. It involves calculation, mastering reality through concepts, and encompassing ordinary life with formal rules, laws, and regulations.

African American religion, it will be used as a special case example in the text. In this chapter, the mythology will be outlined, which will be followed by the religious experience of two of the main leaders of the religion (Chapter Four), a profile of the religious leaders of the Nation of Islam (Chapter Six), and discussions on ritual (Chapter Seven), religious organization (Chapter Eight), and ethos (Chapter Nine). A final note on the Nation will be presented in the chapter on religion and the economy (Chapter Eleven), when I address the question of religion being an inhibitor or a facilitator of change.

The Black Sacred Cosmos

62

As Lincoln and Mamiya (1990) have demonstrated through their research on black American religion, the "black sacred cosmos" has dominated the religious world view of African Americans. They stress that "black people created their own unique and distinctive forms of culture and world views as parallels rather than replications of the culture in which they were involuntary guests" (Lincoln and Mamiya 1990:2). A word that illustrates the parallel nature of black Christianity is the importance given to freedom. As Lincoln and Mamiya (1990:4) observe:

> A major aspect of black Christian belief is found in the symbolic importance given to the word "freedom." Throughout black history the term "freedom" has found a deep religious resonance in the lives and hopes of African Americans. Depending upon the time and the context, the implications of freedom were derived from the nature of the exigency. During slavery it meant release from bondage, after emancipation it meant the right to be educated, to be employed and to move about freely from place to place. In the twentieth century freedom means social, political, and economic justice. From the very beginning of the black experience in America, one critical denotation of freedom has remained constant: freedom has always meant the absence of any restraint which might compromise one's responsibility to God. The notion has persisted that if God calls you to discipleship, God calls you to freedom. And that God wants you free because God made you for Himself and in His image. Although generations of white preachers and exhorters developed an amazing complex of arguments aimed at avoiding too obvious a conclusion, it was a dictum securely anchored in the black man's faith and indelibly engraved on his psyche. A well-known black spiritual affirms that:

Before I'll be a slave
I'll be buried in my grave
And go home to my Father
and be free. . .

African American Christianity has been at the heart of black culture, raising the core values of that culture to an ultimate level and legitimating
them. Many aspects of black cultural practice and some major social institutions "had religious origins; they were given birth and nurtured in the
womb of the Black Church" (Lincoln and Mamiya 1990:7).

The Black Muslims: Sowing the Seeds of Black Nationalism

Although Christianity has played an important role among African
Americans during the twentieth century, it is Islam which has had a
remarkable impact in creating a unique African American religion. There
are three contrasting mythologies of the Black Muslim or the Nation of
Islam that can be categorized as the genesis, interim, and mature belief systems. In the initial mythology, Allah was incarnate in W.D. Fard, a
stranger who came to Detroit from Arabia in 1930 and who was reported to
have been born in Mecca in 1877. Fard (called Master Farad Muhammad)
brought a proto-Islamic faith to blacks in America, but it was Elijah
Muhammad who popularized its mythology.

63

According to Elijah Muhammad, Allah himself is a Black Man — the
Supreme Black Man — and all black men represent Him (Lincoln 1961:73-
80). The original man was black and his history is coextensive with the creation of the earth. White man's history spans only six thousand years,
beginning with the creation of the white race by Yacub, "a black scientist in
rebellion against Allah." In grafting out his creatures' colour, Yacub grafted
out their very humanity. As Elijah Muhammad said of the white race:

> The human beast — the serpent, the dragon, the devil, and Satan —
> all mean one and the same; the people or race known as the white or
> Caucasian race, sometimes called the European race. ... Since by
> nature they were created liars and murderers, they are the enemies of
> truth and righteousness, and the enemies of those who seek the truth.
> (cited in Lincoln 1961:77)

Gardell (1996) adds that this race was believed to be evil by nature,
drained of the divine essence, incapable of acting or thinking decently, and
unable to submit to the law of Islam. Caucasian hegemony is equal to the
evil era of the Devil expressed in colonialism, slavery, racial oppression, and

poverty. In the person of Master Farad Muhammad, and under the direction of Elijah Muhammad, this oppression is beginning to come to an end, and when mentally "dead" black people are enlightened with the true knowledge of the Nation of Islam, which is the Knowledge of Self and God, this supremacy will cease. God will destroy all the "white devils" in an apocalyptic fire, and the earth will be transformed into a black paradise.

After the passing of Elijah Muhammad in 1975, there was a need for a viable successor. Before his death, Elijah appointed his seventh child, Wallace D. Muhammad (called Imam Warith Deen Muhammad), to head the movement (Torque 1993). He rapidly attempted not only to restructure NOI (Nation of Islam) but to adjust it to the mythology of mainstream, Sunni Islam. Gardell (1996) referred to it as "Rapid Islamization Transit." This I refer to as the interim mythology. Wallace's readjustment of NOI was to de-deify Master Farad Muhammad and to de-demonize the white man in order to position the mythology more in line with mainstream Islam, which would consider these early teachings heresy. In effect, he "spiritualized" the more physical aspects of the original mythology. The enemy was not the white man but the spiritual white man who oppressed the black race. In fact, converted Caucasians could be full members of NOI. He called his father a great teacher but not a messenger or a prophet. Master Farad Muhammad was not another prophet (there can be no other later prophet but Muhammad Ibn Abdullah in orthodox Islam) but a great teacher or imam.

The third mythological stage, termed mature, begins with the ascendency of Minister Louis Farrakhan Muhammad. He was born in 1933 in the Bronx and later became the official leader of NOI. He believed that while Wallace led the Nation, it experienced a fall. It was his intent to resurrect the original mythology, structure, ritual, and ethos of the movement.

Besides accepting the original tenets of Master Farad (that he was divine and that the white race was demonic) he argued that man is god and god is man. Gardell (1996) calls the mythology of the Nation *blackosophy*, and outlines it as follows. Elijah Muhammad did not really die but passed onto another human stage of development. He ascended to become the Lamb of God and the Messiah. In contrast, Master Farad achieved the utmost of divinity and no longer needs to grow any more. Farrakhan has not yet achieved full divinity and is called "little Messiah." Being so, he can properly interpret the faith.

The central tenets of the mature Nation are summarized by Gardell:

· the black man is God's creation
· Mr. Yacub, the black scientist, created the white race and is evil
· the black original culture was the cradle of civilization

- white supremacy (coming to an end with NOI) is against the long term divine will
- God is a material being
- man in his exalted state is divine
- to achieve divine-hood, one needs to have a knowledge of self. The phrase: "I-SELF-LORD-AM-MASTER" or I.S.L.A.M. is at the heart of the mythology. If one really knows oneself, then one knows God.
- true anthropology is theology, for all are "gods"
- in essence, the Nation of Islam is a nation of gods (1996:170ff.)

The Nation of Islam was the most recent and most successful of the proto-Islamic cults that helped sow the seeds for black nationalism and black pride. Its myths challenged the myths of white Christianity which often assumed that the white race was favoured by God. The Nation of Islam became the foundation for the development of a large, orthodox, Islamic African American community that presently challenges the Black Christian Church. It is estimated that about 1 million of the 8 million Muslims in the United States are African Americans, and close to 90 per cent of new converts are black (Lincoln and Mamiya 1990:390; Gardell 1996:4). Islam has increasingly become a viable religious alternative to black Christian churches, especially for many black males who seek changes in American society.

Sociologically speaking, black religious myth functions, as does all religious myth, to provide mechanisms for social support, socialization, and social control. But it also has functioned to promote social change. It is culturally produced in a white-dominated society and "simultaneously offers some protection from the elements, provides a sheltered arena for personal development and expression, and allows a controlled level of protest of the external social world" (Baer and Singer 1992:xxii).

| DEFINING RELIGION

We are coming to the end of the second chapter, and still I have not offered a conclusive definition of religion.[9] Instead of beginning this text with a definition of religion, I chose to demonstrate the diversity found in religious world views. I hope that this discussion will help readers to be wary of simple definitions of religion that focus on God or gods, on a particular approach to the material or to the spiritual world, or on a particular mean-

---

9 Blasi (1998) offers an extensive history of the term as well as an in-depth presentation of the substantive, functional, and formal definitions of religion.

DEFINITIONS OF RELIGION

Substantive

Religion is the experiential encounter with the holy and the responsive action of the human being influenced by the holy. – Gustav Mensching (1964:36)

(paraphrased)...the heart of religion consists in the manifestation of the sacred to people. – Mircea Eliade (1959:11)

[T]he haunting realization of the ultimate powerlessness in an inscrutable world, and the unquestioning and thoroughly irrational conviction of the possibility of gaining mystic security by somehow identifying oneself with what can never be known. – Edward Sapir (1960:122-23)

Functional

A religion is a unified system of beliefs and practices relative to sacred things, that is to say, things set apart and forbidden – beliefs and practices which unite into a single moral community called a Church, all those who adhere to them. – Emile Durkheim (1965:62)

Religion, then, can be defined as a system of beliefs and practices by means of which a group of people struggles with these ultimate problems of human life. – Milton Yinger (1970:7)

ing system. What so-called *definitions* of religion tend to be are descriptions of religion rather than hard and fast demarcations.

At the same time, these "definitions" are very useful in coming to a better understanding of religion. Descriptive "definitions," including the widely quoted ones provided in Box 2.3, can tell us much about what religion is, including how it functions and its major forms. It is not without significance that two of the earliest sociologists of religion differed in their opinions about when in their writings it was necessary to define religion. The French sociologist Emile Durkheim provided a widely-accepted formal definition, found in Box 2.3, in his early scholarly writings. His contemporary German counterpart, Max Weber, believed it was possible to define religion only after having studied it extensively. Weber wrote five major books on religion in various parts of the world, but never did provide a definition.

DEFINITIONS OF RELIGION (CONT'D)

A religion we will define as a set of beliefs, practices, and institutions which
men have evolved in various societies, as far as they can be understood, as
responses to those aspects of their life and situation which are believed not in
the empirical-instrumental sense to be rationally understandable and/or con-
trollable, and to which they attach a significance which includes some kind of
reference to the relevant actions and events to man's conception of the existence of the 'supernatural' order which is conceived and felt to have a fundamental bearing on man's position in the universe and the values which give
meaning to his fate as an individual and his relation to his fellows.
– Talcott Parsons (1951:2)

Man makes religion, religion does not make man. In other words, religion is the
self-conscious and self-feeling of man who has either not yet found himself or
has already lost himself again....Religion is the general theory of that world
(the world of capitalism)....its enthusiasm, its moral sanction, ... its universal
ground for consolation and justification ... it is the opium of the people.
                                        – Karl Marx and Friedrich Engels (1964:41)

Formal

Religion is (1) a system of symbols which acts to (2) establish powerful, pervasive, and long-lasting moods and motivations in [people] by (3) formulating
conceptions of a general order of existence and (4) clothing these conceptions
with such an aura of factuality that the moods and motivations seem uniquely
realistic. – Clifford Geertz (1966:4)

BOX 2.3

It is possible to approach definitions of religion from three major positions: substantively, functionally, and formally. A substantive definition of
religion focuses on the essence or nature of religion. Those who employ
substantive definitions tend to emphasize affect or feelings. Religion is an
"experiential encounter" (Mensching), a "manifestation of the sacred"
(Eliade), or a "haunting realization of ultimate powerlessness" (Sapir).
Substantive definitions of religion, much like substantive definitions of
myth, are difficult to establish cross-culturally. Boundaries between the
sacred and secular or the divine and the human are much clearer in western
than in oriental mythology, yet definitions of religion tend to assume this
demarcation. Anthropologist Edward Sapir attempts to avoid defining

religion in terms of western thinking by emphasizing a sense of "ultimate powerlessness" and an impossibility of knowing, but this definition reflects other biases.

Functional definitions emphasize the effects of religion on people and on the social order. They may define religion in positively functional terms with religion providing meaning (Yinger and Parsons), social legitimation (Parsons), social cohesion and integration (Durkheim and Parsons), and a source of morality (Durkheim). Functional definitions see religion as being a product of human activity, which in turn acts back on members of a society in ways that contribute to the maintenance of the social order. It is religion regarded as an important agent of socialization and a guardian of societal values.

Marx's secular social and political philosophy was in direct competition with organized religion of his day, and Marx's definition of religion reflects this tension (Johnstone 1992:110). Marx stressed the dysfunctions of religion, emphasizing how religion is used by the dominant and powerful in society to encourage acceptance of one's lot in life. Marx called religion the "opium of the people," meaning that it served as a kind of narcotic drug administered by the elites of a society to the less privileged.

Functional definitions of religion can stress religion's positive functions in maintaining social control or its dysfunctions in promoting a status quo that exploits a group of people. Non-Marxists tend to describe the functions of religion in more positive terms while Marxists are critical of the role religion has played in perpetuating unjust social situations. Some contemporary Marxists, however, use Marx's framework to describe religious protests that have brought about social change.[10]

Anthropologist Clifford Geertz's formal definition is actually a blend of substantive and functional approaches to religion. He provides a more detailed description of what religion is and how it operates. Symbols — things that represent or remind us of something else — are at the heart of any religion. They have a decided impact on human sentiment which in turn prompts people into action. They are catalysts that elicit "long-lasting moods and motivations." They provide a sense of the "general order of existence" — conceptions that seem very real. Geertz's entire definition is long and quite elaborate, running in its entirety some 46 pages of text. It identifies the general properties of religion, depicting religion as a world view that performs specific functions in society.

68

---

10 Karl Marx had surprisingly little to say about the protest function of religion. His collaborator Frederich Engels, more than Marx, elaborated on the nature of religious protest (Marx and Engels 1964).

In the light of all these definitions, a formal one (that includes both substantive and functional elements) is presented as: "Religion is the individual and social experience of the sacred that is manifested in mythologies, rituals, and ethos, and integrated into a collective such as a community or an organization." This is how religion will be understood in this text.

Whatever else it is, religion offers a way of viewing the world that differs from modern rational and secular thought. With modernization, the boundaries between religion and non-religion have become increasingly more pronounced. The establishing and maintaining of religious boundaries in modern society is the subject of the next chapter.

■ CHAPTER THREE ■

Societal Boundaries and
Religious Institutions

World views represent ways of thinking, and as such lie in the subjective realm of ideas rather than in the objective world of hard facts. Although world views might at first appear very individual and personal, a closer examination will reveal that they require some level of social support for development, maintenance, and dissemination. Creating world views is not a solo enterprise; it is done in interaction with others and within a social context. If a belief system is viewed as being implausible or unrealistic, it is not likely to survive for long. According to sociologist Peter Berger (1969), world views require *plausibility structures* that consist of social interaction and group process. Plausibility structures serve to protect the shared meanings and outlooks of the group.

In western cultures, as we saw in the last chapter, there is an inherent tension between sacred and secular world views. Boundary lines have been drawn in the Levantine religious traditions that are not as apparent in oriental world views. The tension between the larger secular society and religious world views has been described well by sociologists Charles Glock and Rodney Stark as *religion and society in tension*. In their description of this tension between the secular world and religion they note:

> In Judeo-Christian cultures religion is expected to be at odds with the world around it. While religious life must perforce be lived in this world, it is not to be of it. Indeed, it is held to be the duty of priests and prophets to take those who become enmeshed in the trivial affairs of this world and turn them towards the more eternal concerns. Thus, the church is seen to exist in a hostile and evil world, and to have a sacred mission to denounce and resist matters of the flesh, for all this shall pass away. (1965:ix)

Yet despite this ideology that calls for withdrawal from the world, Glock and Stark note that "the majority of religious leaders have been practical men who have gone about the business of managing the mundane interests of religion." As social scientists have long known, the *ideal culture* of a world view is not identical to the *real culture* embodied in the social structure. Nonetheless, world views and plausibility structures are interdependent: world views are dependent on social action and structure for expression and maintenance and social institutions are dependent on world views for meaning and legitimation.

Ideologies (a more generic term that includes religious myths and belief systems) may be about the non-material, but they cannot exist in a spiritual vacuum. They are necessarily incorporated into materially observable social arrangements — what sociologists call "institutions" or "social structures."

72

The struggle between secular and sacred ideologies is thus enacted on the stage of living societies — a tension that may be analyzed in terms of social and institutional boundaries. Just as nations struggle to maintain territorial boundaries, so too do institutional representatives of ideologies seek boundary demarcations favourable to them. The focus in this chapter is on institutions and tensions over boundary formation and boundary maintenance.

| MYTH, RELIGION, AND SOCIAL ORGANIZATION

The mythical world views that we discussed in the previous chapter are, as we have already noted, interdependent with social organization. Religious myths may be regarded as a kind of soul of society, but they cannot persist without taking on the flesh and blood of social institutions. Myths are embedded in the social organizations we know as religion, politics, law, family, the economy, and medicine. In the words of Rollo May (1991:20), "[Myths] are narrations by which our society is unified. Myths are essential to the process of keeping our souls alive and bringing us new meaning in a difficult and often meaningless world."

Although it is impossible to separate completely the subjective dimensions of an institution from its objective ones, breaking religion down into myth and social organization as we are doing is a fruitful academic exercise. It permits us to shift the focus of our analysis away from tension in the realm of ideas toward the struggles found within religious institutions and *between* religious organizations and the larger social order. Objectively, institutions are arrangements of *roles* or patterned sets of social relationships and *norms* or standardized ways of regulating social behaviour. Defined, an institution refers to specific areas of human social life that have become broadly organized into discernible patterns. Institution refers to the organized means whereby the essential tasks of a society are organized, directed, and carried out. In short, it denotes the system or norms that organize human behaviour into stable patterns of activity. (Eshleman, 1994:74)

Each institution has a boundary that demarcates it from other institutions and the society as a whole. According to family-systems theorists, a boundary "defines the system (understood as an institution) and represents the interface, or point of contact between the system and other systems, between the system and its subsystems and supra systems or the environment" (Whitchurch and Constantine 1993:333). The unfolding of the institutional basis for tension that includes boundary issues will be discussed through three major sociological theorists: Emile Durkheim, Max Weber, and Robert Bellah. The common thread in each of these theorists is how the boundaries between religion and the various institutions change throughout time and how religion varies throughout history as it adapts to the larger social environment. Each has an account that can help us to better understand institutional religion in the modern world.

73

The Process of Differentiation: Emile Durkheim

The earliest societies made no real distinction among social institutions. Much like the lowest level of biological life, these societies were simple (having few parts) rather than complex (having many interconnected parts). To use Emile Durkheim's term, folk societies were undifferentiated. Basic to the process of social differentiation is what Durkheim discussed as the *division of labour*. In folk societies, the work tasks to be performed were limited to relatively few, such as obtaining food, preparing it, seeking shelter, child bearing, and child care. These tasks were assigned largely on the basis of sex and age. Religion was not yet a formal organization, but rather it was a world view that was intimately tied to the extended family system. In earliest folk societies, the occupation of priest was yet to emerge, with the patriarch playing the role of religious leader as one of his many roles.

As societies grew in size, there was an increased division of labour, including the emergence of a priesthood and a formal religious structure. The development of a priestly class among the ancient Jewish people may be used as an example. Although Abraham is credited with being the father of Judaism, the priestly class can be traced biblically not from Abraham but from his grandson, Levi (born to Jacob and Leah). It was while the Israelites wandered the desert after the exodus from Egypt that the descendants of Levi were "set apart" by Moses, an act that evolved into a formal

SOCIETY, SPIRITUALITY, AND THE SACRED

priesthood (Exodus 32:29). Through the first stages of Jewish history, the division of labour was very limited (as characteristic of nomadic tribes) and its society was relatively undifferentiated.

Israel began to change and to be differentiated with its liberation from Egypt in about 1250 to 1230 BC. Evidence for this differentiation is documented in a sociological study of Israel from 1250 to 1050 BC by Gottwald (1979). Using a variety of historical sources, he argues that the agrarian-pastoral society of Israel in Canaan included feudalized peasants, mercenaries and adventurers, transhumant[1] pastoralists, tribally organized farmers and pastoral nomads, itinerant craftsmen and priests. However, the differentiation was still nascent, for the religion of Yahweh was coextensive with all of Israel and a crucial instrument in unifying and decentralizing sociocultural patterns important for the optimal functioning of the whole social system.

FOLK SOCIETIES

Folk societies are characterized by what Durkheim termed "mechanical social solidarity." The term "mechanical" refers to a kind of society wherein people act like parts of a machine, indicating little individuality. They are bonded to each other because they resemble one another and share what Durkheim termed a "collective conscience," or a set of "beliefs and sentiments common to average citizens of the same society [which] forms a determinate system which has its own life" (Durkheim 1933:79, 105). Within such societies, religion holds a prominent position because it is an integral part of the collective conscience and has a coercive effect on people's lives. In the words of Durkheim:

> Since these sentiments have exceptional force because of their collective origin, their universality, their permanence, and their intrinsic intensity, they separate themselves radically from the rest of our conscience whose states are much more feeble. They dominate us; they are so to speak, something superhuman, and at the same time, they bind us to objects which are outside of our temporal life. They appear to us as an echo in us of a force which is foreign to us, and which is superior to that which we are. We are thus forced to project them outside ourselves, to attribute what concerns them to some exterior object. (1933:100)

---

1   From the term "transhumance," the seasonal migration of livestock, and the people who tend them, between lowlands and adjacent mountains.

Durkheim (1965) provides a systematic study of the lack of differentiation of religion in folk social settings. *The Elementary Forms of Religious Life* is a theoretical review of the studies of early anthropologists who did fieldwork not only in Australia (among the Arunta, the Loritja, the Kaitish, the Unmatjera, and the Ilpirra peoples) but also in North America (among the Iroquois, the Haida, the Kwakiutl, the Navajo, and others). His central thesis is that totemism is the central characteristic of these peoples and that religion is significantly integrated into their other institutions. Goode's (1951:221) synthesis of the Dahomey, the Manus, Tikopia, the Zuni, and the Murngin gives further evidence of the intricate connection of religion with the economic, political, and familial institutions of these peoples.

Durkheim noted that in folk societies, the boundaries between institutions are permeable and flexible. Because religion tends to be coextensive with the whole society, the religious boundaries and the social boundaries are blurred.

Before we leave Durkheim in this context, it is important to give some empirical basis for his functional interpretation of religion as a source of social integration. Both Durkheim (1965:299ff) and, later, Malinowski (1964:113) contended that folk peoples experienced anomie and social disintegration when a member died. There was a sense of loss and an experience of fractured solidarity. Malinowski (1964:113) writes: "A small community bereft of a member, especially if he be important, is severely mutilated. The whole event breaks the normal course of life and shakes the moral foundations of society." The religious rites of mourning counteract the centrifugal pulls of demoralization, fear, and dismay and functions as a most powerful means of reintegration of the social group's broken solidarity.

THE MODERN WORLD

With the advent of the modern world came much more differentiated societies, each with hundreds upon hundreds of different and specialized tasks to be performed. This differentiation permitted much more personal autonomy than was possible in traditional societies. A young man no longer necessarily follows in his father's footsteps as a shepherd; a young woman has other choices than to be a shepherd's wife. Durkheim believed that this differentiation in work roles serves as a bonding force in modern societies. The new work roles are complementary, causing people to be dependent upon one another in new ways.

As societies became more differentiated, they moved away from "mechanical solidarity" to what Durkheim called "organic solidarity." The increase in the division of labour resulted in individuals being more different from one another than they were in societies characterized by mechanical solidarity. Despite these differences, persons are still bound together by mutual dependencies. The farmer needs the factory worker and the factory worker, the farmer; office workers are dependent on labourers and both rely on political leaders, the police and military workers, bankers, and educators.

Accompanying the development of mechanical solidarity, however, is a shift in awareness or what Durkheim called "social conscience." Increased differentiation could have led to a breakdown of the social bonds that united people. Durkheim believed that social conscience prevented individuals from becoming a "jumble of juxtaposed atoms, between which it [the society] can establish only external, transient contacts" (Durkheim 1933:227). In a more specialized modern society, religion has a specific function of legitimating the morality that creates and promotes social bonds. In other words, religion gradually shifts from being an all-pervasive world view into having a more limited and specialized function.

Increased differentiation makes personal autonomy much more possible than ever before; and, by itself, individual pursuit of self-interest would ultimately lead to the breakdown of the social order. Durkheim wrestled with the question of how the individual could maintain autonomy and still experience solidarity with others. In less differentiated societies a common religious bond was a glue that "united people into a single moral community" (from Durkheim's definition of religion). Durkheim observed that in European societies at the turn of the twentieth century, the nature of religion was changing. According to Durkheim (1965), "The old gods were dying or were already dead and the new ones were yet to be born." Modern society was facing a crisis of myth, and this crisis was rooted in changes in social organization.

As society moved from a relatively undifferentiated mass in which religion played a key role to a highly complex social structure in which religion's influence is diminished, tension increased between religion and other social institutions. In modern societies religion embraces a smaller and smaller portion of social life. According to Durkheim, in earlier societies everything that was religious was social, and all that was social was religious. The two worlds were synonymous. Durkheim went so far as to assert that when people worshipped God or gods, they were in fact worshipping their society. Gradually other institutions, including the political, economic, and scientific emerged, greatly limiting the function of religious institutions. As Durkheim described the process,

> In short, not only does not the domain of religion grow at the same time and in the same measure as temporal life, but it contracts more and more. This regression did not begin at some certain moment of

history, but can follow its phases since the origins of social evolution. It is, thus, linked to the fundamental conditions of the development of societies, and it shows that there is a decreasing number of collective beliefs and sentiments which are both collective enough and strong enough to take on a religious character. That is to say, the average intensity of the common conscience progressively becomes enfeebled. (1933:169-70)

Clearly religion has lost its position of power and prominence in modern society. Do the changes spell religion's eventual demise? Durkheim did not think so. He believed religion would continue as an important force, although it would change radically. Just as societies were subject to the process of differentiation, religion too was increasingly differentiated. While religion in folk societies has the power to unify into a single moral community, religion in contemporary societies is no longer one but many. The pluralism in religious perspectives gives the individual greater autonomy to make moral and religious choices. One need only reflect on the tension in North America as it moves from its European Judeo-Christian base to include religions from other continents, including Buddhists, Hindus, and Muslims, as well as countless new religious movements. Perhaps equally noteworthy are those people who refuse to see themselves as "religious" but who are in quest for deeper "spirituality" (see Bellah, *et al.* 1985; Roof 1993).

As further illustration of the Durkheimian process of differentiation, Parsons (1964) and Moberg (1964) present illustrative examples of the process. Parsons (1964) traces the history of Christianity as a history of differentiation. This differentiation, however, did not follow a linear path. Christianity began differentiated both from Judaism and Roman society. During the medieval period, this differentiation declined, and the Roman Catholic Church became coextensive with the medieval society. From the time of the Reformation, though, Christianity has become more differentiated from within and significantly from the modern society.

Moberg (1964) outlines that Dutch society is differentiated into three *columns* that indicate a vertical pluralism and unity in diversity. The three columns represent the Dutch who are Roman Catholic, Protestant (Calvinistic), and humanistic. Evidence for this pluralism is from the state support of three school systems. In 1957, 34 per cent of parents of school children were Roman Catholic, 28 per cent Protestant and 38 per cent humanistic, neutral or secular. Moberg goes on to discuss that these three columns effect substantial differentiation of the Dutch population into these three groups.

THE CULT OF THE INDIVIDUAL

In his study of "boomers" (Americans born between 1946 and 1964), Wade Clark Roof (1993) makes an important distinction between *spirit* and *institution* that reflects Durkheim's discussion of the "cult of the individual." Roof notes:

> The distinction between "spirit" and "institution" is of major importance. *Spirit* is the inner, experiential aspect of religion; *institution* is an outer, established form of religion. This distinction is increasingly pertinent because of the strong emphasis on self in contemporary culture and the related shift from objective to subjective ways of ordering experience. (1993:30)

In generic terms, Durkheim was aware of this kind of distinction and although he knew that the institutional aspects of religion were being greatly curtailed, he also recognized that this institutional change was being accompanied by greater autonomy for the individual.

For Durkheim (1960), human nature was dualistic, not unlike a two-storey dwelling. The first floor is "purely individual and rooted in our organisms"; the second floor is "social and nothing but an extension of society." Religious (institutional) morality until very recent times had been essential for the functioning of society. It provided the basis for the collective conscience. As religion's moral role became more and more limited in scope, Durkheim sought another form that could function in the place of the collective conscience (Durkheim 1933:169-70). The answer he proposed was the *cult of man or the individual,* a collective moral sense of the worth of each person. It represents a new morality whose seeds were found in the Judeo-Christian tradition but whose secular growth has been facilitated by the climate of post-Enlightenment rationalism.

The rise of new religions in North American society can be used to illustrate this *cult of the individual.* Frances Westley (1983) has demonstrated how the heart of many new "self-help" religions, including Silva Mind Control, EST, and Scientology, promotes a doctrine that celebrates reason and freedom of thought.[2] They teach that the divine is within each person, that it is only as the believer comes in touch with this truth that he or she can achieve full potential. New religions that accentuate the development of personal human potential reflect a shift away from emphasizing the collectivity toward emphasizing the individual (Schoenfeld and Mestrovic 1991). Emerging new religions (as well as the repackaging of many old reli-

---

2   For an extension of this discussion, see Chapter Eight under "cult."

gions) are centred in the individual rather than the community. The primary function of religion may be shifting, as suggested by the *cult of the individual*, from serving to unite people into a community to maximizing individual human potential.

In sum, according to Durkheim, religion in folk societies has loose boundaries, functions to integrate and unify the society, and is relatively undifferentiated from other social institutions. In contrast, religion in the modern world increasingly has distinct boundaries (between itself and the secular social environment as well as from other religious institutions) and functions primarily to enhance personal growth.

The Process of Rationalization: Max Weber

Like Durkheim, Max Weber recognized the critical role played by religion in society as he sought to understand the development of the modern world. A unique feature of his scholarship was the use of historical materials that accented concrete social, economic, and political events rather than the evolutionary theory that was popular at the turn of the last century (Roth 1987). Many early sociologists, including Durkheim, took an evolutionary approach that sought to discover laws of human development. Durkheim, for example, believed that contemporary religion could be best understood by analyzing the religion of folk societies, a task he set for himself in *The Elementary Forms of Religious Life*. Basic patterns found among folk religions were assumed to cast light on the more complex religious beliefs and behaviour of modern men and women. Weber, in contrast, studied in detail many different historical societies, from ancient societies to those in his contemporary world, in order to advance his theory of modernity. In contrast to Durkheim, whose work emphasized the shift in social structures, Weber's theory of developmental history described a shift in world view.[3] The move was from social action based on traditional values to social action based on legal rationality.

The rationalization process affected not only changes in world view but also changes in church authority and structure. Earlier phases of religion commenced with charismatic leaders possessing authority by virtue of their

79

---

3   Weber used the concept of "world view" to avoid the trap of idealism, a philosophical posture that asserts that ideas alone are the real forces of history. In analyzing the role of philosophy and religion in human action, Weber acknowledged the importance of ideals: "Not ideas, but material and ideal interests, directly govern man's conduct" (Weber 1946:280). It should be emphasized here that he was not playing material interests off against the role of ideas. Alexander (1983) notes that Weber saw the structural and materialist interests of societies as equally important as ideas and, at times, even more important.

personal gift. Moses, Jesus, Buddha, and Mohammed all represent charismatic leaders whose followers were instrumental in making the transition from charisma and affective action to more stable traditional forms. With the increasing dominance of rational action, the religious organizations increasingly take on the bureaucratic form of modern society. It is not surprising that many of the fastest growing churches in America are those which have learned well the organizational principles of big business. Bureaucracy, complete with leaders who are credentialed rather than charismatic, is the organizational form of both big business and big church in modern society.

A recent example of the application of the bureaucratic model to current religious organizations is McCann's (1993) work on Christian churches in the United States. His model comes not from within the churches but from models used in interpreting other social organizations, namely a focus on membership, the environment, and the type of work being engaged in. This is a clear signal of the rational mode of organization being applied to modern religious institutions.

In summary, a Weberian institutional theory of social change stresses the "reorganization of institutional life around rationalized bureaucracy" as an important hallmark of the modern world (Meyer 1980:111). Increased rationalization has been accompanied by increases in secularism, religious pluralism, and increased tolerance of religious differences (Lee 1992). Religious change accompanying increased rationalism is also marked by a "disenchantment of the world." Through disenchantment the charismatic quality that once found a place in larger society has been banished to the private sphere by the forces of materialism (Aron 1970:272).

OTHER-WORLDLY VS. THIS-WORLDLY RELIGION

Before closing this section on Weber, I would like to note one other important distinction that is relevant for our discussion of boundaries. Weber differentiated between what he termed "other-worldly" and "this-worldly" religions. According to Weber (1978), some religions teach that the purpose of faith and good works is happiness in some future or "other" world. For example, Catholicism tends to emphasize sacrifice and self-denial in this world for the reward of heaven. Hinduism also stresses a future world through its teaching that living in accord with Hindu doctrine assures a progressive reincarnation until perfection is finally reached. On the other hand, religions such as Confucianism and Protestantism emphasize a this-worldly ethical orientation. According to some Protestant theologies, living a good Christian life will bring desired rewards here and now, including wealth, good health, and longevity. Similarly, Confucianism accentuates filial piety in requiring proper submission to one's father and feudal master. Those who fulfil the demands of submission to authority will, it is held, be blessed in this life (Weber 1951).

Closely corresponding to these two types of religion is Weber's description of two nonrational ways to escape from the "steel-cage" of modern rationalism. These two modes of religious experience Weber terms *asceticism* and *mysticism*. Those individuals who choose the ascetic path chain themselves to some task or selflessly pursue some mission. They turn their backs on an "eat, drink, and be merry" philosophy that promotes a satisfaction of worldly desires. Such people are task-oriented and receive their rewards from the performance of work. The Protestant work ethic provides an illustration of how one might ascetically pursue a call or a vocation out of a sense of duty.

Mysticism, on the other hand, calls people out of the world in its rejection of the idea that anything meaningful can be derived from participation in the everyday world. For the mystic, valid experience derives not from self-mastery (as with the ascetic) but from altered states of consciousness or states of mind, that are far removed from the humdrum of ordinary existence.[4]

81

Weber appears much more pessimistic about the outcome of modernity than Durkheim. Charisma and religious experience, for Weber, are possible escapes from a rationalized and bureaucratized social order, but their long-range efficacy in battling disenchantment with the social order is dubious. Durkheim, on the other hand, appears more optimistic that the "cult of the individual" will provide an antidote for the potential problems of modern society.

The insights of Durkheim on differentiation and Weber on rationalization, rather than being disparate interpretations, are linked together in the modern world. Wuthnow (1987:204) hypothesizes that rationality has an elective affinity with heterogeneous (differentiated) social environments. In other words, rationality is common in those ideological systems which depend upon a wide variety of institutions that have a wide diversity of stimuli. In order to maximize the utility of these stimuli, a high level of rational thought is necessary. He cites Geertz's (1968) study of Islam in Morocco and Indonesia as an example. In a traditional Islamic society, the traditional mode of social action is common under what one may call "Koranic literalism" or strict adherence to the letter of the Koran. However, as both countries moved to modernity, social differentiation occurred in the form of commercial expansion that linked these societies to the larger capitalistic world. As this occurred, rational modes of action expanded as well.

---

4   Both "inner-worldly" and "other-worldly" religion and "mysticism" and "asceticism" are examples of what Weber calls an *ideal type*. See pages 33 and 34.

Beyond Belief: Robert Bellah

Durkheim and Weber were but two early twentieth-century scholars, albeit perhaps the two most important, who related the structural changes in society to important changes in religious organization. Contemporary sociologist Robert Bellah stands on the shoulders of these two giants as he developed a more detailed analysis of the different evolutionary eras through which religion has passed. He begins his analysis by presenting three major assumptions. First, notes Bellah, world views or myths tend to become more differentiated, comprehensive, and rational. Second, religious social action and social organization change in accordance with transitions in myth. Third, these changes in religious evolution do not occur in isolation but rather are related to changes occurring in other social spheres.

Bellah identified five primary stages of religious change: folk,[5] archaic, historic, early modern, and modern. His model is an evolutionary one, "based on the proposition that at each stage the freedom of personality and society has increased relative to the environing conditions" (Bellah 1970:44). His investigations of the relationship of religious institutions and boundaries are much more specific to each of the five eras.

FOLK RELIGION

The distinctive organizational feature of folk religion is its lack of boundaries. The myths of folk religion completely encapsulate the people. The activities of folk religion are not characterized by worship or sacrifice, but rather by participation. The distance between folk believers and its mythical beings is slight, and this distance is further dissipated during ritual activities. All of these factors contribute to the lack of differentiation between religion and other activities in life. As Bellah notes: "Church and society are one. Religious roles tend to be fused with other roles ..." (1970:28). In Weberian terms, folk religion is clearly "this-worldly," with its focus being on the here and now. Weber puts it this way: "religious or magical behaviour or thinking must not be set apart from the range of everyday purposive conduct, particularly since even the ends of the religious and magical actions are predominantly economic" (1978:400).

Despite the differences among American Indian religions, it is possible to talk about characteristics that run through most, if not all, of them that illustrate folk religion. Perhaps the most significant commonality is the merging of the natural and supernatural realms. In the words of Catherine

---

5   Again, I prefer to use the term "folk" rather than "primitive" (Bellah's term) as the former term is more in keeping with current anthropological scholarship.

Albanese (1992:29-30): "This ordinary world for them touched another; in fact, it *was* another.... [In] their religions, Native American peoples were living out their own versions of the ancient idea of correspondence. Their societies were understood to be small-scale replicas of a larger reality that surrounded them. They believed that it was up to them to be the manifest expression of the powers that were nature's secrets."

Albanese elaborates on one Native American people. The meaning of *Kachina* in Hopi rituals illustrates well the intimate intertwining of religious rituals and daily life. The Hopi were among these Native Americans who numbered among the Pueblo, or "village," Indians who lived in the south-western United States. Although they were primarily farmers, they also inherited a variety of hunter-gatherer values, such as an awe of the dead. The Hopi were a people of ritual, with a full calendar of annual ceremonies. Ritual work was the centre of their lives.

83

ARCHAIC RELIGION

Archaic religions are common to much of Africa, Polynesia, and the New World, as well as to the earliest religions of the Levantine region, India, and China. As with folk religions, the world view of archaic religions remains monistic, often having an elaborate cosmology where all things — divine and human — have their place. In both folk and archaic religions, the individual and his or her society are seen as merged within a divine/natural cosmos. A main difference between folk and archaic religions is that the latter's spirit beings are more objectified. Rather than being an abstract force, the spirits in archaic religions have become identified as gods and must be dealt with in some purposive way. These deities need to be propitiated to give favours to the faithful. It is here that true cultic ritual develops, complete with worship, sacrifices, and priests. Archaic religion reveals the first stage of differentiation within the sacred cosmos: rather than the sacred being diffused throughout all nature as in the folk settings, there is now a differentiation between the generic spirit and particular spirits or deities. In addition, these deities tend to be distinct and differentiated from one another.

What is particularly significant, sociologically speaking, is the emergence of a hierarchical two-class system in archaic societies. The upper-status group, which tends to monopolize the military and political power, usually claims religious superiority. At times a priestly kingship evolves — a divine king (such as Nebuchadnezzar of ancient Babylon or the emperor of Rome) — that demonstrates the merging of the natural and the supernatural worlds. The creation of this hierarchy, however, sows seeds of tension between rival groups — conflicts which at times are reflected in myths telling tales of competing deities.

It was with respect to social hierarchies (as a measure of social differentiation) that Guy Swanson (1960) reviewed data from folk and archaic societies and found evidence that certain types of beliefs (some of which are differentiated) were correlated to, for example, different social hierarchies. As referred to in chapter two on mythology, one such correlation was the belief in a monotheistic high god and the existence of a hierarchical arrangement of three or more sovereign groups[6] or groups having ultimate decision-making authority.

The religions of ancient Greece and Rome provide an illustration of archaic religion. Despite important differences, they shared many common features. Both religions were

> polytheistic, both were creedless, neither was attached to any system of ethics, both admitted, though neither required, the use of cult images and other visible objects of worship, both had their holy places and, sooner or later their holy buildings, both had priests and priestesses, yet neither developed a powerful priesthood which could, as such, make its influence felt in politics or even in governing the life of the individual in any great detail; and, perhaps most important of all, both were closely attached to the organization of the State and before that existed, to the family, clan or tribe. (Rose 1959:ix)

The religion of ancient Greece was monistic. It was, in the words of H.J. Rose, "decidedly a thing of every day. The gods were not confined to their temples or to their heaven or nether realm, but were in the streets and houses of the people. Every hearth fire was sacred" (1959:12).

HISTORIC RELIGION

Historic religion, according to Bellah, moves away from the monism found in folk and archaic religions toward a dualistic mythology. These religions are designated as *historic* because they have evolved relatively recently in human history, often coinciding with literacy. Judaism, Buddhism, Christianity, and Islam are all examples of historic religions. Common to these religions (with the exception of Buddhism) is the rejection of the polytheistic pantheon of archaic religions, such as those of ancient Greece or Rome, in favour of one deity. The move toward monotheism has great significance for the creation of boundaries. Replacing the human-like gods with an all-powerful God, the historic era marks the beginning of what

---

6 Swanson uses the term to refer to the elite groups in a society who have legitimate authority and provide political direction to a social group or a society.

Max Weber termed "disenchantment." The sacred is gradually removed from nature and relegated to the heavens or to special holy places. No longer do the gods walk and talk with men and women as they did in the ancient world.

Sociologically speaking, a central organizational feature of historic religions is increased differentiation. Not only is the deity removed from this world, but there is an increased differentiation among classes. From the two-class system of archaic societies there emerges a four-class order: a political-military elite, cultural-religious elite, rural lower-status (peasants), and urban lower-status (merchants and artisans). Religion becomes an organized power base, a force to be reckoned with by both elites and non-elites.

One of the most significant developments within historic religions is the emergence of a clearly structured conception of self. There is a recognition of a *true self*, a responsible and harmonious self, that stands in contrast with the reality of the *empirical self*. Thus, we begin to see a new boundary between this *true self* and the *empirical self*. Personal failures are conceptualized differently in historic religions than in earlier periods; they emerge as transgressions that cry out for salvation. Bellah contrasts historic with archaic and folk religions as follows:

> In primitive [my usage, folk] ritual the individual is put in harmony with the natural divine cosmos. His mistakes are overcome through symbolization as part of the total pattern. Through sacrifice archaic man can make up for his failures to fulfil his obligations to men or gods. He can atone for his particular acts of unfaithfulness. But historic religion convicts man of a basic flaw far more serious than those conceived of by earlier religions. According to Buddhism, man's very nature is greed and anger from which he must seek a total escape. For the Hebrew prophets, man's sin is not particular wicked deeds but his profound heedlessness of God, and only a turn to complete obedience will be acceptable to the Lord. For Muhammad the *kafir* is not, as we usually translate, the "unbeliever," but rather the ungrateful man who is careless of the divine compassion. For him only Islam, willing submission to the will of God, can bring salvation. (1970:35)

Besides this personal boundary, a new boundary emerges. The ideal of historic religions is a separation from and a rejection of the world. Even (as in the case with Judaism and Islam) when believers are enjoined to participate in the world, the faithful are still set apart from the ordinary world by rules and obligations prescribed by their religions. There is a profound dualism that finds expression in both religious and social realms. The differentiation of a religious elite separate from the political power brought a new source of social tension. As Bellah (1970:35) noted: "Whether the confrontation was between Israelite prophet and king, Islamic ulama and sultan, Christian pope and emperor, or even between Confucian scholar-official and his ruler, it implied that political acts could be judged in terms of standards that political authorities could not finally control."

As noted under the discussion of differentiation and Durkheim, Parsons (1964) offers an example of this differentiation in early Christianity. Almost from the beginning, the Christian Church made a strong distinction between itself and the world — particularly the gentile Greco-Roman world. A later church Patristic writer, Augustine (354-430), expanded on this theme in his book *The City of God* (1952).

86

EARLY MODERN RELIGION

The Protestant Reformation beginning in the early sixteenth century is the watershed for the beginning of early modern religion. Catholic religious myth had become quite elaborate, with a heavenly pantheon of Mary, angels, and saints to supplement a triune godhead of Father, Son, and Holy Spirit. These myths had been recorded and embellished in biographies of saints, canon law, papal encyclicals, conciliar documents, and scholastic theology that overshadowed the Bible. Elaborate rituals presided over and controlled by priests were means of enacting the myths within an institutional context. The Protestant Reformation under various reformers who broke with Catholicism set out to reduce this elaborate system of myths and doctrine to biblical teachings alone. Mary, the saints, and the priesthood were diminished in importance, being replaced by the "priesthood of all believers." With the reduction of mediators, believers were encouraged to approach God directly without the intervention of saints and priests (Westhues, 1981). Most importantly, all had the right to interpret the Bible as they saw fit without ecclesiastical mediators.[7]

The two-class religious system of elites (including priests, monks, and nuns) and non-elites (the religious masses) was dropped, and replaced with a system that differentiated those who were saved from those who were not. Since it was impossible to know for sure whether one was among those chosen by God as one of the "elect," good works evolved as an indicator that

7 Max Weber (1958) also observed this process of reductionism — one that he believed had the
   potential of producing extreme loneliness. He writes: "The Father in heaven of the New
   Testament, so human and understanding, who rejoices over the repentance of a sinner as a
   woman over the lost piece of silver she has found is gone. His place has been taken by a tran-

a person was living a life pleasing to God. The segmentation of life into religious activities and non-religious ones was replaced by a sacralization of daily life. As Bellah notes: *"Religious action* was now conceived to be identical with the whole of life. Special ascetic and devotional practices were eliminated as well as the monastic roles that specialized them; instead the service of God became a total demand in every walk of life" (1970:37).

The Protestant Reformation is thus noted for dismantling the elaborate mythical symbol system and the two-tiered religious structure that had characterized Catholicism. In place of the elaborate myths which included human mediators, early modernist religious thought concentrated on the direct relation between the individual and God. This restructuring had the effect of decreasing the role of the community and replacing it with an emphasis on individual responsibility. Although religious myth was still a powerful force, its power was greatly reduced. Changes in ideology, most notably the individuation of Christianity,[8] also spearheaded structural changes. The once-monolithic institution of western Christianity was fragmented into a multitude of denominations — a process of fragmentation that gained speed in the epoch to follow.

One may ask why the Reformation happened and why such significant differentiation and ecclesial boundaries emerged in the first third of the sixteenth century. Wuthnow (1989) offers an interesting sociological theory. He argues that Protestantism, as a *community of discourse,*[9] happened not only because of particular human agents (such as Luther and Henry VIII) but even more so because of the social environment. He provides evidence that the Reformation took root in cities and along trade routes. A critical feature of these areas was that they were loci of change and social ferment: elevated levels of commercial trade, a growth in universities and higher education for more than the clergy, and a decline of princely power. This power began to decline because more than the wealthy began to make

87

---

scendental being, beyond the reach of human understanding, who with His quite incomprehensible decrees has decided the fate of every individual and regulated the tiniest details of the cosmos from eternity.... In its extreme inhumanity this doctrine must above all have had one consequence for the life of a generation which surrendered to its magnificent consistency. That was a feeling of unprecedented inner loneliness of the single individual" (1958:103-04).

8   In light of Durkheim's interpretation of folk societies, individuals have little sense of their own individuality or personhood. As Christianity moved closer to the modern era, there emerged a heightened sense of personal individuality.

9   He uses this term to mean all the written, verbal, and ritual pronouncements that are embedded within a particular social group (1989:14).

money and own land, and there was an expansion of power beyond the small elite. This led to more social and personal autonomy which had an elective affinity[10] with the autonomy that Luther preached. Thus, Wuthnow argues, the religious differentiation is explained, at least in part, because of a much wider social differentiation and because the boundaries of religion are a result of the changing boundaries of the larger society.

MODERN RELIGION

Bellah questions whether "modern religion" is a stage as distinct from the "early modern" stage as are the folk, archaic, and modern stages different from each other. In many ways, however, this period is profoundly different from what preceded it. The central feature of the change that he observed is the collapse of dualism that was so crucial to all the historic religions. In Bellah's words:

> This is not to be interpreted as a return to primitive [folk] monism: it is not that a single world has replaced a double one but that an infinitely multiplex one has replaced the simple duplex structure. It is not that life has become again a "one possibility thing" but that it has become an infinite possibility thing. (1970:40)

Religion of the modern period is a clear continuation of tendencies already evident in the early modern stage. This continuity may be observed in the gradual development of self or the continued growth of the *boundary of the self.* As Bellah (1970:42), expanding on Durkheim's notion of the *cult of the individual,* notes: "The historic religions discovered the self; the early modern religion found a doctrinal basis on which to accept the self in all its empirical ambiguity; modern religion is beginning to understand the laws of the self's own existence and so to help man take responsibility for his own fate." Within modern religions there is a search for personal maturity and social relevance. Salvation from evil and hell has been replaced, in many minds, by salvation from want, poverty, and servitude.

The second tendency begun in the early modern period, religious differentiation and the expansion of boundaries, continues in the splintering of organized religion. "One might almost be tempted to see in Thomas Paine's 'My mind is my church' or in Thomas Jefferson's 'I am a sect myself' the typical expression of religious organization in the near future," states

88

---

10 The term is from Weber and refers to the affinity that ideal types which represent social phenomena have for one another. A classic example is the affinity between the Protestant Ethic and the Spirit of Capitalism.

Bellah (1970:43). Religion has become a voluntary organization in modern society and, with this shift, more a locus on social support than social control. The religious community is a collectivity for encouraging personal search and personal growth rather than a glue that holds the social order together.

More recently, Bellah and his colleagues (1985) posed a Durkheimian question to guide their research on American character, namely, "how to preserve or create a morally coherent life." A segment of their discussion of religion depicts the pluralism found in America. Furthermore, although freedom and individuality may mean somewhat different things to the different respondents, these values are central ones.

Some thirty years has passed since Bellah first lectured on his theory of religious evolution.[11] As we move into the twenty-first century, the trends he identified as *modern* continue. Religious organizations have become even more pluralistic and voluntaristic. Religious beliefs have continued their gradual shift from literal interpretations of religious texts to more symbolic ones (Hoge and Roozen 1979; Roof and McKinney 1987). Most important, the accent on a highly individualistic ethos favouring greater religious subjectivity and personal choice has been on the rise. Self-fulfilment is increasing at the expense of the collectivity. There is a move away from community commitments to a "new voluntarism" (Roof and McKinney 1987), from institutional loyalties to an emphasis on religious experience (Batson and Ventis 1982), from common myths to "fragmented gods" (Bibby 1987 and 1993b).

There is much evidence, then, for a focus on the personal, the ego. There is a boundary between the individual and the religious institution but it is a boundary that allows for much permeability. It is not a boundary that restricts choice but, rather, allows the individual to have a variety of choices.

| RELIGION AND SOCIETY IN TENSION

As societies have increased in size throughout human history, there has been greater differentiation within the social order. In this ongoing evolutionary process, religion has moved from being an all-encompassing world view to being a fragmented institution with limited powers. Differentiation has meant an increase in boundaries — between the individual and the community, between emerging classes or interest groups, between the dominant culture and subcultures, and, finally, between the sacred and the secular. The establishment and maintenance of boundaries is often the

11 Bellah first presented the parts of the paper contained in his 1970 book in a lecture delivered at the University of Chicago in 1963.

product of tension and conflict. With the emergence of a sense of self, for example, boundaries develop to differentiate the individual from the community. With the appearance of social classes, boundaries form to separate religious elites from secular elites and religious elites from the masses. With increased religious pluralism come boundaries to differentiate the cultural values of the various subcultures. With increased rationalization emerge boundaries that more clearly demarcate the sacred from the secular. What follows is a brief presentation on these four dilemmas that have been implicit in my discussion of historical changes observed in modern religion. These dilemmas are intertwined — their boundaries often overlapping — with changes in one affecting changes in the other three. Together they lay the foundation for understanding the religious tension found in the modern world.

90

Personal Boundaries: The Rise of Self vs. the Collectivity

As we have seen, the historic religions have been credited with "discovering self," in affirming a distinct difference between the individual and the social group. The Protestant Reformation and its aftermath provided a doctrinal basis for accepting self, and it is upon this base that religious voluntarism, personal growth, and religious pluralism developed. This increased differentiation between the self (I call this the *boundary of self*) and the social group, however, is not without struggle. There is a persistent tension between human freedom and social control, between individual rights and collective responsibilities, between personal interests and group goals. We are by nature social beings, dependent on one another. At the same time we balk at the loss of freedom intrinsic to our dependency.

This move toward greater individuation, as we have seen, has its roots in historic religion, sprouted new growth during the pre-modern era, and blossomed during the modern period. This trend toward greater individualism began early in America with an accent on self-interest. De Tocqueville (1945) observed that individualism in the early part of the nineteenth century, in the form of self-interest, was interwoven with American religion:

> Not only do the Americans follow their religion from interest [*read*, self-interest], but they often place in this world the interest that makes them follow it.... To touch their congregations, [the ministers] always show them how favourable religious opinions are to freedom and public tranquillity; and it is often difficult to ascertain from their discourses whether the principal object of religion is to produce eternal felicity in the other world or prosperity in this. (1945:Vol II, 135)

This trend was furthered by the American frontier, which had a decisive impact on the shape of American religion. Settlers of frontier regions not only had freedom *of* religion, they were positioned to have freedom *from* institutional religion. Religions thus became voluntary associations rather than the compulsory institutions of earlier eras. Individual freedom of religion had its origins in the very founding of the United States, particularly in what Albanese (1992:120-134) refers to as "liberal" Protestantism.[12] Although this did not achieve its classic form in the United States until well after the Civil War, significant liberal developments were underway on the frontier long before that. As Albanese notes:

> The United States, from the European point of view, was a new land and a wild land. Institutions and attitudes that were taken for granted in the Old World had to fight to make their way in the new. On the frontier, a church was less necessary than a house, and a Bible was less practical than a hunting rifle or axe. (1992:25)

The dilemma of personal versus collective boundaries is basic to an understanding of the role religious experience plays in establishing and maintaining social boundaries. The founders of great religions have been visionaries and prophets, but they inevitably found themselves at odds with the institutional religions of their day. It is this tension between personal religion and religious institutions that is a theme for Part Two, which deals with the dilemmas engendered by tensions between charisma and modern social organization.

Social Boundaries: Homogeneity vs. Heterogeneity

As we have seen in our discussion of Durkheim's and especially Bellah's works (and augmented by Parsons), institutional differentiation gave rise to stratification and competition between strata. Few social boundaries exist in hunting and gathering societies; but as societies move toward an agrarian model, social differences become increasingly pronounced. With the coming of the modern era, however, the rigidity of the boundaries between various social strata is lessened, although inequality continues to persist.

---

12 The word *liberalism* has its roots in the Latin word *liber*, meaning "free." Although the early colonies were hardly "liberal" as we commonly understand the term, the beginnings of religious liberalism clearly can be found there, especially in radical Puritan movements that sought sectarian purity. The seeds of liberalism were found in the colonial Baptist stronghold of Rhode Island, seeds that were nurtured by the deism spread through the Free Masons during the American Revolutionary War (Albanese 1992:120-123).

Sociologists generally agree that there is a continued increase in inequality that accompanies differentiation through the agrarian period of human history, but that it decreases with the rise of individualism in the modern period (Blau 1977). In other words, beginning with the modern era an increase in heterogeneity does not necessarily mean greater inequality. The tension between groups tends to be managed by institutions that emerge to represent special interests. Such institutions promote heterogeneity but can check the tensions generated by inequality (e.g., Coser 1956, 1967; Dahrendorf 1959).[13]

This sociological observation has great relevance for our discussion of religious boundaries in North America. The United States was settled by Puritans, Protestants who wanted to "purify" the Church of England from Catholic vestiges that remained in it. The Anglican Church under Queen Elizabeth I (1533-1603) had sought a middle ground between Catholicism and Protestantism, and it was to the moderate nature of this reformation that Puritans objected. The Puritans themselves, however, did not agree on how this purification should take place. Non-separatists felt they could work within the Church of England for reform; separatists wanted a complete break from the Anglican Church. The Puritans' desire to purge the church from all that was Roman multiplied the two original Christian groups represented in England during the late sixteenth and early seventeenth centuries. These were the people who came to the colonies in search of freedom to worship — a freedom which all too often they desired for themselves but were unwilling to accord others. With them came a proliferation of religious groups — and religious boundaries — with the emergence of Congregationalists, Presbyterians, Baptists, and Quakers among early Puritan settlers (Albanese 1992:106-20).

The American Constitution's guarantee of religious freedom insured that no single religious group would officially have a rank higher than any other. Unlike European countries from which the early settlers had come (and also unlike Canada), the United States would not grant any religion a favoured status. This constitutional provision helped to further religious heterogeneity, with religious groups migrating in search of religious freedom and other groups giving birth to new religions on American soil. Conflict and tension are at times manifested among the different religious denominations — especially between Catholics and Protestants and between old established Protestant religions and newly-emergent religious

---

13 Wuthnow (1988a) argues that within modern Christianity in the United States are special interest groups that provide a personal sense of belonging but also tend to fracture the denominations and the local churches.

groups, but these conflicts have been much less intense than those in societies where people are stratified according to their religious affiliations.[14]

Social boundaries are a topic of special importance for sociologists, and the issues of boundary formation and maintenance will be discussed throughout the next two sections of the text. It is within the frame of the social boundary dilemma that we will discuss tension among groups, including the emergence of new religions, the conflict between political organizations and religious organizations, the interface of class and ethnic stratification on religion, and other issues central to the development and maintenance of group boundaries. The unifying factor in groups, as we have already noted, is shared values. The cultural dilemma to which we now turn explores the extent to which religious values are shared in North American culture and to what extent heterogeneous groups have unique religious world views.

93

Cultural Boundaries: Religion and Religions

In her text presenting a social history of religions in America, Catherine Albanese makes the following poignant observation:

> American religious history ... is the paradoxical story of the manyness of religions and the oneness of religion in the United States. The *manyness of religions* means religious pluralism. It refers to the distinct religions of the many peoples who have come to call the United States their homeland. Conversely, the *oneness of religion* means the religious unity among Americans. It refers to the dominant public cluster of organizations, ideas, and moral values that have characterized this country. (1992:12)

The religion of oneness identified by Albanese is, for the most part, white, Anglo-Saxon, and Protestant (WASP.)[15] All other religious groups are

---

14 Ethnicity is often intertwined with religious identification in some of the most recent struggles. In Bosnia, for example, the Orthodox Christian Serbs are seeking to "purify" the region of Muslim Bosnians and Roman Catholic Croatians. Similarly, the struggle between the Protestants and Catholics in Northern Ireland is more about the historical conflict between the British (Protestants) and the Irish (Catholics) than about religious ideology (see McGuire 1992:205-208). Many so-called religious wars often are more a reflection of national and ethnic issues than religion, although religion may be used to legitimate and intensify the conflict.

15 Herberg (1960:88) calls this the *common religion*, meaning "the American way of life," the overarching sense of unity amid conflict, the love of others, and a symbol of unity.

forced to deal with their boundaries in light of the cultural value system of WASPS. It is important to note that the boundaries we are talking about in this dilemma are not structural (organizational or denominational) ones but rather cultural. The conflict is over values, including (but not limited to) prayer in public schools, abortion, text book selection, and artistic freedom. Such issues cross denominational boundaries to create new cleavages, sometimes overlapping with denominational concerns but more often bringing together partners from different religious affiliations.

The religion of oneness has several expressions, including the so-called "Protestant mainstream" and civil religion. Many religions walk a tightrope as they strive to maintain their cultural distinctiveness that may be in tension with cultural religion.

Observing American religion in the 1950s, Herberg (1960) considers that the central boundaries are between Protestants, Catholics, and Jews. At the time of his writing, 95 per cent of Americans professed allegiance to these religions (1960:46). Of these, 76 per cent were Protestant, 21 per cent Catholic, and 3 per cent Jewish. Protestantism is characterized by denominationalism with a routinized Biblicism. Catholicism was predominantly an immigrant-Irish religion that from its beginning was in tension between local authorities and the Papal authority. The first Jews came to America in 1654 and have been characterized since then as significantly adapting themselves to the American way of life. This adaptation led to the emergence of three "denominations" within Judaism: Reform, Conservative, and Orthodox.

Wuthnow (1988a) updates Herberg's work on differentiation and boundaries to consider what he calls *symbolic boundaries* and what I am calling *cultural boundaries*. In his 1996 publication on support groups in America, he observed that there have been four major structural realignments of American religion since the Puritans arrived on the northeast coast of the United States. The first process begun with the revolution broke the tradition of the state establishment of religion inherited from Europe. The second occurred during the nineteenth century when the hegemony of a small number of Protestant churches dominating the religious landscape declined. In its wake, faith became more democratic and egalitarian, new denominations arose, and Jewish peoples co-existed with Roman Catholics and earlier settled Protestants. The third restructuring process began in the middle of the twentieth century while the fourth, the growth of small groups, is emerging towards the latter part of the twentieth.

Wuthnow argues that American religion is no longer characterized by denominational boundaries or what he terms the declining significance of denominationalism (1988a:71) but, rather, by a whole new set of boundaries that he calls the *restructuring* of American religion. This restructuring crosses denominational lines and is marked by a new alignment of liberalism and conservativism (1988a:164-180). Liberalism is characterized as religion adapting itself to the cultural environment, and conservatism distancing itself from it. In effect, then, the cultural boundaries are between these two new cultural alignments, with the former, liberalism, having permeable symbolic boundaries to the American culture and the latter, conservatism, having boundaries that are not loose and stronger.

The fourth restructuring process is becoming evident in the 1990s. Wuthnow (1996) notes that the small group movement is this new cultural structure. I shall outline this latest process in Chapter Eight under religious organizations.

The Canadian experience has provided a somewhat different religious culture than that found in the United States. The first two charter groups in Canada were the French Catholics and the British Anglicans, who soon became the "two solitudes"[16] (Bibby 1990). Unlike the many-faceted religious mosaic that was found in the American colonies, Canada's religious scene was dualistic from its earliest days: French Roman Catholic and Anglican. Even after the British conquered the French, the Roman Catholic Church continued to receive partial recognition by the British (Westhues 1976). In Quebec we find an even more pronounced relationship between church and Canadian state. Until the "quiet revolution," a modernization movement of the 1960s, there was a virtual union of church and state in this French-speaking province. While the United States may be characterized as having a religious pluralism coloured by the dominance of the WASP culture, in Canada (until very recently) minority religions were in tension with either Anglican Protestantism or Roman Catholicism, both of which had privileged status.

Transcendental Boundaries:
Ordinary vs. Extraordinary Religion

Over the last two chapters, we have been discussing the extent to which different religions make distinctions between "this world" and the "other world." Oriental religion, for example, tends not to regard this world as "really real." It is the spiritual that is real and the material world an illusion. A different type of monism can be found in folk religions in which the spirits are part of the natural order of things. The shift toward dualism, thus making religion an extraordinary phenomenon, accompanied the rise of historic religions. Religious reforms and renewals at times attempt to break

---

16 Bibby made use of the term from a novel published in 1945 by Hugh MacLennan (1978 [1945]).

down the boundaries between these two worlds. While the first three sets of boundaries dealt with the individual, society, and culture, this last set of boundaries deals with the extent to which the transcendent is also immanent.

Catherine Albanese (1992:6-9) has provided an excellent discussion of *ordinary* and *extraordinary* religion. *Ordinary religion* is "the religion that is more or less synonymous with culture"; it "shows people how to live well within boundaries." Ordinary religion is a taken-for-granted world view. It is reflected in intuitive statements and vague sayings about life, such as "God helps those who help themselves," "Whatever will be will be," "Idleness is the devil's workshop." Ordinary religion reveals itself in folkways and mores that are part of a culture, which, when examined, tell us much about the values of a society.

> In other words, ordinary religion is at home with the way things are. It functions as the (mostly unexamined) religion of a community as community. Because it is about living well within boundaries, it values the social distinctions that define life in the community and respects the social roles that people play. It honors the ranks that they hold and the general institutions of government, education, family and recreation to which they assent. In sum, ordinary religion is the religion that reinforces the bonds between members of a society, that provides the social "glue" to make people cohere. (Albanese 1992:7)

Extraordinary religion, on the other hand, clearly differentiates itself from the dominant culture. It is what we are likely to think of when we think of "religion." Its boundaries are firmly drawn to distinguish itself as much as possible from the larger mundane world.

> *Extraordinary religion* encourages a special language that also distinguishes it from the rest of culture, and its sense of going beyond the boundaries often finds expression in universal statements, intended to apply to all peoples. The special language of extraordinary religion maps a landscape that people have not clearly seen. It gives people names for the unknown and then provides access to a world beyond. It assures people that the "other" world does touch this one but is never merely the same as it.

Modernity in the West, as we have seen through Bellah's discussion of the pre-modern and modern stages, has witnessed an increasing separation between ordinary and extraordinary religion. And, as we discussed in our last chapter on myth, this extraordinary religion has been increasingly privatized. This trend is one that I will point to throughout this text. At the same time, the tension between the ordinary and the extraordinary, between a Weberian "this-worldly" as opposed to an "other-worldly" religion, has produced diverse responses. As we shall see through illustrations developed in Part Two, some groups have denied the extraordinary nature of religion, while others have sought to make the extraordinary "ordinary" in establishing religious utopian communities. Institutional efforts to deal with the tension between these two religious forms has contributed to the religious mosaic that is present in North American society.

| SUMMARY

In the beginning was a unified social order where social differentiation was minimal. This primal social mass with boundaries between the self and the social order was functional as humankind struggled against the forces of nature for survival. In time social institutions emerged, with religion being one of the first distinct and differentiated social structures. As history continued to unfold, differentiation continued. Not only was religion differentiated from other institutions, but *religion* became *religions*, with hundreds of religious denominations struggling for their share of the religious marketplace. This increase in the number of religious groups was accompanied by more distinct boundaries between the individual and the larger community. Increased individuation and a stronger sense of self became the hallmarks of the advanced modern social order.

97

Religion, an institution which once played a pivotal role in the public sphere, is increasingly relegated to the private sphere. With increasing individuation and privatization of religion, it has become necessary to note the differences as well as the interrelationship between *religion* and *spirituality*. *Spirituality*, or the *sacred within*, the search for an experience of transcendence, has always been a function of religion, but it now appears to be brought into increased focus as humankind moves into the new millennium.[7] This experience of the sacred and its relationship to institutional religion is the subject matter of the second part of this text.

---

17 Chapter Four will present a more detailed definition of the concept of spirituality.

■ CHAPTER FOUR ■

Varieties of Religious Experience

Trying to define and to describe religion is reminiscent of the story about an elephant and a group of blind men. According to the fable, none of the men had ever before encountered an elephant, and each was able to sense only the part of the animal that was immediately in front of him. Groping in the dark, the blind men felt different parts of the elephant, took note of its sensations, and then described their experiences. The man who felt the tusk announced that the elephant was part of a plow, while the one who patted the trunk claimed that the elephant was a whole and complete plow. The person who examined the head of the animal reported that the elephant was like a pot. The one who felt the ear insisted the elephant was like a harvest basket used to separate grain. The man whose hands glided over the tail described the elephant as a thick rope. The total elephant was beyond the perception of any single blind man.

There is a moral for students of religion in this tale. Even collectively the blind men might have a distorted view of the elephant; but in sharing their perceptions, some of the distortion can be corrected. Although the collective portrait might not be entirely accurate, hopefully it would come closer to the real elephant than any partial description. To some extent, we are all like the blind men, able to describe what we have personally experienced. These experiences may be personal spiritual encounters that we perceive and report in ways influenced by our culture, or they may be concrete human interactions that reflect cultural practices and religious institutions. Our experiential knowledge (or lack thereof) shapes our attitudes and beliefs about what religion is — or what it is not. A feminist Christian, for example, will describe God differently from a traditional evangelical. Both Christian believers will describe God in terms different from those used by a Shi'ite Muslim. Christian and Muslim alike will view the supernatural differently from a Zen Buddhist. A devout religious believer will have different definitions of spiritual reality from an avowed atheist. Approaching religious myths from a social scientific perspective, as we have done in the first part of the text, allows us insight into how others have described the sacred or the holy. If it does not give us a completely valid view of the essence of religion, at least it should leave us more humble about our individual perspectives.

This same tale of the elephant and the blind men may be applied on another level to the social scientific study of religion. Different approaches, including psychology, sociology, anthropology, and social history, describe different parts of the whole. Each represents a particular vantage point, allowing the student of religion to perceive only part of the phenomenon. Studying religious experiences provides one description of religion; studying religion and culture provides another. Those who research religious institutions and religious demographics provide still other perspectives. Scholars who insist that none of these descriptions can be understood without a sense of history provide another vantage point. Only taken together do we have a better understanding of the nature of religion in the modern world.

From yet another angle, the fable reminds us that religion itself is a complex and multidimensional phenomenon. To illustrate its complexity, readers may ask themselves a question commonly asked on surveys: "How religious are you — very, somewhat, or not at all?" Now reflect on the facets of religion that you used to answer the question. You might have interpreted "religious" to mean "orthodoxy," indicating a belief in a transcendent and personal God or in the literal truth of the Bible. Perhaps the word "religious" connoted belonging to a church or synagogue and attending services regularly. "Religiosity" could have suggested a high level of personal devotion, reflected in frequent prayer or meditation, or certain ethical and moral behaviour. You might have interpreted "being religious" as an associational membership in a denomination or as an indicator of a personal relationship with the divine. Most probably you thought of several of these dimensions before responding to the question. Denominational affiliation includes being a member of a community or organization; belief, ritual practices, private devotions, moral code, and experiences each provides a partial view of the phenomenon we call *religion*. The definition that I am proposing (c . Chapter Two) captures all of these dimensions.

The focus in this chapter will be on one particular facet of religion — the experiential dimension which will be termed the *sacred within*. I will consider first the nature of religious experience, noting how it has been conceptualized and researched by social scientists. Thereafter, the science which examines religious experience, psychology, will be introduced. Under that rubric, personality-spirituality types, models, and various kinds of spirituality will be explored.

Before beginning, I will present various definitions useful in understanding the nature of the *sacred within*. To recall, the definition of religion used throughout this text is "the individual and social experience of the sacred that is manifested in mythologies, rituals, and ethos, and integrated into a collective such as a community or organization." The individual experience of the sacred as part of this definition is what concerns us here. In the social scientific study of religion, religiosity refers to religious commitment. Swatos (1998) argues that the term is best operationalized by using what have come to be known as the *5-D* approach to religiosity. This comes from the work of Glock and Stark (1965), who viewed religiosity in five dimensions: ritual, ideology, experience, intellectual, and consequential.[1]

Swatos (1998) uses religiousness as a synonym for religiosity. To present the image that the *sacred within* has a unique identity apart from the *sacred between* and *among*, I am proposing to use the term *spirituality* (hence the title of the text) in a specific way in this chapter and in this text. The way I intend to use the term is to define it as those aspects of religion and religiosity or religiousness that have an internal presence to the individual. It includes such elements as feelings, moods, attitudes, beliefs, attributions, and the like. This definition is similar to James's:

> In the more personal branch of religion it is on the contrary the inner dispositions of man himself which form the center of interest, his conscience, his deserts, his helplessness, and his incompleteness. (1902:29)

There is a more recent precedent for using spirituality in this way. In an attempt to offer clarity to the terms "religiousness" and "spirituality," Zinnbauer and his colleagues (1997) use a sample of 346 individuals who offer their own definitions of the terms and who also respond to established instruments of religiousness and spirituality. They consider religiousness to include personal beliefs such as belief in God or a higher power and organizational beliefs and practices like church membership, church attendance, and commitment to the belief system of an organized religion (Zinnbauer *et al.*, 1997:561). Spirituality is defined in only personal or experiential terms (not institutional or organizational), such as a belief in God or a higher power, or having a relationship between God or a higher power (Zinnbauer *et al.*, 1997:561). These psychologists, however, see an overlap between the two constructs. Both are incorporated into traditional understandings of

---

1 Ritual captures participation in personal and social rites; ideology is an adherence to the principal beliefs of religion; experience is the affective aspect of religion; intellectual involves religious knowledge; and the consequential dimension measures the effect of an individual's religion on other aspects of one's life.

the sacred and the constructs are modestly but significantly correlated with one another (r=.21). Yamane (1998b) says essentially the same thing. Spirituality is most generally understood as a quality of a person whose internal life is orientated toward God, the supernatural or the sacred. Again, the central point is that it is internal to the individual.

This is how spirituality is used here and throughout the text. Religiosity and religiousness will include both internal dimensions of religion (the sacred within) and external dimensions (the sacred between and among).

Religious experience also has a specific meaning in the literature and in this text. Yamane defines it as "the sense, feeling, or perception of being in the presence of the sacred, holy, or supernatural" (1998a:180). It has, essentially, two components: affective and cognitive. This is how the term will be used in this chapter.

102

| RELIGIOUS EXPERIENCE

The differentiation of experience from other indicants of religion can be seen as part of the overall differentiation processes as presented by Durkheim in Chapter Three. Scholars have suggested that in pre-modern religions, religious experience, beliefs, and practices were intimately intertwined. With modernity, more emphasis came to be placed on dogma and organization than on experience. Rather than being something that is "lived," religion commonly became something to be "believed in," "participated in," or "joined." Affective dimensions of religion seemed to lose ground to the rational.

As I have discussed at length in Part One, the advent of modernity (especially the philosophy of the Enlightenment) took its toll on the credibility of religion. In the late seventeenth century, Friedrich Schleiermacher (1988) attempted to justify Christianity against the Enlightenment rationality that threatened its credibility by arguing that religion is best grounded in sentiments, not in ideas. People have experiences that cannot be comprehended within the bounds of the everyday world. As they reflect on such experiences, they come to conceptualize God in certain ways. According to Schleiermacher, science and philosophy may attack religious conceptualizations or ideas but they cannot undercut the experiences themselves (Proudfoot 1985).

Those who follow Schleiermacher accept religious experience at face value. For them, religion cannot be destroyed by rational critique for it is grounded in the experience of believers. It was Schleiermacher who influenced some early social scientists who wrote about religious experiences, including the religious philosopher Rudolf Otto and the psychologist William James (1842-1910).[2]

Nascent Conceptualizations of Religious Experience

I precede the discussion on religious experience with a discussion on the object of religious experience: the sacred. In sociological discourse, it was recognized by both Durkheim and Weber.[3] Durkheim (1974:48) was the first to introduce a distinction in the sacred as inspiring respect and fear as well as inducing love and desire. Weber added that the sacred is "uniquely unalterable" (1978:406). More recently, the British sociologist Nottingham

---

2 Weber's insights on religious experience are also useful. He links religious experience of the individual to the social. His focus is on the relationship between charisma, the affective action of religious leaders, and social organization. Weber's *charisma* appears to be similar to what Otto calls the sacred. As Weber states:

> [Not] every person has the capacity to achieve the ecstatic states which are viewed ... as the preconditions for producing certain effects in meteorology, healing, divination, and telepathy. It is primarily ... these extraordinary powers that have been designated by such special terms as 'mana,' 'orenda,' and the Iranian 'maga' (the term from which our word 'magic' is derived). We shall henceforth employ the term 'charisma' for such extraordinary powers. (1947:400)

Weber terms the individual bearer of charisma a "prophet," citing such religious figures as Zoroaster, Jesus, Muhammad, and the Buddha (Weber 1947:339-40). According to him, charisma cannot remain in its pure form, but becomes routinized or institutionalized.

This is another important dilemma in religious experience: charisma refers to a first-hand experience of the sacred while the routinization of charisma indicates a second-hand experience of the sacred. This insight helps us to understand why religion can be a source of social change and vivacity or an inhibition to change that becomes "dead weight."

In somewhat of a contrast to Weber and to what the psychologists of religion say, Durkheim (1915:417) argues that religious experience is more of a collective one and less an individual one. For example, in his work on aboriginal peoples of Australia and North America, it is when believers in hunting and gathering societies gather together in a ritual, a religious ceremony, that they are carried beyond themselves into another world. It is in this group ritual that they experience ecstasy, enthusiasm, effervescence, joy, interior peace, serenity, and a sense of being "transported into another world."

3 Durkheim (1965) elaborated on social religious experience in his study of aboriginal religions. This will be discussed in Chapter Seven on ritual. Weber's insight into charisma is his road into religious experience. See the discussion on Weber in Chapter Five under the section entitled "Religious experience and social institutions."

(1971) acknowledged that the sacred should be at the centre of a sociological study of religion. This is further professed by Bailey (1998), who considers it to be the key concept in the study of religion.

Otto (1958), from a comparative religion perspective, adds to the interpretation of the sacred (in Latin, *numen*). As depicted in Table 4.1, there are two dimensions: *mysterium tremendum* and *fascinadus* (similar to Durkheim). As a believer approaches the sacred, two kinds of experiences are elicited. The first one is awe and distance. The religious person is in touch with a power, a force that is illustrated by terms such as: august, a shuddering, dread, fear, being overpowered, a sense of being a creature and of relating to the sacred as being wholly other.

NUMEN OR THE IDEA OF THE HOLY

[Based, in part, on Otto (1958)]

MYSTERIUM TREMENDUM *as sense of:*	FASCINADUS *as feeling of:*
awe	wonderfulness
distance	rapture
august	unity
shuddering	hunger or desire
dread	blissful excitement
fear	exaltation
being overpowered	overabundance and plenty
being a creature	being loved
plenitude of being	experiencing mercy
energy	experiencing compassion
confronting a wholly other	experiencing kindness
	being understood

TABLE 4.1

Note that there is an implicit tension, a dialectic even, within the experience of the sacred. One may consider religious experience flowing along an implicit continuum within the sacred. Table 4.2 expresses this continuum:

THE NUMEN

Dread	Fear	Energy	Wholly Other	Being Wonder Filled	Mercy and Love

TABLE 4.2

One may say that, to some extent, what world view one has of the sacred will affect the results of that encounter. If one's world view of the sacred is "dreadful," one is likely to experience dread or fear. If, however, one has a world view of the sacred with attributes of love, mercy, and compassion, one is more likely to experience being loved, accepted, and cared for. Bailey (1998) adds a further clarification. The sacred possesses four characteristics: in experience, it is unique and special; in value, it is all-demanding; in consciousness, it is primordial; and, in communication, it is active and ineffable.

James offers us a similar but contrasting approach in his analysis of religious experience. He considered it to be the genesis of religion, arguing that the founders of every religion had some sort of direct, personal communication with the divine. The "divine," according to James, is "primal reality" that the "individual feels impelled to respond to solemnly and gravely" (James 1902:38). It is the foundation of religious experience, which according to James is

> the feelings, acts, and experiences of individual men in their solitude,
> so far as they apprehend themselves to stand in relation to whatever
> they may consider divine. (1902:31)

James envisioned religious experience as something that exists *sui generis* — as something that is really real. Conventional religion was but a pale reflection of the energizing experience that propelled the saints and prophets. As he describes it,

> It would profit us little to study this second-hand religious life. We
> must make search rather for the original experiences which were the
> pattern-setters to all this mass of suggested feeling and imitated con-
> duct. These experiences we can only find in individuals for whom reli-
> gion exists not as a dull habit, but as an acute fever rather. (1902:24-25)

How Important is the Social Scientific Study of Religious Experience?

One approach to the study of religion has been to follow William James in taking experience as the core of religion. Although this tradition has been criticized for being too individualistic and subjectivistic — often not taking into account the social dimension of religious experience — it has provided an important foundation from which to explore the origins and renewed fervour of religious groups. Many social scientists do recognize that the experiential dimension is an important, albeit often neglected, part of the phenomenon we call *religion* (see Glock and Stark 1965; Stark and Bainbridge 1985). More recently, in his edited volume on the sociology of religion, Greeley wrote, "I feel that sociologists of religion have ignored for too long the experiential aspect of religion" (1995:ix). The need for social scientists to investigate religious experience is also presented by Roof and Taylor (1995), who argue that within contemporary culture there is a renewed interest in religious experience as expressed in new religious movements such as New Age spirituality, Goddess Worship, neo-paganism, eco-spirituality, and "Gen-x" raves. Findings from survey research suggest that religious experiences, in varying degrees and forms, are commonplace. A poll commissioned by *Time* in March 1995 included a question on belief in miracles. Sixty-nine per cent of Americans said that they do believe in miracles.

PSYCHOLOGICAL TYPES AND MODELS OF SPIRITUALITY

There has been an extensive amount of research into the psychology of religion. A landmark article was published by Dittes (1969), who reviewed a wide range of articles on the topic. More recently, Spilka, Hood and Gorsuch (1985) and Paloutzian (1996), among others, have updated this review. Hood (1998) adds to this and offers to the interested student a variety of recent texts. For the sake of simplicity, I shall refer to these three sources in offering an overview of the study of spirituality using psychology of religion as the relevant discipline.

This section will elucidate three areas: psychological types of spirituality, various models of spirituality, and a particular model which is linked to the Weberian approach of this text.

Psychological Types of Spirituality

Hood (1998) discusses a section in his study of the "psychology of religion" on intrinsic-extrinsic spirituality.[4] Tracing its history back to Allport (1960 and 1966), he notes that in spite of criticism (for example from Batson, Schoenrade and Ventis 1993), its use in the measurement of spirituality has dominated much of the empirical study of the phenomenon. Spilka *et al.* (1985) argue that these are motivational dimensions and combine Allport's dimensions with Allen and Spilka's (1967) addition to the literature, which includes a cognitive aspect, and call it committed-consensual. Intrinsic spirituality refers to viewing faith as supreme, orientated toward a unification of existence, honouring universal brotherhood (and, by implication, sisterhood), and striving to overcome self-centredness. Extrinsic spirituality is utilitarian and is sought after for external reasons such as social status and safety from a hostile world.

Committed spirituality is described as the kind of faith that is open, candid, personally relevant, abstract, relational, discerning, and differentiated. The consensual dimension tends to lack a knowledge base, is restrictive, detached, irrelevant to everyday life, concrete, vague, and simplistic.

What Spilka *et al.* (1985) do is to combine the two dimensions, relying on the work of Hunt and King (1971), to include both motivational and cognitive aspects of spirituality. Table 4.3 is a reproduction of this combination.

Spilka and his colleagues use these dimensions as measurements of spirituality, build on them to construct a model of the phenomenon, and review a range of topics to substantiate the validity and reliability of the measures. I shall return to these dimensions as we review varieties of religious experiences and spirituality.

Is there a link between psychological types and religious experience? Poloma and Gallop (1991) provide us with some answers. Their work is restricted to measurements of intrinsic-extrinsic spirituality.

In an American national representative study of prayer, Poloma and Gallup (1991) found that the extrinsics do not tend to pray meditatively (a form of reflective prayer that focuses on the Bible for inspiration) and are less likely to claim an experience of God. They note that 69 per cent of those who are low on extrinsic measures regularly employ meditative prayer as compared to 48 per cent who score medium or high on the measure. Similarly, 44 per cent of those who have low measures of extrinsic spirituality report having frequent prayer experiences of the sacred.

---

4   The author uses the term religiosity or religiousness. See pages 100-102.

Various Psychological Models of Spirituality

Paloutzian (1996) and Hood (1998) outline various models that have been used in the study of spirituality. They agree only on one model, the psychoanalytical. It assumes that the *sacred within* is a response to unresolved conflicts from early childhood and that, in some cases, religion is considered to be delusional but, also, useful in offering a more positive image of religion. It is Hood who assesses the model as the one that is the most dominant in the literature on the psychology of religion and is empirically grounded in clinical studies of spirituality. Paloutzian (1996) sees the model through the eyes of Carl Jung (1875-1961), who believed that there is within each person an unconscious need to look for and to find God. Hood (1998) refers to Jung's work as the genesis of the analytical school.

108

CHARACTERISTICS OF INTRINSIC-COMMITMENT AND EXTRINSIC-CONSENSUAL SPIRITUALITY

(Source: Spilka *et al.* 1985: 19)

INTRINSIC-COMMITTED	EXTRINSIC-CONSENSUAL
Devout, strong personal commitment	"Follows the rules," convenient, called on in crisis
Universalistic, strongly ethical, holds to brotherhood ideals, stresses love of one's neighbour	Exclusionist, ethnocentric, restricted to in-group, chauvinistic, provincial
Unselfish, transcends self-centered needs, altruistic, humanitarian	Selfish, self-serving, defensive, protective
A guide to living, general framework for daily life	Expedient, used when needed, not integrated into daily life
Faith is of primary importance, accepted without reservations, creed is fully followed	Faith and belief is superficial, beliefs selectively held
Faith is of ultimate importance, a final good, supreme value, the ultimate answer	Utilitarian, means to other ends, is in the service of other personal wants and desires

Hood (1998) adds to his list of schools the object relations models (the focus is also on early childhood experiences but tends to be more gender neutral than the psychoanalytical model); the transpersonal models (being based on an explicit assumption that the sacred is real); and phenomenological models (they eschew experimentation and focus on description of religious experience). The last set of models that Hood presents is what he terms the "measurement schools." This is the most empirical of all the models and comes closest to the approach taken in this chapter.

Paloutzian (1996) considers behaviorism and humanism to be other candidates for models. Behaviorism assumes spirituality to be a response to

CHARACTERISTICS OF INTRINSIC COMMITMENT AND EXTRINSIC-CONSENSUAL SPIRITUALITY (CONT'D)

INTRINSIC-COMMITTED	EXTRINSIC-CONSENSUAL
Sees people as individuals, high self-esteem, viewing God as loving, forgiving and positive	Views people in terms of social categories: sex, age status, low self-esteem, viewing God as stern, vindictive
Open to intense religious experiences, views death positively, associated with feelings of power, competence and internal control	Tends to be closed to religious experience, views death negatively, ties to powerlessness and feelings of external control
Uses abstract principles and sees relationships among things	Concrete and literal in outlook and judgement
Discerning, orderly, exact in meaning, clear	Vague, mechanical, routine answers, uses of cliches, obscure in meaning
Complex, differentiated, uses multiple categories, ideas, sees things as on a continuum	Uses few categories, polarized in thinking (black and white on issues), simple ideas
Open, flexible, creative in thinking, thoughtful, tolerant of different ideas and positions	Closed, restrictive, intolerant of different viewpoints, rigid, mechanical in thought

TABLE 4.3

stimuli, that is, a learned behaviour in light of rewards, punishment, association, and imitation. The humanistic school emerges from the tradition that religion is a way for humans to grow, to seek fulfillment, and to become self-actualized. The last model presented by Paloutzian is what he terms "social forces and cognitive mechanisms." This model emphasizes that humans are social beings and that our minds process information before we respond to external stimuli and attribute these stimuli to various causes.

An Attributional Model of Spirituality

Paloutzian's last model is nuanced and specified by what is known as an attributional model of spirituality. I will rely on Spilka *et al.* (1985) to explain it, and then I will link it to the Weberian perspective of the text. Attribution theory is rooted in a tradition of philosophy and psychology that suggests that people have a fundamental need to know, to desire certainty, to look for meaning. The theory is founded upon three bases: motivational, situational, and dispositional.

MOTIVATIONAL. The motivational base is characterized by three elements: that there exists a fundamental motivation for people to make sense of their world; to have cognitive mastery of their environment to protect themselves from harm; and to assign causality to events and situations that affect them positively or negatively. When is one likely to engage in attributions? They are triggered when the meaning of life is unclear, control of one's world is in doubt, and one's self-esteem is challenged.

SITUATIONAL. The assumption of this basis to attribution theory is that human life (including religious life) is lived in social context. Spilka *et al.* (1985: 21-22) say it in the following way: "… most of what we observe in the way of religious belief, experience, and behaviour might result from the circumstances in which these phenomena occur and are studied." Situational factors of spirituality are such elements as contextual factors (for example, people claiming religious experiences are likely to be in a religious collective) as well as event factors such as a personal tragedy happening, a move to another city or state or a natural disaster.

DISPOSITIONAL. These factors are characteristics of people's personalities. They include such things as family background, having a language that can be used to formulate spirituality, levels of self-esteem, images of God, the capacity to see events as either internally motivated or externally controlled, and believing that the world is just.

Does the approach have empirical evidence? Spilka *et al.* (1985) review literature that links attribution theory with intrinsic-committed and extrinsic-consensual spirituality (see above). Those who are intrinsic-committed types make attributions that revolve about a God who is involved in human affairs, and is a loving being in whom one can trust. The same attributions are made by those of high self-esteem and those who sense they are in control over their lives. Studies on prejudice (Allen and Spilka 1967; Allport 1966, cited in Spilka *et al.* 1985) confirm the approach. Those persons rating high on the extrinsic-consensual dimension are likely to blame their failures on others and external forces and are prone to think negatively about minority groups. Extrinsic-consensual types have attributions of God as being impersonal, punitive, and distant. They rely heavily on their own efforts and consider God to be uninvolved in life and circumstance.

How is this approach related to the Weberian perspective of this text? There are three key linkages. As was argued in Chapter Two, people's world views (and a subset, myths) are critical in understanding their behaviour. A world view is similar to people's attributions, of making sense of the world. The second linkage is that of the importance of the social dimension of religion. The Weberian heritage is a sociological one — wherein individual social actors are contextualized in social groups. This is the situational part of the attribution approach. Lastly, the charisma and routinization of charisma continuum is similar to the intrinsic-committed and extrinsic-consensual relation. People who are intrinsic-committed are close to the experience of the sacred (charismatic) while those who are extrinsic-consensual tend to be at a distance from the sacred and exhibit routinized charisma.

VARIETIES OF SPIRITUALITY AND RELIGIOUS EXPERIENCES

There are many varieties of spirituality and religious experiences. I will focus on only three types: psychic experiences, mysticism, and conversion. Where appropriate, I shall outline empirical evidence for the impact of these kinds of spirituality and experiences on other areas of people's lives.

Psychic Experiences

Psychic experiences refer to those experiences thought to be outside what is considered physically possible based on scientific assumptions (McClenon 1998a). They consist of such phenomena as ESP (extrasensory perception), PK (psychokinesis or paranormal action, where one's mind can influence a physical object), and *déjà vu* (the feeling that one has been in a place before).

Greeley (1975), using data collected at the National Opinion Research Center (NORC), used measures which tapped psychic experiences, including *déjà vu*, ESP, clairvoyance, and contact with the dead. He noted with some surprise that "almost a fifth of the American population reports frequent paranormal experiences" (Greeley 1975:5). Only 38 per cent had *never* experienced *déjà vu* and 40 per cent had *never* experienced extrasensory perception ("feeling they were in touch with someone when they were far away").[5]

Do these psychic experiences correlate with other personal or social phenomena? Yes, they seem to. In analyzing the data he had collected on psychic experiences, Greeley (1975:31), for example, found that psychics appear to be more sensitive "in the sense of having higher and stronger feeling levels." They appeared to be more likely to experience the seemingly contradictory feelings of marital tension and positive affect than non-psychics — a finding Greeley attributes to the higher feeling level of psychics. Building on Greeley's study of psychic experiences, Poloma and Pendleton (1991) used the four different types of spirituality (peak, psychic, prayer, and occult) in their research on subjective perceptions of well-being. They sought to determine whether these mystical experiences had an effect on how satisfied people were with their lives, with their sense of meaning and purpose, on happiness scores, and on negative affect (depression, sadness, loneliness, tenseness, and fear). They report that respondents who had peak and/or prayer experiences were more likely to be satisfied with their lives, to feel that life had a meaning and purpose, and to report being happier than those who did not have such experiences. On the other hand, psychics were less satisfied with their lives than non-psychics, and occultists had less of a sense of life's meaning and were more likely to score higher on negative affect. It appears that both prayer and peak experiences have a positive impact, while the occult and psychic experiences have a negative impact, on subjective perceptions of well-being.[6] Poloma and Pendleton are careful in reporting these findings, urging readers to be cautious in their interpretation. Psychic experiences and involvement in the occult need not *cause*

---

5 Bibby (1993b) notes that evidence from two national surveys (one in 1980 and the other in 1990) reveals that 47 per cent of Canadians have precognitions, and 59 per cent have had ESP experiences. In addition, 63 per cent of Canadians surveyed in the mid nineteen-eighties believed "that some people have psychic powers, enabling them to predict events," and 61 per cent affirmed their belief in ESP (Bibby 1987).

6 Unlike Greeley, who focused on psychic experiences, Poloma and Pendleton's multivariate analysis employed all four forms of mystical experience in the same model. Poloma and Pendleton did not find support for Greeley's report that psychics were higher in affective action. They did find that both psychics and occultists tended to be somewhat younger while those with prayer and peak experiences tended to be older than their respective comparison groups. Age was held constant in the multivariate analysis testing for the impact of mystical experiences on well-being measures.

lower scores in well-being. It may well be that those who become involved in less normative forms of mysticism are on the margins of society in yet other ways and this marginality is instrumental in producing the negative findings.

Mysticism

Mysticism can be defined both as a construct and as a measurable variable. As a construct, it is defined as "an oceanic experience" (Freud 1952); "cosmic emotion" and "union with the divine" (James 1902: 78); or "sudden raptures of the divine presence" (James 1902:391). McClenon describes it as a "doctrine that special mental states or events allow an understanding of ultimate truths" (1998b:316). Being abstract, these definitions are not susceptible to measurement. This was made possible through the work, cited by Spilka *et al.* (1985), of Stace (1960) and Hood (1975).

113

Stace (1960) considered mysticism to be noetic (a valid source of knowledge), ineffable, holy, having a positive affect, and paradoxical in that it defies logic. He went on to provide additional criteria of two forms of mysticism, extrovertive and introvertive. Extrovertive includes an experience, an inner subjectivity to all things while introvertive is one which is timeless, spaceless, and selfless. Hood (1975) constructed 108 items which were to tap Stace's criteria, subsequently reducing this number to 38. They tap such experiences as feeling unified into a single whole, holy, peaceful, united with all things.

Do people have mystical experiences or are they restricted to such special people like St. Benedict and Hildegard of Bingen (see Chapter Six)? Using items like those developed by Hood, Back and Bourque (1974) discovered from national samples gathered in 1962, 1966 and 1967 that 31 per cent answered affirmatively to the question: "Have you ever had a religious or mystical experience — that is, a moment of sudden religious awakening or insight?"

Andrew Greeley and William McCready included measures of mystical experience in a national survey. In data collected at the National Opinion Research Center (NORC) in 1972, Greeley and McCready asked the following question: "How often have you felt as though you were very close to a powerful, spiritual force that seemed to lift you out of yourself?" Four out of ten respondents indicated they had had such an experience at least once, with one out of twenty reporting to have had mystical experiences on a regular basis (Greeley 1974). Based on his research, Greeley observed that mystical experiences were more than ecstatic *feelings*; they represented another way of *knowing*. "Ecstasy is basically a cognitive phenomenon," reported

MIRACLES: AN EXTENSION OF RELIGIOUS EXPERIENCE

While traditional churches treat miracles gingerly, it is surely no coincidence that the fastest-growing movement in Christendom places miracles squarely at the centre of worship. The growth rate in the US of the "postdenominational" churches – the Charismatics and Pentecostals – now surpasses that of the Southern Baptists.... "People don't come to listen" explains Peter Wagner, a professor of church growth at Fuller Theological Seminary, "They come to do." The miracles take many forms: besides healing, there are members who have visions, or speak in tongues, or collapse on the ground when seized by the power of the Holy Spirit.

SOURCE: "The Message of Miracles." *Time*, April 10, 1995, p. 38-45.

114

BOX 4.1

Greeley (1974:5), and "the mystic is describing precisely what happens when he says that for the first time he 'sees things the way they really are.'"[7]

Greeley's work on "mystical experiences" suggests that religious experiences are not of a single type. In this pioneering research, Greeley (1974:5) differentiated mysticism from the occult, insisting that "the powers the mystic deals with are totally different from those the witch claims to be in touch with" and that the mystical is "categorically different" from the occult. Research done in England yielded similar results. Hardy (1970 and cited in McClenon 1998b) found that about 33 per cent of respondents answered positively to the question asking if they had been aware of or influenced by a presence or power different from everyday life. Canadians also report mystical experiences. Bibby's (1987) analysis of national studies indicate that 44 per cent of Canadians claim these kinds of experiences.

---

7 Although figures differ depending on the form the question takes, surveys done after the original Greeley and McCready investigation affirm that religious experiences continue to be commonplace. Americans report a wide array of experiences that may be termed "mystical," that is, they transcend ordinary human knowledge through intuition or spiritual ecstasy. A Gallup poll inquiring into "spiritual awakening" reported that one-third of Americans responded affirmatively to the question: "Have you ever had a religious experience — that is, a particularly powerful religious insight or awakening?" This same poll asked people how strongly they agreed or disagreed with the following statement: "I am sometimes very conscious of the presence of God." A total of eight in ten Americans (81 per cent) responded affirmatively, with far fewer (16 per cent) indicating that this statement was not within their personal experience. Another Gallup poll reported that 43 per cent of the respondents had at some time been "aware of, or influenced by, a presence or a power — whether you call it God or not — which is different from your everyday self?" (Gallup and Jones 1989:159-165).

Poloma and Pendleton (1991, 1992), following the work of Greeley, similarly find that there are different types of mystical experience, but they treat "mysticism" as the generic category and identify specific types within the more general category. Mysticism may be rooted in peak, psychic, prayer, or occult experiences. Using the percentages in the data, they were able to compare the frequency of different kinds of mystical experiences (some theistic and others not contingent on a belief in God). Consistent with other studies, Poloma and Pendleton (1991, 1992) report that the vast majority of their respondents experienced (at least once during the previous year) a sense of dynamic peace, awe, and the influence of a higher power. Since Greeley's research did not include experiences specifically rooted in religious practices, Poloma and Pendleton developed items that tap experiences of the God that occur as a result of prayer. Over two-thirds experienced a strong sense of God's peace and presence, divine leadings, and inspirations, and had specific prayer requests answered. Americans are considerably more likely to report paranormal or occult experiences than they are to report peak or prayer experiences.

What are the sources or potential causes of mystical experiences? Several theories have been presented. I shall outline some of them and conclude with the attributional approach of Spilka and his colleagues.

Mystical experiences, albeit in differing forms and intensities, appear to be familiar to most Americans. Scholars, however, are not in agreement as to how to explain such experiences. Psychologists, who use the individual as a unit of analysis, have often sought to explain religious experiences using physiological or other material causes, sometimes reducing their explanations to neurological or chemical responses to physical stimuli (Greeley 1974). Some research in social psychology suggests that the use of drugs, meditation, reading sacred texts, and music are facilitators of religious experience (Batson, Schoenrade and Ventis 1993). Sociologists, whose basic unit of analysis is the collectivity or group, have sought explanations within the realm of observable social factors, including demographic factors (Poloma 1995). Durkheim's (1915) opinion is that individual religious experience is a result of the experience of the social group where participants celebrate rituals that induce emotional highs. Among all three approaches is the researcher's assumption about the nature of such experiences.

Some writers (including James, Greeley, Poloma and Pendleton) accept "as real" the mystical experiences reported by respondents. In other words, they are reluctant to reduce these experiences to other material or social factors. Other researchers are more likely to seek the essence of mystical experiences within the natural realm (including chemical and neurological disorders), with research conclusions that have the tendency to "explain away" the very experience they seek to study.[8] I feel the most fruitful theorizing and research has been done by those who acknowledge the impossibility of determining the essence of mystical experiences scientifically, who proceed to accept the definition of the situation offered by research subjects, and then seek to determine the impact of such experiences on people.

The humanistic psychologist Abraham Maslow (1964) provides a psychological theory of mystical experience that eschews reducing the spiritual to material forces. It places religious experience in the context of a psychology of the whole person — a person with physical, social, and spiritual needs. Maslow (1970:xvi) contends that human beings have "a higher and transcendent nature," and thus religious experiences are a normal part of life. Building on his well-known theory of a "hierarchy of needs," he asserts that it is essential that fundamental needs — hunger, shelter, sex, procreation, interaction with others — be met. These basic needs (D-cognitions) underlie the higher need for self-actualization. The quest for truth, goodness, beauty, order, and the like are reflections of B (Being)-Cognitions. For Maslow, self-actualization commonly comes about through religious experience, which he describes as

> an experience of the holy, of the divine, the indescribable, the eternal,
> of oneness with the universe, of one's littleness; religious experience
> makes one want to give thanks, to surrender, and even to kneel before
> the awesome mystery. (cited in Fuller 1986:168)

Religious experience is a personal and subjective experience that can only be approached scientifically though the second-hand reports of those who are willing to share them. Since the actual experience cannot be tapped directly by researchers, psychological researchers are limited to analyzing reported accounts — accounts that some scholars accept at face value and others do not. An example of the paranormal experiences of the dying, also commonly reported by those who have had near-death encounters, may illustrate the process. Many patients have reported seeing a radiant man clad in white (often described as a "being of light") who induces in them an inexplicable experience of harmony and peace (see for example, Mauro 1992; Woodward 1976). Cross-cultural research indicates that the dying person might *interpret* the apparition in various ways. Someone from the

---

8 Reducing a phenomenon to social or psychological factors is common in social science. Reducing religious beliefs and rituals to social factors in sociology goes back to Emile Durkheim's classic work in which he defines the essence of religion as the worship of society. I concur with Raymond Aron (1970), a well-reputed commentator on sociological theory, who critically states: "To suggest that the object of the religious feelings is society transfigured is not to save but to degrade that human reality which sociology seeks to understand."

Judeo-Christian tradition will probably identify the vision as an angel, Jesus or God; a Hindu may report the radiant being to be a popular deity such as Krishna, Shiva or Deva (Osis and Haraldsson 1977). There is no way for a researcher to know whether any being is in fact appearing or whether different beings appear to different patients. What is significant, however, is that the label attached to the vision is based in the religious culture of the visionary.

A critique of an approach in this text may be that I view the relationship between religious experience and religious institutions in a unidirectional manner (from religious experience to religious institutions). An alternative approach that I also use in this text is the reverse of this direction (from religious institutions to religious experience). This is, essentially, the position of Durkheim (1965), who posits that the social experience of the sacred is initiated within ritual celebrations that have been institutionalized as exemplified by Aboriginal peoples of Australia and North America. More current cases are illustrative. One example of this comes from psychological observations about labelling used by sociologists who work outside the laboratory and inside the natural world. They tend to emphasize that reactions to stimuli are framed by the language and culture of persons who experience them. Yamane and Polzer (1992), using what they call a "cultural-linguistic" approach, shift the focus from inward experiences to providing evidence on how religious institutions promote mysticism. Using NORC data asking how often the respondent "felt as though you were very close to a powerful, spiritual force that seemed to lift you out of yourself," they found support for their basic thesis. The more people are immersed in their religious traditions, the more likely they are to have mystical (peak) experiences.[9] The cultural-linguistic approach focuses on social learning and the role that religious institutions play in promoting mystical experiences. A second example is from a qualitative study of religious experience. Tilley (1994) argues that narratives of religious experience provide evidence that the institutional factor is vital in personal religious experience.

Whether mystical experiences are innate responses of the person to nonmaterial or spiritual phenomena or whether they are the product of physical and social forces, for the present, remains an underlying and untested (although often unspoken) assumption in social scientific writings. Regardless of whether mystical experiences are approached at face value or whether underlying material causes are the primary research focus, the dif-

---

9 This finding fits well with an earlier one based on a study of college students by psychologist Ralph Hood (1970). Hood reported a general relationship between mysticism and church participation, suggesting that "mystical experiences may play a dual motivating role among the religiously committed, serving to maintain an active church orientation while producing dissatisfaction with a particular church membership."

ferent forms of mysticism warrant more attention than they have received to date.

I conclude this section by applying Spilka and his colleagues' (1985) use of attribution theory in helping us to interpret mysticism. They are not alone. McClenon (1998b) acknowledges that attribution theory continues to provide a valuable means for explaining mysticism and other kinds of religious experience.

They argue that the basis for attributions to mystical experience is needs or desires for meaning, control, and self-esteem. Assertions that there is a divine source of mysticism often have life-transforming consequences. In addition, situational and dispositional factors are involved. Intrinsic-committed persons are much more disposed to mysticism than the extrinsic-consensual. There is also evidence that sacred contexts and events are likely to stimulate or "trigger" such experiences. Their theory challenges the view that those who claim mystical experiences are pathological or child-like. Spilka *et al.* see "that those offering these attributions are frequently in very good shape psychologically" (1985:197).

Conversion

The last variety of spirituality to be discussed in this section is conversion. I shall begin by presenting James' thoughts on conversion, update it with Paloutzian's (1996) and Richardson's (1998) insights, review some models of conversion, and conclude by linking conversion with attribution theory.

James (1902:193-203) defines conversion as a change from one aim in life to another, a journey from a divided self to a united self, a new perception of life, and an emotional transformation. For a person to be converted means "that religious ideas, peripheral in his consciousness, now take a central place, and that religious aims form the habitual center of his energy" (1902:196). Paloutzian offers a formal definition as "conversion to an organized set of beliefs that provide a superordinate framework for the individual's life" (1996:145). Richardson (1998) adds that conversion consists of changes involving cognitive, emotional, and belief dimensions.

All three authors subdivide conversion into basically two types. James calls these types *volitional* and *self-surrender*. Paloutzian (with Spilka *et al.* 1985) terms them *gradual* and *sudden*.[10] Richardson moves away from these authors and, in light of the recent controversy surrounding conversions to new religious movements, one he termed *pathological* and the second, *volitional*. Pathological indicates that the person converting is "brainwashed"

---

10 He adds a third called "socialization." Many would not agree with his categorization as it seems to lack the basic element of change from one state to another.

and joins a new religious movement while denying her or his free will. The second type acknowledges the convert as one who freely chooses the new group.

Spilka *et al.* (1985) characterize sudden conversion with three elements: being passive, sensing a strong "otherness," and feeling guilty and unworthy. The sense of passivity refers to being controlled by "something" other than oneself, often in a moment of crisis. The "otherness" is the sacred, the object of religious worship. Lastly, the sense of guilt is a sense of guilt being taken away, a guilt which might have been a trigger to convert.

Gradual conversion is just that — it takes place over a period of time. It still results in a change to a new identity of the self. Good illustrations of this come from the work of Lofland and Stark (1965) and Stark (1992, 1996). Conversion occurs to a new, deviant religious group when, other things being equal, individuals have or develop stronger attachments to members of the group than they have to non-members (Stark 1996:18). He uses this gradual approach to explain how Romans converted to Christianity. In addition, he cites an article on conversion in Holland that reviews twenty-five studies confirming the Stark thesis (Kox, Meeus, and Hart 1991). Spilka *et al.* (1985:206) constructed a table which may better illustrate these two kinds of conversion:

SUDDEN AND GRADUAL CONVERSIONS

(Adapted from Spilka *et al.* 1985: 206)

SUDDEN CONVERSIONS	GRADUAL CONVERSIONS
sudden awareness of the other for meaning or purpose	gradual and increasing search
predominance of negative emotions and feelings of sin and guilt	absence of emotions, especially intense feelings of sin and guilt
passive act of surrendering to a faith perspective	active assent to a faith perspective

TABLE 4.4

The illustration of gradual conversion from the work of Lofland and Stark has become a model of conversion. Richardson (1998b) calls it the "World-Savior" model. Both he and Paloutzian (1996) outline the seven steps that prospective and true converts go through. First, the individual needs to experience enduring, acutely felt tensions. Second, the potential convert must adopt a sacred strategy rather than a profane or secular one to address these tensions. When this strategy is selected, his or her current commitment to conventional religion is experienced as not life-giving. A fourth step consists of a potential convert's sense of a turning point in her or his life and, at that time, meets someone who represents an alternative religious group. After an initial commitment is made, the new convert creates strong bonds to members of the new group and tends to sever bonds with people outside the group. The final step occurs when the convert becomes a "total convert" and identifies completely with the new association.

This is a useful model to try to explain conversions across a wide range of denominations or types of religious organizations. It does not help us, however, to understand the gradual conversion of a person from extrinsic-consensual or intrinsic-committed spirituality. This is where the attribution theory is useful. In light of the theory (Spilka *et al.* 1985:223), many who undergo conversion appear to lack a sense of meaningful direction in their lives, feel themselves to be victims of circumstances, and have low self-esteem. Esteem, sense of meaning, and control are at major lows. Sudden or gradual conversion changes this. Regardless of whether the conversion is within a denomination or a religion, from a church to a sect or a cult, new and positive meanings are achieved. One is "saved." A person moves toward a heightened sense of self, a belief in the sacred that is positive, and a vision that the world is safe. These are changes in attributions.

Other aspects of the theory can also be linked to the Lofland and Stark model. Part of attribution theory is the importance of a social context and the necessity of certain events being present. The social context is twofold: the pre-conversion context is not helpful to the potential convert while the new one is. In addition, according to both attribution theory and the Lofland/Stark model, certain events have to occur. It is necessary that the "seeker" meet someone at a particular place and time who is a member of the new group or has a new kind of spirituality that the person is searching for.

Again, this theory fares well with the Weberian perspective, which locates a person moving from one world view to another. In addition, the new group may elicit a religious experience or an "affective relationship to the sacred and to others." New social bonds are established that might result in the convert's sense of a new identity.

An alternative model of conversion emerges from rational choice theory that I introduced in Chapter One. One such student of the model, Iannaccone (1990), uses working concepts from a household production approach from the tradition of household economics. In simple terms, the concept refers to the production of commodities within a household unit that are not made for exchange or distribution (as in market production) but directly for consumption. This production includes products many of us produce within our homes: food, clean clothes to wear, or an ordered home to live in. The term human capital indicates the skills needed for the production of commodities. Examples of these include cooking, cleaning the house, and driving a vehicle in order to provide goods and services consumed by family members.

Iannaccone translates these terms in the study of religion to "religious production" and "religious human capital." He acknowledges that religious products are difficult to measure, unlike the inputs to religious production. They include such elements as Sunday clothes, sacrificial offerings, time, and labour. His focus, however, is on religious capital: the skills, talents, and training necessary to produce religious products that include familiarity with religious doctrine, rituals, traditions, and members. In addition, this capital is also a product of religious activity such as religious services which are conducted to inspire, instruct, and prepare participants for service.

In this model, he offers an explanation for conversion. He argues that the more similar the group, the greater the likelihood of conversion between religious groups because children receive their religious human capital from their parents and will, therefore, be more likely to move to another group whose members received similar training in religious human capital. He cites several studies to confirm this hypothesis. He concludes:

> ... the human capital approach to religious participation illustrates the threefold contribution of economic theory to the scientific study of religion: integrating numerous predictions within a single conceptual framework; providing theoretical explanations of observed empirical regularities; and generating new hypotheses to guide future empirical research. (1990:313)

| SUMMARY

This chapter has been pivotal to this text and to the Weberian perspective in the study of religion. It consisted of a presentation of the primary object of religion in general and religious experience in particular: the sacred. Religious experience was then defined as being an individual experience of the sacred. Thereafter, various psychological types of spirituality were presented with the addition of several models that have been used in the psychology of religion to interpret these types. The chapter concluded with a review of the literature of the studies on psychic experiences, mysticism, and conversion.

■ CHAPTER FIVE ■

Religious Experience and the Genesis of Religious Institutions

Mystical experience and social institutions are intimately interconnected, and the relationship between the two has long been recognized to be one of tension. According to James, Maslow, and Weber, religious experience is what gives the impetus to religious organization. These social theorists would concur, however, with Berger, who observes: "Whatever else it is, religious experience is dangerous. Its dangers are reduced and routinized by means of institutionalization" (1979a:46). Although religious experience may be "domesticated" (to use Berger's term) by institutionalization, there is an underlying tension between religious experience and religious organization.

For William James (1902:262), it was religious experience or personal contact with the divine that gave the original impetus to a religious organization. The "innocent beginning" is often lost as the "politics and lust of dogmatic rule" take over. If the organization is totally successful, the day of inwardness is over, the spring is dry, and church members, who live a second-hand religion, "stone the prophets in their stead." Abraham Maslow presents a similarly pessimistic outcome when mystical experience encounters the forces of institutionalization:

> Most people lose or forget the subjectively religious experience, and redefine Religion as a set of habits, behaviors, dogmas, forms, which at the extreme becomes entirely legalistic and bureaucratic, conventional, empty, and in the truest meaning of the word, antireligious. The mystic experience, the illumination, the great awakening, along with the charismatic seer who started the whole thing are forgotten, lost or transformed into their opposite. Organized Religion, the churches, finally may become the major enemy of the religious experiences and the religious experiencer. (1970:viii)

Weber is no less pessimistic about the fragility of religious experience than James and Maslow, but his approach is somewhat different. Weber's level of analysis shifts from the individual to the social. His focus is on the relationship between charisma, the affective action of religious leaders, and social organization. Weber's *charisma* appears to be an experience that is at the extreme end of any mysticism scale. This "gift of grace" is not the mysticism we have discussed, but rather rests only on a few spiritual elites. The free-flowing charisma of the spiritual elite becomes the basis for either traditional or legal rational forms of organization that are more institutionally stable than charisma. Religious institutions, like other social institutions, tend to rely on traditional and rational forms of action.

There is a need, as sociologist S. N. Eisenstadt (1968:ix) stresses, to consider how charisma and institution "are continuously interrelated in the fabric of social life and in the processes of social change." In other words, charisma plays a role in the development and transformation of institutions. This process may be demonstrated through select facts from the respective histories of the Shakers and the Mormons. Both represent nineteenth-century indigenous American religions that began after intense religious experiences by their founders. Also important from the sociological perspective, both were nurtured in a common social environment. I shall add to this the religious experiences of Minister Louis Farrakhan, who is central to an understanding of the Nation of Islam.

RELIGIOUS EXPERIENCE AND THE GENESIS OF RELIGIOUS INSTITUTIONS

Charisma in the "Burned-Over District"

The "burned-over district," a section of western New York state, was so named because of the passionate religious zeal exhibited in tent revivals commonly held in the area (Cross 1950). Although a number of theories have been advanced to account for this region's becoming a hotbed of religious activity, a commonly accepted explanation focuses on the socio-economic milieu. The construction and opening of the Erie Canal in 1825, connecting the Great Lakes with the eastern seacoast, opened up new markets for commerce and unprecedented expansion for the western area of New York state. (Between 1820 and 1830, for example, the population of the five counties surrounding the western half of the canal increased 135 per cent as commerce flourished.) This rapid growth brought economic prosperity to the area, but also a weakening of old community bonds.

The milieu created by the flourishing economy of early nineteenth-century New York is familiar to those who study new religious movements. The weakening of community ties is accompanied by a greater individualism that deprives many people of their social moorings. Those migrating into a new area often leave behind family, friends, and community, only to find themselves without meaningful social ties and feeling somewhat estranged from their new world. This social disruption, leaving many without adequate social support or social control, creates conditions that are favourable for religious experimentation and innovation (Foster 1981). It was within this social context that Ann Lee and Joseph Smith introduced their experiences and innovative religions to prospective disciples. Despite the great differences between the two religious movements, they share certain commonalities (Foster 1981). Each had its beginning in the religious experience of its charismatic leader. The leaders, viewing the world as corrupt and on the brink of destruction, were pessimistic about the future. Both felt that the answer to the problems confronting the world was to restore Christianity to its pristine form (although each had a different conception of what model this "original Christian church" should take). Each mystic and founder had a unique vision for establishing the kingdom of God on earth.

Mother Ann Lee and the Shakers[1]

Ann Lee was born in Lancaster, England, in 1736, the illiterate daughter of a blacksmith. At the age of 23, she joined an enthusiastic religious group known as the "Shaking Quakers."[2] The Shaking Quakers, named so because during worship services the members would fall into trances in which they would quiver and shake, experienced persecution for their departure from mainstream Anglicanism. It was while Ann Lee was in prison in 1770 for having participated in worship that was considered indecent and blasphemous that she experienced a vision. In the vision she witnessed the "original sin," which led her to believe that the sexual act was the cause of all evil and suffering in the world. Ann Lee had always felt guilty about engaging in sex with her husband, especially after each of the four children born to her died in early infancy. She was convinced that their deaths were a divine punishment for her concupiscence. During this vision

---

1   The official term is the United Society of Believers in Christ's Second Appearing.

2   It is significant that in 1759 England — much like western New York — was experiencing a time of social change and upheaval characterized by a movement from an agrarian society to a proto-industrial one (Levine, 1984). This spawned a number of religious movements.

a light shone about her, and she claimed that the Lord Jesus spoke to her, becoming one with her in mind and spirit. A few months after her release from prison, Mother Ann Lee (as she was called by her followers) had a divine revelation in which she was directed to America — a place, she was assured, that the Believers would prosper and grow. Mother Ann, together with eight faithful followers (including her husband), moved to New York in 1774 (Morse 1980; Kephart 1987).

Ann Lee had the makings and markings of a charismatic leader, one that could elicit from her followers a commitment to a communal celibate life. Her religious experiences, including speaking in tongues, the ability to heal, visions, and revelations, left her convinced that she was the second coming of Jesus Christ in female form. Through her countenance she was able to convince others that her experiences were more than illusion. An early convert in the United States spoke of Mother Ann as follows:

> her countenance appeared bright and shining, like an angel of glory. The graceful motions of her hands, the beautiful appearance of her countenance, and the heavenly melody of her voice, made her seem like a glorious inhabitant of the heavenly world, singing praises to God. (Morse 1980:23)

As Kephart (1987:190) has astutely noted, the fact that Ann Lee was able to gain any followers in the eighteenth century for a religion in which a woman claimed to be a reincarnation of Christ and which demanded sexual celibacy testifies to her spiritual and charismatic powers. Mother Ann died in 1784, at the age of 48: "Thus ended the short but very remarkable career of a very remarkable person. Through the quiet force of her own personality, she was able to transform a tiny band of ineffectual ecstatics into a respected and rapidly growing religious body" (Kephart 1987:191).

According to Weberian theory, the loss of a charismatic leader often is a fatal blow to a new religious movement. What is needed is the emergence of another leader — one who can systematize, organize, and set the stage for expansion. One of Ann Lee's earliest converts, Joseph Meachem (a former Baptist minister), proved to be the right person for the job following Ann Lee's death. Father Joseph was a brilliant organizer, and one of his first acts was to appoint Lucy Wright to the headship of the "female line." For the next ten years Father Joseph and Mother Lucy provided the necessary stable leadership for the Shakers that nurtured the work begun by Mother Ann Lee. At the time of Father Joseph's death in 1796, there were Shaker communities in eleven locations, with membership totaling over 10,000 persons. Mother Lucy continued in the top position for another twenty-five years, during which time five more societies were established and thousands more people added to Shaker numbers. During its heyday 75 years after Ann Lee's death, the United Society of Believers in Christ's Second Coming, the formal name for the Shakers, had established 19 societies in eight states.

Of significance for this chapter is the attraction to Shaker life offered by revivalistic activities. Foster describes some of these activities as follows:

> Among the types of behavior described in Shaker sources were shaking and trembling, shouting, leaping, singing, dancing, speaking in strange tongues, whirling, stamping, rolling on the floor, crying out against sin and carnal nature, and trance ...
>
> Many of these activities seemed to be clearly beyond any conscious human agency, and thus were seen as manifestations of the supernatural.... Believers saw them as a sign of God's continuing workings in human history and the existence of an authority going beyond the purely man-made. (1981:29)

Religious ritual provided a break from the serious, rigid, and demanding life of a Shaker. It was also in this context that the Shakers were among the forerunners of modern spiritualism, the belief that the living could communicate with the dead. Communication with the spirit world was particularly prevalent in the 1830s and the 1840s, when Mother Ann Lee (now deceased for some 50 years) would come to visit her followers or when Alexander the Great, Napoleon, George Washington or Benjamin Franklin would be their guests (Kephart 1987:212-13). Ecstatic religious communal experiences and vibrant worship accompanied the organization and growth of the Shakers, but charismatic dance increasingly became routine ritual, and spiritualism died down after 1850. The routinization of religious practices described by Desroche was one factor in the demise of the Society:

> The characteristic Shaker dance rituals were slowly modified and eventually abandoned. Instrumental music and more conservative songs displaced the early chants and folk spirituals. The forces of religious ardor, holding compact the life of the sect, were wearing themselves out. (quoted in Kephart 1987:215)

Granted, there were many other socio-economic factors contributing to the decline of the United Society of Believers — factors we will discuss in other chapters of this text. There can be no doubt, however, that this highly successful religious community was marked by charisma from its founding through its early decades of growth. The gradual and then rapid decline of the Shakers after the Civil War coincides with the demise of affective ritual practices. Religious experiences were the highpoint of a very demanding and austere communal celibate life, and they were certainly a drawing card for those attracted to the movement. As the twentieth century entered its last decade, there was but one tiny community made up of a handful of women Believers left (in Sabbathday Lake, Maine). After lasting over 200 years in America, the Society may well be coming to an end.

Joseph Smith and the Church of Jesus Christ of Latter-day Saints

Joseph Smith was born on December 23, 1805, in Vermont, to parents who were both "God-fearing Christians." After frequent moves in search of a better life, the Smiths settled in Palmyra, New York, in the "burned-over" district when Joseph was a teenager. Kephart describes some of the religious groups in the area as follows:

> The Millerites proclaimed that the world was coming to an end. Emanuel Swedenborg announced that he had communicated directly with God. Ann Lee's Shakers renounced sex and marriage, and formed a nearby settlement. Jemima Wilkinson ruling by revelation, built her colony of Jerusalem. John Humphrey Noyes started the Oneida Community. The Fox sisters, claiming to have communicated with the dead, founded the modern spiritualist movement. All of this occurred in Western New York between, roughly, 1825 and 1850. Even the older denominations — Methodists, Baptists, Presbyterians — were torn by schism and dissent. (1987:220)

Joseph Smith reported being disturbed by this "war of words and the tumult of opinions." One day in 1820 the teenage Smith "retired to the woods," asking God to show him who was right, and there he had an intense experience of God:

> I was seized upon by some power which entirely overcame me, and had such an astonishing influence over me as to bind my tongue so that I could not speak. Thick darkness gathered about me and it seemed to me for a time as if I were doomed to sudden destruction. (1957:40)

He then envisioned a pillar of light and saw two personages: one God the Father and the other, the Son. He was told by the former to listen to the Son and not to join any of the religious sects, for "all their creeds were an abomination in his sight" (Smith 1957:48). Smith did not have another visitation for three years. This was the most noteworthy of all his religious experiences since it involved the plates or tablets which are the very foundation of Mormonism. Smith recounts this visitation as follows:

> After I had retired to my bed for the night, a personage appeared at
> my bedside, standing in the air, for his feet did not touch the floor. He
> had on a loose robe of the most exquisite whiteness.... He called me
> by name, and said that he was a messenger from the presence of God,
> and that his name was Moroni; that God had work for me to do....
> He said that there was a book deposited, written upon gold plates. He
> said that the fullness of the everlasting Gospel was contained in it.
> Also, that there were two stones in silver bows — and these stones,
> fastened to a breastplate, constituted what is called the Urim and
> Thummim, and that God had prepared them for the purpose of trans
> lating the book. (1957:49)

Eventually, Joseph Smith removed the plates from the hill and, with the help of the Urim and the Thummim, translated them with relative ease. (The angel Moroni is said to have come back to take the original plates together with the Urim and the Thummim.) The translation stayed on earth and became known as the Book of Mormon.

Joseph Smith had other visitations. In 1827 he returned to the woods together with Oliver Cowdery (an early disciple), and John the Baptist reportedly appeared. After John the Baptist conferred upon both men the Aaronic priesthood and the priesthood of Melchizedek, they had an intense religious experience: "We were filled with the Holy Ghost and rejoiced in the God of our salvation" (Smith 1957:56). In 1830, when Joseph Smith was 25 years old, he gathered with five other young men who had seen the golden plates, for the purpose of founding a church. Joseph Smith announced that he had received a revelation from God which said, "Behold there should be a record kept among you: and in it thou shalt be called a seer, a translator, a prophet, an apostle of Jesus Christ, an elder of the church through the will of God" (Kephart 1987:226).

The church attracted a thousand members in less than a year, but it also attracted vicious persecution. To escape harassment, Smith and his followers moved westward — to Ohio, Missouri, and Illinois — with persecution following them each step of the way. Smith was murdered, at the age of 39, when a mob stormed the jail at Carthage, Illinois, on June 27, 1844. Sociologically speaking, this fledgling church faced an acute leadership crisis with the death of its young, charismatic founder. The movement began to splinter, with several different men taking charge of break-away groups. A second charismatic leader, Brigham Young, emerged to guide the Church of Jesus Christ of Latter-day Saints (the official name for the Mormon Church) into stability and organization.

Brigham Young was born in 1801 in Vermont into a non-religious family, experienced a religious conversion and became a Methodist at the age of 22, and joined the Church of Jesus Christ of Latter-day Saints (LDS) a few years later. His conversion to the LDS was gradual, making a commitment to it in 1832 after he attended a stirring meeting in which there were preaching, testimonies, speaking in tongues, interpretations, and prophecies (Bringhurst 1986). Young describes his new conversion experience as follows:

> their testimony was like fire in my bones; I understood the spirit of their preaching; I received the spirit; it was light, intelligence, power, and truth. (Arrington 1985:29)

Eager to meet the founder of this new religion, Young traveled to Kirtland, Ohio, where Smith was then staying. It was while Young was with Smith that he had the experience of speaking in tongues and sensed the power of God moving through him. Young moved his family to Kirtland, and Smith appointed him as one of the twelve apostles, a leadership group directly under Smith. During this time, Young reported supernatural visions of Peter, Abraham, Jesus, and a host of angels.

One of the next major religious experiences reported by Young occurred after Joseph Smith's martyrdom. In 1847, after Young had assumed leadership of a faction of the Church, he received a revelation on how to organize the believers. He also received instructions to continue the Great Trek to the West to escape persecution and to establish the New Zion. On the morning of July 24, 1847, the Great Trek westward came to an end when Brigham Young caught his first sight of the Great Salt Lake Valley. Followers understood this to be their promised land when Young reportedly said, "It is far enough. This is the right place."

Brigham Young was not only a visionary; he was an able leader and organizer. It is impossible to imagine the success of the LDS as we know it without him. It was under Young's leadership, lasting over thirty years, that the Church of Jesus Christ of Latter-day Saints was firmly established. Today it exists as one of the fastest growing of America's religions (numbering about 9 million worldwide), but also one that has little of the charismatic manifestations of its founders.

Charisma began to be domesticated through "containment" of its fervour even before the death of Joseph Smith. O'Dea (1957:158) reports that there was a significant amount of shared charisma within the community in

Kirtland, Ohio. At times, however, some members claimed prophetic inspiration that challenged the leadership of Joseph Smith. Smith consolidated his leadership by claiming that he alone was the "prophet, seer, and revelator" and by making himself president of the High Priesthood, a move that successfully overshadowed opposition to his leadership. Prophecies of followers were permitted, but they were greatly contained and limited. After Smith's death, Brigham Young gradually took on his master's mantle. It was not until Young began the Western Trek that he was able to proclaim himself "prophet, seer, and revelator." This move paved the way for further containment and institutionalization of charisma, relegating prophecy to the presidency of the church. O'Dea writes:

> Charisma had been successfully contained with the organized structure of the Church and was identified with the functions of the Church office. (1957:160)

Although individual Mormons remain free to receive revelations for their own private lives, it is the Church President who bears the title of "prophet, seer, and revelator," a title which in practice rarely seems to be used. The early charismatic manifestations, including tongues and prophecy, seems to be a thing of the past.

O'Dea's astute observations about the institutional development of the Church of Jesus Christ of Latter-day Saints provided him with the makings to expand the Weberian theory of the routinizing of charisma.

Minister Louis Farrakhan and the Nation of Islam

Following from the presentation of the Nation of Islam's mythology outlined in Chapter Two, we now investigate the religious experience of the current leader, Minister Louis Farrakhan. He was born with the name Louis Eugene Walcott, the son of West Indian immigrants. His youthful religion was in the context of an Episcopal Church where he met a black nationalist by the name of Rev. Nathan Wright. He later became a talented singer and musician and, in a move to Chicago in 1955, met Elijah Muhammad and became an avid follower of the Nation. He moved to New York and joined the temple under the authority of Malcolm X. It was here that Malcolm X challenged him to either continue in performing in nightclubs or to follow Islam. Shortly after that, the manager of the nightclub offered him a lucrative contract. That night, in a situation of doubt, he experienced a vision: "I saw two doors. Over one door was written 'success.' I could look into that door and I saw an amount of gold and diamonds which represented, of course, riches that would accrue. But there was another door, and over that door was the word 'Islam.' And it had a black veil over that door. And in the vision I chose the door of Islam" (Farrakhan, interview in 1989, and cited in Gardell 1996:121).

From that time on, Minister Louis never turned back. He became a committed member and grew, eventually, to become the minister of the Harlem Temple that Malcolm X served, and, subsequently, the leader of the whole Nation. As this vision launched his ministry, so did one in 1985 crystallize for him his belief that he was the "little Messiah." Its importance demands a lengthy quotation from Gardell:

> In the vision, Farrakhan walked up a mountain to an Aztec temple together with some companions. When he got to the top of the mountain, a UFO appeared. Farrakhan immediately realized the importance of the moment. In the cosmology of the Nation, God supervises humanity from a great man-made planet circling Tellus.[3] This planet is known in the NOI as "the Mother Ship" or "the Mother Wheel."... On the Mother Wheel too, are small spacecraft carriers, called "baby planes," piloted by helpers of God. Frequently, the smaller crafts visit earth on various expeditions ordered by God, such as when Elijah Muhammad was rescued from hired assassins in 1975 ... Farrakhan, feeling a bit afraid, asked his companions to go with him but was corrected from the spacecraft: "Just you, brother Farrakhan."... He walked and was placed next to the pilot. ... The spacecraft took off with Farrakhan, who knew that the pilot was sent by God and was to take him to the Mother Wheel. ... After being inside, he heard the well-known voice of the Honorable Elijah Muhammad, which confirmed his being alive. Farrakhan was authorized to lead his God-fearing people through these later days ... the Messiah spoke many things and a scroll full of divine cursive writing was rolled down inside Farrakhan's head. The spaceship shot out of the tunnel and the pilot took the plane up to a terrific height and maneuvered the vehicle to allow Farrakhan to look down on the wheel. He saw a city, a magnificent city, the New Jerusalem, in the sky. Instead of going back to Mexico, the craft carried him with terrific speed to Washington, DC, and dropped him off outside of the city. He walked into the capital and delivered his announcement, the final warning to the United States government. (1996: 132-133)

132

---

3   According to Elijah Mohammad, this man-made planet is 1 ½ miles in diameter and is the locus where the destruction of the enemies of Allah will begin. It is the planet that will display the power of the mightiest God, Master Farad Muhammad. In this heavenly abode, God and some of the divine scientists dwell in a magnificent city, the New Jerusalem, that is a place prepared for the faithful brethren who are to survive the final battle (Gardell 1996:159).

This vision was central to the Nation. It indicated that Elijah Muhammad was still alive, that the Christ would return to punish his enemies in the final battle, and that it was Farrakhan who was the national representative of the Nation and not Imam Warithuddin Muhammad. It further reinforced the mature mythology discussed in the second chapter that Master Farad Muhammad is deified and the elevation of Eljiah Muhammad as the Messenger of God. As we shall see in the chapter on religious organizations, it is from these experiences, in part, that the social infrastructure of the Nation was constructed.

From a Weberian perspective, the most fundamental dilemma of charisma is illustrated by the acclaimed charisma of Anne Lee, Joseph Smith, and Louis Farrakhan, and by what happens after their passing. It means that for the experience of the charismatic person to be passed on to followers, these leaders, typically, provide a mythology, ritual, ethos, and the rudiments of an organization. What happens, however, is that this charisma becomes routinized. It is from this fundamental dilemma outlined by Weber and which O'Dea (1966) expands upon that will form the structure of the second part of this text.

CHARISMA AND INSTITUTION AT THE CROSSROADS

Rather than regarding charismatic manifestations and institutionalization of religion as polar opposites, O'Dea understands them to be in a dynamic and dialectical relationship. As we have seen in the cases of the Shakers and the Mormons, charismatic experiences seem to have decreased with institutionalization. Rather than eradicate the experiences of the founder and early followers, however, institutionalization includes the translation of the experiences into belief systems, rituals, and organization. O'Dea writes:

> Since the religious experience is spontaneous and creative and since institutionalization means precisely reducing these unpredictable elements to established and routine forms, the dilemma is one of great significance for the religious movement. (1970:242)

The Mormons and the Shakers (at least for a time) did find ways to translate the unpredictable mystical experiences of early followers into institutional beliefs and practices. The divine leading experienced by Joseph Smith and later by Brigham Young is an important part of LDS mythology. The ecstatic dancing of the early Shakers evolved into the orderly ritual of later followers. This evolution of institutional forms from charismatic experiences, as I shall demonstrate throughout Part Two, is not limited to the

Shakers and the Mormons but rather is an important part of most religious narratives. Most important, the myth and rituals provide a means for institutions to retain, contain, or renew charisma.

O'Dea (1966, 1970) specifies five dilemmas, each offering a somewhat different approach to the antimony between charisma and institution. These five dilemmas are (1) the dilemma of mixed motivation presented in Chapter Six, (2) the symbolic dilemma, described in Chapter Seven, (3) the dilemma of administrative order, outlined in Chapter Eight, (4) the dilemma of delimitation, expanded in Chapter Nine, and (5) the dilemma of power, elucidated in Chapter Ten. The empirical example, to illustrate these dilemmas, is based on Poloma's (1989) work on the Assemblies of God Pentecostal denomination.

The Dilemma of Mixed Motivation

134

When charisma is at its peak during the early years of a religious movement, followers appear to be motivated by a single-hearted devotion to the goals and ideals of the leader. Both the Shakers and the Mormons had a strong desire to bring about the kingdom of God on earth, and followers were willing to make great sacrifices to further this goal. With institutionalization, however, arises a system of statuses and roles that can generate other motivating factors, including prestige, power, and security. As the original vision becomes more obscure, members often become lukewarm and lethargic — less willing to make the great sacrifices made by their forbears. A tension exists between the vision of the charismatic seer and the institutional practices that develop to promote the vision.

Poloma's (1989:104ff) reference to a prominent prophetic woman pastor, Marie Burgess Brown, provides evidence for this dilemma. In the early years of the Pentecostal movement, Mrs. Burgess Brown was a key leader who had the charisma of leadership as well as the institutional acceptance as pastor (she was a pastor for 64 years). However, during these years and later, there emerged in the denomination increasing pressure not to continue the "female-pastor charisma" and, to the present, even though women can be officially ordained, "the Mrs. Browns in the Assemblies ... are few and far between" (Poloma 1989:105).

The Symbolic Dilemma: Objectivation vs. Alienation

The primary mechanism for keeping alive the vision and religious fervour is religious ritual. If, however, the routinization of ritual is allowed to run its course, the symbol may become a substitute for the religious experience. The routinized symbol loses its effectiveness to elicit and affect the attitudes and emotions of followers. Therein lies the paradox: while objectivation or imposing order on ritual is necessary for continuity, it finally leads to alienation when it fails to provide the nexus between symbols and subjective attitudes. Throughout history there have been examples of responses to the empty reification of symbols. The Reformationists of Europe removed statues and whitewashed religious murals; centuries later after the Second Vatican Council, many Roman Catholic churches simplified their church decor. Quakers moved away from seemingly empty ritual, encouraging complete silence during their meetings to allow worshipers to encounter God; yet the silent meetings became a new ritual. Pentecostals have eschewed publishing an order of the service, allegedly allowing the Spirit freedom to move; but this practice has provided new ritual forms rather than fresh experiences.

Changes in the Sunday rituals of the Assemblies of God illustrate this dilemma. Poloma (1989:187) quotes an observer of the denomination as saying:

> The spontaneity of worship is not as obvious in many congregations as it once was. As the churches have become larger and more urbane, there has been increased demand for a professional clergy, a robed choir, and sophistication in the sanctuary. (Menzies 1971:348)

The Dilemma of Administrative Order: Elaboration vs. Effectiveness

This dilemma, if out of control, leads to the tendency of a structure to over-elaborate — to become an unwieldy bureaucratic machine. Clearly organization is necessary for the vision of the founder to continue. The organization, however, can lose sight of the original vision and become primarily concerned with its own development and growth. Not only can an organization grow to become unmanageable, but structures that were set in place at an earlier time may refuse to bend to change. As O'Dea and O'Dea (1983:60) observe: "Structures which emerge in one set of conditions and in response to one set of problems may turn out later to be unwieldy instruments for handling new problems under new conditions." Whether the problem is characterized by an overelaborate organization or a structure that cannot respond to present-day needs, the result is a potential alienation of office-holders from the rank-and-file members of the religious organization.

In the early years of the Assemblies of God, Poloma (1989:122ff) notes that both in theory and in practice, charisma was diffused both among the leaders and the adherents and was structured in a "loosely cooperative fellowship" that tried to retain this charisma. However, as the denomination grew to such large proportions (numbering, in 1989, 2.1 million nationally), the church has necessarily become more of a bureaucracy. It should be noted, however, that the leaders still try to maintain a charismatic dimension to their leadership structure.

The Dilemma of Delimitation: Concrete Definition vs. Substitution of Letter for Spirit

O'Dea (1966:83) observes that in the process of applying the religious ideal to "the prosaic and concrete, the content of the message may itself appear to take on a prosaic quality and lose those charismatic elements that originally moved men." There is a pit on either side of the narrow charismatic road: one waters down the original message, and the other offers a rigid position that kills the spirit. The dangers of distortion of the faith require the formulation of dogma, but once established, the definitions themselves pose the possibility of another distortion. According to O'Dea and O'Dea (1983:61), the definitions become "a vast intellectual structure which serves not to guide the faith of untrained specialists but rather to burden it." Jesus, for example, repeatedly repudiated the Judaism of his day for its empty legalism, yet Christians repeatedly have developed their own pharisaic practices. The comparative study of religion provides countless examples of petrified doctrine and moral proscriptions, which in time may be challenged. In the course of being challenged, however, there is always the danger of abandoning a core message offered by the prophet.

The struggle to maintain the "spirit of the law" and keep distant from the "letter of the law" has been met with only partial success in the Assemblies of God, Poloma (1989:162ff) contends. Central teachings of the church like "Baptism of the Holy Spirit" and speaking in "tongues" had, originally, a special charismatic flavour. As challenges to these teachings have emerged, they have tended to become more like legal norms void of "the spirit of the law."

The Dilemma of Power: Conversion vs. Coercion

As a religious movement matures, O'Dea observes, it is likely to become intertwined gradually with the public, non-religious culture. This gives rise to the dilemma of power through which leaders may seek ways either to convert or to coerce others to join the movement. Constantine's edict to Christianize the Roman Empire offers a prime example of coercion, as do contemporary efforts by fundamentalist Islamic leaders to restore conservative Islam. Most religions in the West do not have this power to coerce,

136

so they must rely on the voluntary conversion of prospective followers. This horn of the dilemma has its own problems. In order to become attractive to new members and to retain the old, the religion often must accommodate to the secular culture. The charismatic spirit may be eclipsed in the process of providing a growing (or at least stable) membership for a sound organizational base.

Charisma, if it is to endure over time in modern society, will be bureaucratized in some form. It may lead to a bureaucracy that subserves the original spirit (in which case charisma is fostered by the organization) or it may lead to an organization that uses charisma to further the organization (in which case charisma is overpowered by rationality and efficiency). As Stark notes,

> In judging a church, the question cannot be whether it has connected with a certain apparatus of bureaucrats, but whether this bureaucratic apparatus has completely overlaid and stifled the life which it was supposed to assist and to preserve. Only where the latter contingency has become a reality can we speak of the routinization of charisma. (1965:206)

Using survey data (from 1,275 respondents of the Assemblies of God), Poloma (1989:140ff) tests several theses of cultural accommodation. The results are mixed. On one side, there has been accommodation on such original teachings as the rejection of physicians and medicine and prohibitions against public swimming, professional sports, beauty parlours, and the use of jewellery. A more subtle accommodation that Poloma (1989:145) suggests is the lure of narcissistic pleasure and success. However, there continues to be counsel against the use of alcohol, tobacco, non-marital sex, and drugs that present a picture of non-accommodation and the retention of the Assemblies as "a peculiar people, a people set apart."

What I will do in the five chapters in Part Two is to illustrate these dilemmas that address central substantive areas of religion (leadership, ritual, organizations, ethos, and the polity) with data that emerge from the social scientific study of religion and religious studies.

The Dilemmas in the Institutionalization of Religion

■ CHAPTER SIX ■

The Dilemma of Mixed Motivation:
The Study of Leadership

The heart of Chapter Five was the religious experience of founders and leaders of religious movements and the resultant social institutions that flowed from these experiences. This chapter continues the focus on religious leaders with an accent on the tension or dilemma that these leaders experience: the dilemma of mixed motivation.

This dilemma may be illustrated by looking again at the Shakers and the Mormons. As I wrote in Chapter Five, Ann Lee had the makings and markings of a charismatic leader, one that could elicit from her followers a commitment to a communal celibate life. Again, in accordance to Weberian theory, the loss of a charismatic leader often is a fatal blow to a new religious movement. What is needed is the emergence of a another leader — one who can systematize, organize, and set the stage for expansion. One of Ann Lee's earliest converts, Joseph Meachem (a former Baptist minister), proved to be the right person for the job following Ann Lee's death. He was joined in leadership with Mother Lucy to continue the charisma of Ann Lee. Although one cannot read Father Joseph's and Mother Lucy's minds, it does appear that mixed motivations within these leaders is in evidence. Morse (1980), for example, does not write about comparable charismatic characteristics attributable to Father Joseph and Mother Lucy. It could very well be that they kept the top positions not because of a single-minded devotion to the ideals of Ann Lee but, rather, because of the significant prestige that the positions brought to them.

Another example illustrating the dilemma is provided by the charisma of Joseph Smith and the leadership of Brigham Young. To recall (Chapter Five), Smith had three central religious experiences that, in turn, led to the establishment of the Church of Jesus Christ of Latter-day Saints. The first experience was of a revelation of three divine personages: the Father, the Son, and the Holy Ghost. The revelation from this encounter was that he was not to join any of the existent Christian churches. The second major revelation was the call from the angel Moroni to go to take and to translate sacred plates into English which became "The Book of Mormon." The third revelation was from John the Baptist, wherein he was instructed to set up the priesthoods of Aaron and Melchizedek (Smith 1957).

After his death (by martyrdom in 1844), the inevitable question of succession rose. The man of the hour was Brigham Young. As was noted in Chapter Five, this man also had many religious experiences and was also known as a charismatic leader. It appears, however, that after these initial charismatic experiences, Young did not have any more (Arrington 1985). He was, however, a very able leader. His legacy consisted of establishing a pattern of Church government through a quorum of twelve "apostles," creating a communal-cooperative institution that cared for the poorer Mormons, becoming the first governor of Utah, and being known as an astute businessman, colonizer, and persuasive leader. However, some evidence of his motivations being mixed is that he was remembered as being harsh and outspoken, was prone to exaggeration and hyperbole, and was insensitive to those close to him (Arrington, 1985). In addition, he publicly denied that he practised polygyny while being married to two women in 1842 (Bringhurst 1986). Thus, Young appears to be a good example of the dilemma that religious leaders experience: being motivated for honourable and heavenly reasons as well as for desires for power, prestige, and security.

The intent of this chapter will be to use both case studies and empirical research to illustrate this dilemma among religious leaders. Our focus will not be on followers or religious collectivities (to be discussed in Chapter Eight), but on leaders: prophets and priests.[1] To illustrate this dilemma, we will begin by outlining the distinction that Weber (1978) made between prophet (representing pure motivation) and priest (illustrative of mixed motivation). Thereafter, we will look at various kinds of prophets, connect different kinds of religious organizations to prophets and priests, outline current research on clergy, and conclude our discussion on women as prophets and the whole question of women as religious leaders.

A TYPOLOGY OF RELIGIOUS LEADERSHIP: THE PROPHETIC AND THE PRIESTLY

In Chapter Five we investigated the centrality of religious experience as the genesis of religious collectivities. Part of the argument was that from a leader's religious experience emerged a world view or a myth. Weber

---

[1] The term "priest" is a sociological term, an ideal type, and not a profession as is the case of Roman Catholic priests.

(1978:450) adds to this in noting that for the prophet there needs to be a "unified view of the world derived from a consciously interpreted meaningful attitude towards life." Both the religious experience and the world view characterize the leader, whom he calls the prophet. Even at this stage, however, there exists a conflict between the empirical reality and this conception of the world as a meaningful totality that produces tensions in the prophet's inner life as well as his or her external relations to the world (Weber 1978:451).

In contrast to the prophet is the priest, who is more concerned with status and prestige than with charisma. Weber (1978:452) argued that the priest is a product of routinization. The focus of the priest is to secure some permanency of the message of the prophet, to insure the economic existence of the enterprise, and to control the authority of the collective. When we look at historical and contemporary instances of prophets we will see how the institution of the priesthood is related to the charisma of the prophet. This can be illustrated in Table 6.1:

THE PROPHET AND THE PRIEST

(From Weber 1978:439-42)

CHARACTERISTICS	THE PROPHET	THE PRIEST
Authority	a personal call	from tradition
The Source of Authority	from a personal revelation	from an official office
Social Origins	outside of the priestly class	inside the priestly class
Remuneration	little or none	is paid for services
Education	little or none	theological training
Source of Revelation	first-hand account	second-hand account

TABLE 6.1

prophet → charisma
priest → status & prestige

To further illustrate this contrast, Weber added:

> Prophets systematized religion with a view to unifying the relationship of man to the world, by reference to an ultimate and integrated value position. On the other hand, priests systematized the content of prophecy or of the sacred traditions by supplying them with a casuistical, rationalistic framework of analysis, and by adapting them to the *customs* [italics added] of life and thought of their own stratum and of the laity whom they controlled. (1978:460)

In short, then, the prophet as a type of religious leader refers to the person with pure motivations and the priest as having mixed motivations.

A Typology of the Prophet

144

From Weber, two types of prophets can be identified: the founding prophet and the renewer prophet. Beyond that, two others can also be identified from histories of religions: the reforming and the revolutionary types.

Founding prophets claim to bring completely new messages and revelations. Abraham, the founder of Judaism, provides an example of this kind. Renewer prophets preach an older revelation anew with no radical changes (Weber 1978:439). These prophets take an original tradition and attempt to renew it from within, without changing the existing collectivity in any radical way. The tradition is considered to be valid and is the basic source of renewal. The routinized religious collectivity is perceived as needing to be renewed not by something "new" but by a "revolution of tradition" (Hill 1973). Notable examples include Anthony of the Desert (251–356 AD), who is a central figure of monasticism in Northern Africa, and Benedict (480–547 AD), a charismatic leader of the Benedictine order of monks and the Western style of monasticism.

Reforming prophets accept as given some elements of a previous tradition and reform it according to a new revelation. Illustrative examples are Luther, Calvin, and Menno Simons, who sought to reform Roman Catholicism. The fourth type, the revolutionary prophet, began with an established religious tradition but changed it radically according to a new revelation; the result was a "cult-like" collectivity. Jesus of Nazareth, Ann Lee, Joseph Smith, and Minister Louis Farrakhan are examples.

403 - 522 - 3511

1857 Pascal

A FOUNDING PROPHET: ABRAHAM

To present an historical example of a founding prophet, one who brings a new teaching and revelation,[2] I have selected Abraham. Abraham, the founder of Judaism, is also considered the original founder of Christianity and Islam. It is from the original vision of this prophet that emerged, in time, these three significant traditions.

The tradition of Abraham, as recorded in the Jewish/Christian sacred text, saw Abraham as living in the city of Ur (near southern Iraq) during the nineteenth century BC. It is recorded (Genesis 11:31-31) that the father of Abraham, Terah, took Abraham, his wife, and his grandson Lot to Haran, a semi-barren caravan centre on the extreme northern edge of the Arabian desert (Noss and Noss 1984). It is there that Abraham is said to have had his first religious experience. The social conditions of the time were precarious. Noss and Noss (1984:354) note that inhabitants of this region were in constant peril of being attacked by the Akkadian people to the east and the Hurrians to the north. They further documented that some of these peoples actually did immigrate to Palestine where Abraham was to eventually go.

This first religious encounter was in the form of a directive:

> Yahweh said to Abram [his first name], "Leave your country, your family and your father's house, for the land I will show you. I will make you a great nation; I will bless you and make your name so famous that it will be used as a blessing. I will bless those who bless you; I will curse those who slight you. All the tribes of the earth shall bless themselves by you." (Genesis 12:1-3)

Several other experiences followed that: a promise of a covenant and the possession of a new land (Genesis 17); the promise of a son even in the old age of Abraham and his wife, Sarah (Genesis 17); his dialogue with Yahweh over the matter of the destruction of Sodom and Gomorrah (Genesis 19); and the original prescription and subsequent withdrawal of the sacrifice of Abraham's son, Isaac (Genesis 22). All of these religious experiences focused on this man as a founder of what was to become Israel.

2   The originality of the teaching is that he saw the deity in a personal way, that this deity would call forth him and his descendants as a unique people who were bound together as a community, and that this deity would make a covenant, a promise to them that would last for many years.

145

These simple beginnings have had no small effect, since over two billion people follow Judaism, Christianity, and Islam. Cahill (1998) comments on how important was the simple yes to the call that Abraham received:

> So, "*wayyelekh Avram*" ("*Avram* went") — two of the boldest words in all literature. They signal a complete departure from everything that has gone before in the long evolution of culture and sensibility. Out of Sumer, civilized repository of the predictable, comes a man who does not know where he is going but goes forth into the unknown wilderness under the prompting of his god. Out of Mesopotamia, home of canny, self-serving merchants who use their gods to ensure prosperity and favor, comes a wealthy caravan with no material goal. Out of ancient humanity, which from the dim beginnings of its consciousness has read its eternal verities in the stars, comes a party travelling by no known compass. Out of the human race, which knows in its bones that all its striving must end in death, comes a leader who says he has been given an impossible promise. Out of mortal imagination comes a dream of something new, something better, something yet to happen, something — in the future. (1998:63)

REFORMING PROPHETS: MARTIN LUTHER AND MENNO SIMONS

The early church appeared to expand the charisma of Jesus to most of the followers. This collective grew significantly (from one person to an estimated 33 million by 380 AD, as considered by Stark 1996:7) until it, in turn, took on more routinized characteristics. The leaders moved from being prophetic followers of Jesus and became more like priests who were invested in prestige and status. In an historical moment when the church became highly routinized, in the late Middle Ages, two reformer prophets emerged to charismatically offer "new life" to the institutionalized church: Martin Luther (1483-1546) and Menno Simons (1496-1561).

Luther is well known in Christian history as the first to ignite the Protestant Reformation, which had fundamental religious as well as social and economic effects on Western society. Simons was a significant leader of the Anabaptist movement, which is most especially represented by the Mennonite, Hutterite, and Amish peoples.

Luther was a product of monasticism (of the Augustinian Order) but of a monasticism that had become quite routinized. He had faithfully obeyed his authorities and had punctiliously observed the spiritual techniques. He began to believe that the way of the monk was a long discipline of religious duty and effort. Suddenly, in reflecting on the New Testament, he had a conversion experience — an experience of being in a personal and intimate relationship with the divine. He knew this divine not as an object but as a person who cared for, in a concrete way, Martin Luther: man and monk. This was no new truth but the old gospel of grace that had got lost in the highly ritualized, institutionalized, and legalistic medieval catholic church (Dowley 1977).

This experiential conviction never left him. His special gift was not as a theologian but as an evangelist, which was founded on a life of prayer (it is said that he spent three hours at prayer every day) and reading the scriptures (Johnson 1976). From this base, his theological studies of the Christian canonical writings,[3] and his reflections of the state of medieval Christianity, there developed what became known as the three famous Protestant "solas": *sola fide, sola gratia, and sola scriptura. Sola fide* refers to faith alone in Jesus for salvation; *sola gratia* means that it is not by doing good works that one is saved but only by trusting in divine grace; and *sola scriptura* means relying not on tradition to know the divine revelation but only on the Bible. These three tenets became the essential elements in the Protestant sectarian tradition.

One of the reasons why Luther seceded from the Roman Church was that he confronted (like Jesus) a rigid establishment that seemed unwilling to listen. His first confrontation was his nailing of 96 objections on a church door in Wittenberg. Later, he met with a high official of the Roman Catholic Church, a Cardinal; had debates with a Roman Catholic theologian and a well known medieval humanist, Erasmus; and was tried at the Diet of Worms in 1521, accused of heresy. This series of confrontations contributed increasingly to Luther's development into a reform prophet who, eventually, led to the establishment of a sect-like religious collective known to this day as Lutheranism (later history attests, however, that this sect-like collectivity took on more and more church-like characteristics).

Menno Simons was the prophetic reformer of the third arm of the protest against Catholicism (Lutheranism and Calvinism being the first and the Church of England being the second): the Anabaptist movement.[4] Although Simons did not start the movement, he became one of its most outstanding leaders and the one whose name gives us the word

---

3   The term refers to any sacred writings of religions that have primary authority in providing a foundation for faith and morals. Some examples are the Bible for Jews, the Old and New Testament for Christians, the Koran for Muslims, the Guru Granth Sahib for Sikhs, and the Vedic Writings for Hinduism.

4   Literally meaning "later baptism" or the practice of these believers to baptize adults and not infants.

"Mennonite." Simons, a former Catholic priest, emphasized an experiential relationship with Christ. This meant something similar to the religious experience of Luther in having a relationship to the Christ that was personal. He sought to pass this on to followers by encouraging them to be true disciples who used the Sermon on the Mount as their guide and who were open to the inward enlightenment of the Holy Spirit through the baptism of the spirit and reading the Bible (Wenger 1956 and Estep 1963).

The followers of Simons and the other Anabaptists stood not only in contrast to the Catholic church but to Lutheranism and Calvinism as well. Their point of departure from these reformers was that the true church must consist only of the true believers (Bainton 1958). Infant baptism was rejected, in part, because if it were allowed the whole populace would be considered Christian, which would be false (Hershberger 1957). They saw their call not to work through the existent church and state institutions because God was able to work through them personally and not through these institutions. A fundamental conception was to restore original Christianity or the "primitive church" and not merely to reform it. Further characteristics included a focus on an ascetic way of life, not taking oaths, and community living (Bainton 1958).

This significantly reformed church had, and continues to have, a vital place in modern Christianity. Its followers' heritage of courage in the face of persecution, their accent on peace, and their commitment to care for the poor and defranchised continue to be the hallmarks of the original charisma of Menno Simons.

REVOLUTIONARY PROPHETS: JESUS OF NAZARETH, JOSEPH SMITH, BRIGHAM YOUNG, AND LOUIS FARRAKHAN

The third type of prophet is called the revolutionary prophet. This prophetic type emerges when a charismatic leader faces a highly institutionalized religion and is not so much concerned about reforming it but about changing it. This prophet is called revolutionary because he or she begins with an established religious tradition and changes it radically according to a new revelation that he or she claims to have received.

I will use three historical figures: Jesus of Nazareth, Joseph Smith (1805-1844), and Brigham Young (1801-1877) and a contemporary, Louis Farrakhan (b.1933), to exemplify this kind of prophet. There is some debate in the literature considering Jesus as either a reforming prophet or a revolutionary one. Stark (1996) argues for the latter position. His rationale is that when the early Christians believed that Jesus rose from the dead, this myth went beyond simply the reformation of Jewish doctrine, but actually changed it. One could also consider the tradition within early Christianity

148

that Jesus was believed in not only as a prophet (like Isaiah or Jeremiah in Judaism) but also as the Son of God or, in effect, as divine. This would have been revolutionary (indeed blasphemous) teaching and would thus qualify Jesus as a revolutionary prophet.

Two millennia after Abraham (circa 6-10 BC), in a time when Judaism was highly routinized, Jesus of Nazareth entered the historical scene. This man provides us with an illustrative case of the revolutionary prophet: one who accepts as given some elements of a previous tradition (in this case Judaism) and changes it according to a new revelation. Jesus was born at a time in Western history when Rome was the imperial centre of Western civilization. This empire stretched from India in the east to Spain in the west and Britain and France in the north to northern Africa in the south. This political, economic, and social situation became vital for the eventual expansion of Christianity throughout the known world.

Palestine (consisting of Judea, Samaria, Idumea, Galilee, Perea, and Bashan) had come recently under the control of the Romans (c. 60 BC). It was governed by a Procurator (as a representative of the Emperor in Rome) and three Tetrarchies of the family of Herod the Great (about the time of the beginning of the common era or Jesus' birth). Significant antagonism, conflict, and bitterness existed between the Jews and the Romans. This antagonism led to frequent revolts by a group called the Zealots. One of the more noteworthy revolts was led by a Judas who conquered a city in Galilee. This revolt was bitterly crushed by two Roman legions who crucified several thousand of the Zealots (Noss and Noss 1984:415-416).

The Jewish religious climate was also problematic. The religious leaders were, to all intents and purposes, like the institutional priest described by Weber (Table 6.1) above. They were interested in maintaining the status quo and in negotiating with the Romans to achieve as much religious autonomy as possible in the face of the Roman policy of religious intoler- ance. Two key groups held the leadership. The Sadducees, by profession legal experts, had control of the high priesthood and were rich, conserva- tive, linked by complex family alliances, and legalistic. They did not believe in angels, life after death, or in divine intervention (Johnson 1976:15). As somewhat of a contrast, the Pharisees were a lay group who date back to the time of the Maccabees (c. 200 BC) and who led a successful revolt against the Greeks. Johnson (quoting Josephus, c.37-100 AD, an early Jewish histo- rian [1976]) describes them as seeming more religious than the others and more aware of the minutiae of the Law. They used tradition to interpret the sacred texts, and without their leadership the Judaic system could not be made to work at all.

It was against the Pharisees and the Sadducees that the charismatic prophet Jesus levelled his fiercest attack. Matthew (23:13-22) records the words of Jesus:

Alas for you, scribes and Pharisees, you hypocrites! You who shut up the kingdom of heaven in men's faces, neither going in yourselves nor allowing others to go in who want to.
...
Alas for you, blind guides! You who say, "If a man swears by the Temple, it has no force; but if a man swears by the gold of the Temple, he is bound." Fools and blind! For which is of greater worth, the gold or the Temple that makes the gold sacred? Therefore, when a man swears by the altar he is swearing by that and by everything on it. And when a man swears by the Temple he is swearing by that and by the One who dwells in it. And when a man swears by heaven he is swearing by the throne of God and by the One who is seated there.

150 The eventual result of this kind of confrontation was Jesus' crucifixion and death. However, the early followers of Jesus believed that he rose from the dead and that he expected them to carry on his work of reforming Judaism and of spreading this message to the Gentile world. These early disciples soon came into confrontation with the Jewish religious powers and were eventually expelled from participating in the synagogue. It was during this time that this movement became a cult in the sociological sense of the term (see Chapter Eight).

Smith was a revolutionary prophet who, because of several religious experiences, began a new religious collectivity that is fundamentally different from both Catholic and Protestant Christianity. In the first prophetic revelation, he was told to listen to the Son (one of three personages who appeared to him) and not to join any of the religious sects, for "all their creeds were an abomination in his sight" (Smith 1957:48). From these initial revelations and from writings interpreting these revelations, Mormon mythology emerged to stand in contrast to earlier Catholic and Protestant myths. For example, the traditional meaning of the Trinity was that of three persons in one unity. Mormon teaching considers these persons to be three separate personages.[5] These myths are evidence of the revolutionary character of the Smith revelations.

---

5   In addition, there is also a plurality of Gods beyond these three — the mythology of the *Mother in Heaven*. It is understood that there could not be an Eternal Father without an Eternal Mother. Indeed, this Mother is the spouse of the Father (Campbell and Campbell 1988). All people are originally born (their souls) of this union, "in the similitude of the universal Father and Mother, and are literally the sons and daughters of Deity" (McConkie 1979:516). It would appear, however, that the Father, Son (who became Jesus Christ), and the Holy Ghost are still supreme and that they are the only ones adored and worshipped.

Joseph Smith died (he was martyred by a crowd of protesters) at a relatively young age, 39. This was a critical period for the young movement and is especially critical, according to Weber (1978), for succession issues. Who was to lead? Would this new leader carry on the charisma of the prophet or would he act like a priest and be bound by formal norms and concerned about position, prestige, and status? As noted in Chapter Four, Brigham Young became the new leader of the Church of Jesus Christ of Latter-day Saints. One may argue that Young did continue the charisma of his leader but also routinized it (in this way, he is classified not only as a prophet but also as a priest). The evidence of the continuity of charisma is that Young himself had frequent religious experiences as, for example, his belief that he received a revelation about the Great Trek.

Consistent with the goal presented in Chapter Two, I continue the discussion of the Nation of Islam with a look at the central figure of the movement, Minister Louis Farrakhan. He was met in the discussion on mythology as well in our investigation of religious experiences. Here we see him as a gifted leader who, from the documentation from Gardell (1996:139), fits well into what Weber understands to be a charismatic person. He is an eloquent speaker in the wider tradition of African

---

FARRAKHAN AS A CHARISMATIC LEADER

CROWDS HEED CALL TO BLACKS: REBUILD CITIES, FARRAKHAN URGES.

In an atmosphere of racial pride mixed with political anger, one of the largest rallies in US history spread out beyond the Capitol building yesterday as black men congregated to affirm their willingness to work together to improve their communities. The US Park Police, which provides official crowd estimates in Washington, said 400,000 people attended the peaceful rally organized primarily by Louis Farrakhan, the controversial leader of the Nation of Islam. He repeatedly evoked Scripture while excoriating racial relations throughout US history. But in his next breath, Mr. Farrakhan called on blacks to rise above their history of oppression. "We are here to rebuild wasted cities." Throughout the day, the crowd was addressed by a stream of well known blacks, including musician Stevie Wonder, poet Maya Angelou, civil-rights icon Rosa Parks, Washington mayor Marion Barry, and leading members of Congress.

SOURCE: *The Globe and Mail*, October 17, 1995.

BOX 6.1

American preachers. At the rostrum, he is a preacher-artist who uses his gifts as an entertainer to present an extraordinary performance. In his oratory, he fulfills several effective roles: strong warrior, trickster, stern father, heartwarmer, stand-up comedian, encyclopaedic scholar, and the Doomsday prophet. With this charisma, he is able to attract large crowds ranging in size from 10,000 in Boston to 20,000 in Madison Square Garden. Box 6.1 illustrates his powerful charisma.

RENEWER PROPHETS: BENEDICT OF NURSIA AND HILDEGARD OF BINGEN

To understand the impact of Benedict (480-547 AD), some of the historical and social context of the Roman Empire needs to be presented. Constantine (285-337 AD) was the Roman emperor from 312-337 AD (his life and contributions are further expanded in Chapter Ten when we discuss the relationship between religion and politics). He is especially remembered because he became a Christian (312 AD), suspended the persecution of Christians, and announced that thereafter, many varieties of religion besides the state religion of the Empire would be free from coercion and persecution. Stark (1996) does not consider Constantine to be heroic at all. He presents evidence that by 305 AD, the emperor Galerius (emperor from 305-311 AD) acknowledged that Christianity had become so widely received by Romans that a successful persecution was futile. Constantine merely continued state policy.

The edict had mixed blessings. Christians were no longer outcasts and were protected from blatant hostility and persecutions from the Romans. However, as O'Dea and O'Dea (1983:52-53) note, "born Christians" rather than converts made up the membership of the church, and laxness of observance was common. In addition, because the official religion was now Christianity, many people became members not for religious reasons but for reasons of status and position.

In this context, some Christians were disheartened by the laxity. The original fervour and commitment were waning (an example of mixed motivation), and increasingly the church became much more institutionalized and routine. In response, some prophetic renewers like Pochomus (292-346 AD) and Anthony (251-356 AD) emerged. Pochomus was the first to begin and lead a monastery but it is Anthony who is remembered as having given monasticism its special communitarian, ascetic, and celibate character. It is said that he gave away all of his possessions and retired to live as a hermit in the Egyptian desert. In spite of being alone, he fulfilled the teacher's role by serving others who came to him for advice. Even though he was physically withdrawn from the world, he influenced many and effected a number of conversions (Dowley 1977:84).

As Pochomus and Anthony were significant initiators of rejuvenation in Northern Africa, it was Benedict (called Benedict of Nursia, his birthplace in Italy) who "bought" the monastic ideal and worked for ecclesial renewal in Europe. From a source written by Pope Gregory the Great (540-606 AD), we learn that Benedict came to Rome as a young man for a classical education. Dissatisfied with this, he became a hermit. Over a period of time, he had mystical religious experiences in which he sensed a personal and intimate relationship with the sacred. Several men began to come to him and subsequently he began a small community. He later moved to Monte Casino (in central Italy) where he founded the first and most famous of a western (in contrast to eastern and northern African) monastery (Ferguson 1990).

He became noted for his famous *Rule of Benedict* that was the basis for much of western monasticism. In this text (published by Gregory), he outlined a return to Gospel-like simplicity, the encouragement to prayer (to be done seven times a day), hard work, and harmony with other members. Monks were especially to live their lives in the context of an "eternal vision of God" and a "loving identification with Christ." Marty (1959) documented that a keynote of Benedict's system was to create family-like community that emphasized service and sanctity. Van Doren (1991) adds that he built a monastery on compassion, humility, and moderate spirituality, balancing prayer, work, and study; it has become a spiritual treasure of Catholicism. The abbot (the elected leader) was to be a spiritual father and not a rigid authority figure. In addition to this, the monks were to be obedient to the orthodox faith (Ferguson 1990).

The impact of the Benedictines on Western civilization was significant. Van Doren (1991) acknowledges that they organized, sorted, classified, and copied classical texts passed on from the Greek and Roman past. In addition, it was the Benedictine monks who carried Christianity (and with it, civilization) to Britain, northern Germany, and western Spain. It was not long, however, before routinization processes affected the Benedictine monastic movement. Van Doren (1991) notes that the monasteries, like the Christian Church itself, grew rich and that, by the twelfth century, many of them had corrupted the gospel and the simplicity and humility of Benedict.

It was at this stage in Western history that another renewer prophet emerged, and this time it was a woman, Hildegard of Bingen (1098-1179). This remarkable woman was the abbess of several Benedictine women's monasteries. She was noted as a mystical prophet, a poet, a dramatist, a musical composer, a physician, and a political moralist. Hozeski (1994), an English language scholar, in an introduction to a translation of some of her mystical writings, writes of her as one who travelled throughout many parts of the Holy Roman Empire, met with Emperors, conversed with Popes, challenged the laxness of Catholicism in general and the monasteries in particular, and taught university professors and scholars. Besides writing three books on her visions, several biographies, and many letters, she composed a long treatise on physics, documented medical cures, and wrote and collected seventy songs and hymns in a text entitled *Symphonia Armonie Celestium Revelationum* (*The Symphony of the Harmony of Heavenly Revelations*). Her place in a period of history which did not acknowledge the importance of women was striking. Indeed, she exemplifies the role of renewer prophet in addressing mixed motivation in the monasteries and in the church at large. Her legacy goes beyond the church as a figure who shaped medieval institutions in the spirit and simplicity of the original Christian gospel.

Prophets, Priests, and Religious Organizations

154

A special feature of these kinds of prophets is that their uniqueness results in special types of religious organizations that reflect the distinctiveness of the prophets. As we will see in our discussion of the third dilemma, that of administrative order, there occurs the need to continue the charisma of the prophet through a social structure that frequently becomes routinized. Thus the religious leader who is a prophet gives way to the priest. Yet the direction need not be one way. Priests may, in turn, come back to become prophets again in an attempt, for example, to renew the religious tradition that has lost its charisma.

My thesis in this section is that the reformer prophet initiates the sect, the revolutionary prophet the cult, the renewer prophet a movement of renewal, and the priest, who may be a successor of any one of these kinds of prophets, reflects the kind of leadership in the church. We will first define and provide the sociological basis for these kinds of religious organizations and then see how they are connected to the priest and the various prophetic types.

PRIEST AND PROPHET, CHURCH AND SECT

Weber (1946) and Demerath (1965) provide us with elements which distinguish a church from a sect. Table 6.2 illustrates this contrast.

Implied within this typology is that there exists a tension between the religious type and the external environment. Stark (1985) adds to this understanding in reflecting on reasons why there is tension. The church type is in low tension with the social environment and implies accommodation to the external society. One may go beyond this and consider why the kind of leadership that is priestly is most applicable to this kind of religious collectivity. Both the internal and external characteristics of the

CHURCH AND SECT

(from Weber 1946 and Demerath 1965)

	CHURCH	SECT
INTERNAL	professional leaders	lay leadership
	impersonal relationships among members	personal relationships among members
	formal liturgies	informal liturgies
	hierarchical leadership	egalitarian leadership
	inclusive	exclusive
EXTERNAL	accommodation to the external society	no accommodation to the external society
	stable organization	fluid organization
	large fellowships	small and personal
	complex doctrine	simple doctrine
	adapts teaching to the external environment	does not adapt teaching to the external environment

TABLE 6.2

church converge well with Weber's (1978) understanding of the priest-leader. Internally, the priest is a professional who necessarily needs formal theological education. Externally, the priest-leader bases his position on status (as do leaders in the social environment) and receives remuneration (as secular authorities). The position of priest, then, seems to imply compromise and accommodation. In the case of the reformer-prophet it is otherwise. Stark (1985) argued that the sect emerges because of a protest against the accommodative movement of the church. The person at hand would be the reformer-prophet who would lead the emergent sect in this protest.

CULT AND MOVEMENT OF RENEWAL

(from Troeltsch 1931, Brainbridge & Stark 1980, Wach 1967, and Hill 1973)

	CULT	MOVEMENT OF RENEWAL
EXPERIENCE	direct and internal	direct and internal
CHARISMA	frequent	frequent
SOCIAL GROUP	individual	community
TENSION WITH THE EXTERNAL ENVIRONMENT	high tension	moderate tension
TRADITION	a break from it	an adherence to it
IMAGE	radically apart from the "mother" church	church within a church
ORGANIZATION	egalitarian	presence of an authority figure
RATIONALITY	rational	based on faith

TABLE 6.3

THE REVOLUTIONARY PROPHET AND THE CULT

Just as I constructed a typology to distinguish a church from a sect, so also can we construct one to distinguish a cult from a movement of renewal (MOR). I use Troeltsch (1931), Bainbridge and Stark (1980), Wach (1967), and Hill (1973) to construct this typology, illustrated in Table 6.3.

The addition of the cult to the church-sect typology begins with Troeltsch (1931). Troeltsch uses the term "mysticism" to refer to this type. It is characterized by relatively high levels of individualism (with an accent on the direct connection between the individual and the divine), expressed in visions and ecstasy, with little or no dependency upon the religious collective to act as a mediator, and standing in opposition to the Christian doctrines of redemption through Jesus and the incarnation. The charismatic dimension places it in tension with the outside social environment, and the potential to discount the usual doctrines accents the radical departure from tradition. Bainbridge and Stark (1980) take up this theme when they discuss the cult. Their focus is on two central characteristics of the cult: that it is in high tension with the external environment and that it introduces some new revelation into the pool of revelations and actually changes it.

This is the function of the revolutionary prophet — he or she is not only dissatisfied with the high levels of accommodation of the church but also with some of its basic tenets which are believed to be in error. The new revelation through this prophet begins a new religious collective — the cult that is in relatively high tension with the social context and, through its prophet, proclaims an innovative message.

157

THE RENEWER PROPHET AND THE MOVEMENT OF RENEWAL

The fourth type of religious collectivity is termed a Movement of Renewal (see Table 6.3). Its origins go back to Wach (1967) and Hill (1973). When the Church becomes routinized and there arises a leadership which protests this routinization and accommodation, there may emerge not a sect or a cult but, rather, what Wach (1967) calls a "church within the church." He identifies three sub-types, one of which is the most useful for our discussion here: the monastic order. Members of this kind of collectivity desire to live a common life of religious devotion in closer association than appears otherwise possible in a looser association. Membership is exclusive and includes permanent loyalty, obedience, fixed residence, particular dress codes, meals in common, special devotions, and common labour. In addition, members are asked to renounce personal possessions, to embrace celibacy, and to practise asceticism.

An additional characteristic of the Movement of Renewal is provided by Hill (1973:85-103). He developed the concept of "revolution by tradition" to account for the "innovative nature of tradition." Hill comments:

> A "revolution by tradition" can be described as the attempt to realize
> in the present or in the immediate future a basis for authority which
> has the sanction of precedent. The relevant tradition will be claimed
> to have "always existed" but to have been neglected or usurped by
> those at present in positions of authority with the result that the latter
> can no longer claim legitimacy. (1973:88)

From this, we can note that a Movement of Renewal stays within the original church organization and the leaders (and members) endeavour to renew the collectivity by invoking something of the tradition as a source of this renewal. The genesis of this kind of collectivity is best represented by the renewer prophet who is interested in a return to a purity of the past — to the past when there was little accommodation and routinization.

Having laid the foundation of the kinds of religious leaders, prophets and priests, it is important now to update this by investigating more recent and current research on religious leaders. This will be the focus of the next part of this chapter.

MIXED MOTIVATION: RETAINING THE PROPHETIC VISION IN TENSION WITH INSTITUTIONAL ROLE OBLIGATIONS

We begin this section by looking again at Weber (1978), who developed another typology of the prophet and the priest. This is illustrated in Figure 6.1:

THE PROPHET AND THE PRIEST CONTINUUM

(From Weber 1978:442-451)

Prophet...The Lawgiver...The Preacher...The Pastor...The Teacher... Priest

FIGURE 6.1

The lawgiver (Weber, 1978:442) is called to office when there are social tensions. The lawgiver's role is to try to resolve the conflict between status groups by producing a new sacred law of eternal validity. This role is "in-between" the prophet and the priest. The example Weber gives is Moses in Judaism. A contemporary example is the meeting of the bishops of the Roman Catholic Church in Rome from 1962-1965 for the Second Vatican Council. They were like priests in that they represented the hierarchical structure of the Church, but were also like prophets, for the documents they produced (like "new laws") were thought to be charismatically inspired.

The preacher is close to the prophetic end of the continuum but Weber argues (1978:464) that this declines when the revealed religion has been transformed into a priestly enterprise. Preaching endeavours to recapture the charismatic dimension of the prophet. Weber notes that this has been an emphasis of Protestantism. A contemporary example is the centrality of preaching to modern Protestantism. Documentation is provided by the work of Swenson (1990), who observed that the two symbols central to a sect-like Pentecostal church in Western Canada are the "word-podium" and the "music-podium" which, together, accent their central liturgy.

Poloma's (1997) study of a renewal movement in Toronto provides us with another illustration of the charismatic nature of the preacher. She attests that church members and visitors are reminded that the "Holy Spirit" is the one moving in the service, not the preacher. The pastor was quoted as saying: "Don't run after me; I have nothing to give you. It is the Holy Spirit whom you must seek." According to Poloma, it appears that prestige and monetary considerations have not routinized the preachers to the point of becoming priests. In conjunction with this role of preaching, there is a concomitant other role: the pastor. This role is as a counsellor to pass onto the congregational members an interpretation of the sacred tradition and the myth. Examples Weber gives are the rabbis of Judaism, the father confessor of Catholicism, the pietistic pastor of Protestantism, the guru of Hinduism, and the *imam* of Islam. In contemporary Christianity, this role is central because most clerics are also pastors.

The teacher comes closest to the priestly end of the continuum. This person is distinguished from the prophet in that he or she is a transmitter of the revelation that is already acquired. The authority base is no longer charismatic but, rather, a commission from the congregation or someone in a higher authority. Some examples Weber gives are Confucius in China and Zwingli and Calvin in Protestantism. Confucius' (551-479 BC) most well known texts are the *Analytics*. He considered himself not to be a creator but a transmitter of more ancient teachings and revelations: "I'm not born a wise man, I'm merely one in love with ancient studies and work very hard to learn them" (Noss and Noss 1984:269). Zwingli (1481-1531) received his source of Reformation theology from his studies of the New Testament and the early Church writings. Calvin (1509-1564) was known as a synthesizer who took up and reapplied the ideas of the first generation of reformers (Dowley 1977). Both men seem to fit the Weberian type of a teacher.

As we look especially at such topics as role strain among contemporary religious leaders, I will illustrate them with the help of the Weberian typology. The difference is that, for Weber, there were different persons for different roles. The modern cleric has to fulfill a multiplicity of roles. This typology is useful, especially when applied to clergy who have many roles, to help us to understand this first dilemma of the O'Deas, that of mixed motivation. We will look at tensions and dilemmas that clerics experience and then address two kinds of leaders: the social action prophetic activist and clerical and lay leaders within modern Christianity.

159

Tensions within the Priestly Role

Carroll (1992) considers contemporary religious leaders as *theotokoi*, or bearers of the sacred in the midst of life who have a status that has a *sacred aura*. This status, however, is not simple and has inherent tensions and dilemmas. One such tension is the multiplicity of roles as indicated by Blizzard (1956): administrator, organizer, intimate counsellor, preacher, liturgist, and teacher. Later, Blizzard (1958) updated this analysis by estimating that the average clergy person devotes 40 per cent of his/her time to administration, 25 per cent to pastoral counselling, 15 per cent to community organization, and 20 per cent to being a preacher and leader of the liturgy. To this list, Reilly (1975) adds another role: that of the prophet. Her perception of this role is one of innovation, and she adds that younger ministers, at least for Roman Catholic priests, were heavily committed to the prophetic role. What the multiplicity of roles concept does is to help us to understand that within the same person is a tension of the prophetic and the priestly. On one hand, the priestly role "pulls" the cleric to administration, pastoral counselling, and liturgical leadership, whereas the prophetic role "pushes" the cleric to preaching and innovation.

Whitley (1964) and Chafant *et al.* (1984) add that there exists a great deal of role ambiguity among contemporary clergy. In somewhat of a contrast to Weber (who saw different people in these various roles), this current research focuses on the tension of role conflict wherein one person is pulled in different directions. Whitley (1964) suggests three reasons for this. Because there is such a multiplicity of expectations, there is no concise definition as to what the *real* role is. As a consequence of this lack of precision, the minister him/herself is unable to develop an appropriate self-image. Lastly, this self-image is also dependent upon the wider cultural context as well as upon what is expected from the official church itself. In effect, modern clergy seem to experience a whole range of motivations, both pure and mixed (thus reflecting the prophetic/priest dilemma), in their multiplicity of roles.

This multiplicity of roles is also reflected in the relationship between clergy's public and private life. This is illustrated in the research on clergy families when the religious leaders negotiate their professional roles with their familial roles. The problems of time together, family privacy, financial stress, and related issues were documented in several studies in the 1970s and 1980s (Presnell 1977; Mace and Mace 1980; Orthner 1986). Norrell's (1989) recent summary of research on clergy families emphasizes never-ending tasks, insufficient days off, inadequate family time, congregation-centred concerns (the needs of spouse and family notwithstanding), keeping internal psychological or family problems secret, being superhuman models, and many other conflicts associated with the time and stress demands of the ministry. These factors are widely documented in many studies of the "family factor in ministry" (London and Allen 1985-1986; Glenn and Kramer 1987; Lee 1987; Lee and Balswick 1989; Marciano 1990).

In a recent study of evangelical (and some Roman Catholic) clergy and their families in Canada (Larson *et al.* 1994),[6] one finds analogous results. Thirty-two per cent of the married ministers were very happy with their ministry, but a majority (63 per cent) believed that ministry makes marriage more difficult for their spouses. About 80 per cent of both ministers and their spouses agreed with the statement: "being a minister is something like being married to both the church and my spouse." This tension results in stress: clergy indicated that they believe that being a minister conflicts with their responsibilities as spouse and parent.

Tension and stress are present not only in married clergy's lives but also in Roman Catholic celibate clergy's lives. In an introduction to a study of sources of stress of Catholic priests, Hoge, Sheilds and Soroka write:

> The Catholic priesthood is an occupation with unusual stressors. It demands a vow of lifetime constancy and commitment, a vow of obedience to one's bishop or superior, and a promise of celibacy and sexual chastity. The priest is subject to direct authority of superiors. His profession is an especially large part of his total identity. In addition, the diocesan parish priest normally lives on the parish grounds and is seen by his parishioners as being available at any time, seven days a week, so that he cannot clearly demarcate work time from leisure time, work space from private space. The job of a priest is usually unbounded and sometimes ill-defined. (1993:3)

These authors, in their study of 511 priests, found that the central sources of stress for these clergy included overload, excessive responsibility, and organizational problems (having little control over decisions, no connection between responsibilities and rewards, and lacking clear directives in ministry). In a study of Catholic clergy in Canada, Swenson *et al.* (1994), 39 per cent of priests reported a struggle with a sense of inadequacy in the typical pastorate. Forty-four per cent of priests said that they had never experienced ministry burnout, while 37 per cent of them said that they grapple with it occasionally or often. For these Canadian priests, stress does not seem to be a major factor.

---

6 This was a nationally representative sample (N = 1260) of married evangelical clergy and 80 celibate Roman Catholic priests from one province.

Further insights into the Catholic priesthood were outlined by the inclusion of a symposium in the spring 1998 edition of the *Sociology of Religion* journal. Here the guest editor (Chang 1998) acknowledges the contribution of Richard Schoenherr, who has studied the problem of the decline of the priesthood for about 25 years. Schoenherr (with Young 1993 and cited by Chang 1998) collected data from 1966 until 1984 and found that there was a net loss of 300 active clergy each year. He considered this to be an institutional crisis because of the integral link between Catholicism and the Eucharist, the central public ritual of the faith. Without a priest, this central ritual would be eroded and, possibly, lost. With this decline, then, who is in pastoral control? Evidence seems to be the laity. Chang (1998) cites Murion (1992), who found that about 20,000 lay and religious workers are employed at least half-time in half of the 19,000 parishes in the United States. Except for celebrating the Eucharist, they perform many of the priestly roles done previously by the clergy.

In the special edition of *Sociology of Religion*, three articles address issues and concerns about the Catholic priesthood. Young (1998), who was the co-author with Schoenherr of the original study published in 1993, updates this earlier work. He utilizes data from the 1996 Official Catholic Directory. Based on data from 1995, he estimates that by the year 2015, in comparison to 1966, the decline of clergy will be 38 per cent under optimistic conditions and 61 per cent under pessimistic ones. This has major implications for the future of the Catholic Church in the United States, to be discussed below.

Is there evidence of a declining number of clergy in other countries? Vilarino and Sequeiros Tizon (1998) believe this is so in Spain. They find that the decline is just as evident but its reasons and implications are different from those in the United States, because there is a stronger tie between the State and the Church in Spain. Priests in Spain leave the priesthood because they hold liberal views and they want to marry. As more lay persons do the work of the celibate clergy, the traditional patriarchal control of the celibate clergy is losing ground. This results in tension, as one group loses control and an emerging one assumes it.

Is there a similar story in Canada? Swenson (1998) does not address the question of clergy decline (although he implies it with evidence from the Calgary diocese in Western Canada) but does raise the issue of celibacy. He reviews church history on the emergence of celibacy in the Western Catholic Church and finds that support for and against it has varied throughout the nearly 2000-year history of the institution. Typical reasons presented for celibacy (e.g., more time for parishioners, more spirituality, and a deeper devotion to Christ) have not been tested empirically. Using data from 80 Roman Catholic priests and 1,294 evangelical, married clergy, he found no significant difference on measures of religiosity and commitment to parishioners. In unison with Schoenherr and Young, he contends that there is little evidence to continue the requirement of celibacy.

Strains of the Prophetic within Religious Organizations — Social Action vs. Spiritual Mysticism

Two current illustrations of leaders who are prophetic are those who are pacesetters in social action and spiritual mysticism. The former is represented especially by the more liberal church leaders who address such issues as gender inequities, race and class inequalities, and poverty. The latter is more common as a conservative expression in the charismatic movement that emphasizes personal renewal, religious experience, and the creation of spiritually renewed communities and congregations. These two foci illustrate what Wuthnow (1988a) calls the structural realignment of modern American religion into liberal and conservative alliances. Our concentration in this section will be on the racial justice issues, representing the liberal agenda, and the charismatic movement that illustrates the conservative programme.

SOCIAL GOSPEL AS SOCIAL ACTION[7]

People living during the years 1890-1914, both in the United States and Canada, witnessed a heightened interest among the educated classes in the need for societal reform. The focus was to meet the challenge of rising social problems associated with industrialization and urbanization (Wuthnow 1988a). A central component of this came to be known as the social gospel. Allen (1970), a social historian, outlines the social gospel as:

> [that which was] to forge links between proposed reforms and the religious heritage of the nation(s), in the process endowing reform with an authority it could not otherwise command. At the same time it attempted to mould religious and social attitudes thought necessary for life in a world reformed. Still more fundamentally, it represented the complex of ideas and hopes which lay at the heart of reform.... There are many standpoints from which the reform movement can be viewed, but only when it is looked on as a religious expression, striving to embed ultimate human goals in the social, economic, and political order, is the success and the failure of reform fully appreciated.

---

7 Social action here refers to the activity of adherents to the social gospel movement who consider the vitality of the social dimension of the Christian myth in contrast to the more traditional Protestant accent on the individual. The term is in contrast to the Weberian understanding.

During the World Wars and the Great Depression, the vitality of the social gospel went into decline. In the post-war years (1945-1960), with increased economic prosperity, religion in the United States and in Canada experienced growth in a number of areas: high rates of participation (in the United States, 50 per cent weekly attendance and in Canada, 61 per cent for the bulk of the 1950s), the construction of churches, an increase in the size of the ecclesial bureaucracies, and a high demand for clergy (Wuthnow 1988a and Mol 1976).

However, around 1960, there emerged a relatively new kind of religious-social phenomenon: special interest groups. From 1960 to 1988, some 300 new special interest groups joined American religious circles (Wuthnow 1988a:112). It was in this context that the social gospel was revitalized, along with the emergence of spiritual renewal special interest groups with a focus on evangelism, personal salvation, personal piety, and individual morality. The social gospel promotes direct action and justice similar to the way in which it focused on the social problems of the turn of the century. The focus now, however, is not a result of industrialization and urbanization but, rather, because of racial inequities and ethical issues related to the presence of the United States in South East Asia. My example of the prophetic social gospel leaders will be from those clergy involved in the civil rights movement and, more recently, issues surrounding refugees.

The central concern of the civil rights movement, in which many clergy participated, was racism and the discrimination of African Americans. Pettigrew and Campbell (1958-59) document such a case that illustrates well the notion of mixed motivation as well as the tension between being a prophet and a priest. Several clergy were motivated by the social ideal of integration (as a prophetic stance and a pure motive) but found themselves needing to succumb to the desires of the congregation. They resolved their tension and dilemma by calling on the need for brotherly love but not getting involved in direct social action. An example of the social action prophetic leaders who maintained a charismatic stance is Martin Luther King Jr. This nationally known leader appears to have been moved by a pure motive, by a religious "calling" in the civil rights movement (McGuire 1992:236). Harris (1987) noted that if the congregation supported the pastor's prophetic call as a civil rights activist, then the leader held firm to the calling. However, if the congregation did not support the pastor, he endeavoured to balance the ideals of the prophetic call to social activism with the need to please his congregation (evidence of mixed motivation and the priestly role).

Another kind of prophetic social activist leader are those leaders involved in the *Sanctuary Movement*. There are some 50,000 clergy, professional layworkers, and lay persons providing sanctuary to Central American refugees (Johnstone 1992). They are not only in a tension relationship to their congregations but also in conflict with the United States Immigration and Naturalization Service (INS) for performing illegal acts. It is this kind of tension that Hadden (1969) calls "the gathering storm in the churches" and Hoge (1976) terms a division within the Protestant church. At issue is that position that religious leaders take in relation to the members of their congregations. Hadden (1969:148-49) noted that, in a survey, 49 per cent of the respondents felt that "clergy should stick to religion and not concern themselves with the social, economic, and political questions." The pastors and the congregation are in two different worlds: in terms of the prophetic-priestly polarity, it seems that the pastors are committed to a prophetic role on some social issues whereas the people represent a more priestly orientation. Further evidence of this polarity exists in Canada within the United Church of Canada[8] where the clergy are quite liberal while the bulk of the membership is conservative (Bibby 1987).

THE CHARISMATIC MOVEMENT AS A MYSTICAL MOVEMENT

As noted above, the second type of special interest group that is part of the restructuring of American religion is the conservative orientation (Wuthnow 1988a). These special interest groups are characteristically conservative in theological views, and they emphasize personal salvation, piety, morality, and evangelism (Wuthnow 1988a:132). A common form of social expression for these groups is in the form of a Bible Study. Wuthnow (1988a:119), for example, cites data showing that 25 per cent of the American population is involved in some sort of Bible study group. Beyond these groups is another significant special interest group called the Charismatic Movement. Swenson and Thompson (1986) call this contemporary movement a movement of renewal within modern Christianity. Poloma (1997) documents a short history of the Pentecostal-charismatic movement beginning with the Welsh Revival (1903-1904), burgeoning with the Azuza Street Revival (1906-1913), and animated through the Latter Rain Movement (1948), the Charismatic Movement of the 1960s and 1970s, and the Third Wave of the 1980s. All of these revivals were characterized by participants experiencing the Baptism of the Holy Spirit,[9] and a manifesta-

---

8 In 1925, the Congregational Church, the Methodist Church, and most of the members of the Presbyterian Church in Canada united into one large national Canadian church.

9 A conversion moment wherein the person experiences a divine presence, joy, and a religious fervour (Swenson 1972 and McGuire 1982).

tion of the gifts of the Holy Spirit.[10] The Charismatic Movement during the 1960s and the 1970s affected many churches: Episcopalian, Presbyterian, Lutheran, Baptist, Methodist, and Roman Catholic (Swenson 1972; Poloma 1982). A common vehicle for this was the Full Gospel Businessmen's International that "brought" the charismatic message to both clergy and lay people of these churches (Armstrong 1971).

On the whole, there appeared to be a quiet acceptance of these leaders and adherents within the churches.[11] On the other side, however, there is also evidence for tension. Rev. Dennis Bennett was forced to resign from a church in Van Nuys, California, because of congregational opposition and went to pastor a church in Seattle where the congregation was less opposed (Bennent 1971). Unlike the social action prophetic leaders who were predominantly clerics, most of the leaders within the charismatic movement are lay. They do not seem as much in tension with the members of the movement as they are in opposition to some theologians and clerical leaders.

Some evidence of tension and of clerical opposition to the charismatic dimension is noted by Brunner (1970), Maxwell (1971), Swenson (1972), Ford (1971), and Fichter (1975). Brunner (1970:190), an evangelical theologian, argued that the baptism of the spirit and the gifts of the spirit are "hardening instruments" that encourage division within congregations. Maxwell (1971), representing a common evangelical fundamentalist interpretation, wrote that these charismatic manifestations are not authentic for they "came into disuse in the early church." In the study by Swenson (1972), Episcopal and Lutheran clergy expressed significant concern about this movement. Ford (1971) critiqued the more organized arm of the Roman Catholic movement, the communities, and noted that there exists a "new church" wherein lay leaders take on roles of ordained clergy. Fichter (1975), in a study on the Roman Catholic movement, saw leaders and adherents in tension with their bishops. Forty-five per cent of the respondents said they would continue to meet even if the local bishop prohibited their gatherings.

There is also some evidence that the leaders within the movement experience mixed motivations. Fichter (1975), Thompson (1976), and McGuire (1982) all argued that this is evident among some of the leaders. Poloma

10 Such gifts as glossolalia (speaking in tongues), healing, speaking in a prophetic manner, and the like (Swenson 1972 and the Christian text, I Corinthians 12-13).

11 This is evidenced among Lutherans (Sherrill 1964), Presbyterians (Jensen 1963), Southern Baptists (Kelsey 1964), American Baptists (Sherrill 1964), Methodists (Sherrill 1964), and Roman Catholics (O'Connor 1970).

(1982) adds to this that as the intentional communities[12] become more organized, more routinized characteristics among the leaders emerge. In illustrating this dilemma, Poloma (1997) goes beyond the Charismatic Movement to investigate what has come to be known as the "Toronto Blessing." Just as the earlier movements focused on glossolalia and evangelism, this new movement has manifested itself, among its members, in physical demonstrations such as laughing, jerking, shouting, and rolling. However, the central mythological message is God's mercy and unconditional love. In the tradition of Berger and Luckmann (1966), this mythology is legitimated by what they term a second-level legitimation represented in proverbs, moral maxims, and traditional sayings. A central one to this congregation is "That we may walk in God's love and give it away."

The Toronto Airport Christian Fellowship (the locus of "The Toronto Blessing" and the source of a revival reaching global dimensions) tries to retain the charismatic moment of pure leadership motivation by arguing that all members have equal access to "The Spirit." It discourages a "cult of personality," since, after all, it is the "Holy Spirit" who is the leader, not the preacher, the team pray-ers or other pastoral staff. Poloma notes that "for the immediate present, it appears that prestige and monetary considerations still take a backseat to the satisfaction of being able to serve in the spread of this global revival" (1997:261).

What has been argued here is that lay leaders (and some clerics) within the charismatic renewal face some tension with their official churches on the one hand and with their congregations on the other. Beyond that, both clerical and lay leaders within the renewal experience tension between single-minded devotion and mixed motivation. The latter seems to be most evident in the more organized spheres of the movement — within intentional communities wherein the leaders (called coordinators in Catholic communities) are professionals. That is, they become paid pastors and are subject to status pulls and routinized charisma in full-time ministry.

| WOMEN AS PROPHETS AND PRIESTS[13]

Women's place in religious organization in general and leadership in particular is of special importance in the sociology of religion. I shall begin

---

12 These are communities created by persons who voluntarily make a commitment. Within the Catholic Charismatic Movement, several large communities have emerged which resemble the hierarchical nature of Roman Catholic, Episcopalian, and Orthodox churches.

13 It is important to reiterate that this term does not refer to priests in the Roman Catholic, Anglican or some of the Greco-Roman religions, but to the construct as outlined by Weber.

with Weber to set the place of women's roles as prophets and leaders, look at the place of women in the founding of religious movements, and outline some of the key issues surrounding women as priests in the modern world.

Weber (1963:104) argues that in the religion of disprivileged classes, there is a tendency to give equality to women. In addition, the role of the woman as a prophet is common in the early stages of the religions that grew from Buddha, Christ, and Pythagoras. However, Weber observes, after the initial charismatic stage is passed and routinization occurs, "a reaction takes place against pneumatic manifestations among women, which come to be regarded as dishonourable and morbid." Weber's perception is reflected in the O'Deas' first dilemma that we are looking at now. It seems that as both the leadership and the community of followers experience routinization, there are mixed motivations as well as what I am calling a process of *masculinization*. In the light of Weber's insights, masculinization is a form of the routinization of charisma. This process sets the stage for our discussion. Such masculinization continued up to the recent past, when the feminist movement within Christianity and Judaism has challenged it. We might call this recent phenomenon an attempt to regain the original charisma of women having a more salient place in modern religion, or a *feminization* of the clergy. I hope to exemplify these processes in the discussion that follows.

Ancient Judaism is usually depicted as being patriarchal. However, several texts from the Jewish canon attest to egalitarianism between men and women, allowing women to have a central place in the social life of the Israelites. The Song of Songs exalts egalitarian eroticism between a man and a woman. Chapter 31 of Proverbs presents a "modern" view of women, in which women are free to do business, are given a fruit of their labour, and are managers of their households. Stark (1996), in his sociological study of the rise of Christianity, concurs with the Weberian view that early in the religious tradition, women had a special place. He points out that the early church was especially attractive to women who enjoyed far higher status than did women in the Greco-Roman world. He offers several pieces of evidence.

First of all, because of female infanticide practised in ancient Roman society, with men having almost life-and-death power over women and children, there was a disproportionate number of men to women (an estimate is 131 and 100). The Greco-Roman world was not a safe place for women for they were more likely to be killed in infancy, to be divorced, or to be victims of incest, the "double standard" of marital infidelity, and polygyny. The Christian value system rejected the double standard, cohabitation (which left women vulnerable), divorce, and female infanticide (indeed any infanticide). In addition, widowhood in the Greco-Roman society meant that the woman was required to remarry so as to pass on her former husband's estate to a new man. In Christianity, widowed women were honoured and cared for financially by the Church.

In addition, Christian women were not encouraged to marry until they were in their twenties, when they were better able to make adult decisions. In the Roman world, women were three times more likely to marry before the age of 13 than were Christian women. Finally, Stark (1996) reviews early literature that accords leadership roles to women, which is in contrast to the medieval Church.

Later examples of this process appear in the person of Hildegard of Bingen (see above), the Franciscan movement (a thirteenth-century, medieval monastic movement) and the Quaker reforms (a seventeenth-century radical movement in England). As Mack (1987) states, St. Francis (founder of the Franciscans) and Fox (founder of the Quakers) were very open to allowing women to have active roles during the early period of the movements. However, both later Franciscans and Quakers saw "women as transitional figures ... coming to prominence in the early stages of egalitarian fervour, receding into obscurity with the reemergence of structure" (Mack, 1987:121).

Relying on several sources,[14] Warner (1993) argues that social feminism of the late nineteenth century was an outgrowth of the evangelical Second Great Awakening (1795-1835). It was during the first third of the nineteenth century that the gender order of the "separate or two spheres" was constructed. As the economy moved away from family economies (wherein men, women, and children worked together in small enterprises, especially farms) toward the differentiation of manufacturing, women, together with their pastors, created a vision of womanhood which entailed protecting culture and morality. Even though women agreed that their role was in the home, they did not restrict their domain to it and developed extra-domestic roles. They created powerful, local, and nationwide single-sex organizations with a feminist flavour. A well-known example is the Women's Christian Temperance Union (WCTU).

In a recent study on women and religion, Weiss Ozorak (1996) argues that even though women do not feel equal to their male counterparts in organized religion (an indicator of masculinization), they are still more religious on a number of measures and have a sense of empowerment. In her case study of sixty-one middle-class, Catholic, Protestant, Jewish, and Unitarian women, the psychologist notes that her subjects emphasized the importance of a caring community and made attributions of God as a friend and confidant rather than as a cosmic ruler or judge. She quotes a Methodist woman: "Religion is about finding the centre that I think all of us have. And through that centre we relate to each other in ways that are

---

14 Cott 1977, Ryan 1981, Epstein 1981, and Smith-Rosenberg 1985.

helpful ... to try to create, to try to move forward. The power that occurs from that is God power" (1996:27).

According to Poloma (1989), masculinization processes are also at work in the Assembly of God denomination. Women like Aimee Semple McPherson, a founder of the Four Square Gospel Church, and Marie Burgess, a pastor of an Assemblies of God Church in Chicago for forty years, were vital leaders in the early years of these churches. However, as the years passed, women were systematically barred from the clergy in the Assemblies of God. Poloma (1989:108) argues that the Assemblies have bowed to pressure from conservative, evangelical churches under the influence of biblical literalism and have restricted ordination to men.

Ann Lee and the Shakers

In Chapter Five, I outlined Ann Lee's special prophetic gift. She saw herself as the Christ incarnate in female form and exhibited such charismatic manifestations as speaking in tongues, healing of others, and experiencing visions and revelations. As I noted, one of Ann Lee's earliest converts, Joseph Meachem, organized the Shakers into two authority gender lines: male and female. Stein (1992) observes that Shaker history was partially characterized by conflict between subgroups and personal aggrandizement of leaders (a clear example of mixed motivation).

It seems that two processes were in parallel growth among the Shakers. On one hand, there is evidence for the evolution of mixed motivation as illustrated by Stein's work. On the other hand, we saw in Chapter Five that Meachem, the immediate successor of Lee, established a male and female leadership pattern. One may argue, then, that the salient role of women was institutionalized early in the movement and the masculinization process did not occur.

Women, New Spiritualities, and Islam

There is an additional body of literature that addresses other issues of religion and gender such as new spiritualities and Islam. Neitz (1998) notes that women have created women-centred, relatively small and unorganized religions that emerge from neopaganism[15] and the feminist movement. The participants worship female deities and celebrate nature rituals. The claim is that these women feel empowered and are constructing a new union of femininity, religion, and self.

---

15 As part of new religious movements, the social phenomenon refers to a revival of paganism, especially of the Greco-Roman variety. It emphasizes a belief in many deities (sometimes in symbolic terms) that include, especially among female ones, that nature is sacred, and that the

By now, the reader will be aware that religion is multidimensional and that there are significant differences and variations between Christian and Jewish denominations and among participants within each denomination. A similar story is discovered in Islam. This world religion is also multidimensional and there is wide variation among believers within the faith. The relationship between women and Islam is also quite varied. Two articles which address the question of gender and Islam are relevant to our discussion.

The research on women and Islam reviewed here that focuses on differences within Islam illustrates a dual tradition within the faith that is also acknowledged by Bellah (1970:154) in his study of Islam. On one hand, the Koran, the sacred text of Muslims, states that a woman was created by Allah with man (Koran 60), and is to be treated as a man with justice because she has similar rights (33). The Koran counsels men to treat women with kindness (62), and states that women are to be seen as blessings to men (192). On the other hand, even though women have rights similar to men, they are inferior in status (33), men have authority over women because Allah has made man superior to women (64), men have the prerogative of divorce (33, 386-398), and they are allowed to have several wives, especially if the women have children and are currently widowed (60).

171

Campbell (1964:445) makes a similar point in his study of Occidental religions. A Shi'ite text views woman as being created as a temptress while Fatima, the daughter of Mohammed, is revered and honoured throughout the Islamic world. Moaddel's (1998) research reflects this dual tradition. He argues that in India and Egypt, where Islam has experienced modernization resulting in what he terms "Islamic modernism," adherents have encouraged women's education and their involvement in social affairs and have spoken out against polygyny and exclusion. He theorizes that they have created an Islamic discourse that is rooted in the Enlightenment and is channelled through unique historical and social structures in Egypt and India. On the other hand, Iran, after the revolution of 1979, denounced all the provisions for female equality that were common under the leadership of the Pahlavi (see Chapter Ten). Under the Ayatollah Khomeini's fundamentalist, hierarchical regime, veiling of women in public was re-introduced, and all the reforms granted by the Pahlavis that benefitted women were reversed.

The dual tradition of women's roles is also reflected in a national survey done in Kuwait in 1994 and published by Meyer, Rizzo, and Ali (1998). In the survey of 1,500 Kuwaiti citizens, they find support for their hypothesis

feasts to be celebrated are seasonal ones. Newport (1998) adds that neopagans believe that many religions are radically and irreconcilably different; that no one person has more or less authority than the other; and that they are the ones holding the true faith, which is the ancient folk religion.

that Islamic orthodoxy is a predictor of allowing women to vote, but Islamic religiosity is not. Islamic orthodoxy is a composite construct of several items that reflect this orthodoxy.[16] In contrast, Islamic religiosity is measured by another set of items that tap religiosity.[17]

Meyer *et al.* (1998) point out that is not just religion that predicts extending the franchise to women. Other factors include being Sunni and having a high social status, and social embeddedness between and within the Shi'ites and the Sunnis. If a citizen adhered to a school of thought from the Shi'tes of Iran, he would be less likely to support the franchise. On the other hand, if a citizen had links to Sunnis of Egypt, he would be more likely to support the extension of political rights to women. The authors conclude that it is important to specify what it is in Islam that is either supportive or unsupportive of women's rights: "In short, Islamic beliefs and positive views toward increasing women's political rights, in general, and towards the democratization process in particular, operate within structures of group life and stratification systems of nations, such as Kuwait" (Meyer *et al.* 1998:143).

Clergy Women

One might say that the second-wave feminist movement that has resulted in many churches opening up their leadership to women is an attempt to regain the lost charisma of female leadership common in the early years of a religious movement. Here I discuss the role of women as clerics, concluding with a theory from Chaves (1996) of why some churches have been more likely to ordain women than others.

Several studies that Warner (1993) reviews present a positive answer not only from the current situation but also from the past. He notes that religion has long provided the moral leverage necessary for women to be in leadership positions and to have a sense of empowerment. Among Catholics in the 1960s, devotion to Saint Jude led women to break off rela-

---

16 The items include: it is a duty to help those confused about religion; it is important to help people become enlightened about religion; the world would be a better place if more people held my religious views; the world's problems are aggravated by the fact that so many people are misguided about religion; all Muslims must work together to face the Western challenge against Islam; and Islam does not separate politics and religion (Meyer *et al.* 1998: 135).

17 The construct consisted of these items: families should insist that women wear veils; men should have beards; Western clothing is more practical than traditional clothing; divorce is okay if two married people cannot get along; and people should choose political candidates for their political experience, not their religious sect (Meyer *et al.* 1998: 136).

ORDINATION OF WOMEN

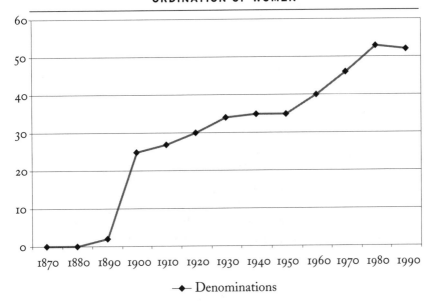

—◆— Denominations

Source: Chaves (1996:842)

FIGURE 6.2

tionships with "mean" boyfriends and reject unwanted medical treatments (Orsi 1990). In rural Missouri, young Pentecostal women were able to travel and leave home, and current Pentecostalism gives some women opportunities as religious entrepreneurs (Lawless 1988).

Chaves (1996) outlines both a descriptive and theoretical presentation of the ordination of women. After showing how more and more churches have ordained women, he then offers a theory of why some churches have ordained women and others have not. His argument is as follows. Noll (1992), referred to by Chaves, notes that the Association of Women Ministers was formed in 1919 to secure equal opportunity for women and was influential in changing rules in several churches. Hole and Levine (1971) add that around the start of the second wave of feminism,[18] the National

---

18 There is some debate as to how many "waves" or different stages of women's movements have existed in the United States and Canada. Chaves considers the "first wave" to be the early twentieth-century suffrage movement whereas the "second wave" is the more recent movement which has broader goals such as equal pay, equity in the family, equal protection for rights of women, equal access to higher education, and more egalitarian policies for access to professions.

PROFESSIONAL WOMEN

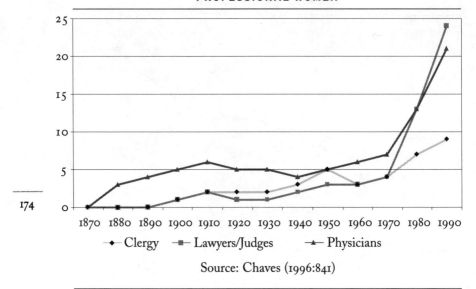

Source: Chaves (1996:841)

FIGURE 6.3

Organization for Women established an Ecumenical Task Force on Women and Religion that sought equal opportunity of access to the clergy.

Carroll (1992) notes that the ordination of women has increased at a rapid pace since 1970. Chaves (1996) offers us a graph that illustrates this growth (see Figure 6.2). There were 21,000 ordained women clergy in the United States in 1986, a three-fold increase since 1970. In Canada, there is also evidence for this increase. The first woman to be ordained was in 1936, in the United Church of Canada; in 1993, 25 per cent of ordained United Church ministers were women. Ten per cent of Anglicans priests are women. However, there are none in the Roman and Ukrainian Catholic churches (because of the ban on ordaining women) and there are few in Baptist, holiness, and Pentecostal churches (Nason-Clark 1993).

Even with these increases, Carroll (1992) acknowledges and Chaves (1996) observes (see Figure 6.3) that this increase is still considerably behind the proportion of women in law or medicine. Is there support for the ordination of women? Is there evidence, then, that the presence of women has made a difference in the churches? Is there evidence that there has been an attempt to regain the feminine charismatic image?

Surveys give us some answers to these questions. Lehman (1987) conducted a national survey in England in 1984 of the following churches: Church of England, the Baptist Union, the Methodist Church, and the

United Reformed Church. Forty-five per cent of the respondents definitely agreed (38 per cent probably agreed) to the following statement: "A woman's temperament is just as suited for the pastoral ministry as is a man's." Respondents saw no difference on which gender performed the following tasks: senior pastor (51 per cent), assistant pastor (73 per cent), preaching a sermon (78 per cent), and leading a pastoral prayer (89 per cent). Lehman (1987:69-70) summarizes:

> From these data it seems clear that most church members in these denominations in England are comfortable with modern consciousness as it manifests itself in pressures of changes in church leadership. The prospect of ordaining women — a very recent innovation in church history — is something they can live with. They appear satisfied that they can adapt to this departure from tradition and that the church will be none the worse for it.

175

An earlier study was conducted by Lehman (1985) on the United Presbyterian Church of the United States in 1980. Thirty-nine per cent of the respondents definitely agreed (43 per cent probably agreed) to the same statement in the English study: "A woman's temperament is just as suited for the pastoral ministry as is a man's." In a range from 39 per cent to 86 per cent, respondents saw no difference in which gender performed the following tasks: senior pastor (51 per cent), assistant pastor (39 per cent), preaching a sermon (66 per cent), and leading a pastoral prayer (86 per cent). Lehman (1985:51) summarizes in a similar way to his study in England:

> The basic picture in these data is that most people are fundamentally and philosophically open to women in ministry, including specifically the ordained ministry. Yet many of them do have reservations. It is a "mixed bag."

The "mixed bag" is reflected in the differences between the English and the American study. The American Presbyterians are less open to women being ordained than the English. Lehman, in his English study, does not try to account for these differences. However, in both the United States and England, the more church members manifested modern attitudes or consciousness (indicated, especially, by levels of education), the more open they were to the salient role of women (Lehman 1985: 108 and 1987:88).

This "mixed bag" imagery is even more salient among Assembly of God adherents. Poloma (1989:112), in her statistical study of both lay and cleric respondents, notes that even though 82 per cent of members were not opposed to women's ordination, only 31 per cent felt that women should be permitted to be church elders. What this means is that members offer

BEHIND MILLION MEN, BLACK WOMEN: "NO GIRLS ALLOWED" REQUEST LEAVES COMMUNITY DIVIDED.

The Million Man March has drawn thousands of African-American men to Washington. But black women stand divided on the event...Sylvia, owner of a restaurant in Harlem, acknowledges that her employees said they are in favor of the march. Another black woman says: "I really think it is a wonderful movement as far as the men are concerned." On the other hand, longtime civil rights activist Jewell Jackson McCabe notes that the march is a hoax, a way for Farrakhan to claim leadership of the black community.

SOURCE: CNN US News posted on the Web, October 16, 1995

176

BOX 6.2

verbal support to the ordination of women but, in fact, do not give them room to serve as an ordained minister. This imagery is more striking when one looks at the Nation of Islam. Here it is even less than a question of a mixed bag, for there is a strong mythology of the role of women that is significantly conservative. Gardell (1996:59, 283) notes that women's roles are primarily to be wives and mothers and that they are not to be included in the hierarchical leadership structure. They are urged to dress modestly, to obey their husbands, and take great pride in raising children (see Box 6.2 for additional reflection).

Another question to consider in this overview of clergy and women is whether to restrict it to the ordained. Wallace (1992) researched women in the Roman Catholic Church who, although not being ordained, did virtually everything in rural Catholic parishes and were recognized as legitimate pastors by the local bishop. She acknowledges that this is quite remarkable given the patriarchal structure of this church and the conservative stand of Rome in not giving women access to the priesthood. Wallace offers several reasons for this. First, Vatican II (1962-1965) gave official recognition that the medieval institution needed to be updated to the modern world in areas that were changeable. Second, major demographic transitions have presented a very practical need for lay leadership: there is a severe shortage of priests.[19] The third reason she offers is the contemporary women's movement. First of all, she presents national data that reflect an American Catholic population that is over 50 per cent in favour of granting ordination to women (Hoge 1987). Second, women's groups within the church

19 For data, see the section under "Tension in the Priestly Role," pp. 160-162.

have lobbied for pastoral letters from bishops that condemn sexism and order gender-neutral documents.

During 1989, Wallace conducted her own research on twenty women of eighty who were either currently in pastoral roles or were so in the recent past. All had to have been appointed by their bishops for inclusion in the study. There was an equal distribution between laywomen and nuns. These women endeavoured to do the work of a caring pastor: knowing people's names, showing affection, visiting parishioners, showing personal warmth, being willing to work in collaborative rather than authoritarian leadership, and empowering members to be more active in the life of the parish. The appointment by the local bishop was authentic. Shortly after the new pastor arrived, he came to conduct an initiation ceremony that legitimated her role. However, in spite of the parochial and diocesan support, these women leaders experienced constraints, conflicts, and tensions. The primary source of the conflict was on the institutional level. Even though they did most of the pastoral work, they were not allowed to baptize, marry, conduct funerals, nor, especially, be the celebrant at the Eucharistic celebration. When the Sunday liturgy was conducted, a priest had to come in for that function. They experienced tension in this role: on the one hand, they were given significant authority but, on the other hand, their authority was subordinate to the ordained priest who, being the Eucharistic leader, had more "power" than they did.

Wallace's work is an indicator of a much wider phenomenon. Murnion (1992 and cited in Chang 1998) found in a survey that 85 per cent of full- or part-time lay workers were women. This seems to be significant evidence that a new feminization of Catholic leadership is very much in the making.

In Canada, one would expect that evangelical clergy would be quite conservative in their support of the ordination of women. However, Larson and his colleagues (1994) found that 59 per cent of evangelical clergy support their ordination. (Yet a similar story could be told for evangelical ministers in Canada as for Assembly of God members in the United States: they verbally support ordination but, in fact, very few women are ministers: only 3 per cent of ministers in the sample were women.) This support is somewhat higher for Roman Catholic priests (62 per cent) but not significantly. Since the mean age of the priests surveyed was 60 years old, this could be a reason why only 62 per cent support women being ordained (Swenson et al. 1994).

Carroll's (1992:293) review of some of the literature on women clergy responds to our question about whether women's presence does make a difference. Charlton (1978), in a study of ordained women, discovered that women were trying to challenge a male model of leadership by adding feminine characteristics to the role. She found, however, limited evidence for this happening. Ice (1987), in a case study of 17 clergy women, paints a different picture. She argues that clergy women have distinctively feminine leadership styles and that their influence will move the church away from patriarchal and hierarchical forms of polity and introduce a more egalitarian, personal, and collaborative style. Wallace (1991), in a study of Catholic women administrators, gives credibility to Ice's work. Carroll (1992:294) concludes that there are not enough data to provide definite conclusions. My hypothesis that women clergy are regaining a lost charismatic past is lacking consistent evidence. However, it should be noted that there is some evidence for this happening in the modern movement of the ordination and legitimation of women in clerical positions.

There is evidence, then, for the "mixed-bag" metaphor. However, to extend this thought, it is appropriate to ask why some churches have ordained women and some have not. Chaves (1996) presents a theory and a test to answer this question and others. He relies on a recent approach to organizational change called the "new institutionalist" theory, developed by Powell and DiMaggio (1991). In short, the theory considers that there is a "loose coupling" of formal rules with everyday practice and that these rules are likely to have a source outside of the organization. This suggests that organizations are dependent upon elements from the external environment rather than upon internal social mechanisms. The examples that Chaves (1996:844) uses are (1) that even though some churches do not allow ordination of women, there are increasing numbers of women seeking pastoral positions; (2) women have performed and continue to perform leadership roles within the denominations which forbid access to ordination; and (3) even if women are ordained, their positions are met with both male clerical and congregational opposition. His theory, then, is based upon what is happening in the outside environment as well as what is happening within the organization.

Using a database of 92 American churches, Chaves uses what is called an "event-history analysis" which tests the likelihood of either an event occurring or "changes of state." What is measured is a "hazard rate," which is the rate of movement from one state to another, in this case, the rate at which a church allows ordination for women. The results reveal that both what was happening in the external and internal environment influenced the likelihood that the church ordained or did not ordain women. Externally, both first-wave and second-wave feminism had an effect on the likelihood of ordination. Internally, women are likely to be ordained in those churches which were recently founded (theorizing that those churches which have been recently founded have no long history of male-only ordination), those which were non-sacramentalist (arguing that the more sacramentalist a church is, the more it is tied to a masculine image of ordination), those

NEW ROLES FOR JEWISH WOMEN

Although women have always been important in the Jewish faith, they traditionally have served only background roles during religious ceremonies, such
as the Passover Seder. But a women's Seder to be held in Dallas and in other
parts of the country next week will give a definite feminist twist to the story of
the exodus of the Israelite slaves from Egypt.

"Women will be sort of celebrating their own liberation at this Seder," said
Joel D. Brooks, executive director of the American Jewish Congress'
Southwest Region, sponsor of the Dallas Seder, which began four years ago.
Participants in the Seder will name their mothers and grandmothers, aunts or
other women who have been significant in their lives. Rabbi Nancy Kasten,
who led the women's Seder last year, said the rituals are part of a trend to
rediscover major roles of women in history and culture.

"Like in many areas of our society, women's contributions have been overlooked or belittled," said Kasten, associate chaplain at Southern Methodist
University.

Although generally accepted, the feminist Seders, which originated in New
York and California a little over a decade ago, can be misunderstood,
Kallenberg said.

"It's kind of controversial," she said. "I took a friend last year and she went
home. She thought it was anti-male." But Kallenberg, who will also take part in
more traditional Seders, said the ceremony is merely an affirmation of women
and the major roles they have played in religious history.

SOURCE: http://www.ssnewslink.com/doc/images/small_logo.gif, April 19, 1997.

BOX 6.3

which were not literalist in biblical interpretation (because the more fundamentalist a church is, the more likely it is to take verbatim the biblical
imagery of the subordination of women to men) and those which allow
more independent authority to women in leadership positions within congregations.

Summing up his article, Chaves offers some informative insights. In the
early period (from 1850 to 1917), conflicts over the ordination of women
emerged because small numbers of women wanted to speak and take leadership within the churches. This is also substantiated by Warner's review.
In the period between 1920 until 1970, the source of conflict was a top-
down, "mandated" decision to ordain women. From 1970 to the present,
however, it is female seminarians and theological students who have been

forming organizations, mobilizing constituencies, and disrupting normal organizational processes that continue to refuse a full recognition of women as clergy. Chaves adds that the ordination of women is part of the "Western cultural account" (Meyer, Boli, and Thomas 1994), from which comes the notion that individuals have a distinctive moral standing *as individuals* and not as members of "natural" groups (families, races, genders, classes). It is interesting that what he is saying here is that the ordination of women is rooted in the modern, secular world and not within the mythology, the ethos, and the ritual of the sacred. One might say that the process of recapturing the charisma of women is accomplished not by a "revolution of tradition" (Hill 1973) but by assimilating to the modern agenda of gender equality.

In an attempt to summarize current research on female clergy in the contemporary Protestant church, Chang (1997a) introduced a symposium on the topic that included articles by Chaves and Cavendish (1997), Nesbitt (1997), Charlton (1997) and, the symposium organizer herself, Chang (1997b). Rather than detailing each of the contributors, I will rely on Chang's (1997a) summary of their insights.

Chaves and Cavendish update Chaves' earlier work cited above (1996) and argue that the feminist movement's influence on the ordination of women has not been a simple linear progression and that the institutions who ordain women learn from their social environments and, in doing so, redefine the terrain and issues of political struggles.

Nesbitt, in her findings based on a study of male and female clergy from the Episcopal and Unitarian churches, indicates that although more women are being ordained, they do not have equal occupational achievement rates as men. Sadly, she notes, clergy social status has been reduced with the inclusion of women. Charlton followed a number of female students from the time they were in the seminary in 1977/78 to 1994. She found that 50 per cent had left the ministry, some were on leave, and many others were seriously contemplating leaving the pastorate.

There is better news from a study by Chang (1997b). She provides data from 15 Protestant denominations and 4,900 respondents on the topic of finding a first position as a clergy woman. She found that women take longer to formally enter the new career, but they have made substantial gains when one looks at transitions across successive cohorts, and the longer women (as well as men) looked for work and did not find it, the more their chances of success diminished.

All these studies indicate a common finding: the continued presence of tensions and dilemmas for these women. Chang (1997a) reviewed other research and found that even though the ordination of women on the institutional level is accepted and encouraged, many of them do not find work, and when they do find work, they experience a lot of opposition to their ministry, and, if married with children, do not receive the support that a man would. In addition, there is evidence that Nesbitt's finding of lowered status is confirmed by other studies. This review confirms the "mixed bag" imagery that was discovered in previous studies. Even though women have gained much through entering the "male" clergy, they have done so at great cost and have not received the benefits that their male counterparts have.

By way of a conclusion to a review of the research done on Christians, clergy, and gender, Nason-Clark offers us some thoughts:

> What would a church look like if it took the responsibilities of Christian men and women as equal partners in sharing their faith and the responsibility for leadership? The gender breakdown of the local church board or governing council would not differ from the nursery roster; the proportion of women on the platform would approximate the proportion of women in the pew; the language and liturgy of worship and instruction would be inclusive of the diversity amongst believers; the full expanse of the church's ministry would have men and women serving as partners, on the basis of talent, willingness to serve and spiritual maturity; and the programs offered to the congregation and the local community would represent the full range of needs and experiences of ordinary women and men, boys and girls alike. The full inclusion of men and women in active lay service can only be accomplished by rethinking the power and prestige conferred by ordination. (1993:230)

| CONCLUSIONS

Insights from Carroll (1992) and Nason-Clark (1993) provide us with reflections on the presence of the dilemma of mixed motivation and continued tension and struggles of religious leaders. Carroll (1992) uses Wuthnow's (1988a) restructuring thesis that we looked at in Chapter Three. Carroll considers three processes occurring: (1) the redefinition of clergy not only as clergy man but also as clergy woman; (2) the blurring of the distinction between the clergy and the laity (the decline of clericalism); and (3) a reinterpretation of truth and faith in light of the postmodern world consciousness.

The first reflection of Carroll's is what we have just looked at in our investigation on gender and religious leadership. Women's entry into the ministry could very well challenge the sacred role of the minister as being solely a man's role. This has created a new dynamic, a clash of symbols that involves an entry of the feminine into what has been a sacred masculine domain. Again, the dilemma is one of balance. It would seem that because most modern societies consider women and men equal, women should be included in church leadership.

Carroll's second reflection is his discussion on the decline of clericalism: the conception of the church as being the People of God rather than a hierarchy, the emergence of teams of leaders in churches (including laity), the decline of available priests in Roman Catholic parishes (see also Nason-Clark 1993:231), and the growing intolerance with unchecked power not only in religious institutions but also in any sphere in contemporary society (Nason-Clark 1993:232). The dilemma seems to be that of a contrast between a hierarchical structure and an egalitarian, democratic one. If one retains only a hierarchical structure, one runs the risk of continued clericalism; however, if one emphasizes only the democratic or egalitarian model, one meets the problem of what de Tocqueville (1945) called the *tyranny of the majority* and the movement toward mediocrity.

The third reflection concerns the clergy's role as interpreters of truth and the faith. In light of postmodern thinking, one finds that certainty is undermined, doubt is institutionalized, and everything seems open to revision. Nason-Clark adds that the modern cleric is not the only professional able to meet the spiritual needs of members: family therapists, psychologists, and social workers compete with the minister. These other professionals challenge the cleric as being the only one able to interpret the human condition. The call of clerics, Carroll maintains, is more a call of what Giddens (1991) calls *reflexivity*. Clerics should be open in interpreting the religious tradition by using a variety of sources: the sacred text itself, theological commentaries, their own and others' experiences, and modern science. Carroll (1992:301) writes: "reflective leaders are … attempting to restructure their interpretive role to bring religious faith to bear meaningfully on the complex issues of living in this time of high modernity."

A dilemma is involved here as well. If one interprets the sacred tradition as a sealed tradition and the leader clothes him/herself in the authority of *theotokoi*, then one runs the risk of alienation from one's congregation. On the other hand, if the leader is open to too many sources, the risk is that the tradition loses its essence and "the baby is thrown out with the bathwater."

I conclude our chapter where we began. Both historically and contemporarily, the role of the religious leader is one of a dilemma of mixed motivation. Sacred traditions call for leaders who are single-hearted in devotion; pure in mind, heart, and body; and models of the tradition for the followers. Only occasionally is this fulfilled in reality. The challenge, however, continues to be set before these leaders: to be to the present-day believers what the original founders were in the beginning.

182

CHAPTER SEVEN

The Symbolic Dilemma: The Study of Ritual

This chapter offers a look at another central feature of religion: ritual. In the context of viewing religion as a dilemma, ritual is what O'Dea refers to as the symbolic dilemma. In summary form, in the genesis of a religion, prophets hope to continue the experience of the sacred in their own lives as well as in the lives of the followers. In doing so, it becomes objectivized for the sake of continuity. However, in the process it tends to lose its effectiveness and results in alienation. Therein lies the paradox: while objectivation is necessary for continuity, it finally leads to alienation when it fails to provide the nexus between symbols and subjective attitudes.

Keeping the nature of this dilemma in mind, this chapter will accomplish the following. First of all, I will analyze ritual with a focus on defining the phenomenon. Carrying on the tradition of this book in giving both a substantive and a functional definition to both religion and myth, ritual will also be presented from both a substantive and a functional viewpoint. Then, I will connect ritual to myth and, subsequently, to religious experience. I will describe Durkheim's theory of religion, which connects social religious experience, ritual, and myth. Thereafter, I will present anthropological and sociological studies of ritual connecting ritual and myth.

Following this, I will illustrate the symbolic dilemma (routinization processes) by interpreting it in the light of the substantive and functional definitions of ritual. The attempts at de-routinization will be illustrated by looking at recent examples of routinization and attempts at retaining charisma in the modern charismatic movement as well as in traditional Pentecostal churches. The chapter will conclude with an empirical look at the psychological and social effects of group and private ritual.

| AN ANALYSIS OF RITUAL

In the last part of Chapter Two, I provided both substantive and functional definitions of religion. Again, a substantive definition of religion focuses on the essence or nature of religion. Those who employ substantive definitions tend to emphasize affect or feelings. Religion is an "experiential encounter," a "manifestation of the sacred," or a "haunting realization of ultimate powerlessness." Functional definitions emphasize the effects of religion on the people and on the social order. People may define religion in positively functional terms with religion providing meaning, social legitimation, social cohesion and integration, and a source of morality. Marxist definitions of religion stress the dysfunctions of religion, emphasizing how they are used by a dominant group to exploit other groups of people.

    When we looked at myth, we saw that it could be understood in a similar way (Chapter Two). Again, the substantive approach attempts to define the essence of a myth. It seeks to clarify and illuminate. The functional approach, on the other hand, seeks to determine what effects myths have on the lives of people and the larger society. We noted, with Campbell, that myths have cosmological, sociological, and psychological functions. The cosmological account helps the believer to "make sense" of the world and her or his place within it (very similar to Yinger's [1970] concept of religion providing meaning). The sociological function is to provide social control, social support, and socialization of youth or new members into a society or religion. The last function that Campbell identifies is the psychological one wherein myth may initiate the individual into a reality of his or her own psyche, guiding a person toward spiritual enrichment or well-being.

    In a similar way one can analyze ritual. From several anthropologists and sociologists of religion, both a substantive and functional view of ritual will be presented.

A Substantive Definition of Ritual

Geertz (1966:28) describes ritual as consecrated behaviour in some sort of ceremonial form. This form may be simply a recitation of a myth, the consultation of an oracle or a decoration of a grave. Human expressions of ritual activity consist in particular moods and motivations. In ritual, the "world is lived and is imagined." The sociologist Davis outlines religious ritual as being

> highly circumscribed to time and place, expressive of internal attitude, symbolic of unseen powers. It can include any kind of behaviour known, such as the wearing of special clothing, the recitation of cer-

tain formulas, and the immersion in certain waters; it can include
singing, dancing, weeping, bowing, crawling, starving, feasting, reading etc. (1948-49:534)

Hargrove (1989:49) offers a simple definition: "ritual is repeated symbolic
behaviour," a behaviour in which the religious participant meets his/her
mythical hero.

Durkheim (1915:226) and Smith (1956:265) present a similar outline of
the substantive meaning of ritual and note that within ritual a bond of
friendship, communion, and unity connects the ritual observer with his/her
god. Durkheim adds that rites are rules of conduct which order participants
to have a special comport in the presence of the sacred (1915:43) and that
rites help people to forget the real world and transport them into another
world where everything is more at ease (1915:380).

In the light of these contributions, I offer the following as a substantive
definition of ritual:

> Ritual is repeated consecrated (sacred) behaviour that is a symbolic
> expression of the moods and motivations of religious participants and
> unseen powers. Ritual forms a bond of friendship, community, and
> unity with the believer and her/his god. Finally, ritual transports the
> participant into another world (the world above) wherein there is
> peace and harmony.

To illustrate this definition, I will use Watts' (1954) study of myth and ritual
within pre-Vatican II Catholicism and Poloma's (1997) study of the
"Toronto Blessing" in contemporary Canada. In pre-Vatican II
Catholicism, the historical myth-event of Christ takes on an eternal dimension that is not restricted to two thousand years ago but is something peren-
nial, both in all time and beyond all time. This church follows an annual
cycle called "the Church Calendar" which begins with Advent, a period of
preparation for Christmas, symbolizing one's personal death and the permanent coming of Christ's kingdom, and continues with Lent which pre-
pares the participants for the death/resurrection myth of the Christ. The
third period is the post-Easter period wherein the church members are
reminded of the "mysteries" which they just experienced ritually. The final
period is a post-Pentecost time wherein the participant reflects upon the
long period of history when the church exists in this "world under the
"power of the Holy Spirit." The cycle begins again to repeat the previous
periods.

The rituals are repeated over and over again and carry with them a sacred
character. In Advent, for example, the believers are encouraged to be in

touch with moods and motivations conducive to that period: to remember their mortality and to prepare for eventual death. The rituals also serve to put the believer in touch with the "Christ" in whom bonds of friendship, unity, and communion are strengthened. Lastly, because reliving past historical events is not of this world, but because, in Watts' words, "time itself is delivered from mere inanity by being lived *sub specie æternitatis*,"[1] (1954:2) the ritual observer is transported into another world while still living in this world.

Poloma (1997) depicts ritual as a medium of the "Divine Presence." In describing a worship service that includes a substantial amount of music, loud praise, and laughter, she quotes one of the pastors as saying: "Worship is a personal and intimate meeting with God in which we praise, magnify and glorify Him for His Person and His actions. It is the act of freely giving love to God. We meet God and He meets us" (Sinnott 1995). The experience of this pastor is an illustration of the "bonding between the believer and the sacred."

186

A Functional Definition of Ritual

As with a functional definition of religion and myth so also a functional definition of ritual accents what ritual does — its function both for the individual and for the social group or society of which the believer is a part. Eight functions of ritual can be identified from the literature: (1) remembering, (2) social bonding, (3) regulating the moral behaviour of members, (4) socialization and changes in social statuses, (5) psychological development, (6) bonding to nature (the ecological function), (7) being empowered, and (8) evoking the nefarious. The remembering function recalls to the believer that which tends to be easily forgotten: the mythologies of the past. In social bonding, the ritual observer is bonded to her/his god and so also is bonded to other members of the social group or the society.

Another function is one of regulation of behaviour. For social life to be possible, it has been long understood by both anthropologists and sociologists that there needs to be some sort of common base, some sort of common value or moral foundation that integrates individuals. A number of authors (to be identified shortly) argue that because ritual activity is repeated activity and because it is a "moral force," it acts as a socially controlling agent on individual persons. Ritual also serves the individual to develop psychologically. In one way, it may help to elicit as well as to control emotions and, in another way, contribute to individual well-being.

---

1   Literally, "in the form of or with the appearance of eternity."

Another sociological function of ritual is present when individuals are in the process of being socialized into being active members of a society or are changing statuses. The literature on ritual terms these "rites of passage" and include such rituals that surround birth, puberty, marriage, and death.

The ecological function of ritual is not common. What is understood by this is that for some religious participants, rituals put them in touch with nature, with the natural ecology. They function to form some kind of communion with the earth, the fields, waters, etc. This function will be illustrated with an investigation of Aboriginal American religion.

The seventh function is empowerment. The argument here is that when participants gather together they experience something they do not when they are alone: empowerment and a sense of having received a supernatural power. The last function is negative and is the invocation of the nefarious. As religion can be dysfunctional (see the discussion of Marx in Chapter Twelve) both for individuals and groups (societies as well), so also can ritual. This function will be illustrated by some studies of witch-hunting rituals of early America.

RITUAL AS REMEMBERING

Ritual functions to remind both individuals and social groups what their heritage is, what their past was. It serves to remind the participants of the myths, the stories, and the past events that affect the present reality. Davis writes: "Ritual helps to remind the individual of the holy realm, to revivify and strengthen his faith in this religion" (1948-49:534). Berger (1969) begins his functional definition of ritual by arguing that people tend to fear the prospect of chaos: both cosmological and social. Ritual serves to remind them that, in the light of religious myths, this chaos is "pushed back" by a repeated number of reminders. In short, ritual "makes present the past" (1969:26).

Watts (1954), Wallace (1966), Durkheim (1915), and Eliade (1959) present a common theme of remembering. Watts (1954) describes Christianity in the form of a ritual reliving of the Christ-story through the seasonal cycle of the ecclesiastical year. For Wallace (1966), ritual connects the myth of the past with the reality of the present. For him, ritual recalls a major cosmological theme: a theory of the origins of the universe and the pantheon (the divine population of the heavens). Durkheim (1915:372) says it well: "The rite consists solely in recollecting the past and, in a way, makes it present by means of a veritable dramatic representation." Eliade (1959) adds that it is by way of ritual that the believer constructs a sacred space that reproduces the work of the gods.

Two illustrations may be useful here. Eliade (1959:30-31) describes the Vedic[2] ritual for taking possession of a territory. The ritual consists of setting up a fire altar consecrated to Agni (a Vedic deity). By the erection of the altar, Agni is made present, and communication with the world of the gods is assured. Beyond that, the erection of the altar to Agni is the reproduction of the original Creation. In other words, the enactment of the ritual is to remember the past, to do again what the gods did in the beginning, which was to create the universe.

Geertz (1966) provides us with an example of a collective ritual from Bali (an Indonesian island east of Java which has been Hindu since the seventh century AD). Two key actors represent *Rangda* (a satanic figure) and *Barong* (a comic figure). The contest continues over a long time with one figure gaining the upper hand at one time and the other at another time. Most of the tribal members participate actively and are drawn near to the two main figures. As they participate, they move into a mass trance and enter "into the world of Rangda and Barong." The ritual functions to make the participants "remember" the original conflict between these two figures and to be present with them in that conflict. Rangda reflects the cultural trait of fear, whereas Barong represents playfulness, exhibitionism, and extravagance: both realities close to the life experience of the people.

A last example of ritual as remembering is illustrated by the fasting and holy day celebrations of the Nation of Islam. The fasting, enacted by all the faithful, occurs during the month of December as a kind of "counter-remembrance" of not celebrating the false birthday of a dead prophet (Jesus Christ). Two holy days are commemorated that remember important birthdays: the Saviour's Day of February 26 to recall the birthday of Master Farad Mohammad, and the second Saviour's Day, the birthday of Master Elijah Muhammad, October 7.

RITUAL AS SOCIAL BONDING

Central to the sociology and anthropology of religion is the social dimension of religion. The study of ritual reinforces this perception. Ritual functions to bond persons together, to increase levels of social cohesion, and to augment social solidarity. Smith (1956:263) reflects this tradition: "in renewing by a solemn act of worship the bond that united him [the participant] with his god, he also renewed the bonds of family, social and national

---

2   Of or pertaining to the Vedas. Veda literally means "knowledge." The Vedas are any of the oldest sacred writings of Hinduism including psalms, incantations, hymns, and formulas of worship incorporated in four collections called the Rig-Vedas, the Yajur-Veda, the Sama-Veda, and the Atharva-Veda (Webster 1982:1816).

obligation." Smith observed the sacrificial ritual common in Semitic religion where members ate and drank together as part of the ritual. He writes,

> By admitting man to his table the god admits him to his friendship; but this favour is extended as one of a community, to eat and drink along with his fellows, and in the same measure as the act of worship cements the bond between him and his god, it cements also the bond between him and his brethren in the common faith. (1956:265)

Durkheim extends this function beyond the eating and drinking dimension of ritual to other kinds of social interaction. He notes:

> Rites are something more than movements without importance and gestures without efficacy — the apparent function is to strengthen the bonds attaching the believer to his god — they at the same time really strengthen the bonds attaching the individual to the society of which he is a member. (1915:226)

Another example is provided by Kertzer (1988:20-21). The Mohegan Indians of New England had been struggling to find an identity ever since their tribe was outlawed by the state legislature in 1880. By 1930 they had lost much of their identity and bonding through intermarriage, language loss, and cultural demise. The Mohegans solved this crisis by stressing rites and symbols that identify them as Aboriginals and Mohegans. The central rite is the annual pow-wow in which native dances are performed, local crafts are displayed, and native clothes are worn. These repeated rites, then, functioned to create unity and bonding among members.

An additional example from First Nations peoples is the rite of the Sacred Pipe. Paper (1989) gathered together evidence that the most central and most universal rite of the North American Aboriginals is the smoking of the Sacred Pipe. The rite has many elements that do not vary substantially from tribe to tribe and from region to region. At an appropriate time (for example in council), the Sacred Pipe is ceremoniously filled with tobacco and the shaman[3] lights it from a fire. Then, he raises the pipe up to the zenith and down to the nadir as well as pointing it to the east, west, north, and south. Thereafter, he passes it to all who are present and each smokes. The various gestures have great significance. Raising up to the zenith symbolizes an offering to the deities and a resultant communion with them. The pointing to the earth signifies a unity with the earth,

---

3   A person who acts as intermediary between the natural and supernatural worlds, using magic to cure illness, foretell the future, control spiritual forces, etc.

whereas the circle pointing is a sign of unity with the whole of the universe. The sharing of the pipe is the sharing of lives: therein is the source of bonding and unity among the participants. Paper (1989:36) writes: "Basic to the ceremonial use of the Sacred Pipe is that it is passed among the participants: it creates social communion; it joins all into a sacred circle."

Another example of social bonding through ritual is given by a case history accounting of a coven, a witchcraft ritual in a modern setting by a practitioner (Starhawk 1988). She writes:

> There is a fire. The people are gathered on the dancing ground. The priestess sings a chant; the drums begin. The people respond, with their voices, their bodies; chanting and moving in the pattern of the dance. From their voices, their bodies, arises the power to call down the Orishas, the Gods. Moving together, singing together, the people are one. The drums and the power unite them in a common bond, relinking them with each other, with the ancestors who down through time have chanted, have danced in this way, with the land that supports the people and the spirit that enters into them. There is a circle. The people hold hands; they chant together to the Goddess, the Gods. Now one is inspired to begin a chant; now another. They move together in a dance. The power moves through them, uniting them in a common bond with each other, with the land that supports them and the spirit that enters into them. (1988:154)

The central function of this ritual is community building. This bonding is further augmented after the ceremony by the participants eating and drinking together. The image of the circle is quite central: it symbolizes a communion with the divine as well as with one another. It also is a sign of equality and a lack of hierarchy (in another place in this text the author describes the many formal roles; these roles are rotated among all members periodically).

RITUAL AS REGULATING MORAL BEHAVIOUR

Durkheim (1938) has argued that a unique feature of social groups, of societies, is the presence of social facts. These facts are considered to be every way of acting that is capable of exercising an external constraint on the individual person. Human behaviour, then, is affected by these facts that are coercive in nature and tend to regulate the behaviour of societal members. Religion in general and religious ritual in particular function in this way — being kinds of social facts which act as an external constraint upon the believer. Durkheim states: "the true justification of religious practices does not lie in the apparent ends which they pursue, but rather in the invisible action which they exercise over the mind and in the way in which they affect our mental status" (1915:359). He adds that rites "serve to remake individuals and groups morally" (1915:370).

More recently, Wuthnow (1987), using a cultural analytical approach, sees that the central function of ritual is moral. Ritual is that which maintains moral order or "regulates and defines social relations" (1987:107) and is "a symbolic expressive aspect of behaviour that communicates something about social relations, often in a dramatic or formal manner" (1987:109). In the tradition of Durkheim, then, the moral function of ritual is to put order into human relationships, to provide a code whereby men and women can live and interact together.

There seems to be some doubt, however, as to the effectiveness of these rituals in regulating moral behaviour in the modern world. Willits and Crider (1989) conducted a longitudinal study of the effects of beliefs and rituals among high school students. While the students were in high school, the rites and beliefs of the parents did affect the life orientation and morals of these young people. However, ten years later, it was found that at best the parents' religious rites and beliefs had an indirect effect. On the other hand, there is also evidence to the contrary — that some rituals are effective in moral behaviour. Poloma and Gallup (1991), in a national study on prayer (as a private ritual), noted that those who prayed meditatively (measured as those who spend time quietly thinking about God, who "feel" the divine presence, who worship and adore God, and who try to listen to God) are the ones who are most likely to forgive others who hurt or abuse them. They seem, then, to put into action a moral dictum of Jesus: "forgive one another seventy times seven."

RITUAL AS SOCIALIZATION AND CHANGES IN SOCIAL STATUSES

Some of the earliest work done on ritual by anthropologists was on rites of passage. Van Gennep (1960) argued that all cultures have a class of rituals that celebrate the transition of an individual from one social status to another. He notes there are three stages: separation, transition, and incorporation. Wallace (1966:105) explains them: "In separation, the individual is taken from a place or group or status; in transition, he is sacred and is subjected to procedures of transformation; and in incorporation, he is formally installed in the new place or group or status." I will present a case study on marriage to illustrate this function.

THE RITUAL OF MARRIAGE

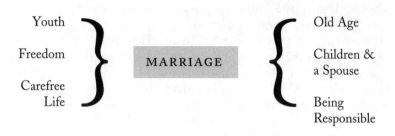

Youth

Freedom

Carefree
Life

} MARRIAGE {

Old Age

Children &
a Spouse

Being
Responsible

FIGURE 7.1

Kligman (1988), an American ethnographer, presents a case history of marriage rites among a peasant village community in the northern region of Romania, "Ieud Maramures." The whole text is devoted to an in-depth analysis of the marriage rite, which is central to the life of these people. Although the centralized socialist government was trying to modernize the region, the peasant people held strongly to traditional beliefs, practices, and social behaviours. Traditional rites of marriage and funerals were still strong when Kligman did the study during 1978 and 1979.

In this village, marriage constitutes the ideological basis of social and sexual relations by transforming and restructuring identity and social interaction. The marriage rite is a central rite that lasts for three days. The whole ritual orders and controls the transition from being single to being married by providing a means to reorganize the economic, political, and social aspects of the social relationships and to articulate the nature of the social consciousness of the people. The ritual involves a wide variety of people: the extended families of both the bride and the groom, close neighbours, guests of honour, and peers of the bride and the groom. Because the community is patriarchal, the marriage affects the bride the most for she must change more than the groom. The wedding becomes a vehicle for the legitimation of the position of women, and the values and norms of the culture are focused within the drama itself. Marriage symbolizes a loss of virginity of the woman (the man loses his as well but it is not celebrated). This loss represents the death of an old status and the arrival of responsibilities that entail hard work and serious cares. Figure 7.1 illustrates the process.

Using Van Gennep (1960), Kligman analyzes the ritual according to the three phases of separation, transition, and incorporation. The separation stage consists of the marriage preparation, the "dance of the groom's flag," the "dance of the bride's crown," a symbolic ritual of bride bargaining, the dressing of the bride, and the mutual asking of forgiveness from both sets of parents. The dance of the groom's flag consists of the friends of the groom gathering to sew together a flag the evening before the wedding. This flag is a symbol of colourful vitality and power between men and women. It is patriarchal in nature and is the dominant marriage symbol. It is carried by a flag bearer who leads the groom; together they go to the home of the bride on the day of the ceremony and lead the bridal entourage into the church. It is in the home of the bride that the "dance of the crown" ritual is celebrated. Here the bridesmaid, with another woman, holds the crown (made of flowers) and leads a dance of both men and women. The crown is a symbol of the bride's virginity and is shown to friends and the future husband.

The transitional stage consists of the actual church ceremony, post-ceremonial meals, gift exchanges between wife-givers and wife-takers, and rituals of asking for the bride. After the church ceremony, the bride returns to her parents' home. It is late in the night when the groom comes to the house and asks the father for his bride. After many tries, the father "gives" over the bride to her new husband. After this, a meal is shared. Here the families are gathered, and a roast chicken is prepared. All but the bride eat, for the passing and the eating of the chicken symbolize the virginity of the bride.

Now that the transfer from the family of the bride to the family of the groom has taken place, she is brought to the groom's house, where she is symbolically undressed. Processes of incorporation into adult status commence. The woman now moves from a status of freedom and carefreeness to being a child-bearer and having full adult responsibilities. The husband is also no longer free and is also a full adult.

RITUAL AS PSYCHOLOGICAL DEVELOPMENT

O'Dea and O'Dea (1983) provide us with an interpretation of religion being a response to people's experiences of "limit situations" or feelings of contingency, powerlessness, and scarcity. Ritual practices can, as noted by Smith (1956), Kluckhohn (1972), and Hargrove (1989), reduce the anxiety produced by these feelings. Kluckhohn argues that rites remind believers of how the ancients managed. These ancients (he uses the example of the Navaho people) met similar "limit situations" and conquered them. If the rites are performed properly, the participants can also reduce anxiety and be at peace.

Durkheim furnishes us not only with a functional understanding of ritual directed toward society (bonding and moral regulation) but also with a psychological function of well-being. He notes that when the Australian aboriginal repeats rites over and over again, the result is not only a material good but also a sense of well-being. He writes that after performing the rite "they take away with them a feeling of well being, whose causes they cannot clearly see, but which is well founded. They feel that the ceremony is good for them; and, as a matter of fact, they reforge their moral nature in it" (1915:359).

Smith (1956) and Wilson (1982) add another dimension to the psychological function of ritual: the expression of emotion. Among the Semites, Smith observes, emotional gaiety and rivalry were commonplace. It was at such times of public ritual and sacrifice that participants cast off their cares and rejoiced before the god. Several research examples may help us to understand this function. McGuire (1982), in her study of Catholic Pentecostals, and Swenson (1972), in his study of the charismatic movement, saw that in the central rite of the people — the prayer group — there was a common experience of power, emotion, and release. In a more dramatic way, Morse (1980) documented the Shaker Sunday service. In the gathering, participants are seen to turn their heads from left to right, to cry in ecstasy, to shed tears, to fall down on their knees, and to rest quietly on the floor (see Chapter Five).

Wilson (1982:34-35) adds that ritual not only facilitates emotion but also regulates it. These two functions are related. Ritual stimulates certain types of emotional expression. After a response is elicited and expression is encouraged, then the emotions are channelled: "We may say that ritual manages the emotions: it provides the occasion and the means for their decorous and controlled expression" (1982:35). In the light of our thesis of routinization of charisma, we would argue that the earlier stage of emotional expression is common when the ritual is not routinized and is at its "charismatic" stage. For the Shakers and the charismatics, the ritual tends to elicit relatively high levels of emotion. However, at later stages (evidence for this is from the later Shaker communities and the more developed covenant community prayer meetings within the charismatic movement) the ritual tends not so much to elicit emotion but more to regulate it (see Chapter Five for evidence of the Shaker routinized Sunday ritual).

RITUAL AS BONDING TO NATURE:
THE ECOLOGICAL FUNCTION OF RITUAL

This function is not commonly recognized in the research literature. It was discovered in research on Aboriginal American religion. As is well known from native studies, the aboriginal peoples of America and Canada have a profound respect for the natural environment. Paper (1989) describes the ecological and cosmological meaning of the Sacred Pipe. The bowl of the pipe (made of stone) is a miniature cosmos that is female. The tobacco is put into the bowl in minute pieces that symbolizes bringing the entire cosmos into the bowl itself. The stem (made of wood) of the pipe is male in nature and is symbolic of the trees and the sky.

When the Sacred Pipe is smoked in a formal ceremony, there is signified a connection of the self (the participant) with the world of social relations (fellow participants, family, clan, and nation), to that of animals who are extensions of social relations (nature is depicted in personal, familial terms), to the earth, to the sky, and to the whole of the cosmos. This ritual, in effect, then, is understood to integrate people with nature, for all things are "relatives."

RITUAL AS EMPOWERMENT

Durkheim wrote that a central function of ritual is empowerment:

> believers ... feel that the real function of religion is not to make us think, to enrich our knowledge, nor to add to the conceptions which we owe to science others of another origin and another character, but, rather it is to make us act, to aid us to live. The believer who has communicated with his god is not merely a man who sees new truths of which the unbeliever is ignorant; he is a man who is stronger. He feels within him more force, either to endure the trials of existence, or to conquer them. It is as though he were raised above his condition as a mere man; he believes that he is saved from evil, under whatever form he may conceive this evil. (1915:416)

Durkheim focuses here on a central feature of religion in general and ritual in particular — empowerment. It is important to consider his background theory of religion to place this in context. This we will do shortly when we look at how myth, ritual, and experience are connected. Suffice it to say now, there is evidence that ritual celebrations do have the effect of empowerment. Two studies will be used to illustrate this. Both McGuire (1982) and Swenson (1990) gathered evidence that when some Christians experience the charismatic gifts and the "Baptism of the Holy Spirit," they receive a sense of empowerment.

McGuire (1982:7) identifies four characteristics of power among participants of Catholic Pentecostals within a prayer group ritual: the power of God is given directly to ordinary human beings (one need not be a professional cleric); individuals have the power to see the relevance of religion in their ordinary lives; this power has a strong experiential component; and all these beliefs (and rituals) compel members to seek out a community of fellow believers.

Swenson (1990) argues that through the central rituals of a small, evangelical/charismatic church, individuals give witness to being empowered. The four key rituals are holy communion, the Sunday worship service, adult baptism, and membership ceremonies. The Sunday worship service is the rallying point, the core ritual that focuses within a few hours the drama of the people's Christian myth, the charismatic heritage, and empowerment for service. There are two pulpits in this ritual service: the "Word Podium" and the "Music Podium."[4] "The Word Podium" symbolizes the importance of the literal word as found in the Christian scriptures. It is in this setting that the senior pastor spends about half-an-hour in teaching, exhortation, and preaching. This "Podium" is a focus of faith, of life, of empowerment, and of action. The message is reported as being practical, at the heart of people's hurts, and a balm to soothe the brokenness experienced by members throughout the previous week. Not as important, but still central, is the "Music Podium." Nearly equal time is given to worship songs. These have an effect of "clothing" participants with praise, wherein something happens in the spiritual realm, and the worshipper communicates with the divine.

In short, these rituals are vehicles of empowerment: assisting the participants in feeling stronger, less alienated, and more ready to serve others. It should be stressed that in both cases, empowerment, although it is personal, is directed to the social group in which the whole group (or church) becomes empowered as well.

RITUAL AS EVOKING THE NEFARIOUS

There are certain kinds of rituals which function to bring harm, hurt, and even death to others who are considered enemies or evil. Curses and witchcraft[5] are common examples. Sociologically, one may see these kinds of rituals as creating boundaries between the immediate social group and the "outsiders." I will look at some examples of witch-hunting rituals to illustrate the function.

Feminist scholars have identified medieval witch hunts as the worst examples of misogyny. Women were declared witches and burned at the stake for many reasons. Hughes (1971:252) outlines some of them: for talk-

---

4   The term was given by an informant who was involved in the music ministry.

5   McGuire (1992) makes a distinction between white and black witchcraft. The former is used for only beneficial purposes such as healing. In contrast, black magic is used by its practitioners for both beneficial and evil ends. However, some practitioners of witchcraft do not see the negative aspect, and the distinction does not reflect the reality of witchcraft rituals and beliefs.

ing back to their husbands or a priest, for stealing, for prostitution, for adultery, for bearing a child out of wedlock, for masturbating, for lesbianism, for child neglect, for scolding, and for involuntary miscarriage. The nefarious ritual consisted of identifying, prosecuting, and executing the women. The estimated number of victims is relatively high: from 100,000 (Monter 1977) to one million (Dworkin 1977).

How can we explain, from a sociological perspective, why this happened? A possible explanation is to consider the nature of medieval society. As will be discussed in Chapter Ten, the medieval world was a hierocratic[6] society, in which sacred institutions were dominant. This domination led to the use of coercion and violence to induce people to conform. Those who did not conform were sought out, tried, prosecuted, and, as in the case of witch hunts, killed. Women were considered in many ways to be non-conformist. Because the medieval world was as patriarchal as it was hierocratic, they were more likely to be victims than men.

A case study of a hunt for the so-called "Malefic Witch" (a term used to describe any witch of this time and place) of pre-Salem New England in about 1650 will illustrate a typical ritual of witch-hunting. Weisman (1984), an historian, noticed a common characteristic among most of the women accused of witchcraft: they were older, single or widowed, and poor. The ritual process began with one person accusing a particular woman whose normal relationships with the community had been ruptured. The accusation was countered by the accused which, sometimes, took on the form of curses, threats, and being outspoken in public. The actions of the accused led to more accusations from the larger community, and she began to be labelled a "witch" not only by the one accuser but also by the rest of the community. Weisman interprets this level of accusation in terms of a symbol of conflicts within the community itself: between those who had means of living and those who did not. The woman became a "scapegoat" for the fears and conflicts of the village. The next stage involved the juridical system of the colony. Courts were set up and witnesses for and against the accused were heard. If the evidence gathered confirmed the accusation, she would either be imprisoned or executed — depending on the severity of the "witchcraft."

A Summary of a Functional Definition of Ritual

Ritual encourages people to remember what they so frequently forget about their religious heritage: their myths. It tends to create bonding and com-

---

6   The term refers to the rule or government by priests or religious leaders.

munion between members and the social group thus constructed. Conversely, ritual is also a source of social control, a mechanism of social-ization, and a means to acquire a new status and a regulator of moral behav-iour. For the individual person, ritual practices create well-being and offer a vehicle of emotional release. However, they also tend to channel and to regulate emotion. Rituals, especially among folk peoples, Aboriginal Americans, and some New Age adherents,[7] integrate the participants with organic life, the earth, the land, the water, and the sky. A sixth function of ritual is empowerment. The spiritual is understood by most religious adher-ents as being redolent of energy or power. Through ritual, this power is captured by the participants and they feel a sense of empowerment. Lastly, ritual has also a dark side. Even though it may function positively in estab-lishing group boundaries, it also produces harm and destruction to individ-uals who are targets of that ritual.

THE CONNECTION BETWEEN MYTH, RITUAL, AND EXPERIENCE

In Chapter Two, we looked at religious world views or myths. Religious experience was investigated in Chapter Four. Here I shall build on this ear-lier work and connect myth, ritual, and religious experience.

The examples used in Chapter Five were religious collectivities that emerged from the individual experiences of Ann Lee and Joseph Smith. From those initial experiences, the world views or myths were constructed. The mythology of the Shakers or the Mormons did not precede the expe-rience but, rather, the mythologies succeeded the experience. This is quite evident upon an analysis of these religions. However, in the case of folk religions, the story is much less clear. We do not have historical accounts of individual, charismatic persons being the originators of these religions. Even in the case of the modern New Age Movement, we do not have clear evidence that the movement emerged from any particular person. The focus on the Weberian perspective, then, needs to take us in a different direction. Durkheim has provided us with a precedent for this. His focus was not on individual religious experience but, rather, on group or social religious experience. This is the genesis of his analysis of folk religion.

What I hope to do in this section is to present a theory of the connec-tion between social religious experience, myth, and ritual; summarize the anthropological data on the connection between myth and ritual; and out-line the connection between experience, myth, and ritual using Wuthnow (1987) as the focal author.

---

7   This relatively new movement will be discussed in detail in Chapter Thirteen.

Durkheim's Theory of Religion[8]

The Weberian perspective of this text may be criticized in that I have focused on individual religious experience in our interpretation of religion. This is the case for the more historical kinds of religion such as Buddhism, Islam, and Christianity, for each of these begins with a charismatic person. However, religion is much wider than that. For most of the history of humanity upon earth, folk religions that were part of hunting and gathering and agrarian/pastoral societies were much more common. Our search, then, for the meaning of religion in general and ritual in particular needs to include folk societies as well. Anthropologists have provided us with significant volumes of evidence to attempt an interpretation. The search will focus on Durkheim (1915), who analyzed the folk religion not only of Australia but also of North America.

Durkheim begins his study of folk religion with the analysis of totemism.[9] Essentially, Durkheim's argument follows this line of reasoning. Each tribe of the Australian mainland had an emblem which was the totem of the tribe. This totem (most frequently symbolic of an animal or a plant) represented both the local, central deity of the tribe as well as the tribe itself. This totem was not inert but had a spiritual power that was believed to have real effects in the lives of the clan members. Figure 7.2 gives a graphic illustration of Durkheim's analysis. Further, this totem illustrates not only the two-fold symbolic dimension but also the fact that the deity and the clan are in fact one. As Durkheim notes,

> The god of the clan, the totemic principle, can therefore be nothing else than the clan itself, personified and represented to the imagination under the visible form of the animal or vegetable which serves as totem. (1915:206)

This is where we get the famous Durkheimian reductionist understanding that religion is society (see Chapter One). To be fair to Durkheim, however, his seemingly immediate leap to this conclusion is not as simple as he describes it in this part of his text. The actual reason why he believes that

---

8 There is some debate among some students of religion that his data from Australia and North America are problematic. Evans-Pritchard (1965), an anthropologist who has studied religion extensively, discards his theory on the ground that the evidence is flimsy and the data second-hand (cited in Alexander 1982:76).

9 Rivers (1968) adds to Durkheim's use of these people as typical of folk religions by noting that totemism is central to other folk religions as well as those found in Australia.

the clan participants are actually worshipping their clan in worshipping their god is because of social religious experience connected to ritual.

We already saw that Durkheim considers that it is belief and ritual within a community that is at the heart of religion (see Chapter Two, Box 2.3). Why do the believers actually believe that the deity is real? They do so because of ritual and a common social religious experience. Rather than disregarding what William James had to say, Durkheim (1915:417) receives the psychologist's interpretation that religious experiences are real. His nuance, however, is that the experience is a collective one and not an individual one. It is when folk believers gather together in a ritual, a religious ceremony, that they are carried beyond themselves into another world. It is in this group ritual that they experience ecstasy, enthusiasm, effervescence, joy, interior peace, serenity, and a sense of being "transported into another world." Durkheim implies that because of the group experience (not possible as an individual) in the celebration of ritual, the believers adhere to a conviction that the deity, filled with energy and power, is real and present to them. Also, this presence is felt as a locus of moral control. However, it really is not the deity which is the source of the religious experience but, rather, the clan, the social group itself.

THE DUAL SYMBOLISM OF THE TOTEM

(adapted from Durkheim 1915)

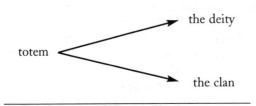

FIGURE 7.2

In addition, it is from these collective ritual experiences that the collective consciousness and the mythology emerge. It is obviously difficult to put a time on this. After the mythology is somewhat crystallized, ritual takes on a new function (the remembering function, above) — recalling what the beliefs are and adding further to the integration between myth, ritual, and group experience. In summary form, then, Durkheim argues that in the context of ritual, participants experience something much greater than themselves. This "greater" is understood to be the deity. From this, a mythology emerges.[10] However, the mythology, now constructed, acts as a moral force upon the individuals. Future ritual practices recall the mythology and the group is further recreated.

---

10 This is the same conclusion that Parsons (1968) comes to in his reading of Durkheim and writes: "Hence the tendency is to think of ritual as the primary element of religion and religious ideas as secondary rationalizations, explanations, and justifications of ritual" (1968:437).

THE SYMBOLIC DILEMMA: THE STUDY OF RITUAL

The Anthropological Evidence

Although there is a debate as to the direction of the connection between myth and ritual and which has priority (Hargrove 1989), the anthropological evidence seems to be weighted toward the precedence of ritual. Wallace (1966), Smith (1956), and Watts (1954) argue that it is out of ritual that myth occurs. Obviously the anthropological data are not available to present a chronological priority of ritual over myth, but it does seem to point to what Wallace calls an "instrumental priority." As he states, "we have argued, ritual has an instrumental priority; the goals of religion are to be achieved by performing rituals; myths are merely extremely valuable, and regularly employed, auxiliary equipment" (1966:106).

He is joined by several other anthropologists. Boas notes: "The ritual itself is the stimulus for the origin of the myth ... the ritual existed, and the tale originated from the desire to account for it" (1938:617). Raglan adds: "Religion consists in the due performance of the rites. Religious belief is belief in the value and efficacy of the rites, and theology, apart from some forms of mystical theology, consists in giving reasons why the rites should be performed" (1949:47). Raglan (1956) offers a theory of why myth succeeds ritual. Ritual stands on its own if the effect of the rite is forthcoming. However, if it is not forthcoming (as the ritual was to bring forth rain and it did not rain), there is some reason for it. The construction of the myth and the story behind it are created to give an account of the ritual. Watts (1956) reminds us of a "Catholic Principle" that reflects the precedence of ritual over myth. The "Principle" is *Lex orandi est lex credenti*. This simply means that the law of worship (a rite) is the law of faith. It has been long understood in this religion that the faith (the myth) is expressed in who and what the people worship.

Others interpret the relationship interactively by not giving precedence to either. From his work among the American Navahoes, Kluckholn (1972) notes that myth is a system of word symbols whereas ritual is a system of object and act symbols. The Navahos performed rituals, according to his interpretation, to heighten the awareness of the common system of sentiments. In summary form, he writes:

> ... myth and ritual have a common psychological b? sis. Ritual is an obsessive, repetitive activity — often a symbolic dra∵ atization of the fundamental "needs" of the society, whether economic, biological, social, or sexual. Mythology is the rationalization of these same needs, whether they are all expressed in overt ceremonials or not. (1972:105)

MYTH, RITUAL, AND THE TOTEM

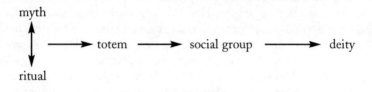

(adapted from Kluckhohn 1968, and Durkheim 1915)

FIGURE 7.3

In a way, Kluckhohn agrees with Durkheim in that he connects myth and ritual together with the social group. Both of these authors would theorize that myth and ritual are best understood as emerging out of the society they are embedded within. Rivers (1968) has a similar interpretation. He notes that because the totem is central to folk religions and because the totem is a symbol of the clan or the society, both myth and ritual are indirectly connected to society by means of the totem.[11] This is illustrated in Figure 7.3. Finally, Geertz (1966) describes ritual as consecrated behaviour and myth as consecrated world view. They are connected in that ritual is understood to be a symbolic fusion of an ethos (a way of doing things) and a world view (a way of viewing things).

Other authors do not speak of the precedence of myth over ritual but do give definitions that connect the two. For Hargrove (1988), ritual is repeated symbolic behaviour whereas myth is an explanatory verbalization. In addition, ritual is used to make the myth more real, and myths seem to have developed to explain, justify or reinforce existing rituals. Wallace (1966), although he gives precedence to ritual over myth, also contrasts and compares the two religious phenomena: "Myth, in the most general sense, is the theory of ritual, which explains the nature of the powers, prescribes the ritual, accounts for its success and failure. Together, they are religion" (1966:107).

The Sociological Evidence

Two sources help us to understand the connection between myth and ritual in the modern world: Berger and Luckmann (1967) and Wuthnow (1987).

---

11 Hargrove (1988) says a similar thing in noting that the structures of myth reflect the structures of the society and (from Turner 1967) that rituals symbolize the nature of the relationships of groups within the particular society.

The former authors do not speak directly of ritual but they do theorize that the origins of world views (both sacred [myths] and secular) are socially constructed through human interaction and communication. Their basic thesis is that knowledge emerges through social interaction. When social interaction is regular, consistent, and long term, a common way of thinking and believing emerges. Language is the most important vehicle for this thinking and believing to become a systematic way of viewing the world. They write: "Language … constructs immense edifices of symbolic representations that appear to tower over the reality of everyday life like gigantic presences from another world. Religion, philosophy, art, and science are the historically most important symbol systems of this kind" (1967:40). Their final point, that religion is a central symbol system, is most important. In an extension of their thinking, I argue that religious social interaction that is regular, consistent, and long term is really ritual. It is from this ritual that a "symbol system" emerges or, in my words, a mythology. This kind of interpretation seems to explain, at least in part, why some anthropologists argue that ritual takes precedence over myth.[12]

Wuthnow (1987) presents a reverse view: ritual as a consequence of myth. He uses four categories to describe human cultures: subjective culture, structural, dramaturgic, and institutional. Subjective culture refers to the system of beliefs, attitudes, opinions, and values. Subjective culture responds to the problem of meaning and is defined as "a belief system that is mediated by individuals' experience" (1987:11). The structural approach to culture states that, as these subjective elements of culture are objectified, there emerge patterns of relationships among these elements. The dramaturgic category of culture consists of utterances, acts, objects, and events. A special kind of this category is ritual. The last category is the institutional one, in which subjective elements of culture become structured and are articulated in some form of drama (as in ritual) such that they crystallize into institutions which focus on actors, organizations, and the use and distribution of resources.

For Wuthnow, the primary function of ritual is moral order. Beyond that, however, is the function of reminding the participants of the meaning that forms the mythology of the believers:

> The narrative structure of ritual also plays a critical role in the capacity of ritual to reaffirm pluralistic values. Rituals tell a story: a message

---

12 We can also extend this to individual religious experience. I have theorized that from individual religious experience (we may call this private ritual), the mythology emerges. It may be said that the person who has this experience is in "interaction with the divine," and it is from this interaction that myth emerges.

of intentions and values dependent on a larger mythology of shared experience, but communicated in graphic, iconic imagery rich in connotative potential, thus amenable to high variable interpretations unlike strict conceptual terminology. (1987:135)

In a way, Wuthnow presents a sociology of religion that begins with experience (the locus of meaning), continues with structure (the ordering of the world and the cosmos), followed by ritual (the regulation of moral order and the remembering of the myths), and concluding with the construction of institutions (the institutionalization process of religion which results in religious organizations).

Can we reconcile these different pieces of evidence? Does ritual precede myth or vice versa? One way to interpret this discrepancy is to consider different types of religion: folk and historic. It may be that in folk religions (studied predominantly by anthropologists) myth flows from the social experience of the sacred in ritual. For folk religions, then, ritual precedes myth. I call this the Durkheimian perspective of ritual. Historic religions (Buddhism, Judaism, Christianity, and Islam) begin with a charismatic figure. It is the leaders' individual experience of the sacred which appears to become codified in myth. The myth is relived, is remembered in ritual. Thus, for historic religions, myth precedes ritual and may be termed the Weberian perspective of ritual.

| THE ROUTINIZATION PROCESS

In this section I will examine the routinization process that has occurred within ritual in light of our analysis of ritual as well as provide a case history of the process through the study of the Charismatic Movement in the United States.

Some General Reflections

It is not infrequent in popular culture to consider anything to do with ritual as being dead and empty. This may be due in part to the predominant religion in the U.S. being Calvinistic Protestantism, which reacted strongly to the highly routinized ritualism of the Catholic Church toward the end of the middle ages. In many ways, Calvinistic Protestantism reacted so strongly to Catholicism that it not only jettisoned the emptiness found in medieval Catholic rituals but also the very rituals themselves were abandoned. This cultural heritage was also reflected in sociology through the deviance studies of Merton (1957). Merton used the term "ritualism" to refer to the deviant person who does not believe in the goals either of the society or of an institution but "goes through the motions" by doing the ritual required of him, but without attaching any true meaning to the ritual. The action is empty and carries with it no true substance.

In light of our understanding of the symbolic dilemma presented by O'Dea, I would consider ritualism the most routinized form of ritual or alien to recreating the sacred experience. I have presented an interpretation that ritual is important in keeping alive the original source of the ritual, either the experience of the group as in Durkheim's understanding or the experience of a charismatic person as Weber and James would interpret it. The dilemma, again, is that the objectivation of the religious experience is vital for continuity, but if it runs its course, the meaning behind the ritual loses its power and fails to provide the nexus between symbols and subjective attitudes.

Using the substantive and functional definitions of ritual, I attempt to understand the routinization process better. From Geertz (1966), Hargrove (1989), Durkheim (1915), and Smith (1956), I constructed the substantive definition of ritual provided earlier in this chapter. It is at this level that ritual is the least routinized. The ritual is present to contain the religious experience, particularly the communion between the participants and the divine. This stage, the "earliest stage" of ritual, is the least alien. However, if the ritual is allowed to be disconnected from the experience, then the participants no longer have a sense of a communion with the divine.

We also may find the two ends of the continuum present in ritual when we analyze the functional definition of ritual also provided earlier in the chapter. For most functions, we find evidence for levels of routinization. For example, in the function of remembering, words and gestures which really do connect the participants with their history, their original myths result in communion. However, if the ritual is mere words and motions, then the connection does not occur. Another example is the rites of passage. It may be argued that among North American Christians, whose divorce rates are close to the societal norm, the ritual of marriage as a rite of passage seems to be empty of meaning and power. It may be said that if the Christian marriage ritual actually evoked a religious experience of bonding with the divine and of a bonding between the married couple, these marriages might be more stable.

In the next section of the text I will review some recent research on the charismatic movement as it has attempted to de-routinize ritual. This will be followed by an examination of group and private ritual, prayer, which illustrates minimal routinization.

The Routinization and Attempted De-Routinization
of Ritual in the Charismatic Movement

I have noted that rituals are a common element in religion. As Watts (1954) indicates, ritual has been a central feature of Christianity, particularly Roman Catholicism. It is reasonably common knowledge that these rituals have become very routine over centuries of use and misuse. One of the purposes of the Second Vatican Council (1962-65) was to "renew" the official liturgy of the church. In fact, liturgy was the first document discussed and promulgated. Shortly after, throughout the world, liturgical reform within the Catholic Church was common. One may see this as an attempt to de-routinize ritual, to "regain" the charisma, and to reduce alienation. However, shortly after this renewal, some Roman Catholics were still not satisfied with this renewal: it appeared to them that it did not go far enough. In other Christian circles, there was a movement that constructed another ritual format that attempted to significantly reduce alienation and introduce charisma. This movement later became known as the Charismatic Movement.

Liturgical critics of the rites within the Catholic Church have spoken against the alienation of these rites. The Roman Catholic Charismatic Movement is seen as a response to this alienation. The teaching of the religious rite called "The Baptism of the Holy Spirit" is seen as a response to the alien nature of the sacramental rite of confirmation. In this rite, the "Holy Spirit" is evoked but there seems to be little evidence of that invocation. However, when individual believers are prayed for in the rite of the "Baptism of the Holy Spirit," there appears to be an effect using the gifts of the Holy Spirit, especially, glossolalia or "tongue speaking" (Neitz 1987).

O'Connor (1971), a Catholic theologian of the University of Notre Dame, was quick to try to situate this new rite within the Catholic tradition (saying for example, that the Baptism of the Holy Spirit is really the sacrament of confirmation becoming effective) and to argue that it had some historical precedents. In the Catholic tradition, there are several rites such as praying for healing, laying on of hands, and the like. These rites took on new meanings and substance within this movement. The most prominent one was to lay hands on others who were sick and to see them restored to health. Neitz (1987) in her study of Catholic Charismatics and Meredith McGuire (1988) in her investigations of ritual healing in suburban U.S. give credence to these observations. In short, these new rites or renditions of older rites may be seen as attempts to regain the substance of the rite: the reliving of the religious experience.

Prayer: Do Private and Group Rituals Make a Difference?

A national sample of adults conducted by the Gallup Poll (Poloma and Gallup 1991) and a study done on members of a Charismatic Pentecostal Church (Poloma and Hoelter 1998) provide the basis for our question on the potential effectiveness of one type of ritual: private prayer. In the first study of 1,030 respondents, the authors categorized those who pray privately (accounting for 88 per cent of the sample) into four categories: ritual prayer, conversational prayer, petitionary prayer, and meditative prayer.

Ritual prayer is characterized by the questions in the survey that ask respondents if they either use a book of prayers or if they recite memorized prayers. Nineteen per cent responded in the affirmative. The question "Do you ask God for material things that you may need?" indicated the category of petitionary prayer and 42 per cent answered "yes." Conversational prayer and meditative prayer had a more complex set of questions. Conversational prayer means talking to God in your own words, asking God to forgive sins, asking God to provide guidance in making decisions, and thanking God for blessings received. Eighty-four per cent acknowledged praying in this manner. Lastly, meditative prayer captured the deeper dimensions of the private ritual and was indicated by answers such as spending time quietly thinking about God, spending time feeling a divine presence, time worshipping and adoring God, and trying to listen to God speak to you. Over half (52 per cent) of those surveyed gave an affirmative response.

The question is, however: are these types of prayer effective? In other words, do they contain a sacred substance (a charisma) that is reflected in human experience? Three major effects are recognized: religious experience, political activism, and forgiving others. Significant correlations were found between all the types of prayer and religious experience. However, meditative prayer showed the strongest correlation ($r=.51$).

Two categories of political activity were identified: those activities orientated to particular candidates and local issues and those focused on national problems. Results reveal that those who prayed more (particularly those who prayed meditatively) were more likely to be involved in activities related to the candidates and local issues than those who

RITUALS AMONG CANADIANS

CANADIAN RELIGIOUS RITUALS

Nationally, 29 per cent of Canadians pray on a daily basis. Thirty-seven per cent of Atlantic Canadians pray every day in contrast to those in BC whose percentage is 20. Twenty-three per cent of Canadians attend religious services at least once a week and 20 per cent read the Bible or other religious writings at least weekly.

SOURCE: *Macleans*, April 12, 1993:37.

BOX 7.1

prayed less. Lastly, it was found that those who pray ritually, meditatively, and colloquially are more likely to forgive those who hurt them than are those who do not pray in that way.

The authors comment that "Prayer is an important part of the lives of Americans, and it appears to have positive effects in their lives" (1991:105). In this way, the sacred is kept alive in the lives of these people and many seem to have effective religious experiences and reduce the inherent danger of ritual being alienated.

The second study was conducted with 918 members of a congregation called "The Toronto Airport Christian Fellowship." In an earlier study on the same church, Poloma (1997) (see earlier in this chapter) had outlined the meaning and impact of the worship service. Here, she and her colleague (Poloma and Hoelter 1998) investigated another form of ritual and asked whether group prayer is effective in the lives of the participants. In a multiple regression analysis, after controlling for other relevant factors, they found that when members prayed in a group setting they experienced spiritual healing (representing healing in the divine-human relationship). Both these studies reveal that group and private ritual do appear to make a difference in the lives of people.

| CONCLUSIONS

In response to the question, "Can charisma be continued through ritual?" I would say: it depends. Ritual activities themselves seem not to be able to continue the charismatic moment. Other factors seem to come into play. In this chapter, I have outlined the substantive and functional meanings of ritual. Thereafter, I argued how intricate the connection was between myth, ritual, and religious experience. The chapter ended with reflections on research into how the Charismatic Movement revived social rituals which had become alien to so many adherents and how group and private prayer seems to have a life of its own to continue the vitality of charisma in the lives of many American and Canadian women and men.

In Chapter Eight we will investigate the dilemma of administrative order, which will lead us to the study of religious institutions.

The Dilemma of Administrative Order: The Rise of Formal Organizations

Chapter Seven ended with some reflections on how to keep alive the sacred in the challenging onslaught of ritualism that has the potential of alienating religious believers. This chapter presents another challenge within religion: how to maintain order within collectivities without that order inhibiting freedom and effectiveness.

The dilemma of administrative order, which O'Dea and O'Dea (1983) subtitle "elaboration versus effectiveness," if out of control, leads to the tendency of a structure to overelaborate — to become an unwieldy bureaucratic machine. Clearly organization is necessary for the vision of the founder to continue. The organization, however, can lose sight of the original vision and become primarily concerned with its own development and growth. Not only can an organization grow to become unmanageable, but structures that were set in place at an earlier time may refuse to bend to change. As O'Dea and O'Dea (1983:60) observe: "Structures which emerge in one set of conditions and in response to one set of problems may turn out later to be unwieldy instruments for handling new problems under new conditions." Whether the problem is characterized by an overelaborate organization or a structure that cannot respond to present-day needs, the result is a potential alienation of officeholders from the rank-and-file members of the religious organization.

What I intend to do in this chapter is to introduce the reader to the meaning of an institution or an organization by relying on sociological theory that emerges from the work of Berger and Luckmann (1966) and Mott (1965). A definition of a religious organization will follow. The chapter will be focused on elaborating on the various kinds of religious organizations (church, sect, cult, movements of renewal, and denominations), some illustrations of transformations from a cult to a denomination and a sect to a denomination, a review of the research on people who switch from one organization to another or who disaffiliate completely, and an investigation of a new type of religious organization, the interest or support group. Lastly, we will ask the question and provide some food for thought about whether charisma is able to be maintained within organizations.

The Elements of an Organization

According to Weber (1978), the very heart of a society and the scientific study of that society (sociology) is social action. In Chapter One, I noted that Weber speaks of social action insofar as individuals attach subjective meanings to their behaviour. Beyond that, this action also takes into account the behaviour of others and is thereby oriented in its direction (Weber 1978:4).

As social interaction continues on a regular, consistent basis, a certain amount of routine emerges. Berger and Luckmann (1966) call this the *face-to-face situation*. This consistent interaction results in the construction of typifications or a typing of others. One may see these typifications as expectations of behaviour that others have upon you. Mott (1965:24) calls these expectations *norms*: "the rules or standards that govern interaction." Roles are an extension of norms. Within any social situation, each person has obligations or standards of behaviours (norms) that are associated with a role. Mott (1965:26) considers a role to be a collection or a cluster of norms. A social organization, then, may be described as a cluster, a complex of roles. Moreover, within the organization, there exists a ranking of roles which places individuals who occupy roles in a hierarchy.

Some mainstream sociologists extend this definition to include the notion of function. Westhues (1982) adds that the institutionalized forms of social interaction within and among a wide variety of societies entail a goal, a function to accomplish. For example, every society must establish, maintain, and defend its own internal order, for chaos contradicts the very definition of a society. The organization, the institution that provides for this function, is the polity or the political system. With this background, when I use the term social organization or social institution I mean the following:

> A social organization or a social institution is a complex, or a cluster of ranked roles which, in turn, are a complex or a cluster of expectations of behaviours within a social interaction setting. In addition, it is focused by a common goal or a function to fulfil.

The Elements of a Religious Organization

In Chapter One, I outlined Weber's categorization of social action. The third type was that of affective social action, which I noted as being at the core of religion. This is the locus of charisma, and the routinization of charisma is the way affective social action is transformed into either traditional or rational/legal social action. This is the heart of the process of organization or the construction of religious institutions. As above, when charismatic or affective social action becomes regular and consistent, norms, roles, and ranks emerge. I may, then, give a preliminary definition of a religious organization as a routinized form of charismatic social interaction that results in a cluster or complex of ranked roles.

However, I also understand a social organization to be focused on a goal, a function to be fulfilled. I outlined the various functional definitions of religion and myth in Chapter Two and the functional definitions of ritual in Chapter Seven. Although there is substantial variation in these functions, it seems that the concept of relationships or social interaction seems to synthesize all of them. One might say that religion functions to create relationships of an individual to the sacred, the cosmos, nature, others, and oneself. I then define a religious organization as:

211

> ... a cluster or a complex of ranked roles that are, in turn, a cluster or a complex of norms that are routinized elements of charismatic or affective social action focused on creating relationships of an individual to the sacred, the cosmos, nature, others, and oneself.

Wuthnow's (1987) work is useful in providing us with a way to envision how myth, ritual, and religious institutions are connected. As we saw in Chapter Seven, he uses four categories to describe human cultures: subjective, structural, dramaturgic, and institutional culture. It is his final category of the interaction of the organization with the external environment which expands our understanding of religious institutions. He writes:

> The process of becoming an institution involves developing a relatively stable means of securing resources, an internal structure for processing these resources, some degree of legitimacy with respect to societal values and procedural norms, and sufficient autonomy from other institutions to be able to establish and pursue independent goals. (1987:169)

With this in mind, then, I expand the definition of a religious organization to include a mechanism of legitimizing the securing and processing of external resources. These resources are procuring and retaining members of the organization and the material necessities to operate the same. Lastly, the religious organization would need to have a certain level of autonomy to enable the individual person to create relationships with the sacred, the cosmos, nature, others, and her/himself.

Before I leave the discussion of defining a religious organization, it is important to add that a distinction can also be made between a substantive and a functional definition of a religious organization. A substantive definition consists of a religious organization that facilitates both the individual and collective experience of the sacred while a functional definition embodies a religious organization that serves to provide social solidarity, integration, global well-being, and meaning.

THE EMERGENCE OF FORMAL RELIGIOUS ORGANIZATIONS

This part of the chapter outlines how sociologists of religion have categorized and specified religious formal organizations. One might argue that religion becomes formalized according to different ways of meeting the need to have an elaboration of roles and institutionalized procedures on one hand and to maintain the charismatic element on the other hand. The literature provides us with four basic ways that formal religious organizations emerge: the sect, the church, mystical organizations (which include the cult and the movement of renewal), and the denomination. These different types will be outlined.

The Sect

There is a long tradition in the sociology of religion of defining what a sect is. Weber (1978:1121ff.) argues that the first moment of the routinization of charisma is the formalization of a small group of followers of a charismatic leader. He notes that the pure type of charismatic rulership is unstable and there is a desire, especially by the followers, to transform charisma and charismatic blessing from a unique, transitory gift of extraordinary times and persons into a permanent possession of everyday life. He writes:

> The turning point is always reached when charismatic followers and disciples become privileged table companions, as did the *trustis* of the Frankish king, and subsequently fief-holders, priests, state officials, party officials, officers, secretaries, editors and publishers, all of whom want to live off the charismatic movement, or when they become employees, teachers and others with a vested occupational interest, or holders of benefices and of patrimonial offices. (1978:1122)

The sect appears to be the kind of formal organization that is "closest" to the charismatic moment of a religion. In another place, Weber (1946) defines the sect as admitting only members who are true believers (those who are the converted), having a leader whose authority is based on a charisma and not on an office, being predominantly lay, and tending to be democratic or egalitarian.

Troeltsch (1931:331) describes the sect as a small group; accenting personal, inward perfection; aimed at personal fellowship; renouncing the idea of dominating the world; having an attitude of indifference, toleration or hostility to the outside society; being connected with lower classes; being detached from the world; appealing to the sermon of the mount as the spiritual ideal; and being fundamentally democratic. Demarath III (1965:37-39) adds to this the following elements. The leadership of the sect is charismatic and non-professional as well as being perceived as somewhat eccentric by non-members. The standards of the sect are stringent and include conversion and signs of salvation. The fellowship is intimate and is an exclusive moral community. Ritual is less important than spontaneity and the personal testimony more vital than any sacrament. The sect stands in a non-accommodative relationship with the external society. It is animated by a distinctive doctrine and is unwilling and incapable of capitulation. Clark (1948), in his study of the church and the sect in Canada, notes that the sect is marked as an exclusive organization and is separate from the larger society.

Later authors (for example, Yinger 1970 and Wilson 1969) extend the meaning of sect in a continuum from those sects which are closer to the charismatic moment and are not well organized to those sects which are very well organized. I will not detail these extensions here but will only say that the original typology of the sect-church continuum had been misused. Coleman (1968) reviewed the existing material on the typology and concluded that the endeavour to fit it with available data was futile because there was so much variation. He refers to one author (Eister 1967), who advocated the abandonment of the typology because the distinction was bankrupt, unproductive, and confusing. Coleman hoped to discover the heuristic value of the typology and argued for the use of the term "organizational precariousness." The sect is precarious because in endeavouring to maintain pristine purity and charisma and to provide social order, it frequently becomes too organized and evolves into a more formal religious organization.

A further characteristic of the sect is its relationship to the church type. Several authors (Wach 1967; Mann 1955; and Wilson 1970) use the term "protest." Wach (1967) terms the kind of protest against the laxity and "over-accommodative" nature of the church a "radical" protest. The result is a separate religious organization that distances itself from the church-type.

Stark and Bainbridge (1979, 1985) endeavour to move the typology to a theory. This is an important difference; these scholars utilize the church-sect-cult typology to present a theory of secularization and counter-secularization processes. During this century studies have presented arguments for and against the thesis. In their theory, Stark and Bainbridge (1979, 1985) took into account both secularization and sacralization processes, which they termed the self-limiting process of secularization. In our terminology, we would call this the attempt to regain the lost charisma and to reduce the formalization processes inherent within religious organizations. Stated simply, they maintained that secularization is a fact in modern society; however, it is self-limiting. They argued that as secularization and rationalization increase, there is a concomitant movement to recognize the limitation of these processes, especially in regard to issues of meaning. In churches, sacralization processes develop which challenge and mitigate the overall thrust of the secularization process. As in the case of sect formation, protest movements emerge from within established churches.

In the tradition of the church-sect typology, the church type is described as a religious organization in a low state of tension with its environment. A sect type, on the other hand, is considered to be in a high state of tension with its environment (Stark and Bainbridge 1985:141). According to this theory, in the beginning stages of secularization, members protest, break away, and search for a more other-worldly form of religious commitment.

A summary of a definition of the sect seems to encompass three domains: leadership, membership, and the relationship, to the environment. A sect is:

> A religious organization that includes members who are considered to be converted, who follow stringent rules of behaviour, who form a small, primary and intimate group, who opt for spontaneity rather than for formalized ritual, and form an egalitarian moral community. The leaders of the organization protest against the "over-accommodative" nature of the church type and tend to be lay, charismatic, non-professional, and adhering to clear doctrinal statements. As a whole, the organization stands in a high-tension relationship to the environment and is organizationally precarious in that it endeavours to maintain the pristine message while providing a sense of social order. As an organization, it tends not to accommodate to the external environment and may take a stance of indifference, intolerance or hostility towards that environment.

Table 8.1 illustrates the characteristics of the sect:

ELEMENTS OF A SECT

KIND OF LEADERSHIP	KIND OF MEMBERSHIP	RELATIONSHIP TO THE SOCIAL ENVIRONMENT
lay	those who claim to be converted	high tension
charismatic	they tend to follow stringent rules	non-accommodative to the environment
non-professional	they form primary groups	organizationally precarious
	tend to be spontaneous	indifferent to the environment
		intolerant of the environment

TABLE 8.1

Before the sect type is illustrated, it is worth considering if this sect is closer to the substantive or functional understanding of a religious organization. I am placing it on the substantive end of a continuum between substantive and functional because an essential feature of the sect is that it intends to reform a religious tradition by going back to its source (the sacred). Its additional genius is not to accommodate to the secular environment.

To exemplify the sect type, two cases from Alberta will be presented. Although O'Toole (1996) argues that the sect is not the predominant form of Christianity in Canada, neither in the past nor the present, this does not mean that the sect is without merit as a vital religious form in the nation. The examples presented here include the main features of the sect type as outlined in this definition. Also, the first example, of vibrant sects during the years following World War I, the Great Depression, and after World War II, enables us to understand case histories of sects that both protest against the more traditional churches and respond to widespread social unrest. The second example, that of a modern sect in central Alberta, illustrates a protest against a modern church as well as an organization in high tension with the external environment.

Mann (1955), a former sociologist from the University of Toronto, researched churches, sects, and cults that reveal a somewhat unique feature of religion in North America. In common with most other religious awakening and reform in North America, the Alberta case is not unique. However, its distinctiveness is that from this religious ferment emerged a vibrant political movement called the Social Credit Party that was the government in the province from 1935 until 1971. The political base of the party was predominantly evangelical Christianity, and William Aberhart (the founder of the party in Alberta) was also a pastor and radio evangelist. I will come back to this party when we look at the connection between religion and politics in Chapter Ten.

In 1946, there were an estimated 228,190 members in all Protestant churches in Alberta. Of these, 53,790 or 24 per cent were members of evangelical sects (Mann 1955:30-31). These sects were inheritors of the fundamentalist movement of the early part of the century which was unified by a very strident protest against modernity (especially the theory of evolution). They were united doctrinally in that they shared a tight ascetic code of morality and belief in the literal truth of the Bible, in the personal second coming of Christ, the existence of a fire-and-brimstone hell, and in necessity of a dramatic conversion experience. Other characteristics included hearty congregational singing, enthusiastic preaching, a congregational form of government, a unanimous attack against modernism, and a condemnation of the coldness, formality, and class consciousness often found in the churches (Mann 1955:27-32). A special characteristic is that these sects grew at the expense of the more established churches. These converts, or "switchers," came from such churches as Roman Catholic, Orthodox, Methodist, Baptist, United, Lutheran, Presbyterian, and Anglican. However, the switching did not tend to occur over a wide range of denominational differences. Frequently, Mann argues, the converts tended to follow ethnic lines such as German Lutherans joining German sects: "In general, shifts in religious conviction followed lines of least ethnic, religious, and social resistance: new Canadians attached themselves to sects composed of their own ethnic group" (Mann 1955:34).

As noted above, the liturgies celebrated by these evangelical sects were lively, enthusiastic, and vibrant. Mann (1955:45) observes that the informality and friendliness may have accounted for some of the sects' appeal to farmers as well as to highly mobile urban people. This religious practice offered lonely and marginal people a simple way of certifying their belonging to a tight-knit group.

Another example of a sect is one located in a mid-sized city in Alberta. The sect emerged at a very different time in Alberta than the ones illustrated above. It was formed from several charismatic prayer groups within the United Church of Canada. For about ten years, members of these prayer groups served in several United Church congregations in the hope of "renewing" the churches. Increasingly, their protest became nullified without any changes happening. Also, the United Church of Canada was going through modernization processes such as questioning the literal meaning of the Bible, speaking of God in inclusive language, and allowing practising homosexual persons to be ordained ministers. Several members of these groups left the denomination and eventually invited a minister of a Pentecostal church (of the Fellowship of Christian Assemblies) to pastor the nascent congregation. From a small number (40 members) in the early 1980s, the sect had grown to over 300 members by 1991. Swenson (1991) argues that there is significant evidence that most of these members came from the mainline churches (especially Roman Catholic, United, and Anglican) because they experienced deligitimation[1] from their previous commitments.

Both the Mann and Swenson studies challenge the Bibby and Brinkerhoff (1973, 1983, 1994) thesis of the circulation of the saints.[2] Their research on evangelical churches in Calgary during the 1970s and 1980s reveals that most of the growth of the evangelical congregations came from successful youth socialization and movement from one evangelical church to another. Mann and Swenson's data reveal that membership increase came not from other sects but, rather, from mainline, church-type denominations. I would suggest that the sect in central Alberta drew on people from the mainline churches because many were members within these churches before, had a conversion experience within them, but did not receive support from them. They eventually became alienated and left to create and join the sect. The Bibby and Brinkerhoff data reveal people who have always been evangelical but who were "circulating" from one sect to another.

The Church

In light of Weber's routinization process that we outlined above, one may argue that the church type of formal religious organization is a type further

---

1 The term refers to those devotees who have become disillusioned from their current religious affiliation and consider that it is no longer a legitimate institution.

2 In their 1994 study, the authors nuance their original thesis. Although the data continue to reinforce the thesis, there have been recent changes in that there has been an increase of non-evangelical community membership.

removed from the charismatic moment.[3] Figure 8.1 illustrates this. I shall use the same authors that gave us an understanding of the sect to define the church type. Weber (1964) describes the church as an institution whose membership is composed of those who may not experience a conversion but who are baptized, usually as infants. The charisma of the leader is not a personal one, but rather, is a charisma of the office. The leaders are priests or ministers who are professionally trained, and the organization tends to be ranked according to a hierarchical structure.

Troeltsch (1931:331) characterizes the church as being conservative in doctrinal matters, dominating the members, and to a certain extent accepting the secular order. It tends to be universal in that it endeavours to cover the whole of a society. The church appeals to the upper classes for support and utilizes the state to accomplish some of its goals. It stabilizes and determines the social order. The religious practices are marked by asceticism and are aimed at preparing the members for the supernatural end of life.

Demerath III (1965:37-39) adds to this the following elements. This kind of religious organization has a professional leadership, a relatively impersonal fellowship, and has lax criteria for membership. Ritual is important, and the sacraments are the central kinds of rituals. The church accommodates itself to the secular order with a posture of adaptive compromise and leads to organizational stability and a large following. It needs to share its membership with other institutions which may, in turn, increase the potential for secularization processes within the organization. Clark (1948) adds that the church seeks the accommodation of religious organization to the outside community and looks for the welfare of the society at large.

Coleman (1968) applies the term "organizational precariousness" to the church that has a built-in tension of dissatisfaction with its organization "weight" that encourages organizational breakdown. Stark and Bainbridge (1979 and 1985) argue that the church, in relation to the external environment, is in a low-tension relationship.

From all of these authors, using the same domains as the sect, I define the church in the following way:

> The leaders of the church usually are priests or ministers who are professionally trained and hold not a personal charisma but a charisma of office. Authority is "top-down" in a series of hierarchical rankings. There tends to be a liaison between the religious and the secular leaders. The religious leaders seem to be concerned about the welfare of

---

3 This interpretation is substantiated by the work of Berger (1995) in his reading of Weber's (1978) comparison of the church and the sect.

THE CHURCH AND CHARISMA

sect   church

→

charismatic moment   routinization of charisma

FIGURE 8.1

the larger society. These leaders tend to be conservative in doctrine, especially in traditional societies, but move toward liberalism in the modern world.

Members are mostly members from birth and have an ascriptive status. The people appear to be socially controlled by the leaders, large in numbers, and there is a relatively high level of organizational stability. Ritual is more important than spontaneity and the fellowships lean toward impersonality and a kind of collectivity. Church members tend to be ascetic in religious practices in traditional societies but are much more relativistic in the modern setting.

The church accommodates itself to the external environment and thus may become overly secularized. It has a level of low tension with this environment and because of its bureaucratic "weight" tends to break down. Table 8.2 illustrates this definition.

Before an example of the church type with a Canadian illustration is presented, it may be useful to know how important this organizational type has been to the development of Canada as a whole. O'Toole (1996), in an essay on religion in Canada, makes a cogent argument that the evolution of Canadian religion has followed the European model rather than the American one. In the spirit of revolution, the United States has been dominated by the sect as the most common kind of religious organization. In contrast, religion Canadian style has had strong roots in the social establishment common in the church type of organization. It has had, especially historically, strong links to commanding political, business, and cultural elites. This has had a continued impact, O'Toole argues. About two-thirds of Canadians consider themselves to be members of the Roman Catholic, Anglican or United Church. This has not changed even with the introduction of non-Christian religions as well as with the growth of secularization. Citing Statistics Canada (1993) and Maclean's (1993), O'Toole notes that 80 per cent of Canadians self-describe themselves as Christians. Of them, 20 per cent belong to conservative Christian sects while a full 80 per cent still adhere to one of the "Big Three": Roman Catholic, Anglican, and United.

ELEMENTS OF THE CHURCH

KIND OF LEADERSHIP	KIND OF MEMBERSHIP	RELATIONSHIP TO THE SOCIAL ENVIRONMENT
priests	from birth	low tension
professionally trained	ascriptive status	accommodative to the environment
in a hierarchical order	more likely to be controlled by leaders	organizationally "over-weighted"
in liaison with secular authorities	ritual is more important than spontaneity	tends not to be indifferent to the social environment
conservative in traditional times but liberal in modern times	tend to be part of impersonal social groups	

ascetic in traditional times
and relativistic in modern times

TABLE 8.2

Yinger (1970:257-258), dissatisfied with the simplicity of the church/sect typology, adds further refinements to the continuum. He distinguishes the church type into *the universal institutionalized church* and *the universal diffused church*. The former has all the major characteristics of the above definition with the additional fact that it is co-extensive with the whole of society, as in Christendom of the middle ages. The second type also has the same characteristics but is only one type of religious organization in a complex, modern society. Within modern Christianity, there are currently no examples of the former type. Within Islam, however, there are contemporary examples in Saudi Arabia and Iran.

Nonetheless, the rural parish church of Quebec of relatively recent past is an example. Miner (1939) presents an ethnographic analysis of this type of religious organization. St-Denis is a rural parish community about eighty miles downstream from Quebec City. Although the history of the community goes back to 1695, it was formally established as a parish in 1833. The economic base was entirely agricultural, with the centre of the social life of the community being the parish itself. Because the civic boundaries of the community were co-extensive with the parish, we can rightly call St-Denis a universal church. The parish was the "first point of reference" of the people into which is enmeshed the family. The family type was primogeniture (inheritance given to the first son). All of the other children (ranging in number from 5 to 7) were to leave the farm. One was to become a priest, another a nun, and the rest professionals or emigrants to the northeastern part of the United States to work in the textile industry.

When Miner was writing, the role of religion was very powerful. Sacred beliefs supported the time-tested, successful right behaviour. The Sunday ritual, the Mass, was the key ritual attended by virtually every person in the parish. In this setting, the priest (called the *curé*) presented directives for a righteous life. This ritual functioned to create solidarity and cohesiveness within the group of believers. This ritual was augmented by sacred feasts which brought further integration. One such example was a celebration in the autumn called All Souls' Day. In this ritual families were integrated with their ancestors in a series of prayers for the deceased. This kind of religious organization permeated the daily life of its members, was present as a powerful means of social control, and created social solidarity and cohesiveness among a people. However, it was out of step with modernity, which emphasizes individual choice and personal freedom.[4]

Since the time that Miner completed his work, St-Denis has not changed much but Roman Catholicism beyond the village has changed dramatically. O'Toole (1996) informs us that the church has moved from a triumphalist position to an exile or abdication from the centre of Canadian Francophone life. It has been displaced by the state in education and health care, has experienced a drastic decline in clergy, and is beset with an increasingly large number of members who do not frequent religious services. In addition, these Francophone Catholics dissent from official church teachings on matters of birth control, legalized abortion, and premarital sexual activity.

On the other side, however, a full 86 per cent of Quebeckers identify themselves as Roman Catholics. The organization itself has also changed to include liturgical flexibility, ecumenical dialogue, and a compassionate concern for social justice. The more central institution in the lives of Francophones is the Catholic parochial school. Even though the adults do not go to church on Sunday, they send their children to the schools still under the directorship of the Church. Citing Lemieux (1990), O'Toole writes:

4   Ten years later, Miner returned to the parish. Already by this time modern values and technology were invading the tight community.

> Raymond Lemieux suggests that, in contemporary life, it [Quebec Catholicism] has acquired a multi-faceted character. It has become a diffuse, churchless faith which simultaneously supports a vague, almost subliminal civil religion of reassuring familiarity and a privatized popular religiosity whose discrete spiritual quests evoke and involve "religious effervescence, emotional communion, affirmation of universal values and explosion of imaginary." (1996:123)

Before this section is completed, it is worth indicating that the church is best illustrated by a functional definition of the religious organization. This is for two reasons. The church is an example of routinized charisma or the sacred and is defined as that type of religious organization that accommodates itself to the secular environment.

Mysticism

This introduction to religious typologies takes us beyond the more established one of the church and sect to include the cult. Before we discuss that, however, I go back to the work of Troeltsch (1931), who introduced into the sociology of religion a term which is organizational in nature (not a spirituality as in the case of James): "mysticism." From this early work by Troeltsch we can distinguish two types of mysticism: the cult and movements of renewal. The former is well established in the current literature, the latter less so. I will here outline the typology of mysticism from Troeltsch and then look at the cult and at movements of renewal.

Mysticism brings us back to religious experience wherein the religious leader or the individual has a personal sense of the divine presence. Troeltsch (1931:729ff) outlines it with the following elements: an insistence upon a direct inward religious experience, taking for granted the externals of religion (such as rites and dogmas) and either rejecting them or supplementing them with the experience, expressing itself in ecstasy and frenzy or in visions and hallucinations, and having a concentration on the purely interior and emotional side of religious experience. Sociologically, members tend to be individualists with little concern for the welfare of others.

The main tendency of this individualism is toward quietism and abandonment. The purpose of the collective, the group, is personal and only for the edification of the individual. Mysticism does not create social solidarity, community, or social cohesion but, rather, individual spiritual growth.

THE CULT

From Troeltsch's outline of mysticism, several authors have focused on two elements of this original type: personal religious experience and individualism. I will select central researchers who have presented elements of a cult that we will utilize here: Becker (1932), Mann (1955), Westley (1983), Stark and Bainbridge (1979 & 1985), and Johnstone (1992). I will then illustrate an example of a cult using Westley's work on cults in a modern, urban setting (see Chapter Three).

Becker (1932) was the first to use the typology referring it to a loose association of individuals with a private, eclectic religiosity. He describes the cult as a form of social organization of non-official religion (see McGuire 1992). Mann (1955:6-7) contrasts sects with cults. Whereas sects emphasize the recovery of primitive, first-century Christian doctrine, cults blend alien religious or psychological notions with Christian doctrine with a view to achieving a more adequate or modern form of faith. It is this blending or syncretic feature that distinguishes the cult. Members defend this kind of independent existence by choosing different elements of the Christian religion with non-Christian beliefs. A sect is indifferent or opposed to many secular goals such as worldly prestige, popularity, and wealth, but a cult accepts such values. The ultimate goal of the cult is individualistic and accents harmony, happiness, and success.

Westley roots an interpretation of cults in the work of Durkheim (1915, 1951, and 1969). As we saw in Chapter Seven, Durkheim argues that it is the gathering of believers that is the source of religious belief. Religion, in traditional societies, is pre-eminently a collective phenomenon. In the modern world, however, the collective activities of societal members become far fewer. In line with other sociologists, the unit of society in the modern world is no longer the group but the individual. In a religious sense, the individual becomes sacred, and the kind of religion of the modern world is more and more the worship of the individual. Westley (1983) uses this element of modern religions especially to characterize the cult. She describes these modern cults with the following characteristics: a rationalized economic structure (fee for service), an emphasis on individual development, a partial involvement of members, and a transient community life (1983:87). The belief structure corresponds to these sociological characteristics: an emphasis on science and technology, a concern with contamination and purity, and a belief that one's personality is a composite of many past personalities.

Stark and Bainbridge (1979, 1985) add another characteristic of the cult. They argue that the cult is like the sect in that it is in a high-tension relationship with the environment. It differs from the sect type because the

223

cult's protest against the church turns to a non-conventional belief system or to a deviant religious tradition (deviant to the society under investigation). My reference to Joseph Smith and nineteenth-century Mormonism is an example of a cult using this kind of characteristic. Robertson (1992) extends the deviant element of a cult. He notes that the cult emphasizes the new — a new revelation or insight believed to be inspired by a supernatural agent. There is an attempt on the part of cult members to contrast themselves with the more traditional and orthodox religious groups (either churches or sects). He also adds the presence of a heightened level of individualism. Cults diverge from churches and sects in that they tend not to develop a strong organizational structure and are informal and small.[5]

Using these authors, one can identify several elements which converge around three domains: deviant beliefs, a focus on the individual, and a relationship with the environment:

> A cult is a belief system which is deviant from the traditional religious doctrines of the host society. Members tend to blend non-traditional with traditional tenets that make it syncretic. There is a special focus on the individual who becomes almost sacred. This emphasis on the individual leaves the association thus formed in a loose, informal, organizational structure. Finally, the cult stands in a high-tension relationship with the external environment.

Table 8.3 illustrates this definition.

Before I proceed to discuss examples of cults, a further distinction into types of the cult is necessary. Paloutzian (1996) accepts the definition of cult as presented thus far. He adds another meaning of the term and calls it "a destructive cult." By this he means a cult that seeks to control and radically alter the personalities of their groups. There is much controversy about using the term in this way. To give some credibility to his description, Paloutzian provides evidence from some members who have left the Moonies or the Unification Church. Critics of using the term "cult" in this way would argue that ex-members are not the ones to ask since they may be exaggerating their sense of a loss of identity. There does seem to be some evidence, however, to classify some noteworthy cults in this light: the Jonestown cult, the Solar Temple, Heaven's Gate, and the Branch Davidians. In the case of Jonestown, the Solar Temple and the Heaven's Gate groups, members committed suicide — the kind of suicide that

---

5 There are some exceptions to this. The Jonestown cult and the recent Branch Davidians of Waco, Texas, are examples of very close integration of members enmeshed in a strong hierarchical political structure.

ELEMENTS OF THE CULT

DEVIANT BELIEFS	KIND OF MEMBERSHIP	RELATIONSHIP TO THE SOCIAL ENVIRONMENT
tend to be deviant from the religious doctrine of the host society	through conversion	high tension
beliefs are selected from several sources	achieved status	high and low accommodation to the environment
	the individual is the sacred	

TABLE 8.3

Durkheim (1951) would call "altruistic suicide" or a suicide that indicates a willingness to take one's own life for the sake of the group.

Campbell (1998) adds another term that is useful for our understanding of the phenomenon. He uses the term *cultic milieu* to refer to a society's deviant belief systems, rituals, and associated collectivities, institutions, and individuals. Additionally, it is characterized by all the worlds of the occult, magic, spiritualism, psychic phenomena, alien intelligences, lost civilizations, and faith healing or nature cures.

With this background in mind, I will illustrate this ideal type with two empirical case studies of new religious movements, one in Montreal and the other in the United States, the Nation of Islam. Westley (1983) researched six groups in Montreal that are categorized as being part of new religious movements[6]: Scientology, Psychosynthesis, Arica, EST, Shakti, and Silva Mind Control. It is beyond the scope of this presentation to detail the unique elements of these religions. Instead, I will present the common characteristics such as beliefs and organizational features.

---

6 Although there is a wide variation of new religious movements, Wilson (1976:63) provides us with a general definition: that salvation is gained by becoming acquainted with a special, perhaps secret, knowledge from a mystic source; that ultimate salvation and knowledge come from the liberation of powers within the self; that real salvation is attained by belonging to a saved community, whose life-style and concerns are utterly divergent from those of worldly people.

225

Using several authors (Stone 1976; Ellwood 1973; Gaustad 1974 and Bach 1973), Westley (1983) presents the following common characteristics of these groups: being drawn from the encounter group/therapy tradition; the idea of pre- and post-existence in a spiritual state; the idea of a plurality of worlds, each with its own spirits and angels; the Renaissance notion that divine consciousness is continuous with humans; the intimate connection between the body and the mind; bodily conditions seen as direct reflection of mental states; and being part of the human potential movement which emphasizes individual changes from an intense group encounter. In short, these groups, which are the *cult of man,* are

> a mixture of the late stages of the human potential movement, the positive-thought movement, and the occult traditions. The point of agreement of all six of these is that it is the human individual who is seen as sacred, as all powerful. This sacred power is seen as located deep within the individual personality. Actions in the outer world become significant, not in themselves, but only in terms of their impact on this inner self. (Westley 1983:38)

There are several distinguishing organizational features that these six groups share. To participate in the group activities, fees for services are asked. Rather than have teachings on certain themes common in churches and sects, the fee for service is offered in exchange for a course on a certain topic. Membership transience is another feature of these groups. In fact, as long as the individual grows or develops, the continued presence of the group is not necessary. Partial commitment or involvement is also common. One can come and go at will and one will not be asked "Why did you miss the gathering last week?" (Westley 1983:39-58).

The belief system corresponds to this informal, loose kind of organization. Faith (such as trust in a supernatural power or person or adherence to basic doctrines) is substituted for learning scientific technology (one is reminded of the turn of the century cult, Christian Science). Rather than focusing on healing that would integrate one into a community (as in the case of members of the Catholic Charismatic Movement), it is purification from polluting ideas, especially negative ones, that is important for members of these groups. In this way, these particular groups are gnostic[7] in a fundamental manner.

---

7   The term is from the Greek, *gnosis,* a word that simply means "knowledge." The mythology that extends the meaning of the term is gnosticism. Its origins go back to Egyptian religion which had a central tenet, "He who knows himself, knows the All." Other important features include the teaching of the Divine Man, (a man who was both human and divine); Sophia or

The Nation of Islam has a similar mythology but a very different kind of organization that is not at all loose but is rather tight, hierarchical, and structured. The mythology of the Nation was discussed in Chapter Two and some of its ritual in Chapter Seven. Before I proceed to discuss the organizational features of the movement, it might be worth commenting on Gardell's (1996) interpretation of its mythology, for it has relevancy to its organization. He considers it to be fundamentally gnostic, with roots in Sufi Islam,[8] Manichaeism, and Druze religion.[9] The Nation's belief system, like Gnosticism, is hidden, esoteric, and veiled. It can be presented but only in symbolic and mystical terms. Evil is a spirit that travels in human bodies and is, especially, manifested in the white person. There is the great cycle of time that looks something like the following. In the first cycle of time, there was paradise and an essential unity between God and man, for God created himself in the form of man. The second great cycle began with the creation of the white race (in gnostic terms, the separation of the divine and the human) when the black person lost his or her knowledge of self. The third stage begins with a period of enlightenment when saviours (Masters Farad and Elijah) show that the way to unity again is to become aware of one's inherent divinity. This mythology can be interpreted only by messengers who have been appointed to do so. In the case of the Nation, this is Minister Louis Farrakhan. From this belief, the hierarchical nature of the Nation flows. As depicted in Figure 8.2, Minister Farrakhan is the primary authority figure who has deputies to carry on specific ministries. There are elected representatives from all the NOI mosques throughout the United States. In the upper regions of the hierarchy, two ministries should be noted: the ministry for women and the one for defence. The former is headed by a woman

227

THE ORGANIZATION OF THE NATION

Minister Louis Farakhan

National Council of Labourers:
Finance, Commerce, Defense, Women, Education, Youth, Health

Elected Representatives from the Six Regions in the United States

FIGURE 8.2

the feminine manifestation of the divine essence similar to the Divine Mother; having special knowledge available only to a few; a strong distinction between the spiritual and the material; and, lastly, a symbolic reading of canonical texts from Judaism, Christianity, and Islam (Eliade 1995).

8   Ascetic, mystical Islam.

9   An independent sect situated mainly in Lebanon, Syria, and Israel, that is an offshoot of Islam.

(called the MGT Captain or national instructress of women). The defence ministry holds a key position — a military male cadre of highly disciplined men who "defend" the Nation. They are not aggressors but protect the name, property, and assets of the people. In Farrakhan's words: "we will whip the hell out of any that comes against us, short or tall, armed or unarmed" (cited in Gardell 1996:142).

Gardell (1996) notes that the resurrection of the Nation after the "fall" with Wallace Muhammad began in small study groups within members' homes and in rented halls. By the mid-1980s, there was such a boom that mosques were created throughout all of the states in the United States. To become an official member mosque of the Nation, at least 40 people apply to the headquarters and agree to abide by the rules and regulations of Minister Farrakhan and his chiefs of staff. Each mosque has a leader who is similar to the imam[10] of mainstream Islam.

228

In concluding this section on the cult, is it to be considered an illustration of the substantive understanding of a religious organization or the functional one? I would say that it can be both. It can be considered to represent the substantive dimension because it does not accommodate itself to the environment. On the other hand, it can be considered to be closer to the functional if it creates a mythology that is focused on, for example, control of persons as in the case of the Nation of Islam.

THE MOVEMENT OF RENEWAL

We saw in Chapter Six the characteristics of a movement of renewal. Its central feature is a protest from within an existing church that does not involve a secession or a schism but rather a desire and mobilization to change the tone, the emptiness, the routinized charisma of the church through a renewal of a tradition. The renewal movement members strive hard to maintain connections with the authorities of the church. Table 8.4 reflects the characteristics of a Movement of Renewal or MOR.

A current example of a MOR is the Catholic Charismatic Movement. Swenson and Thompson (1986) did a content analysis on key texts and magazines of this movement from 1967-1976. Using Wach (1967), Hill (1973), and O'Dea and O'Dea (1983) as a theoretical base, they reviewed Catholic Charismatic spokespersons such as Ranaghan and Ranaghan (1969), Ford (1970), O'Connor (1971), Clark (1971, 1976), and Ranaghan (1971), and Byrne (1971) to illustrate that the Catholic Charismatic Movement is a movement of renewal.

10 Arabic IMAM ("leader," "pattern"), the head of the Muslim community; the title is used in the Koran several times to refer to leaders and to Abraham.

ELEMENTS OF THE MOR

LEADERSHIP	KIND OF MEMBERSHIP	RELATIONSHIP TO THE SOCIAL ENVIRONMENT
lay	through conversion	high tension
not professionally trained	achieved status	low accommodation to the environment
in strong relationship with the church	join to primary groups	non-schismatic in relationship to the church
a renewal of tradition	desire a strong relationship with the church	
	the organization tends to be informal	

TABLE 8.4

All of these spokespersons write of the need for members of the movement to remain loyal to the Roman Catholic Church in its leadership and its core beliefs. In their writings, Swenson and Thompson (1986) also observed that to legitimate the charismatic dimension of this movement in the eyes of both the followers and the church hierarchy, leaders take great pain to locate the charismatic dimension in the traditions of the Catholic Church. Such "sacred pasts" consist of the New Testament, the early church, the monastic movement, and the mystical saints of the medieval period. A recent past was the Vatican II council in the early 1960s. Relying on the documents (Abbot 1966), these charismatic leaders make a case that the highest authority in the Catholic Church, the gathering of all the bishops and the Pope, approved of the vitality of the charismatic gifts.

But what of the movement of renewal, substantive or functional? I would argue that it approximates the substantive dimension for the same reasons as the sect: the quest for authenticity (for the sacred) and the non-accommodative nature of the religious organization.

This completes our investigation into cults and movements of renewal. The last organizational type, common in modern societies, is the denominational one. I will outline its main features and then present a case history of one such denomination: the United Church of Canada.

A TYPOLOGY OF THE DENOMINATION, THE CHURCH AND THE SECT

(Source, in part: Martin 1962:4-10)

CHARACTER-ISTICS	CHURCH	DENOMINATION	SECT
salvation dilemma	one way	several ways	one way
unity dilemma	through institutional means	through experiential means	through right doctrine
order dilemma	achieved separate from as well as linked to the social environment	achieved through a pragmatic relationship with the social environment	achieved separately from the social environment
sacramental dilemma	the sacred is within symbols	sacred among the people	sacred in the text
marital dilemma	marriage is a sacrament	marriage is not a sacrament	marriage is a contract
eschatological dilemma	individual	individual	only for the converted
individual dilemma	collective choice	individual choice	individual choice
moral dilemma	through works	through faith and works	through faith

TABLE 8.5

The Denomination

The term denomination was introduced into the sociology of religion by Niebuhr (1957). It is seen as one type of routinization of charisma that represents an accommodation to the class divisions within a society. He argues that a sect exists only for the period of time of the reformer. Soon after the death of the reformer, the sect begins to accommodate itself to the host society, and the denomination emerges. The denomination, then, is a routinized sect that reflects the class, ethnic, and racial divisions in a society.

Martin (1962) updates this. He notes that sects do not necessarily become a denomination but may continue for many generations as, for example, in established sects. What is unique about the denomination is that it has some features that are common to the church and sect type as well as having characteristics unique to itself.

Martin provides us with a way to distinguish the denomination from both the church and the sect types. Table 8.5 presents this distinction. This table has been substantially taken from Martin as acknowledged above. I have added, however, the concept of dilemma that I consider implicit within Martin's typology.

As can be seen from this table, the church type and the sect type represent polar extremes of each of these elements. The denomination, however, tends to try to balance the extremes (except in some instances where it accepts the extreme either of the church or the sect). This overview of the denomination illustrates the core thesis of the whole text: that of tension. Here the tension is about organizational choices that result in the various configurations of these types. One might argue that the denominational alternative is an endeavour to capture something of the sacred of the sect while avoiding the weight of the bureaucracy of the church.

Rather than presenting my usual summary definition of the different types of religious organizations, I choose to select Martin's (1962:11) own definition of the denomination[11]:

> [it] ... does not claim that its institutional borders constitute the one ark of salvation, its concept of unity is a unity of experience and its historical sense is likewise a unity of experience rather than an institutional succession. Its attitude to organization and to cultic forms tends to be pragmatic and instrumental, while its sacramental conceptions are subjective. This subjectivity is related to a fundamental individual-

---

11 Some later work has been done on developing this type (Berger 1961, Morioka and Newell 1968, and McGuire 1992). However, these more recent references do not add anything substantially different than Niebuhr and Martin.

ism. In the field of eschatology its conceptions are traditional and in the field of moral theory its conception of the relation of faith and works is dynamic but balanced. (1962:11)

With this definition as a background, I will illustrate this type with a church from Canada: the United Church of Canada. It was created on June 10, 1925, by a unification of three churches (Presbyterian, Methodist, and Congregational) and one small amalgam, the General Council of Local Union Churches. Grant (1967) argues that the union was not so much a result of ecumenism (it had not yet been born) but, rather, one of exigency and practicality. Canada was still an expanding country at this time. Vast lands with small populations left rural areas with many churches in competition with one another, and each with few members. Union, then, made pragmatic sense.

232

The *Basis of Union* (the document that forms the foundation of the union of the various churches) presents a presbyterian polity[12] wherein each congregation and pastoral charge (there were 4,200 congregations in 1990 and 2,400 pastoral charges or one or more congregations under a minister) has a representation and a voice in one of 98 presbyteries. Each presbytery, in turn, has its own elected representatives in the conference (a union of thirteen local presbyteries). Finally, each conference has its elected persons to the national church, the General Council, wherein major decisions are made (Morrow 1923 and Grant, Chambers, Forrest, Greene, Lee and White 1990). One of the ways the early founders found consensus is that each church would not develop its own "brand" of Christianity. In other words, there were to be no "Wesleyans" or "Calvinists." A consequence of this meant a lessened emphasis on "ours" and "theirs" (Grant 1967:101).

Morrow (1923) outlines a history of the discussions within each of the churches that eventually led to the union. The *Basis of Union* (Morrow 1923:322-327) established both the doctrinal and political basis of the new church. All representatives agreed that the union was to be based upon the faith given by the apostles and prophets of the New Testament with Jesus Christ as the "corner stone." The Bible was understood to be the primary source and ultimate standard of the faith. In addition, the representatives held allegiance to the early creeds and the teaching of the reformers. The document goes on to detail the common beliefs regarding God, revelation, the divine purpose, creation, the sin of man, the grace of God, the divine-human nature of Jesus, the Holy Spirit, the need for regeneration, faith,

---

12 This is the kind of organization that emerged from the Calvinistic Reformation. In a nation state, the church is divided into geographical units called presbyteries. Congregations subsist within these presbyteries.

repentance, sanctification, and prayer. The doctrines of the law of God, the meaning of the Church, the sacraments, the ministry, fellowship, and the teachings of eschatology all follow basic reformation theology.

A significant contrast is found in the (unofficial) currently accepted "doctrines of faith." Grant *et al.* present a creed in the following words:

> We are not alone, we live in God's world. We believe in God who has created and is creating, who has come in Jesus, the Word made flesh, to reconcile and make new, who works in us and others by the Spirit. We trust in God. We are called to be church: to celebrate God's presence, to love and serve others, to seek justice and resist evil, to proclaim Jesus, crucified and risen, our judge and our hope. In life, in death, in life beyond death, God is with us. We are not alone. Thanks be to God. (1990:160)

From this creedal document, one is able to see how the leaders of the United Church take a middle-ground approach that is quite indicative of the denominational type. This church sees itself as only one way among many to salvation, being pragmatic, seeing the divine presence in others, emphasizing personal choice, and combining both faith and works. The routinization of sect to denomination is also evident. From a sect type of doctrinal stance common in the beginning of the church to a much wider basis of faith in the 1990s, one can see how much the church has adapted itself to the external culture.

O'Toole's (1996) reflections on the United Church add further credence to this interpretation. Even though 11.6 per cent of Canadians affiliate with this church, this figure is a decline from 20 per cent in previous times. In addition, only 16 per cent attend religious services on a regular basis. Mythologically, the church exhibits a moderate progressivism that tries to steer between extreme liberal and conservative belief systems. This has become, indeed, its most crucial challenge. On one hand, conservative members are concerned about the maintenance of orthodox doctrine and sexual morality while the liberals are committed to social justice, equity, and inclusiveness. The importance of inclusiveness brought the church to near crisis in the late 1980s when professed homosexuals were given freedom to be ordained as ministers. Although a full-scale schism did not occur, there continues to be a high level of tension between the conservatives who are becoming more marginalized.

There is recent evidence, however, that the denomination is leaning more to a left position and not a middle one. Rev. Bill Phipps, the current moderator of the denomination, challenges orthodox United Church teachings. In contrast to a New Testament text that says: "In his body

[Jesus Christ] lives the fulness of divinity" (Colossians 2:9), Phipps says: "I believe that God is more than Jesus. God is huge, mysterious, wholly beyond our comprehension and beyond our total understanding. Jesus does not represent or embody all of God, but embodies as much of God as can be in a person." The resurrection should not be taken literally but, rather, "it is the belief in transforming energy that calls us into the world to follow Jesus who, we say, gives life over death." And, finally, "heaven and hell are what we create on earth" (*Maclean's* 1998:43).

Summary Statements

Concepts which are central to our understanding of these various types are tension, accommodation, and protest. Using Figure 8.1, above, one may argue that a religious organization begins from the charismatic moment when the processes of routinization commence. The sect appears to be the closest type to this moment. As the sect accommodates more and more to the cultural environment (in a state of tension), the church type may emerge (as in the case of the post-reformation churches) or a denomination (as in the case of churches during nineteenth-century America and documented by Niebuhr).

As the church type moves more to the extreme of accommodation, some members and possibly a reformer, renewer prophet, or revolutionary prophet protests the accommodation. The kind of response to the tension and accommodation directs the kind of organization. In the case of the reformer, a sect emerges; the renewer prophet, a movement of renewal, and the revolutionary prophet produce a cult. The denomination is seen as standing midway between the sect and the church: an accommodation that settles on a balance of the polarities as part of the accommodative process of the church and the non-accommodative process of the sect. In this way, one may consider that the denomination has both a substantive and functional dimension.

| ILLUSTRATIONS OF TRANSFORMATIONS

I have presented a possible way of understanding the transformation processes involved in movements between various organizational types. In this section I will focus on two types of transformations: from the cult to the denomination and from the sect to the denomination. Both types are ways of interpreting the routinization processes. Both types begin with a charismatic moment either through a leader (as in the case of the Mormons) or through a wider social/charismatic movement as in the case of the Assemblies of God, an American Pentecostal church. I will first look at the case of the Mormons and then follow up with the Assemblies of God.

From the Cult to the Denomination: The Case of the Mormons

I refer the reader back to the discussion of the genesis of the Mormon Church in Chapters Five and Six. The argument there was that both during the life of Smith but especially after his untimely death, routinization processes were occurring. O'Dea (1957) used the term "the containment of charisma" to refer to the choice of the Mormon leadership to restrict charisma or revelation to the Church president. What I will do here is look at some more recent research on the Mormons to see the direction in which the routinization processes have gone and to argue that the church has moved from a cult to a denomination in many ways.

O'Dea (1957) takes the position that even though the frontier has been conquered and that Mormons, like many other Americans, are a "people of plenty," there continues to be a vitality and life within the church. He does concede that routinization has occurred but that this routinization continues to be confronted with new tensions and challenges. One difficulty that Mormons face (as do other churches) is the continued response to accommodation. It seems that the Mormons have responded with the compromise of the denomination: that of the middle-ground balance of polarities, i.e., not choosing the extremes of the cult or the over-formalization of the church, but rather the middle ground of the denomination. This I intend to show in the following pages.

According to several authors and observers of Mormonism it is commonly understood that the religion went through significant transformations around the end of the nineteenth century and the beginning of the twentieth. Two major realignments seem to have taken place: the emergence of a bureaucracy and changes in some of the basic faith tenets. Both of these processes illustrate the transformation of the religion as a cult in the nineteenth century that was in high tension with the American society and held non-traditional beliefs to a denomination with low tension and the denial of some non-traditional beliefs in the twentieth century.

In Chapter Six we saw some of the new teachings of early Mormonism. Many of these same teachings continue through to the present. Several things illustrate the fact that nineteenth-century Mormonism had elements of the church and cult types. Shipps (1985) reviews the major Conference addresses of the church; in 1916, the president (Joseph F. Smith) announced that the Church of Latter-Day Saints was "The Lord's true Church," that the people were "God's People," and that outside of this church there was no salvation. Cultic beliefs were also promulgated: that God is not a spirit but a material being of the male gender and that each believer moves toward an eternal goal which is that of "eternal progression" or the transformation of each man and woman into the "godhead" (Shipps 1985:143-149).

Three other central positions of the religion during the nineteenth century contributed to its being in high tension with the American culture: the doctrine and practice of polygyny,[13] the creation of a new Zion or the coming of utopia, and the establishment of a theocracy in the Utah territory. Shepherd and Shepherd (1984) did a content analysis of all the major speeches of the church presidents from 1830 to 1979. What they were looking for were the kinds of themes that changed according to the years. They argue that there were three main sources that contributed to the transformation of nineteenth-century Mormonism to the Mormonism of the twentieth century: external social pressure, internal growth and success, and secularization.

External pressures led the church to change its polygyny tenet when, in 1890, President Woodruff, as "prophet and revelator," announced that the church would no longer sanction the practice and issued what came to be known as the "Manifesto." Also, at the peak of the civil rights movement, the church lifted the ban on the ordination of black males to the priesthood. In response to the accusation of exclusivism, the official church no longer strove to build a utopian society in a theocratic political system but now emphasized individual moral reform similar to the conservative evangelical Christian position.

Internal pressures also changed the religion. Its leaders mitigated the emphasis on exclusivity and were less likely to proclaim so strongly that LDS was the one and only true religion. Secularization processes have also taken their toll. Using Berger's (1969) analysis of secularization, Shepherd and Shepherd (1984:183-193) provide evidence that a large bureaucratic structure has evolved within Mormonism that resembles secular bureaucracies. Beliefs have also changed. Although the core doctrines (like revelation, divine intervention, authenticity of the Book of Mormon, the divine atonement of Jesus, the universal resurrection, and the immortality of the soul) have not changed, other tenets have (see above regarding polygyny and black male ordination). The Shepherds see that from 1889 to 1979, the

---

13 Shepherd and Shepherd (1984:81) quote from a speech of the First Presidency at the October Conference, 1885, which provides the basis for polygyny: "We cannot withdraw or renounce it. God revealed it, and He has promised to maintain it, and to bless those who obey it."

These authors go on to say that this practice was a divine commandment on which the members' personal salvation depended and which could not be set aside without violating God's will.

accent on belief distinctiveness has declined and the focus on end-times theology or eschatology has also declined.

Using the elements as outlined in Table 8.4 one may be able to understand to what extent, if any, the Church of Jesus Christ of Latter-Day Saints has become a denomination. As for the dilemma of salvation, a middle road has been chosen. We saw that in the nineteenth century, the church was very exclusivistic. Throughout the twentieth century, however, this has declined. On the question of unity, LDS appears to be somewhat midway between the church type and the denomination type. Unity of the institution under the authority of the central headquarters continues to be important. On the other side, with the increased emphasis on individual religious experience, there is a movement toward unity of experience among members.

Organizationally, we observe that the authority of the religion, especially in the hands of the president, is considered to be divinely inspired. Yet evidence of pragmatism is abundant. It may mean that in the theology of the religion (the ecclesiology), the belief that the authority is rooted not in divine approbation but in the routine and day-to-day operation of the church pragmatism is the norm.

Sacramentally, LDS is close to the church type. A condition for membership in the church is baptism. The more striking sacramental tenet of the church is found in the interpretation of marriage. Marriage is very central to the theology of the church and is considered to be of eternal duration (if a couple is married in the temple). Changes in eschatology have definite signs of increased denominationalization. In the nineteenth century, utopian beliefs were very salient (hence the name of the religion). However, as noted above, the focus is more on individual eternal destiny more like the denomination type.

Shipps (1985:148) argues that LDS is especially a corporate church in that "the unit of exaltation"[14] is the family and the whole church. However, "the unit of salvation" is in fact the individual. Shepherd and Shepherd (1984) add that personal prayer time and personal revelations have had increased salience within the General Assemblies during this century. The dilemma of the faith and works appears to be in the middle with a balance of faith (considered to be a knowledge of the fundamental truths of Mormonism) and moral reform.

237

---

14 This means that one not only needs to be a baptized Mormon but must continue to be a faithful follower in order to be exalted or raised up to eternal life.

From the Sect to the Denomination: The Case of the Assemblies of God

From the outline of the sect as a type of religious organization, the church called the Pentecostal Assemblies of God can be qualified as being a sect in its inception. Beginning in 1914, through a gathering of three hundred persons, the church has grown to an estimated two million members with over ten thousand congregations and 22,584 ordained clergy (quoted in Poloma 1989, from Jacquet 1988).

With this growth, there is evidence that the church has become more and more like any other denomination in the United States. This is given credibility on several counts. Poloma (1989), in her analysis of the denomination, sees that the structure is a combination of the congregational nature of the denomination as well as the presbyterian model. The General Assembly is made up of elected pastors from the local, regional, and state levels. This reveals the democratic nature of the organization which is a characteristic of the denomination. In addition, much of the "work" of religion is not guided by charisma (from scriptures, revelation or prayer) but from an American way of doing things: pragmatism.

| SWITCHING AND DISAFFILIATION

An additional and important question to ask about religious organizations is to inquire why people "switch" or move from one kind of religious organization to another, or from the various kinds of groups (for example, Catholic, Protestant, Jewish, Islam or New Religious Movements) to others. Beyond that, why do some leave the religious organization into which they were socialized into no affiliation at all?

Since a landmark study done in the 1960s by Stark and Glock (1968), there has been a significant amount of research on the topic of switching and disaffiliation. I shall review a selection of this research that documents both the patterns and the complexities of the social phenomena. The review will conclude with some reflections on seeing these patterns and complexities through the lens of Weber's charisma and routinization of charisma.

Stark and Glock (1968), using a sample drawn in California, discovered that about 40 per cent of their sample switched and that the following patterns were occurring: men and women moved from more conservative churches and sects to more liberal and upwardly mobile denominations like the Episcopalians, Presbyterians, and Congregationalists. Those groups which lost membership included Methodists, Lutherans, non-Christians, and those with no affiliation. The reason they gave, as noted by Roof and Hadaway (1979), was theological. Believers moved upward because the

238

destination denominations were more liberal and had demythologized belief systems which were more conducive to modernity.

In Calgary, Bibby and Brinkerhoff (1973) found evidence for little switching but for increased growth within evangelical sects. Their research was sparked by a position stated by Kelly (1972), who documented evidence that conservative churches were growing at the expense of the liberal ones. They explain growth not because people were leaving mainline Canadian churches (particularly Roman Catholic, Anglican [Episcopalian], and United Church of Canada) or coming from disaffiliates, but because these congregations were able to socialize their youth well and members were moving from one evangelical sect to another. For the latter reason, they use the term *Circulation of the Saints*.

Hadaway (1978) argues, from several General Social Surveys conducted between 1973 and 1977, that even though there was a general pattern of movement from liberal to conservative affiliations (as noted in his and Roof's study below), the patterns are more complex. Baptist and Lutherans were more stable than other mainline churches, but at the extreme of the conservative continuum, many members were switching. This offers some explanation for these new patterns. It could be that the Lutheran and Baptist stability is realized because they tend to concentrate geographically, the Baptists in the south and the Lutherans in the Mid-West. With such high concentration there would be fewer alternatives and people would be more likely to marry endogamously (thus precluding switching because of one's spouse being of another group).

Roof and Hadaway's (1979) research is similar to Kelly's. Using General Social Surveys from 1973 to 1976, they found that, in contrast to Stark and Glock (1968), the mainline churches or more liberal ones were losing members to sects and that more and more were disaffiliating themselves entirely from mainline religions. Those who lost members include United Methodists, United Presbyterians, and the United Church of Christ. The Southern Baptists, Mormons, Jehovah's Witnesses, and various Pentecostal and other sects gained members.

Why the discrepancy? Wuthnow (1976 and cited in Sherkat 1991) believes that the 1960s stand out in contrast to earlier and later decades, because in that decade, the counter-culture was born and new religious groups were emerging. This may explain, in part, why many religious nones[15] became affiliated but does not seem to give an account of why liberal churches were growing. A better explanation may be that Stark and Glock's study was regional and the Roof and Hadaway one was a national

---

15 Those who do not have any religious affiliation.

sample. Something may have been present in Northern California that was not common in other parts of the U.S.

Newport (1979), in his use of national studies from 1975 to 1976, adds to the discussion. His research gives further reasons for the phenomenon of switching. First of all, he discovered that switching was substantial. Of the 30 per cent who switched, 38 per cent moved out of the religious system altogether, leaving 18 per cent who did change. The most common reason cited for switching was a change from one's affiliation to that of one's spouse (religious exogamy). Newport noted that 40 per cent of all those who switched did so for that reason. According to different groups or denominations, Baptists, Roman Catholics, and Methodists lost members, while Episcopalians, Presbyterians, and sects gained. This evidence confirms data from Stark and Glock (1968) as well as from Roof and Hadaway (1979). Movement is not consistently from liberal to conservative or vice versa.

A later article by Hadaway (1980) adds a further reason for switching. Using a 1978 Gallup Poll, his analysis included measurements of religiosity or religiousness (measured by ritual participation and religious experience) that discriminated between the switchers and the *stayers* (those who did not change). The switchers were more religious than were the stayers. In fact, 60 per cent of the switchers were religious seekers and were more likely to be evangelicals. Roof (1989) asks the question of the number of times that switchers do switch. In his analysis of the 1988 General Social Survey, he found that 33 per cent of those who switched had switched more than once. The reasons the respondents gave for their mobility was religious exogamy (they changed because of their spouse) and other family members and friends. This confirms a network theory of conversion first presented by Lofland and Stark (1965)

In reviewing the literature on switching from the 1960s until the 1980s, Sherkat (1991) synthesized the research and found that there had been five sets of theories used to explain the phenomenon: status theories (upward or downward mobility to higher or lower status denominations); family structure (marriage and socialization of children); network theory (from Lofland and Stark [1965] on the tendency to convert because of family and friendship social networks); denominational characteristics (if a denomination is liberal, moderate or conservative); and generational characteristics (age differences). He used the same database as Roof (1989) and found evidence to support all five theories. People switched to increase status, because of the faith commitment of their spouses, due to friends and relatives, because they were attracted either to the liberal or conservative teachings of the other affiliation, and because they were young. Of all, the strongest predictor was religious exogamy.

Hadaway and Long Marler (1993) asked the opposite question on switching: why do adherents not switch or why are they stable? Using a range of General Social Surveys from 1973 to 1990, they confirmed the earlier finding of Hadaway (1980) that the switchers are more religious than are the stayers. They read the Bible more, pray more frequently, attend church more often, give more money to the church and are more likely to say that they are "*born again*." Other reasons are given for those who stay. They are more likely to be socialized into their denomination from early childhood and are more likely to marry someone from their same affiliation. The switchers had marginalized church affiliation when they were young, had parents who were married exogamously, and had irregular contact with relatives.

Bibby and Brinkerhoff (1994) returned to their study of the 1970s to see if their original findings held true (1973). They used comparative data from a revisit to 16 of the original 20 congregations they surveyed in 1970. They found few differences. Reaffiliates (those from other evangelical churches) made up 70 per cent of the congregations, birth was down somewhat to 17 per cent, and proselytism up modestly to 13 per cent. However, they offered some new reflections to their original thesis of the *circulation of the saints*. Even though the circulation thesis is accurate, the Conservative Protestants (using evidence from the Calgary study and national studies) are demonstrating impressive vitality in managing to maintain 10 per cent of the national religious market. They do this by continuing to hold their youth and through modest increases in evangelism. Mainline Christianity (Anglican, Roman Catholic, and United Church) are not even doing that and are losing ground in membership and commitment.

Hadaway and Long Marler (1996) considered that there was a problem in using the father's affiliation in estimating the rate of switching, which greatly exaggerates the actual rate of movement from non-affiliation to affiliation. Evidence for this was discovered in their analysis of the 1988 General Social Survey. One needs to take into consideration the wide range of family types in today's social landscape. Of particular note is the fact that the biological father is frequently absent, and it is thus necessary to use data that taps the mother's affiliation.

Sherkat and Wilson (1995) update the research on social status theory with the use of the New Paradigm in the social scientific study of religion (see Chapter One). They argue that high-status parents socialize their children into high-status denominations (of the church type), and that those who have "been left behind" by an upwardly mobile group tend to switch to a sect that is more conservative. Also, they found that those who seek out and want a strict religion choose conservative denominations. The authors note that it is the change in social status that prompts changes in affiliation.

The original discovery by Hadaway (1980) that those who switch are more religious is confirmed in a study of Presbyterian youths by Hoge, Johnson and Luidens (1995). Reasons given for those youths changing to affiliations close to the Presbyterian tradition include religious exogamy (again, changing to the religion of their spouses) and moving to a new city. Those who switch to traditions further removed from Presbyterianism do so because they are dissatisfied with the church's teaching. Those who move outside of the church are also more religious than those who switch to a church doctrinally close to them.

Musick and Wilson (1995) continue the interest in religious exogamy. Using the National Survey of Families and Households (1987-1988), they confirm previous studies on the centrality of religious exogamy in determining switching. Those persons who are part of a liberal denomination are more likely to switch to a more moderate or conservative group for reasons of marriage whereas those from relatively conservative groups (Methodists, Mormons, and Pentecostals) are less likely to move and become, especially, Catholic. On the other hand, a Catholic is more likely to opt out of religion altogether (disaffiliate) than convert to a spouse's Protestant faith.

Much has been learned about the phenomenon of switching from about thirty years of research. We know more of the rates of, directions of, and the reasons for switching. One finding stands out that gives credibility to charisma and routinization processes. It has been found that switchers tend to be more religious than non-switchers. One could argue that the switchers are closer to the charisma of Christianity, and the stayers to its more routinized form. It may also be reasoned (although not measured in these studies) that the switchers are more intrinsic-committed, while the stayers are extrinsic-consensual.

| THE INTEREST AND THE SUPPORT GROUP

The Interest Group

In Chapter Three, under the subtitle of cultural boundaries, we were introduced to the work of Robert Wuthnow. There we discovered that he observed three major restructuring processes of American religion. Within the third process, interest groups became more and more salient as an alternative to large churches (Wuthnow 1988a:100-131 and 1988b:496).

This is not a new organizational type but, rather, a group that attracts members because of a common cause or purpose. Wuthnow (1988a:104) describes it as "becom[ing] a vehicle for articulating religious themes in relation to issues of broader social significance." Although they are not new in American religion (some nineteenth-century examples include the Women's Christian Temperance Union, the Anti-Saloon League, and the Oxford Movement in England), their growth has been significant since 1960 with an increase of 300 new organizations (Wuthnow 1988a:112). There are numerous kinds, including Bible study groups, religious coalitions against nuclear warfare, prison ministries, holistic health, positive thinking, group therapy, healing ministries, and the like. The Canadian experience is also like this. Bibby (1987:126) does not use the term "interest groups" but he has this in mind when he argues that Canadian affiliates tend to choose from a whole variety of options from home Bible study groups to anti-abortion lobby groups.

Wuthnow (1988a:128-130) offers an interpretation that builds on my thesis of tension and dilemma. He notes that just as there has been a decline in the saliency of denominationalism in the United States and an increasing process of centralization, there has also been discontent with this. A response to this dilemma of the administrative order has been a protest. This protest has not taken the form of a new sect, cult or denomination, but rather a new form: "the interest group." Within this group, members feel a sense that they are involved, that they have a connection to others in primary relations, and that they can join forces to meet a common goal. Wuthnow (1988a:125) writes: "the growth of special purpose groups in American religion since WWII has undoubtedly contributed positively to the revival of religious commitment."

However, even the interest groups are not immune to routinization. These groups emerge as protest movements with concomitant grass-roots enthusiasm (revitalized charisma). This enthusiasm becomes institutionalized in professional staff roles which leads to considerations of career advancement, salaries, budgets, and organization preservation. Another problem emerges in the relationships of interest groups with one another and the particular congregation and/or denomination. They carry with themselves a strong potential for fractionalization and competition. Also, they may tend to follow the fissions common in the public sphere on such issues as pro-life/pro-choice, ecology/work, gay rights/heterosexual rights, and the like.

The Support Group

Wuthnow (1996) argues that there is currently a fourth restructuring or realignment of American religion: the emergence of the small group movement (see Chapter Three for the first three). Using a national survey that included 1,000 respondents involved in small groups, 900 who are not, and in-depth interviews with a smaller number, Wuthnow concretizes the concept of the small group and its importance in late twentieth-century American society.

From these data, Wuthnow estimates that about 40 per cent of all Americans belong to a small group that meets on a regular basis. They encompass a wide variety: Sunday school classes, Bible study groups, Alcoholics Anonymous and other twelve-step groups, youth groups, singles groups, book discussion groups, sports and hobby groups, and political or civic groups (1996:4). This translates into hundreds of thousands of small groups, not a small number. The majority of these are religious; two-thirds have some connection to churches or synagogues. Wuthnow restricts his research to those of the Judeo-Christian tradition. If one added those involved in New Religious Movements or the New Age Movement, the numbers would be even more impressive.

Stories tabulated from this research project reveal that those who have joined these groups testify that their lives have been enriched, they have found new friends, received warm emotional support, and have grown in their spirituality. Many have overcome major addictions. Others reveal that their identity has changed and they feel much more positive about themselves. Two major themes capture the various experiences of the participants: the quest for community and spirituality. Wuthnow adds a third theme: how the movement is contextualized historically and socially into the American society.

Belonging or being part of a community has been a central theme of the sociology of religion since its inception, especially through the insights of Durkheim. This is a central theme and quest of small group participants. The small group is characterized as purposive, intentional, and voluntaristic. In this sense, small groups are different from families, ethnic affiliations, and neighbourhoods. Members tend to offer and receive emotional care rather than physical or economic support. They are exposed to a network of care and support as well as to an ideology or a mythology of the group. I shall return to this in the section, below, on the quest for the sacred or spirituality.

Emotional support is defined as encouragement rather than criticism or guidance. Certain norms have emerged: tolerance of diversity and selecting a group more for what one can receive than give is also common. Members tend to be substantially committed but with options. They would not likely devote their whole life to the group or alter their career plans to accommodate the needs of the group; if they find that the group is burdensome or unfulfilling, they may leave. A hallmark of the movement is to enable members to adapt to the emotional pressures of family, relationships, work or school. Wuthnow notes that both strengths and weaknesses characterize the movement:

To their credit, they provide us with small portable sources of inter-
personal support. Their weakness lies in their inability to forge the
more enduring bonds that many of us would like or to strongly resist
the fragmenting forces in our society. (1996:16)

The second major theme of the movement is the quest for the sacred.
Participants claim that their faith has become more important to them and
that they have found others with whom they can pray and share their spiritual struggles. Wuthnow considers that the kind of spirituality emerging
from the movement is redefining how Americans image the sacred. The
deity is seen to be a god who loves them, cares for them, is interested in
their lives, accepts them, and pastors them. Wuthnow observes that the
world view or mythology of the group which sees the sacred as personal,
intimate, kind, and loving is correlated with the importance of intimacy in
human relationships.

245

The quest for and the reception of the sacred do not simply happen.
These groups prescribe rituals for growing closer to the sacred. Books are
studied, the Bible is reflected upon, and prayers are said together. Being
disciplined in one's spiritual life is another common norm in the groups.
Something is said of the goal but the dominant impulse is the sharing of
the joys of the journey. The signs of the presence of the sacred are real and
pragmatic: in feelings of security, peace, happiness, and a good self-image.
An interesting pattern of spirituality is emerging that is in contrast to the
kind common in the denominations: "the kind of faith that focuses heavily
on feelings and on getting along rather than encouraging worshipful obedience to or reverence toward a transcendent God" (1996:19).

Wuthnow's third theme is an interpretive one: linking the small group
movement to American society. His primary thesis is that the movement
fits well with trends already at work in American society and is not in a con-
frontational stance with secular culture. Some of the cultural values
included in the movement are democracy, variety, pragmatism, voluntarism, and the diminished honour of authority (small-group leaders are
more like facilitators than authority figures).

Smaller groups have a distinct advantage over churches and sects. They
require virtually no resources other than a place to meet and time offered by
the participants. They can meet the needs of members (both communal and
sacred) without paying rent, supporting a minister, priest or rabbi, or
underwriting the expenses of a national bureaucracy.

The small-group movement has taken on organizational forms common
in America and has adapted them to a new social situation. They have been
successful in making possible what Durkheim (1933) calls *secondary groups*
and de Tocqueville (1945) refers to as *free associations*. Wuthnow says that

the small-group movement is effecting a quiet revolution in American society. It provides a kind of social interaction that many busy people who are also rootless find attractive without making significant changes to their lifestyle. These groups may be interpreted as functioning as a glue in holding the society together as well as being a solvent that provides a way for people to break from other kinds of social groups which held them in some kind of bondage. They seem to perform a difficult dual function: providing both social support and freedom at the same time. As we have seen in the study of religion thus far, this is a relatively rare achievement.

I conclude with a quotation from Wuthnow, who sees the movement at a critical juncture:

> In my view, the small-group movement is now at a critical juncture in its development. To date, despite the various criticisms I have already raised, its social effects have been largely beneficial. The movement has provided caring and support for millions of Americans who were suffering from addictions, personal crisis, loneliness, and self-doubt and has helped them rebuild their lives. It has been a source of vitality for many religious organizations by providing reasons for people to join these organizations and to start thinking about their spiritual journeys. The movement has skilfully deployed its resources for people to reach virtually all segments of the population.... Consequently, it is now poised to exercise even greater influence on American society in the next decade than it has in the past two decades. The resources are there: models have been developed, leaders have been trained, national networks have been established, and millions of satisfied participants are ready to enlist their friends and neighbours. (1996:26-27)

In the light of the Weberian thesis of charisma and routinization of charisma, there appears to be sufficient evidence to indicate that the charisma is being revitalized. This charisma is not only restricted to the small groups themselves but also to the religious organizations that they tend to be part of. Further, members of these small groups appear to represent intrinsic/committed spirituality. It remains to be seen if members will be able to retain this charisma and intrinsic/committed spirituality or go the way of so many movements towards routinization and extrinsic/consensual spirituality.

THE STRUCTURAL ADAPTABILITY
OF RELIGIOUS ORGANIZATIONS

Warner (1993), in his presentation of a new paradigm in the sociology of religion, argues that religious organizations have structurally adapted to political and economic organizations by becoming increasingly centralized and heavily bureaucratized. They have done so by moving from a centripetal focus (a movement toward centralization) to a centrifugal one (toward de-centralization).

In the case of mainline Protestantism, the centripetal processes (resulting, especially, in the growth of the National Council of Churches) began after the Civil War and continued through to the end of the Vietnam War. Referring to Hutchison (1989), mainline Protestantism looked more and more like a protected establishment. McKinney and Roof (1990) argue that as denominational and ecumenical budgets have been cut, mainline headquarters have relocated to smaller urban centres away from the large metropolitan regions. A further illustration of the centrifugal process is what Wuthnow (1988a) refers to as the "declining significance of denominationalism." Warner (1993) comments that as the centrifugal force moves people away from denominations they are "reshuffled into new combinations" such as the "restructuring of religion" toward interest groups.

An additional centrifugal process is what Warner calls "*de facto* Congregationalism.*" This means that the local religious community is in fact defined by those who assemble together rather than by those who live in the same geographical area. Even within the Roman Catholic Church, the archetype of the parish and bureaucracy is moving more and more in the direction of the gathering concept. Warner refers to the social historian Jay Dolan (1985), who notes that this process has long historical roots in American Catholicism. This is also evident in Judaism, significantly through the increased involvement of women (Prell 1989) and among immigrant Muslims who see their congregational leader, the *imam*, as much more than just a prayer leader (Waugh 1992).

CONCLUSIONS: THE QUESTION
OF THE MAINTENANCE OF CHARISMA

This chapter has focused on the third dilemma of institutionalization identified by O'Dea and O'Dea (1983). A central issue is the dilemma that in order for a religious organization to be effective it needs some sort of organizational structure. Thus, some level of routinization is necessary. However, if the routinization processes increase, the original charisma is lost and what is left is an over-elaborate organization or bureaucracy that tends to be self-perpetuating. The key seems to be some sort of balance.

The object is to have enough routine to make effective the religious organization but also to maintain a certain element of the charisma as well. This chapter has illustrated how difficult it is to obtain this balance.

Religious organizations seem to be only partially successful. There appears to be a tendency to extremes of instability (as in the case of the sect and the cult) and to over-elaboration (as in the case of the church). Four attempts have been made to construct a balance: the movement of renewal, the denomination, the interest groups, and centrifugal processes. Even here, however, the success has only been partial. I would contend that these dynamics will likely not cease in the near future and that religious organizations will continue to have to struggle with this dilemma in a search for more ways to maintain the charisma while being organizationally effective.

CHAPTER NINE

The Dilemma of Delimitation: The Study of Ethos

This chapter charts another path into the domain of religion: the study of ethos in general and religious morality in particular. I have drawn other paths into the terrain of the sacred through religious experience, myth, ritual, and organizations. My theory and review of the scientific study of religion led me to argue that the genesis of religion is in religious experience, both social and personal, which is followed by the construction of a mythology to explain that experience. Rituals are fashioned to continue that experience through one's life-course and to pass it on to succeeding generations. Thereafter religious organizations emerge for the maintenance, framing or housing of religious experiences, myths, and rituals.

Within these organizations are other paths which Geertz (1973) calls *ethos*. One may see this as a cluster of behavioural codes including values, norms, morals, and laws. Anthropologists and cultural sociologists have referred to values as providing a general orientation to life while norms outline more specific kinds of behaviour. Another way in which we may look at norms is to consider them as "the rules or standards that govern interaction" (Moot 1965:24). A particular species of a norm is what Sumner (1906:80), a founder of American sociology, terms the *more* that has the authority of facts (1906). Mores, or moral codes, carry more weight and channel human behaviour according to effects: rewards for conformity and punishments for disobedience. Laws are specific norms and mores that are codified by some state or societal authority. The cultural analyst Robert Wuthnow (1987) adds another important element to an understanding of morality: the provision for social order in a society. This recalls Durkheim, who also saw morality as a basis of social solidarity. In religious circles, these mores have even more of an impact because they carry with them some sort of sacred approbation and legitimacy. A popular term to describe them is an *ethic*, and a collection of ethics would be called an *ethical system*. For example, as in the case of the ten commandments of Judaism, conformity means long life and prosperity, and disobedience connotes suffering, a shortened life, and poverty (see Deuteronomy 28).

Like myth, ritual, and organization, the purpose of the ethical or moral system is to channel and to keep believers close to the original religious experience, the pristine charismatic moment. This we may call the *spirit of the law*. To enable a moral code to be operative in people's lives, a process of *delimitation* is necessary. Delimitation refers to a provision of limits to a fluid and illusive religious experience that functions to specify human behaviour as closely as possible to religious experience. Further, in the process, *elaboration* frequently results.

O'Dea and O'Dea (1983:83) explain it in the following way. In the process of applying the religious ideal to "the prosaic and concrete, the content of the message may itself appear to take on a prosaic quality and lose those charismatic elements that originally moved men." There is a pit on either side of the narrow charismatic road: one waters down the original message, and the other offers a rigid position that kills the spirit. The dangers of distortion of the faith require the formulation of dogma, but once established, the definitions themselves pose the possibility of another distortion. The definitions become "a vast intellectual structure which serves not to guide the faith of untrained specialists but rather to burden it" (O'Dea and O'Dea 1983:61). Jesus, for example, repeatedly repudiated the Judaism of his day for its empty legalism, yet Christians have developed their own pharisaic practices. The history of religions provides countless examples of petrified doctrine and moral proscriptions, which in time may be challenged. In the course of being challenged, however, there is always the danger of abandoning a core message offered by the prophet.

This, then, is another one of the dilemmas of religion: delimitation. Using this as the framework, I plan to outline the intricate connection between myth, ritual, and ethos. Anthropological and sociological research will illustrate this connection. Thereafter, I will provide a morphology of morality that was constructed in a review of the literature from religious studies, anthropology, and sociology. Where appropriate, the dilemma of delimitation will be used to illustrate the morphology. Then, research on Buddhism in Burma,[1] Roman Catholicism in the West, and recent new religious movements in California will provide the empirical basis for the dilemma and will enable us to understand the vital place of ethos in religion. Lastly, using the work on the restructuring of American religion by Wuthnow (1988a) that I outlined in Chapter Three and Chapter Eight, we will see how different religious world views elicit various ethical systems.

---

[1] The official name of the country is now Myanmar.

Within this restructuring framework, I shall include a brief discussion of the morality of the Nation of Islam.

THE CONNECTION BETWEEN MYTH, RITUAL, AND ETHOS

There appears to be general consensus among anthropologists and socio-logists of religion that the moral or ethical dimension is central to the understanding of religion. Dissenting voices to this include the nineteenth-century anthropologist Edward Tyler and the functionalist anthropologist Bronislaw Malinowski. Tyler (1929), in his study of folk religions and ani-mism, argued that ethical laws stood independent of animistic beliefs and rites. He was joined by Malinowski (1932) who relegated religion to the ultimate ends of the Argonaut peoples and saw it as practically divorced from the functional aspects of everyday life.

251

Influenced by Yinger's (1959) outline of the connection between religion and morality, the Rice University anthropologist Edward Norbeck (1961) saw some basis for Tyler's and Malinowski's positions. For example, he found that, among the Inuit, morality is relatively removed from religious myths and to break a moral code is not to entail after-life punishment. However, in contrast to Tyler and Malinowski, Norbeck discovered that for the Manus peoples of Melanesia, morality is intricately tied to religion. Strict moral codes govern sexuality. To illustrate, one is guilty of sexual transgression even if one inadvertently sees private parts of the opposite sex. Laziness, theft, and disobedience to elders incur illness as a punishment from the ancestral spirit. He writes: "Any moral transgression is thus the concern of everyone and the compulsion to follow the code is strong. Public accusations of guilt, confession, and expiation also bring shame and loss of social prestige and serve to strengthen the supernatural sanctions" (1961:184).

The bulk of the evidence does reveal that there is a substantial inter-con-nection between myth, ritual, and morality in religion. Inspired by Geertz (1973), Figure 9.1 illustrates this connection.

I begin with the heart of religion, the sacred that is interactively linked to myth, ritual, and ethos. Geertz (1973: 126ff) explains the connection between myth, ritual, and ethos in the following way. Religion consists of a myth, a ritual, and a code. Myths provide believers with what "is," the fac-tual, a view of reality, and the ethos is the "ought" that flows from the myth. He writes:

> A people's ethos is the tone, character, and quality of their life, its moral and aesthetic style and mood; it is the underlying attitude

toward themselves and their world that life reflects. Their world view [in my terms, myth] is their picture of the way things in sheer actuality are, their concept of nature, of self, of society. It contains their most comprehensive ideas of order ... the ethos is made intellectually reasonable by being shown to represent a way of life implied by the actual state of affairs which the world view describes, and the world view is made emotionally acceptable by being presented as an image of an actual state of affairs of which a way of life is an authentic expression. (1973:127)

These world views, however, are not merely in the ideal realm. They are represented in symbols such as a Buffalo totem of the Sioux peoples of the American Great Plains, the cross of Western Christianity, the icon of Eastern Christianity, the serene Buddha statue in Burma or the crescent of Islam of Saudi Arabia. As we saw in Chapter Seven, rituals dramatize, make present, and express the myth through ceremonies. This is to enable the practitioners to have a religious experience. Thus, the connection between myth, ritual, and the ethos is profound. In other words, myth makes meaning of the cosmos, ritual enacts the myth, and ethos provides the quotidian channel to live out the myth. Again, one comes full circle. Ideally, if believers know the myth in an experiential way, enact it through ceremonies, and live it out in daily life, they increasingly come in contact with the sacred.

What I propose to do in this section is to provide empirical evidence for these connections. My thesis is that myth and ethos mutually reinforce one another, and ritual reinforces ethos. I will provide evidence from anthropological studies on folk and Eastern religions (Buddhism in Burma) and recent surveys in North America.

THE SACRED, MYTH, RITUAL, AND ETHOS

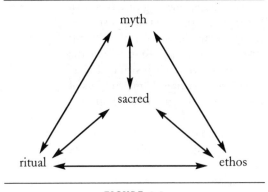

FIGURE 9.1

Connections in Folk Religions

Goode (1951) reviewed four folk peoples and outlined their religious systems: the Dahomey of Africa, the Tikopia of Polynesia, the Zuni of New Mexico, and the Murngin of Australia. Goode explains the connection between myth and the ethos. The social character of religion is not only horizontal (implying the ethical or moral) but also vertical: between the believers and their deities. Social values are, at the same time, ultimate values linking the person to the sacred. He notes that folk gods have the same notion of what is good and evil as does the tribe, for "as long as the group is living according to precept, the general action of the spiritual entities is expected to be beneficial, not inimical" (1951:44). The precept that is closest to the sacred is to protect the holy from the profane. One needs to honour the sacred as in the case of the Tikopia. During a sacred ceremony, the people are forbidden to talk about mundane matters. One may argue that one of the most basic precepts in religion is: "You shall not let the profane intrude upon the sacred." Among the Dahomey of Africa, the ancestral spirit called *Sir Ghost* guards the family and supervises the morals of the kin. If, for example, there is a sexual offence (for example, adultery), *Sir Ghost* will send an illness to the offending party. Confession and some sacrifice to the deity need to be offered to compensate for the offence. The basis of morality among the Zuni of New Mexico is honour; honour to the elders expresses honour to the deities.

253

The most extensive analysis of the connection between myth, ritual, and ethos in folk religion is from Durkheim (1915) in his secondary analysis of the tribal peoples of Australia. His interpretation can be illustrated by an extension of Figure 9.1 and shown here as Figure 9.2.

With Durkheim, even more so than with Geertz, ethos is central to religion. If we recall, the totem is the focal religious symbol for Durkheim. This symbol is the symbol of the sacred *par excellence* that reflects the animal or the vegetable holy to the tribe. Again, the tribe is named after the totem, and the most basic taboo of each tribe is that they should not eat of the totem, for this is an intrusion of the profane into the sacred. Again, the totem can be identified with the social group, and, thus, worship of the deity in the totem is really the worship of the group.

A special feature of the totem is the presence of a moral force that is believed to reside within the totem. To impart this moral force to the believer, it is necessary to celebrate a ritual. In this ritual, members frequently

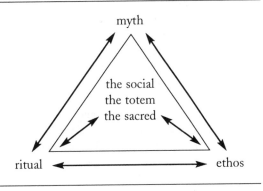

THE SACRED, THE SOCIAL, MYTH, RITUAL, AND ETHOS

myth

the social
the totem
the sacred

ritual ⟷ ethos

FIGURE 9.2

gather, recall their ancient myths, and are empowered in a kind of sacred effervescence. In this environ, the individual receives the power to obey the moral order of the tribe that is believed to be enacted by the sacred. In fact, when the believer obeys the codes, he feels empowered and full of confidence, courage, and boldness in action (1915:211). Thus there is a profound connection between belief in the totem (the myth), the ritual of a common celebration (to enact the myth), and an empowerment from the totem to obey the moral codes which, in turn, provide the believer with more power.

Of course, Durkheim notes, this deity is none other than the society itself which is the source of social control that "acts" upon the individual to enforce conformity. He writes:

> As long as scientific analysis does not come to teach it to them, men know well that they are acted upon, but they do not know by whom. So they must invent by themselves the idea of these powers with which they feel themselves a connection and from that, we are able to catch a glimpse of the way by which they were led to represent them under forms that are really foreign to their nature and to transfigure them by thought. (1915:209)

Finally, the presence of a moral force is so salient to Durkheim's anthropology and sociology of religion that he calls the religious gathering a "moral community" in his definition of religion (see Chapter Two).

Connections in Eastern Religions: The Case of Buddhism in Burma

Buddhism has an ancient history and preceded the emergence of both Christianity and Islam. Founded by the revolutionary prophet, Gautama Buddha (c. 563 – c. 483 BC), Buddhism shares with the other Eastern religions a monism that does not posit a separate creator deity (see Chapter Two on religious myths). Throughout its long history, Buddhism, like Christianity, has gone through many transformations and creations of different versions (sects of systems). Two major schools are identified: *Theravada* (the Lesser Vehicle or the way of the elders) and *Mahayana* (the Great Vehicle). The *Theravada* school predominates in Sri Lanka, Thailand, Burma, and Indo-China. The *Mahayana* alternative is the Buddhism of North Asia in China, Korea, Japan, and the Himalayas (Noss and Noss 1984 and Florida 1994).

The anthropologist Spiro (1982) illustrates the linkage between myth and morality through his field work among the *Theravada* (*Hinayana*) Buddhists of Burma. In this work, Spiro identifies four types: Nibbanic,

Kammatic, Apotropaic, and Esoteric. Each provides evidence of the vital linkage between myth and ethos.

Morality is at the very heart of Buddhism for it is one of the three stages of salvation: *sila* (morality), *samadhi* (meditation), and *prajna* (wisdom). However, salvation from the world of suffering (in the hope to reach the "land of no suffering or nirvana") is centred on meditation in the original teaching of Gautama. Through meditation, one becomes detached from all things, both internal desires and external troubles. In the state of detachment, then, one practises the great precepts of Buddha, especially compassion toward all creatures.

Buddhism received the myth of *Karma* or the process of rebirth from Hinduism. Salvation consists of being freed from the karma that would reduce one's social status in the next life. For example, through meditation and following the precepts, one can achieve a better state in another life. Eventually, one is freed completely from Karma to enter Nirvana or eternal peace, calm, and the total cessation of suffering. Spiro argues that for the various kinds of *Theravada* Buddhism in Burma, this process and goal are quite different.

255

Nibbanic Buddhism (after *nibbana*, nirvana) is the closest version to approximate the path of the Gautama. It is the Buddhism of the monks who meditate for long hours each day. They obey the five precepts (actually, in some cases eight or ten) as a means to achieve nirvana: "morality is primarily a form of spiritual discipline; it is a means to the attainment of a certain psychological state which is the first condition for the achievement of nirvana" (Spiro 1982:47).

Kammatic Buddhism (after *Kamma*, one's Karma) is a routinized form of Buddhism which focuses not on achieving Nirvana but, rather, on improving one's karma. These adherents strive not so much to renounce desire and pleasure, to eliminate rebirth, but to have a *better* rebirth. The central process is not meditation as in the case of Nibbanic Buddhism but, rather, following the precepts. It is in this form of Buddhism that the linkage between myth and morality takes the form of a "salvation by works." It is doing good works and not transgressing the precepts that a better karma is assured in the next life. The most positive "good work" is giving to others and protecting living things from death. There are some interesting local customs of morality. For example, if a man commits adultery (breaking the third precept), he will be reborn with a small penis, whereas if a woman does the same, she will be reborn a prostitute.

Apotropaic Buddhism (from the Greek, a ritual designed to avert evil) moves Buddhism away from other-worldly mysticism to inner-worldly asceticism, to use the Weberian term. The focus is on this world, the everyday and the mundane. Both morality and ritual (Nibbanic and Kammatic Buddhism do not accent ritual) are designed to ward off evil and to protect the faithful against calamity and illness. In contrast to the previous forms of Burmese Buddhism, this folk Buddhism acknowledges the presence of evil spirits that one needs to be protected from. Falling just short of believing that Gautama Buddha is a deity there to save them, they believe that the Buddha has "infused" protective power in His statues, in various rites, and in obeying the precepts.

Here, then, we see the unity and the interconnectedness of myth, ritual, and morality. The myth states that the world is suffused with evil spirits and that there is power in the Buddha statues, the monastery, the Buddhist teachings, and the precepts. By adhering to various rituals like reciting prayers, making offerings to the Buddha images or to the relics of the Buddha, and reciting the beads (repeating, for example, texts from the sacred canon) as well as obeying the five precepts, one is protected from evil in this life.

The fourth Buddhist form in Burma, Spiro calls *esoteric* or *chiliastic*[2] Buddhism (1982:162). In the tradition of the church-sect-cult typology that I investigated in Chapter Eight, esoteric Buddhism may be called a cult in that it is a syncretism of traditional Buddhist beliefs, local animistic practices, and quasi-secretive sects. Even though the Buddha is not a deity, his return is expected (theologians of Nibbanic Buddhism see Gautama Buddha as the fourth incarnation of the Buddha, and the fifth Buddha will bring on the eternal kingdom of the Buddha). However, there is also a belief in a mythical magician or *Weikza* who has enormous supernatural powers. For esoteric Buddhism, morality is secondary while the practice of magical rites to invoke the Weikza is primary. In this case, morality is connected less to myth than ritual.

Connections in the West: Current Research Linking Myth, Ritual, and Morality

Survey research documents a reasonably long tradition of linking myth, ritual, and morality. Gerhard Lenski (1963), in the late 1950s in Detroit, conducted research with 656 Roman Catholics, Protestants, and Jews. He found that devotionalism (as measured by personal communication to God through prayer and meditation) was associated with an ethic of helping or humanitarianism. Allport (1966), in his study of religion and prejudice, found that even though religious affiliates were more prejudiced than non-affiliates, members who were most active in their churches were least prejudiced.

---

2 The term refers to millennialism or religious belief that focuses on the coming of the divine kingdom, the future order, the future heaven on earth.

Later research is consistent with these studies of the 1960s. In a 1973 survey of San Francisco Bay area residents, Piazza and Glock (1979) found linkages between myth (measured by images of the divine), ritual, church attendance and daily prayer, and morality. Morality was measured as a willingness to perform compassionate acts. Those who had what the researchers called a "personal view of God" or a belief that God was active in their lives were more likely to attend church and pray and more likely to lend money to a co-worker without interest and give money to a stranger for bus fare. Morgan (1983) adds further credibility to the linkage between ritual and morality from data from a national representative sample ($N=1,467$). His findings reveal that those who pray frequently or those who have integrated prayer into their day-to-day lives are more likely to "stop and comfort a crying child," be a "good listener," "get along with loud and obnoxious people," and "turn the other cheek," than those who do not.

Lastly, the national study conducted by the Gallup organization (see Chapter Seven; Poloma and Gallup 1991), reveals similar results. Poloma and Gallup extend the measure of prayer beyond mere frequency to types of prayer: ritual prayer, reading from a prayer book or reciting memorized prayers, and conversational prayer, talking to God in one's own words. Two other types include petitionary prayer, asking God for favours, and meditative prayer — think about God, feel a divine presence, worship God, and try to listen to God speaking. A bivariate analysis[3] reveals that those who pray meditatively are more likely to forgive others who have hurt them and are less likely to nurture resentments than are those who use the other forms of prayer.

Summary of the Myth, Ritual, and Morality Connection

My thesis of this section is that there is a substantial linkage within religion between myth, ritual, and morality. By using anthropological evidence from studies of folk societies, religious studies of Buddhism, a case study of Burmese Buddhism, and survey findings of modern America, there is significant evidence that there is this linkage.

| A MORPHOLOGY OF MORALITY

As I researched the many studies of morality and religion, I detected an interesting pattern that illustrated the O'Dea and O'Dea delimitation dilemma. In the first and second parts of the text, I have given both sub-

---

3   The type of analysis that investigates to see if there is a significant relationship between two variables.

stantive and functional definitions of religion, myth, and ritual. In a morphology or typology of morality, we also discover both substantive and functional elements. A substantive understanding of morality is a precept or moral code that is proximate to the sacred. The example given is from Goode (1951), who uses Durkheim's distinction between the sacred and the profane which is at the core of this text. Almost universally among folk peoples, Durkheim (1915) and Goode (1951) observe that the "profane must not intrude into the sacred." More particularly from Durkheim (1915:43), we learn that there is a whole range of interdictions that protect and isolate the sacred from the profane. One might construct a moral code that would reflect the reality: "You shall not let the profane intrude into the sacred."[4]

Functional morality is what morality is to do, is to accomplish. Within functional morality, seven different forms appear: empowerment, bonding, ecology, social integration, worldly success, social control, and alienation. What I intend to do in this section of the chapter is to represent these seven types with empirical examples. I shall begin with the first function of morality: empowerment.

The Function of Empowerment

The focus on morality in Durkheim's work is on social control. Not only do moral codes come from the gods to induce conformity, they also empower the conformists. To be an effective member of a society, Durkheim (1915) argues, one must conform not only externally but also internally. In the process of internal conformity or socialization, one becomes elevated and magnified. In addition, these moral codes become "moral powers" within us, and we develop a moral conscience. By conforming to the codes, one senses a protection from the deities, and one has confidence to meet the challenges of everyday life.[5]

A case study of American Pentecostals further illustrates this function. In a non-representative sample of Pentecostals, Gerlach and Hine (1970) gathered data from 230 respondents, all of whom acknowledged being empowered with "the Holy Spirit." This empowerment is believed to enable the Pentecostals to commit themselves to each other, who, in turn, add more of a "pool of power" to the church.

---

4   Another example of the substantive meaning of morality is from the Decalogue of Judaism. Of the ten commandments, the first three are ordinances specifically related to honouring Yahweh or the central sacred element of the religion.

5   This is reflected in the sacred text of Christians, the New Testament. It is told that after Jesus rose from the dead, he sent his Holy Spirit to his disciples. If they obeyed his precepts, they would be empowered from "on high" to continue his mission upon earth.

The Function of Social Bonding

The example of this function comes from Goode's (1951) analysis of the Murngin of Australia. These people consist of a large clan of about 40-50,000 members who live in a geographical region comprising 360 square miles. The religious and social centre of the clan is a large water hole which is believed to house the unborn children. It is necessary that parents obey the codes of their clan in order to free the spirits of the children to become incarnated. After birth, a child must follow the age-graded codes of his or her gender. In doing so, the child becomes bonded to his or her group. As an adult, a man grows into spiritual manhood and in so doing, increases bonds with his fellows. Thus, by following the moral codes, he builds a bond with the spiritual world and with the world of his clan.

Empirical evidence of this bonding and how it affects morality is given from the Detroit study of Lenski (1963). He found that people who were "communally involved," measured by how many of one's close friends and relatives are members of the same religious group as a measure of social bonding, showed changes in behaviour in their everyday life.

259

The Ecological and Cosmological Function of Morality

This function of morality connects believers to nature and to the cosmos. As obedience to moral precepts bonds people to brothers and sisters, so does obedience bond them to the earth, the water, the sky, the animals, and the stars. For example, Eliade (1959) argues that by following the codes of sexual intimacy, one becomes bonded to the heavens, for the heavens are to the earth as the male is to the female. Or, when one lives out a married life, one represents the divine wedding to the whole universe.

The clearest example of this function is from the Aboriginal peoples. Before European contact, there were an estimated 4-12 million people in North America who spoke 550 different languages. Even though there was a wide ethnic variation, they all shared some fundamental myths, rituals, and ethical codes. The social historian of American religion, Albanese (1981, 1990), describes it in this way. "Nature Religion," the central concept, is a descriptor of a mythology of connectedness: the world and the cosmos are redolent with power, vivacity, unity, and purpose. The view is fundamentally a relational one that connects individuals, societies, nature, and the universe into a sacred tapestry. Unlike the Apotropaic Buddhism of Burma, the material world is a sacred world, a safe world, a world "peopled" with mysterious persons.

The fundamental value and explicit moral code for all these people, in a term coined by Albanese (1990:26), is "the harmony ethic." In pragmatic terms, one is to respect and honour everything: animals, plants, the earth, water, and fellow humans. The well-being of all persons depends fundamentally upon how well one lives out this basic precept. Not to honour nature (to kill more than one can eat, cut down more trees than necessary, fish beyond the dietary needs of one's group) is to cause disharmony with one's fellow brothers and sisters. A specific code that is common among the Aboriginals is to apologize to an animal if one has to kill it in order to live.

The complementary ethic to this is what Albanese calls the "ethic of reciprocity" (1990:27). If you follow the harmony ethic, you will, in turn, be treated well by your fellow humans and by nature; indeed, the whole cosmos will be gracious to you. This harmony and intricate connectedness is illustrated in Figure 9.3.

260

The Function of Social Integration

Another function of morality is social integration. It is argued that as members of a social group, a tribe, or a religious organization honour the moral codes that are common for all the members, they will integrate more and more into the whole of the community. For the Inuit of the north, it is very important to avoid breaking the religious taboos. If one does, the spirits will be angered and will take their anger out on the members of the group (Norbeck 1961:177).

Another example of morality influencing social solidarity is among the Kammatic Buddhists of Burma whom we met before. In what is called a Buddhist lent, people go on a pilgrimage throughout local villages to collect articles and money to give to the monasteries. The manifest function of the practice is to gain merit for one's better future karma, but the latent function (to use Merton's famous term) is the creation of village solidarity. In fact, Spiro (1982) notes that being a Buddhist adds to the solidarity of the whole Burmese society, for to be Burmese is to be Buddhist.

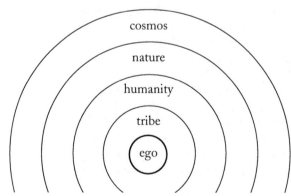

THE HARMONY ETHIC

cosmos

nature

humanity

tribe

ego

FIGURE 9.3

The Function of Worldly Success

A further categorization of morality is reflected in religion's tendency to affect change in people's mundane world. Religion is pragmatic and is effective, at least sometimes, in providing believers with a better place in life. Weber's (1958) study of Protestantism and the genesis of capitalism is a classic expression of this function. He argues that the Protestant ethic (as represented by the Calvinistic ethic of hard work and diligence that would bring eternal rewards) has a latent function: to empower people to succeed in wealth and status. It is too simplistic to think that if one adheres to this ethic one will prosper financially. However, the ethic becomes a moral force, a power to work hard, to be honest, to save, not to steal. An offshoot of this is success in the world. Weber goes to great lengths to present credible evidence to substantiate the thesis and his work has been replicated in many research projects since his time. I shall detail the thesis in Chapter Twelve.

261

To illustrate this function further I turn again to Spiro's work among the Burmese. Kammatic Buddhism best epitomizes the function of worldly success. However, it is not worldly success in the present life that matters but worldly success in the next rebirth. By following the Buddhist precepts, one can look for a long life in the present incarnation and a better life in the next. If these precepts are not followed in this life, however, one may be reborn as a less than desirable person in the next life. For example, if one steals, one will be born a pauper in the next life.

The Function of Social Control

As Weber's work best illustrates the function of worldly success, so does Durkheim's research illustrate morality as social control. In fact, as we have seen, it is at the very heart of his theory of religion. Society is a moral force coercing members to conform. It is in this conformity that society is made possible.

Norbeck (1961) portrays this function well in his analysis of the Manus people of Melanesia. The Manus, as we saw before in this chapter, are very strict in regard to sexual mores. Each family has a guardian spirit who keeps a close eye on the actions of the family members. If members are obedient to the precepts (Norbeck identifies sixteen), they will have wealth and a long life. If they transgress, they will become ill, live a short life, and be poor. Nordeck (1961:184) writes of the power of social control among the Manus:

Any moral transgression is thus the concern of everyone else and the compulsion to follow the code is strong. Public accusation of guilt, confession, and expiation also bring shame and loss of social prestige and serve to strengthen the supernatural sanctions.

Most of the research using morality to control people is found in the literature linking religion and politics. In the next chapter, I will investigate this relationship more closely. The basic thesis is that political regimes use religion as an instrument of power and enforce it through the medium of religious morality (especially those that protect the power of the regime). Yinger (1957) refers to the Russian Orthodox Church of 1915 being used by the aristocracy to control the people. MacIver and Page expand this interpretation: "The religious codes often emerge as powerful engines of control to maintain the interests of the established order against the processes of change, as when the Russian Orthodox Church became a bulwark of the tyranny of the Russian Tzars" (1957:318).

262

The Moral Function of Alienation

The last function that we identified is really a dysfunction: alienation. This is taking elaboration to the farthest extreme where religion results in negative outcomes both for individuals and the social groups or institutions in which they reside. Berger (1967) explains it in the following way. Religion (and religious ethics) is a product of social construction that occurs in conversations between persons, groups, and institutions. In the process of this construction, some projections can become so reified as to appear objective and not dependent at all on social creation. The actor does not act but is acted upon and is but a passive receptor in the process. If this involves codes of behaviour, these codes become "alien" to the person and are dysfunctional to him or her.

A good historical example is the publication of *Malleus Malificarum*[6] in 1486 by two German medieval theological professors[7] (Buckland 1993). In

---

6   A detailed legal and theological document regarded as the standard handbook on witchcraft, including its detection and its extirpation, until well into the eighteenth century. Its appearance did much to spur on and sustain some two centuries of witch-hunting hysteria in Europe. The *Malleus* codified the folklore and beliefs of the Alpine peasants and was dedicated to the implementation of Exodus 22:18: "You shall not permit a sorceress to live."

7   Two Dominicans: Johann Sprenger, dean of the University of Cologne in Germany, and Heinrich (Institoris) Kraemer, professor of theology at the University of Salzburg, Austria, and inquisitor in the Tirol region of Austria.

this document, the authors outline how to identify and prosecute women who are suspected of witchcraft and sorcery (Mahoney 1987). These particular codes illustrate how far removed morality can be from the sacred, and they are used not only to control people but also to imprison them. This is the ultimate extent of the elaboration of ethos.

A Summary of the Functions of Morality

Morality takes on many different forms within religion. In this review, we saw that it varies from extremes of delimitation to elaboration. Our argument was that a substantive interpretation of morality locates it close to the centre: in the sacred. As it becomes delimited and elaborated, it moves increasingly away from this centre until it becomes a dysfunction to persons and societies.

263

FROM DELIMITATION TO ELABORATION TO DELIMITATION: EVIDENCE FOR THE CYCLE

In this section of the chapter, I hope to substantiate the dilemma of delimitation by looking at Buddhism in Burma, Roman Catholicism in the West, and some new religious movements in the western United States. Coming shortly after the charismatic moment of a religious inception is the necessary process of delimitation. Thereafter, there is a strong tendency for elaboration. However, as elaboration produces little religious life, a protest may emerge which attempts to bring the religious ethos back to a delimited state. The following three interpretations will illustrate this.

The Case of Buddhism in Burma

Spiro's (1982) anthropological study of Burmese Buddhists was adopted to illustrate the myth-ritual-morality linkage and is also used to characterize this cycle. Noss and Noss (1984) write that shortly after Gautama's death, a representative group of disciples gathered to provide a Buddhist sacred canon. Although there is an historical debate as to when this canon was established, it is nonetheless true that the delimitation process began. Morality in its delimited stage is illustrated in Burma with Nibbanic Buddhism. Here, morality is seen as a discipline to prepare one to meditate better and, in turn, to achieve nirvana. However, in the course of time, this delimited stage led to an elaboration stage with the development of the other three types of Burmese Buddhism: Kammatic, Apotropaic, and Esoteric. In the case of Kammatic Buddhism, morality becomes not so much tied to meditation, but is a means to acquire merit. The merit is to give one a better life in the current incarnation and a better life in any future reincarnations.

For Apotropaic Buddhists, obeying the moral precepts is elaborated even further. Here, obedience will act as a barrier to tragedy and hurt in a world inhabited with evil spirits. Finally, the most extreme form of elaboration is among those of Esoteric Buddhism. The elaboration process is accentuated by a mixture of normative (traditional) Buddhism and local animistic principles and customs. In this case, morality is a magical means not only to achieve a worldly end but also to do evil to enemies.

The attempts of delimitation are also alive in Burma. The presence of Nibbanic Buddhism within the monasteries reminds the lay people of a better way. Nowhere in the world, Spiro (1982:397) notes, are clergy as honoured as they are in Burma. The Burmese term for monk is *hpoung:ji*, which means, "the great glory." These "Sons of Buddha" are addressed in terms that one would address Gautama Buddha. The moral code of honour is the central code in social interaction. This is morality of the people, and they go to great lengths to venerate monks and sacrifice for them. Spiro quotes a Catholic missionary who lived in Burma in 1900:

> The best proof of the high veneration the people entertain for the Talapoins (Monks) is the truly surprising liberality with which they gladly minister to all their wants. They impose upon themselves great sacrifices, incur enormous expenses, place themselves joyfully in narrow circumstances, that they might have the means to build monasteries with the best and most substantial materials, and adorn them with all the luxury the country can afford. (1982:401)

Spiro adds further that from the Burmese point of view, their honour of the monks follows from what they believe them to be: remnants of a spiritual charisma. Morality, then, takes on a role bringing a believer in touch with the sacred in the person of the monk. The implication of this goes a long way in Burma. As one honours the monk, one honours one's parents and anyone who has authority in one's life. This becomes a source of social order and integration for the whole of the society.

The Case of Roman Catholicism in the West

Another historical example of the cycle of delimitation-elaboration-delimitation is the history of moral theology in the Roman Catholic Church. The Jesuit spiritual theologian John Mahoney (1987) documents this history. A reasonable consensus appears in the history of Christianity that for the first two to three centuries of the religion, the elements of charisma were alive.

Thus, we can reasonably argue that in this early period, morality was delimited. However, in about the fifth or sixth century, this began to change, and a long history of elaboration began. There are several examples that Mahoney gives. In what are termed the "Celtic Penitentials," there appeared what became known as "moral casuistry," which refers to a minute analysis of human acts to see if they accord to a rigid rule of behaviour. They were typified as, in Mahoney's (1987:7) words, "an appallingly rigid systematized approach to sin." The elaboration process continued in the sexual morality of Augustine of Hippo (354-430 AD). Mahoney observes that his theology is frequently flawed by melancholy, disgust, and even brutality toward the human in his or her sinfulness. He argued that not only is one forbidden to have pre-marital or extramarital sex, but if one has sex within marriage without the explicit purpose of procreation, one sins.

For centuries moral casuistry and an ambivalence toward sex even within marriage has captured the minds and actions of countless Catholics. However, delimitation processes began to shift Catholic moral theology. Changes were triggered during the last thirty years with the Second Vatican Council (1961-1965) when theologians were urged to offer new directions in moral theology with a return to the Christian scriptures and works of the Fathers of the Church. Thereafter, moral theology tended to become Christocentric, a morality not of the law but the spirit, not a code of precepts, but rooted in relationships beyond the individual.

The first result of this was the publication of *Humanæ Vitæ* on July 25, 1968. Even though the encyclical does not allow for artificial contraception, it did place love at the centre of marriage, and the authors saw marital sex as an expression of this love. Moral theologians began to ask questions like: which particular clusters of circumstances, like electrons around a morally neutral nucleus, make a critical moral difference? There emerged within moral theology a heightened appreciation of sexuality and marriage, and sexual activity was seen as a sign of two in one flesh.

Another theologian, Pinkares (1995), analyzed the *Catechism of the Catholic Church* and a recent encyclical, *Veritatis Splendour,*[8] which further exemplifies the delimitation process within Roman Catholic moral theology. Central to both documents is the accent on Jesus' Sermon on the Mount (rather than the moral precepts), an emphasis on interior conscience, and an acknowledgement that morality needs to be contextualized within various cultures, social structures, and times. The documents made some use of the social sciences in the development of the texts.

---

8 The catechism is the most recent one officially published by the Roman Catholic Church (United States Catholic Conference, 1994) and the encyclical, made public by John Paul II in 1993 (Libreria Editrice Vatican, 1993).

The Case of the Counter-Culture
and its Responses in California

Tipton's (1982) study of three religious groups which emerged in the 1960s portrays a final example of the delimitation-elaboration-delimitation cycle. These groups grew as a response to many disappointing excursions of young people into the counter-culture in the tumultuous period of 1960-1970.

Major political, social, and economic upheavals characterized the 1960s in the United States. The country was in the midst of a war that was highly controversial and was protested by many. African Americans moved to assert their rights as human beings and as American citizens. Women, in an effort to gain social equality, mobilized in protest over patriarchal power and sexism. As a result, there were major shifts in the culture of the land and, in particular, the moral basis of the society. For many young people, the moral order was elaborated beyond measure, and they challenged the institutions which channelled that order. Tipton (1982:29) writes: "A profound change did occur as a result of the cultural conflict of the 1960s — the de-legitimation of utilitarian culture, and with it the stripping away of moral authority from the major American social institutions: government, law, business, religion, marriage and the family."

As a response to that, many young women and men protested in the form of adopting what Tipton calls "American Culture III" — a culture that emphasizes subjective experience, love without law, peace without organization, harmony without authority, intuition without reason, freedom without constraint, good without evil, and simplicity without complexity. Certain proverbs describe the morality: "Make love, not war," "get in touch with yourself," "express your feelings, not repress them," and "enjoy the freedom and peace of the moment." The counter-culture expresses an attempt at delimitation in a radical way. However, many of the excursions of these young people into this uncharted social landscape led to further disappointment — especially the communal living alternative, where it was discovered that there is not love without law, peace without bureaucracy, harmony without authority, intuition without reason, freedom without constraint, good without evil, or simplicity of life.

A response to this, Tipton argues, is to turn to alternative religious systems which do not reflect the rigid moral structures of established religion and retain enough moral order that young people can make sense of their world. Three new religious movements provided this for many: a charismatic Christian sect, a Zen Buddhist spiritual centre, and the Erhard Seminar Training (EST) series intended to free people from anxieties and

266

life concerns. Tipton analyzes each of the three groups in great detail by relying on a variety of case study techniques.

Although in each group different paths delimited ethics or made a moral sense of their worlds, they all shared some common patterns. Each had an explicit, unified ethic, and all three offered to their adherents a road out of a conflictual culture through "heartless rules on one side and the deep blue sea of boundless self expression on the other" (1982:234). These alternative religions offered community as the context of personal and social identity and a moral vision of society as a whole. Each sought this in various ways. The Christian sect offered symbolic political power to the powerless ex-hippies and the powerless lower-middle class. Zen enabled its members to live with the conventional society by living out an alternative way of life as they sought to influence its further course. EST provided a model of psychological change to social institutions, for members were encouraged to accept the social system as it is, acknowledge themselves as its cause, and participate in it according to its rules in order to change it (Tipton 1982:243).

The Cycle of Delimitation-Elaboration-Delimitation: A Summary

In modern Burma, medieval and modern Roman Catholicism, and new religions in California, we find a pattern of the cycle. In all cases, we find that there is a period of delimitation, a stage of elaboration, and finally a movement back to delimitation. If past history is anything to go on, the future should illustrate a continuation of this cycle. One thing we know for sure is that the human religious spirit is not stagnant — there is always the quest for deeper authenticity. Moral systems are very prone to elaboration and rigidity. These examples help us to understand that there is a way to retain the spirit of the law, the spirit of the ethic, without an antimonial alternative.

THE RESTRUCTURING OF AMERICAN RELIGION: THE CASE OF MORALITY

I bring this chapter to a close by looking at clusters of morality that seem to centre on what Wuthnow (1988a) terms "cultural structures." Recall that in Chapter Three under the subtitle "cultural boundaries," I outlined his reasoning. He argues that American religion is no longer characterized by denominational boundaries or what he terms the declining significance of denominationalism (1988a:71). In regard to both personal and social morality, in the late 1970s there seemed to be little evidence to

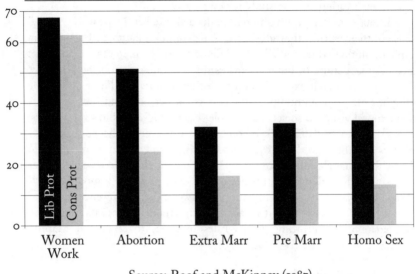

MORALITY AND RESTRUCTURING

Source: Roof and McKinney (1987)

FIGURE 9.4

support denominational differences on personal and social moral issues. For example, he notes that on attitudes to abortion, one finds that about the same proportions in all of the major denominations expressed approval or disapproval (1988a:87). With the decline of denominationalism comes a whole new set of boundaries that he calls the *restructuring* of American religion. This restructuring crosses denominational lines and is marked by a new alignment of liberalism and conservativism (1988a:164-180). Liberalism is characterized as religion adapting itself to the cultural environment whereas conservativism distances itself from this environment. In effect, then, the cultural boundaries are between these two new cultural alignments with liberalism having permeable symbolic boundaries to the American culture and conservativism having boundaries that are tighter and more impermeable.

A way to illustrate this restructuring is to see if Christian morality is clustered around these centres. Theoretically, one would think that more conservative ethics would cluster in the conservative structure, and more liberal ethical positions would cluster around the liberal structure. This theory seems to have an empirical base. For example, Roof and McKinney (1987) compare a range of moral issues not only along denominational lines but also along a continuum of liberal to conservative lines.

MORALITY AND RESTRUCTURING IN CANADA

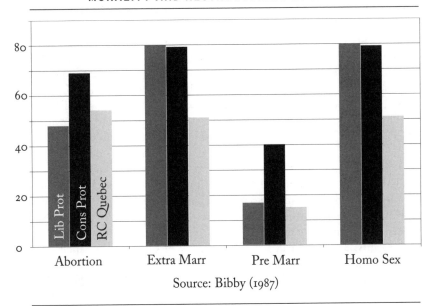

Source: Bibby (1987)

FIGURE 9.5

Figure 9.4 was constructed from Roof and McKinney's analysis of morality and denominations. Their data come from eleven different General Social Surveys (GSS) from 1972 to 1978, 1980, 1982, and 1984. This figure uses only two categories: Liberal Protestants and Conservative Protestants. Their categories are more expansive and include moderate Protestants, Roman Catholics, Jews, and smaller groups like the Mormons and Jehovah's Witnesses.

In this figure, "Women Work" means "women working if husband can support her"; "Abortion" refers to "Favour abortion for any reason"; "Extra Marr Sex" indicates "Extra-marital sex not always wrong"; "Pre Marr" means "Premarital sex not always wrong"; and "Homo Sex" means "Homosexuality is not always wrong." The authors add more to their tables. A conclusion, both from this sample chart and the other issues they refer to, shows there is a significant difference between the two groups. However, their data do not quite fit Wuthnow's two-part restructuring thesis. Roof and McKinney find that Roman Catholics and moderate Protestants form a "middle" group that seem distinct from their end points.

In Canada, we find a similar story. As noted in Chapter Three, there is less variation between major denominations, and most Canadian Christians belong to what Bibby (1987) calls "The Big Four": Roman Catholic,

Anglican, United Church, and Conservative (those churches which are either evangelical or charismatic). He also has correlated a number of moral and social issues on denominations with data that he has been gathering for about twenty years across Canada. Figure 9.5 is an illustration of these data.

So that there can be a comparison between items cross-nationally, I used the same variable names in Figure 9.5 as in Figure 9.4. Also, for the sake of comparison, I collapsed the Canadian affiliations, Anglican and United, into liberal. Also, because there are significant differences between Roman Catholics in Quebec and those outside Quebec, Roman Catholics within Quebec appear in this figure. Lastly, there was no comparable item about women in the public sphere and thus this item was not included.

Evidently, there are similar restructuring patterns in Canada as in the United States: a clustering of liberal attitudes with liberal churches and conservative attitudes with conservative churches. Similar to the Roof and McKinney data from the United States, there is a middle ground. Not shown in this figure but evident in Bibby's data is that there is also a middle ground in Canada: Roman Catholics outside of Quebec, Lutherans, and Presbyterians. A feature not in the United States, however, is a strong ethnic-Roman Catholic difference. The Roman Catholics in Quebec are just as liberal as the Anglicans and the United Church members. One might argue that in Canada there is a new form of cultural structure that has an ethnic dimension in contrast to the United States.

In summary, there is partial evidence from these data for the two-fold restructuring thesis of Wuthnow both in Canada and in the United States. In both countries there is a middle ground. In the United States, it is among the moderate Protestants and the Roman Catholics. In Canada, the middle ground consists of Roman Catholics outside of Quebec and those of Lutheran and Presbyterian persuasion. Unlike the United States, however, at least when it comes to morality, Quebec Roman Catholics stand in close union with liberalism in Canadian Christianity.

Beyond the Christian dimension, the Nation of Islam is a further example of this restructuring on the conservative domain.[9] Gardell (1996:59) informs us that members of the Nation are to marry endogamously, be conservatively dressed, work hard, and shun alcohol and drugs. Women are to dress modestly, obey their husbands, and take pride in raising children. Children are to study hard and avoid the street culture and senseless play.

Additional elements of the Nation's ethos include pronatal morality, norms against homosexuality, traditional gender roles, obedience to author-

---

9 Gardell (1996:346) notes that the ethical system of the Nation is quite compatible with Protestant, white, conservative middle-class Americans.

THE RESTRUCTURING OF CANADIAN RELIGION

CANADIAN LIBERAL
AND CONSERVATIVE DIFFERENCES

A *Maclean's* poll conducted in 1993 finds evidence for a conservative-liberal split. As United Church leaders accommodated to liberal values like speaking out on social issues and accepted homosexual clergy, rank and file members rebelled and 20 per cent of the United Church membership felt that the Church was too liberal. As the general population becomes more liberal on social issues, it is the most uncompromising conservative churches that are flourishing. Although they only make up 8 per cent of the Canadian population, 75 per cent of Conservative Christians believe that homosexual behaviour is morally unacceptable (compared to only 40 per cent of Roman Catholics). They are the only group of Christians in which the majority disapproves of premarital sex and they are the strongest opponents of abortion – 41 per cent say it should be permitted only when the mother's life is in danger.

SOURCE: *Macleans,* April 12, 1993:34-35.

BOX 9.1

ity (both religious and state), and a subordination of the individual to the Nation. Gardell writes:

> the NOI hails traditional family values, loyalty to the nation, and obedience to God. They applaud the decent, hardworking, honest, God fearing heterosexual, who should be neatly dressed, polite, modest, law-abiding, and respectful of authorities. They encourage self-help and mistrust social welfare, value a God-centered education with emphasis on discipline and learning and are epistemologically convinced of nonrelative universal truths that form the basis for knowledge. They are nonsmoking, nondrinking, clean-living moralists who shun sexual promiscuity, excessive partying, and decadent behaviour. (1996:346-347)

| SUMMARY AND CONCLUSIONS

We have come full circle in our investigation of ethos in general and morality in particular. It has been discovered that there exists an intricate linkage between myth, ritual, and morality. We have also seen that on the continuum between delimitation and elaboration, there are both substantive and functional dimensions of morality. We saw further that religions frequently go through the processes of delimitation, elaboration, and back to delimitation. Recent studies illustrate that in modern Canada and the United States, morality seems to be clustered around two poles: liberal and conservative. Finally, consistent with our introduction to mythology and the example of the Nation of Islam, we saw that this new religious movement considers morality to be central to its life.

In Chapter Ten, I investigate the final dilemma of O'Dea and O'Dea: the dilemma of power or coercion versus conversion. This dilemma will enable us to understand the linkage between religion and politics.

■ CHAPTER TEN ■

The Dilemma of Power: The Relationship Between Religion and Politics

As indicated in the closing remarks of Chapter Nine, we continue to investigate the linkages between religion and society through the lenses of the O'Deas' dilemmas by looking at the fifth and final one: the dilemma of power. In this chapter I outline the connections between religious and political institutions.

To understand this dilemma, let us recall the O'Deas' interpretation. As a religious movement matures, it is likely to become intertwined gradually with the public, non-religious culture. This gives rise to the dilemma of power through which leaders may seek ways to either convert or to coerce others to join the movement. The prince Vladimir (d. 1015 AD) of Russia, who ordered the mass baptism of the people, is a prime example of coercion, as are contemporary efforts by fundamentalist Islamic leaders to restore conservative Islam, as in Iran or Algeria. Most religions in the west do not have this power to coerce, so they must rely on the voluntary conversion of prospective followers. This kind of response to secularization is the recent phenomenon of the privatization of religion. This horn of the dilemma has its own problems. In order to become attractive to new members and to retain the old, the religion often must accommodate to the secular culture. The charismatic spirit may be eclipsed in the process of providing a growing (or at least stable) membership for a sound organizational base.

To regain the charisma, a frequent sectarian or cultic response occurs. On the other hand, charisma, if it is to endure over time in modern society, will be bureaucratized in some form. It may lead to a bureaucracy that subverts the original spirit (in which case charisma is fostered by the organization) or it may lead to an organization that uses charisma to further the organization (in which case charisma is overpowered by rationality and efficiency). As Stark notes,

> In judging a church, the question cannot be whether it has connected
> with a certain apparatus of bureaucrats, but whether this bureaucratic
> apparatus has completely overlaid and stifled the life which it was sup-
> posed to assist and to preserve. Only where the latter contingency has
> become a reality can we speak of the routinization of charisma.
> (1965:206)

As we saw in Chapter Six, Christianity began with the revolutionary
prophet Jesus. After several centuries, this new sect became like a church,
which we saw as a type of religious organization that accommodates itself
to the social environment. I shall outline two kinds of responses to this
accommodation. In the first case, I shall look at Constantine, whose imperial involvement in the early church developed a paradigm called
Cæsaropapism (Weber 1978 and Marty 1959) and which may also be called
the *secular paradigm*. Another response was a further accommodation on
the part of the Christian church wherein the religious collective used the
state to achieve its own end. From Weber (1978), this is called a hierocratic
response,[1] which may be referred to as the hierocratic paradigm. Table 10.1
illustrates these alternative responses.

TWO RESPONSES TO ACCOMMODATION

NAMES OF RESPONSES	MEANING OF RESPONSES
The Secular Paradigm or *Cæsaropapism*	The State Use of Religion
The Hierocratic Paradigm	Religious Use of the State

TABLE 10.1

Beginning with the Reformation, another kind of religious-political
response is identified: communal withdrawal. As we saw in Chapter Six,
Luther and Simons were reform prophets who reacted to a highly accommodated and bureaucratic church in the later years of the medieval period.
One response to this bureaucratized religious institution was withdrawal, as
in the case of the Anabaptist Reformation of the sixteenth century. Table
10.2 depicts this response.

---

1   The term refers to the rule or government by priests or religious leaders. Weber (1978:1161) uses
    it as a form of cæsaropapism. However, this is incorrect; as was seen above, cæsaropapism is
    the subordination of priestly to secular powers.

ONE RESPONSE TO BUREAUCRACY

NAMES OF RESPONSES	MEANING OF RESPONSES
Collective or Communal Withdrawal	No Political Involvement

TABLE 10.2

Modern religious-political responses have a somewhat different nature. Their reaction is not so much to religious accommodation as to secularization. Four kinds of responses are identified: the privatization of religion, that is, a personal withdrawal from the political sphere; religious political activism; the division paradigm, which is the separation of the state from religion; and civil religion. Table 10.3 presents a pictorial representation of these four responses to accommodation and secularization.

FOUR RESPONSES TO SECULARIZATION

NAMES OF RESPONSES	MEANING OF RESPONSES
Privatization	Personal Withdrawal
Political Activism	Engaging in the Political Sphere
The Division Paradigm	Separation of the Church and the State
Civil Religion	Religious Mythology and Ritual that Supports the State

TABLE 10.3

SECULAR REGIMES AND HIEROCRATIC RULERS

According to Weber (1978), in his many studies of the relationship between religion and society, there has been a long history of tension and antagonism between political and sacred authorities. This tension commences, especially, at the stage of permanent settlements. He reflects that the city god or patron saint is indispensable for the beginning and continuation of every political community. In war, the triumph of one's own god is the definite confirmation of the ruler's victory and an effective guarantee of the obedience of the subjects. As will be outlined below, the tensions seem to

be endemic to the relationship, and in historical times, patterns of this tension can be identified.

The Secular Paradigm or Cæsaropapism

The secular paradigm, or Cæsaropapism, is illustrated by the period of time
from Constantine, the first Christian Roman Emperor (272-337 AD), until
the last emperor of the Roman West, when the empire fell to barbarian
invasions (476 AD) under the leadership of Romulus Augustulus. The
paradigm had a much longer history in the East from the time of the first
Christian Emperor to the fall of the Czarist state in Russia in 1917. Marty
(1959:141) defines it as "the monarchial control over ecclesiastical affairs;
particularly, it connotes the intrusion of a civil officer into the sanctuary,
the crossing of line from the imperial to the priestly." In Russia, Marty
continues, it means that the church was in some way a *department of state
organization.*

276

The paradigm commences with the conversion of Constantine in 312
AD, when he was reported to have seen a vision in the heavens of a
Christian cross that gave him encouragement to fight and win against a
usurper to the throne, Maxentius. Thereafter, he treated Christianity as a
favoured religion. Many were his accomplishments: he instituted Sunday as
a holiday, established December 25 as the celebrated day of Christ's birth,
forbade the bloody gladiatorial combats, built churches, and forbade the

---

THE WEDDING OF RELIGION AND POLITICS IN RUSSIA CONTINUES

CHURCH BOLSTERS RUSSIAN NATIONALISM

On a wide range of foreign and domestic issues – including nuclear disarmament, the
political union of Russia and Belarus, and the eastward expansion of NATO – the Orthodox
church is reinforcing the increasingly nationalist slant of Russian politicians.... In domestic
affairs, the church has bolstered the chauvinistic mood of Russian politics by pushing for
restrictions on foreign missionaries and smaller religious sects.... Critics say the church
today is continuing its tradition of cozy links with the Kremlin. The patriarch often appears
side by side with President Boris Yeltsin at key political events... as a reward for its loyalty,
the church has been allowed to participate in lucrative state-authorized financial schemes,
including a tax free revenue... the church owns 40 per cent of the shares in the oil-export
industry... the church's conservative and authoritarian tendencies are linked to its rejection
of the fundamental reforms that were introduced by Western religions.

SOURCE: *The Globe and Mail,* A1 and A15, May 31, 1997.

BOX 10.1

building of new pagan temples (Todd 1979 and Latourette 1975). Two accomplishments stand out as central to our discussion. First, he allowed Christian clergy to use donations given to the state that put them on par with the pagan priests. Many laymen became priests thereafter, which exemplifies the dilemma of mixed motivation. Nonetheless, this does indicate growing accommodation of Christianity in the Empire. His second accomplishment was his edict of toleration wherein all religions were free to function without fear of reprisal.

Evidence for the secular paradigm is that Constantine and his Christian imperial successors tended to be significantly involved in the business of the church. It was Constantine who ordered the gathering of the Nicene Council (325 AD), presided over the first session, and introduced the term *homoousios* ("of one essence") to describe the personhood of Jesus (Todd 1979). His successors (except for Julian who was not a Christian) continued to be very active in the life of the Church.

An example of extreme Cæsaropapism occurred during the reign of Gratian (shared with two others from 375–378 AD), when a strict Christian sect in Spain was accused of heresy and immorality. The local secular authority responded. The leader of the sect (a Priscillian) was tried in civil court and was executed with six of his followers (Todd 1979). Although the church reacted to the practice, this dual connection between church and state against dissenters became a model during the medieval period

The secular paradigm or the Cæsaropapal model is well illustrated in the Eastern Church,[2] particularly in Russia. In 860 AD, the Moravian prince Rastislav asked the Byzantine Emperor to send missionaries to the Slavs. The Emperor obliged and after a short period of missionary activity, two monks, Cyril and Methodius, earned great success. A state Church was instituted and became very common in the East. In 988, Vladimir sent envoys to Islam, Latin Christianity, Judaism, and Eastern Christianity to investigate which one would best suit his purposes for a national religion. He chose Eastern Christianity and ordered the mass baptism of all Russians. This is a classic example of the use of power not to persuade conversion but to coerce it. Between 1451 and 1452, Constantinople fell to the Turkish Muslims, and the primary seat of Eastern Christianity was evacuated. Moscow then came to be known as the "Third Rome": the centre of the Russian state as well the spiritual centre of the East (Steeves 1979).

277

---

2   Early in Christian history, two models of Catholicism evolved, a Western and an Eastern tradition. The West tended to follow the Latin culture whereas the East, the Hellenistic. The Latin version tended to be more scholastic (taking a cue from Aristotelian philosophy) and legal (following after Roman Law), whereas the East tended to be more ascetic and mystical in the tradition of Plato.

From this time on, Orthodox Christianity became the state religion until the fall of the Czarist regime in 1917.

Marty (1959), in his short history of the Christian Church, gives further credibility to this paradigm with the reinforcement of Cæsaropapism in the person of Peter the Great of Russia (1672-1725 and Czar from 1682-1725). He set up the style of religious-political linkage that continued through to the Bolshevik Revolution of 1917. He was heard saying, "I am your patriarch." He reorganized monasteries and schools, reformed parish life, and infused religious instruction with a polite and subtle rationalism. The revenues of the Church were under state control, and the clergy were not much more than vassals of the state. He even went so far as to abolish the Patriarchate in 1721 and established a synod of bishops under the watchful eye of a layman who came to be known as "The Czar's Eye."

278

This paradigm illustrates an extreme of the dilemma of power. As the sacred institution adapts to the secular society, the secular world enters into the very life of the sacred. In this case, the charismatic role of the religious institution is substituted for the political power of the state, and the latter leads or tries to rule the former. In relationship to the O'Dea dilemma discussed here, this paradigm is a clear illustration of the use of power for conversion.

The Hierocratic Paradigm

Although the hierocratic paradigm was not actually used until the medieval period, it was born in the fourth century and was salient right up to the Protestant Reformation of the sixteenth century. Two events occasioned this. Theodosus (emperor from 378-395 AD) objected to the persecution of Jews in Rome and commanded that the bishop responsible should restore a burned synagogue. Ambrose (340-397 AD), a bishop of Milan, forced Theodosus to capitulate to him, and the Jews were not recompensed. A second instance was more dramatic. In 390 AD, the people of Thessalonika murdered a military commander. Theodosus sent a Roman campaign against them, and 7,000 people were executed. Ambrose excommunicated Theodosus, who was not reinstated into the church until he publicly repented (Todd 1979). There was a growing awareness in Western Christianity that the emperor (and the secular authority) was inferior to the sacred authority. This became the model of church-state relationships through to the end of the medieval period.

The model, however, went through many turns. In the ninth and tenth centuries, the West was, again, in crisis and turmoil. Lay investiture (the practice of a lay or secular leader choosing a priest, bishop or pope) was common. It was not until a reform movement within the monasteries that the direction of control began to change. The Cluniac order, founded in France in 910 AD, led a reform of the hierarchy. One such priest, Hildrebrand (1020-1085) became Pope Gregory VII; he outlined the hierocratic paradigm in 1065 in a document entitled *Dictatas Popæ* which forbade lay investiture, stated that the pope was superior to secular rulers, and declared that papal power was absolute (Clouse 1979).

The paradigm reached its zenith during the papal reign of Innocent III (1161-1216) in the Fourth Lateran Council of 1215, which established the mastery of the papacy over nearly every feature of Latin Christianity. A special outcome of this church-state marriage was the crusades. Begun in 1095 under the campaign of Pope Urban II (1042-1099), kings, princes, and soldiers embarked on a "holy war" to free the Holy Land from the power of the Muslims. Seven to eight crusades (from 1095-1270) resulted in only one successful victory led by the Holy Roman Emperor, Frederick II (1194-1250), in 1228-29 (Clouse 1979). Not only did the crusades not accomplish their goals (Islam gained permanent control in 1291) but they further alienated Eastern Christians because of the barbaric behaviour of Western soldiers.

An interesting anecdote should be added to our discussion involving the sociological use of myth discussed in Chapter Two. There were several theological supports offered to the hierocratic paradigm. Alcuin, an Anglo-Saxon theological scholar of 800, argued that the Pope was spiritually superior to the emperor of the Holy Roman Empire. Innocent III presents a poetic analogy of the paradigm. In the heavens, he writes, there are two illuminaries: the sun and the moon. On earth, there are also two illuminaries: the pontifical authority and the secular ruler. The moon is an image of the secular ruler while the sun is symbolic of the Pope: "The royal power derives its dignity from the pontifical authority: and the more closely it cleaves to the sphere of that authority the less is the light with which it is adorned; the further it is removed, the more it increases in splendour" (Innocent III in *Sicut universitatis conditor*, October 1198, quoted in Clouse 1979:256).

The paradigm was further reinforced through the theological thinking of the most famous scholastic cleric, Thomas Aquinas (1225-1274). He argues that the secular power does not depend on the spiritual power and that kings are not vassals of the pope (in contrast to Innocent III) but rather that the church is still the higher power and kings must be subject to priests, bishops, and popes. In addition, it is the duty of the state to put heretics to death (thus giving a theological basis to the later infamous inquisition [Matson 1987]). Here we see another example of the use of power for conversion in the fifth O'Dea dilemma.

Most of the effects of the paradigm were negative, particularly the crusades and the later inquisition. There were, however, some positive effects.

An example of this was the leadership of King Stephen of Hungary (969-1038 AD) who, according to an historical account, sought the welfare of his people. The Divine Office, a Roman Catholic prayer book, describes the relationship:

> My beloved son, delight of my heart, hope of your prosperity, I pray,
> I command, that at every time and in everything, strengthened by your
> devotion to me, you may show favour not only to relations and kin, or
> to the most eminent, be they leaders or rich men or neighbours or
> fellow-countrymen, but also to foreigners and to all who come to you.
> By fulfilling your duty in this way you will reach the highest state of
> happiness. Be merciful to all who are suffering violence, keeping
> always in your heart the example of the Lord who said: "I desire mercy
> and not sacrifice. Be patient with everyone, not only with the power-
> ful, but also with the weak." (1975, Volume IV: 1328-1330)

The Secular Paradigm Revisited in the Reformation

The Reformation marks the "crossing of a religious Rubicon" that has shaped Christianity in profound ways since the sixteenth century. A socio-political effect was the realignment of Europe into political-religious regions. Linder (1979) notes that tensions and animosities ran so deep that there were two major series of war and conflicts during the 1540s and then from 1618 to 1648. The latter came to be known as the "Thirty Years War"; it began as a religious struggle with political overtones and ended as a polit-ical struggle with religious overtones. This fits well with the secular para-digm.

A way of settling the tension was for princes, the political leaders of var-ious states and smaller regions, to choose which faith (Roman Catholic, Calvinist or Lutheran) his subjects would adhere to. This is a classic exam-ple of the extreme end of the O'Deas' fifth dilemma, conversion through force. A major consequence of this was the establishment of the principle *cuius regio, eius religio*, i.e., whatever is the religion of the monarch or prince, all members within his region are to have the same religion. The secular authorities promulgated laws that forbade any public worship of the reli-gion that was not approved by the local political authority (Marty 1959).

As above (in the secular paradigm), the fifth dilemma of O'Dea is well illustrated by the use of coercive power to convert rather than to persuade and elicit a voluntary response.

The Hierocratic Paradigm Revisited in Modern Iran

In Chapter Two, I mentioned that Islam is one of the western religions that belongs to the Levantine cultures that border on the eastern side of the Mediterranean sea. Born in the seventh century through the prophecy and evangelism of Muhammad (571-632 A D), Islam grew from a small following of dedicated disciples to number in the hundreds of millions in the twentieth century. Two major traditions have reflected this growth: Sunni and Shi'ite Islam. The Shi'ites argue that proper interpretation of the Koran lies with those who are in the lineage of Muhammad's son-in-law. The last descendent was a Mohammund al-Mahdi (the twelfth Imam) who is said to have disappeared in 874. He is considered to be the Lord of the Age and is to reappear in the End of Time (see Noss and Noss 1984).

A modern example of the hierocratic paradigm is that of the Islamic Revolution that commenced with the reign of Ayatollah Ruhollah Khomeini in 1979. I will outline the major features of the revolution and indicate how it reflects the hierocratic paradigm of the religious leaders having control both of religion and the state.

Shi'ite Islam was established as the state religion in Iran from the foundation of the Islamic-Safavid Empire dating from 1511. Throughout subsequent years until 1722, the Shi'ite hierocracy lead the state in both secular and religious terms. Arjomand (1988) notes that when the Empire collapsed in 1722, the Shi'ite leaders were forced to subsist on their own and concern themselves only with sacred matters. From 1925 until 1979, the country was led by the Pahlavi Shahs who were committed to the modernization and secularization of the state. This culminated in what was known as the *White Revolution* or the *Revolution of the Shah and his People* of 1963. Even though the Shah was a religious figure (The King of Islam), the Pahlavi Shahs disengaged the Islamic hierocracy from secular policies, sold resources to foreigners (considered against the Islamic policy of selling property to infidels), gave the franchise to women, and handed over educational functions to the state.

To the youthful Khomeini, this was anathema and was tantamount to a step toward the abolition of Islam, the delivery of Iran to the Baha'is who were agents of Zionism and American imperialism, and the promotion of prostitution and destruction of the family by giving the franchise to women. From 1962 until the revolution, Khomeini set out for himself and his Shi'ite followers two goals: to avenge themselves against the Pahlavi dynasty and to turn the tables on Westernized intellectuals who had cheated the Islamic hierocracy in all the important religious traditions for the maintenance of the "true religion."

CHALLENGES TO ISLAMIC POLITICAL FUNDAMENTALISM

"Khatami! Khatami! You're the hope!" [shouted thousands of ecstatic Iranians] as they rushed toward a 54-year-old black turbaned cleric, nearly crushing him as he mounted the podium inside a mosque. In the election campaign that began four weeks ago [May 1, 1997], Mohammed Khatami was a sensation. Surveys showed his support climbing from 13.9 per cent to 20.2 per cent to 52 per cent on election eve... Who voted for Khatami? Iranians fed up with political and social restrictions, women chafing at dress codes, twentysomethings denied satellite dishes and dispirited citizens who never saw a reason to vote – until Khatami came along... Khatami ... a liberal theologian, a politician who speaks of freedom, a family man with an avuncular grin and a scholar who has worked in the West and is said to be at home in English, German, and Arabic. That's quite a contrast to the severe and sober ayatollahs who have governed since the 1979 Islamic revolution.... "In the beginning, we needed militants. Now we need people who can build the country. We need a man like Khatami."

SOURCE: *Time*, June 2, 1997, p. 32–33.

BOX 10.2

Arjomand (1988) continues to argue that the Ayatollah was definitely a charismatic leader who was thought to be the true follower of Mohammed in the person of the Twelver, the hidden Imam of the Age. After the revolution, Khomeini became the ruler of Iran on behalf of the hidden Imam, established an Islamic theocracy, and eradicated Occidentalism as an enemy not only of the people of Iran but of Islamic faith. The mythology (see Chapter Two) that gave legitimacy to the movement was a fundamentalist-millenarian world-view that included Khomeini as the resurrected Hidden Imam, God (Allah) as the inspiration of the revolution, and Satan as anyone who opposed the revolution.

In light of what we have learned thus far about secularization and various responses to it, Khomeini represents a charismatic leader in general and a *renewal prophet* in particular, and the revolution a *revolution by tradition* (see Chapter Eight). The Iranian revolution is a good illustration of how religion responds to secularization in terms of establishing a hierocratic model of the linkage between the secular (the state) and the sacred (Islam) and how it illustrates the use of power and control in conversion rather than free acquiescence.

| A RESPONSE TO BUREAUCRATIZATION:
| COMMUNAL WITHDRAWAL

In Chapter Six, I looked at several kinds of religious leaders, one of whom was called a "reformer prophet." One such reformer prophet was Menno Simons, a major leader in the Anabaptist Reformation. This will be the case example of communal withdrawal.

This movement[3] was a significant movement that developed outside of the mainstream Protestant Reformation. The potent arms of both the Roman Catholic and Protestant churches visited it with the severest of penalties and persecutions (Bainton 1958). Yoder and Kreider (1979) argue that the core of the movement was the opposition to the intrusion of the state into the life of the Christian church and the church's call on the state to do its work (as was common in the second main alternative to secular- 283 ization). Anabaptists saw their call not to work through the existent histor-ical structures of church and state but to offer a whole new alternative: to restore original Christianity to what they called its pristine form without linkages to secular authorities. Further characteristics included an empha-sis on an ascetic way of living, the repudiation of taking of oaths (which merited much persecution from the state), abstention from any force in religion, a dedication to a way of life of suffering, and community living (Bainton 1958). There was a belief in the experience of regeneration and a general indifference to the political world (Williams 1962).

What can be gleaned from this short analysis is that the radical reform-ers chose not to intersect with the secular polity and to keep separate not only from the established churches but any state authority. Is this true today? There is variation among modern-day Anabaptists. Two groups that have maintained the radical separation from the state are the Amish and the Hutterites. Both groups live in rural areas and are relatively discon-nected from the secular authorities around them. The Mennonites (who are quite heterogeneous) have become another Christian denomination and are more like other Christians in their political involvement as citizens of Canada and the United States.

Is this depiction of the Anabaptist withdrawal typical of the various types of Anabaptism? Sawatsky (1992) thinks not. He sees certain kinds of Mennonites in the twentieth century, Transformist Anabaptists, as empha-sizing the liberation of men and women from oppressive social, political, economic, and ideological structures. They tend to be impatient with normal political processes and advocate some form of political activism such as confrontation or nonpayment of taxes.

---

3 Derogatorily called so by their opponents and meaning "later baptism" (Yoder and Kreider 1979).

In linking this analysis to the fifth dilemma, the religious-political motive is voluntary: individuals are given the freedom to become members of the religious group and are not coerced into it.

RESPONSES TO SECULARIZATION IN THE PUBLIC SPHERE

I begin by presenting a short profile of the secularization theory. In the final chapter of the text, I shall investigate the validity of the theory. Here, however, I will present secularization as a baseline from which to consider political-religious responses to it. My main thesis is that with increased religious accommodation to secularization, four central responses can be identified (as outlined in Table 10.3, above): privatization or personal withdrawal from politics, religious political activism, the division response paradigm, and civil religion. I begin with Berger's definition of secularization, stressing the institutional or objective aspect of the process: "By secularization we mean the process by which sectors of society and culture are removed from the domination of religious institutions and symbols" (1969:107-108).

This focus of secularization begins with what Nisbet (1966) terms the *philosophes* of the Enlightenment period. He notes that a common feature of this position was a disdain for institutional religion of any kind. The platform was a rational one: there is no logical or empirical basis for religious convictions or beliefs that inform these sacred institutions. This tradition was given a sociological basis through the work of Comte (1798-1857). His thesis was that secularization was a natural process of the growth of societies from a religious (and superstitious) genesis, to a rational middle ground (based on philosophical and erroneous assumptions), and, lastly, to a positivist stage wherein truth was discovered through the use of the positivist sciences.

As I detailed in Chapter Three, Durkheim (1965, 1969) is not so convinced. His thesis is that religion in a traditional form (folk, classical, and Christian) needs to give way to a new form of religion in tune with modernity, that is, the cult of the individual or the worship of the individual human being as the locus of the sacred. Weber also does not predict the eventual collapse of religion in modernity (see Roth 1987). He, like Durkheim, argues that religion will change through the processes of rationalization; disenchantment with religious institutions, beliefs, and ethics will be more akin to a rational mode of acting and less akin to a supernatural mode. However, at selective moments of history, the charisma which became routinized through reason may "break through" in various institutional forms in renewal movements or the birth of sects.

The Privatization of Religion, or Personal Withdrawal from the Public Sphere

One response to the secularization of religion in a society is to try to reduce the tension by "keeping religion to yourself" and not engaging in any public manifestation of one's belief. Musing on this, Berger (1967) argues that religion in the modern United States is a private institution that is not linked to the public sphere. He contends that a significant consequence of modernization is the creation of the private sphere or a domain of personal life that is separated from the major political and economic institutions. In this sphere, the individual is expected to fulfill him or herself in a number of voluntary relationships (1967:369ff).

This is represented especially by the family. Religion has gone through a similar process in that secularization has "driven" religious institutions and symbols out of the public social areas. Berger adds that this process has several implications. First, religion is no longer able to challenge the autonomy of the state which has become a rigid, powerful, and highly-structured institution. Second, the economy is also effectively divorced from religious influence. Third, religion is most relevant in "leisure-time activities" in which the individual is able to have a significant amount of choice. Fourth, religion has found a social proximity to the family in the private sphere, reflected in the ideology of familialism.

Do Berger's reflections bear empirical verification in recent research? Two sets of literature will be reviewed to illustrate a positive response to one of his observations and a negative response to another.

The third position allows the individual believer significant latitude of belief. This is illustrated by what Roof and McKinney (1987) call a "new voluntarism." Other sociologists of religion use similar terms to reveal the same reality. Greeley (1977) comments that what has emerged within Catholicism is a "selective Catholicism." Marciano (1987) characterizes modern religion as an integration arising from a combination of elements of personal biography and ecclesial beliefs, values, and norms. Similarly, Bellah et al. (1985) speak about the individualist tradition in American culture that influences religious orientations and commitments.

Roof and McKinney (1987) add the following elements to the definition of American mainline religion today: the quest for self, the inner life of impulse and subjectivity, the emphasis on a highly individualistic ethos favouring greater religious subjectivity and personal choice, and the disestablishment of the institution of religion. These same authors write that "commitment to Self has grown at the expense of community, disrupting especially loyalties to traditional religious institutions" (1987:33). They say that to understand what is happening today on the religious scene one has to be aware of the implications of greater individualism and voluntarism (1987:9). In Canada, a similar process is described by Bibby (1987); believers tend to select personally relevant aspects of their religion, resulting in a fragmentation of their belief system.

Berger's fourth implication does not have as much empirical basis. Booth and his colleagues (1995), in a recent review of the linkage between religion and the family, find a relatively weak empirical link. This is substantiated by an earlier review done by Larson (1991), who calls the linkage between religion and family phenomena a "tenuous connection." To test the linkage on various measures of religion and marital quality, Booth *et al.* (1995), using data from a 12-year longitudinal study of 2,033 married persons and drawing from the two last waves (1988 and 1992), find a similar result. They find little support that on various measures of religiosity there is an increase in marital quality.

Political Activism: Liberal and Conservative Political Responses to Secularization

Religion and politics continue to be connected in the modern world, which is often characterized as being secular. Throughout the text, there has been a synthesis of evidence to argue that religion is still present in the personal and social lives of many people, particularly in the United States and Canada. This is reflected in several political movements which are significantly informed by two forms of Christianity: liberal and conservative (to use Wuthnow's terms in his restructuring of American religion). I shall use as cases one example from the liberal emphasis that emerged out of the first part of this century in the social gospel movement which became the Cooperative Commonwealth Federation (CCF) Party of Saskatchewan and, later, the federal New Democratic Party (NDP). Two examples will reflect the conservative emphasis: the Social Credit Party of Alberta and the New Religious Right of the United States.

My thesis here is that these two forms of Christianity respond to the secularization process in two different ways. The social gospel movement reflects the church model of response (to use Weber's [1978] and Troeltsch's [1931] categories) as an adjustment to the social environment and tries to build bridges between the two. The conservative response is to emphasize the differences between Christianity and the world in more of a sectarian mode. Both responses illustrate the dilemmas of the sacred in a profane environment.

A LIBERAL RESPONSE

I begin our investigation here by looking at what has come to be known as the social gospel movement. Beginning about the end of the nineteenth century and the first part of the twentieth century, many liberally minded Protestants recognized that the modern industrial state was not serving marginalized people. Hargrove (1989:266), a sociologist of religion, notes that the social gospel developed out of a need to care for the rights and the needs of the poor and the downtrodden. She quotes Bennett (1955:20-21), who provided a mythological basis for this movement. Elements of this include: faith in God as Lord of history; recognition of the commandment of love as a call to act to improve the living conditions of others; a call to repentance — to transform what can be changed for one's neighbours' sake; a Christian understanding of sin which recognizes that anyone will pursue personal or in-group interests, that those interests are accountable by others, and that no person can be trusted to run the society for the benefit of all; and a recognition of one's neighbour as a whole person in the context of the community, so that action will be taken in a broader frame of reference.

Allen (1973) traces the social gospel movement in Canada from the 1890s. He notes that proponents of the movement considered that Christianity involved a passionate commitment to social involvement and a desire to champion the disinherited. In a liberal mode of thinking, the sacred might very well be the secular and the secular the sacred. The *Kingdom of God* was not a far-off goal but rather something present wherein adherents are challenged to harness themselves to social problems and carry the yoke of social concern (1973:17). Allen profiles leaders, churches, and regions in Canada to present a picture of the social gospel movement between 1914 and 1928. In his conclusion, he reflects on what were some of its effects. Even though it was not accepted fully in the Protestant churches (predominantly Anglican, Methodist, Presbyterian, and Congregationalist), it did bring on a broad range of social reforms such as legislation that aided the underprivileged and contributed to the creation of social work as a profession (1973:352).

It is from this background that the Cooperative Commonwealth Federation (CCF) of the province of Saskatchewan emerged. The well-known sociologist, Seymour Lipset (1959) informs us of the emergence and growth of this political party. The party (formally established in 1932 in Calgary) had three basic roots: rural socialism, urban socialism, and the social gospel. Rural socialism had a long history, dating to the early part of the century. Its origins emerged in a joint effort by farmers to sell grain not to private markets but to cooperatively owned grain companies who represented the needs of the farmers and not of big business from eastern

Canada. In addition, the farmers united to form an association called the
United Farmers of Canada that was inherently socialist in nature. In 1929,
a small group of trade-unionists and teachers formed the Independent
Labour Party (ILP) of Saskatchewan. To augment a power base, the two
organizations joined forces with other socialist Canadian organizations in
1933 to become a new political party known as the Cooperative
Commonwealth Federation.

The social gospel connection comes through J.S. Woodsworth, a former
Methodist minister and avid advocate of the movement. He was a prominent leader and author who, in 1918, resigned from the ministry and
devoted himself to the socialist cause (Allen 1973:49). In the 1930s, he was
the national leader of the CCF. It was during the late 1930s, however, that
the original radical stance of the CCF in Saskatchewan was modified (Lipset
1959:111ff).The second impact of the social gospel came with the 1941 election as party leader of Tommy C. Douglas, another former minister and a
member of the Baptist Church. Douglas (1973), in an autobiographical
essay, writes of his time as a pastor in Weyburn, Saskatchewan in the 1930s.
He organized a food bank, a clothing depot, and an unemployment agency.
The tragedy and difficulty of the depression of the 1930s gave impetus to
the CCF party because many people cooperated to make a quality life for
themselves. He writes:

> The cooperative movement grew by leaps and bounds during that
> period. People helped each other in a score of little ways. They rallied
> to each other. They came close to each other for warmth and comfort
> and companionship. (1973:170)

He was a charismatic leader and a religious prophet for social reform.
While a pastor, he met a woman who was too poor to pay for health care.
He promised her that if he ever came to power, he would see to it that
health care would be provided for the poor and the rich alike. As we shall
see shortly, he held good his promise.

In 1944, Douglas and the CCF did gain power in a provincial election.
Immediately, the party began to extend social services such as social security and health and education services, legislate security of lands for farmers, and increase farm commodity prices (Lipset 1959). Of special interest
was provision of health care for residents. Lipset argues that the most
important single reform of the government was socialized medicine. And,
in keeping with Douglas' promise and a mandate of the party, in 1947, a free
hospitalization plan was inaugurated for all residents. It was not until 1962,
and after the CCF became the New Democratic Party (NDP) in 1961 in

Canada (it was still the CCF party in the province), that the Saskatchewan government introduced coverage for medical care.

As one can see, the impact of the social gospel in the political landscape in Canada is real. Indeed, Lipset (1959:136) recognizes the importance of the social gospel in the CCF. He notes that from the time of its founding to the present, the party has had a moralistic and religious emphasis: "The CCF stresses its support of Christianity and the fact that many of its leaders are religious; and it makes political capital of the fact that some churches are anticapitalist" (1959:136). Although it would be an exaggeration to say that the social gospel was the only driving force for socialized medicine in Canada, it is nonetheless true to say that it did have a definite impact on the future shape of medical care in this country.

CONSERVATIVE RESPONSES

Two historical responses inform our discussion here: the Social Credit political movement of Alberta and the New Religious Right in the United States. Both are conservative responses to secularization and economic and political problems.

The Social Credit Movement

The Social Credit party was begun by a charismatic leader by the name of William Aberhart (1878-1943). Born into a Presbyterian family in Ontario, he became a teacher and moved to Calgary, where he became a high-school principal, ran a successful Bible study program, and founded the Prophetic Bible Conference in 1918. This eventually led to the development of the Calgary Prophetic Bible Institute which trained young Baptist men and women as evangelists and church workers. His reputation grew in the 1920s with his establishment of a radio program dedicated to evangelism and millennial theology. This became immensely popular and he began to combine bible prophecy (millennialism) with Social Credit doctrine in 1933. He led the party and was swept to political power in Alberta in 1935, in the midst of a drought and a depression (Thomas 1977).

He was a typical charismatic leader who was able to capture an audience through rhetoric, enthusiasm, and humour. His message appealed to listeners who had an evangelical persuasion and who were looking for an answer to the social chaos of the Depression. His political success was closely tied to his religious success, as followers of sectarian evangelicalism listened attentively and followed without question (Miller 1977). His success is owed in part to the economic situation in Alberta under the sieges of the Great Depression and the Great Drought of the 1930s. Much of his political jargon was directed against the capitalists of the East who were considered responsible for the economic downturn of a prosperous Alberta. Mann (1955), a sociological observer of sects and cults in Alberta, observes that the preacher-turned-broadcaster denounced the greed and unscrupulous moneylenders of eastern financial interests and wealthy churches. This he turned into a popular outlet for many marginal and economically depressed Albertans.

Aberhart's new political party, the Social Credit, owes its name, philosophy, and practice to a party in England with the same name in the early part of this century. The basic principle of the party was what was known as the *A + B Theorem*. "A" payments are made to individuals of private firms as wages, whereas "B" refers to payments to other firms to cover capital costs, etc. "A" (incomes) is always less than A + B (total costs of production), so stimulus is needed to maintain consumption. To reduce the discrepancy, consumers would be issued a credit that would enable them to consume more in order to live well. This credit, as interpreted by Aberhart in Alberta, would be in the form of a dividend to all people to increase their purchasing power. In Aberhart's own words, the "state shall be viewed by its citizens as a gigantic joint-stock company with the resources of the province behind its credit" (Bell 1993:62). Each citizen would be given a certain amount of money (as a credit) that would allow him or her to purchase necessary goods and materials. This credit would come from a small tax levied on each product and service offered in Alberta.

Thus, with the charismatic authority of Aberhart, the religious following of most Albertans, the ideology of the social credit philosophy, and the socio-economic need of the province's people, the Social Credit governed the province from 1935 until 1971.

Ironically, the basic principle of the party was never realized. Aberhart claimed that the reason why he could not institute social credit was because the federal government would not permit him to do so and the banks were unwilling to give him his much desired credit. How then could this party remain in power for such a long time? One interpretation is that the support for the party was among the working class of Alberta (documented by Bell 1993) and farmers. The farmers did not put much credibility in the credit system but they liked the conservative religious base of the party. Ernest Manning, a protégé of Aberhart, was the premier from 1943 to 1968 and continued the Aberhart heritage of being both a state leader as well as an evangelist.

In addition, attention was turned away from political niceties during the Second World War. After the war, and with the production of oil in Alberta taking off in 1947, Alberta enjoyed unprecedented economic prosperity. By the end of the war, the radical nature of Social Credit was gone, though Albertans continued to be attracted to the conservative and religious nature of the party.

The New Religious Right
There is a current climate of conservative ideology and practice in many western countries today. Even liberal parties like the Democrats in the United States and the Liberals in Canada have become more right-wing than left. Part of this conservative swing has religious underpinnings in the form of what has come to be known as the New Religious Right. One of the first sociological analyses of the movement was a book edited by Robert Liebman and Robert Wuthnow (1983). In this text, several authors outline the ideology (or mythology), the organization, and the cultural environment of the movement.

Himmelstein (1983:15-18) presents three elements of the ideology of the movement: economic libertarianism, social traditionalism, and militant anti-communism. Economic libertarianism is classic capitalism with the assumption that if the market is left to itself, the interaction between rationally self-interested persons will yield prosperity and social harmon, and manifest personal and social goods. Thus, the welfare state needs to be dismantled, since it interferes in the economy. Social traditionalism is more focused on religion. Its premise is that social ills have emerged with liberal support for abortion, the Equal Rights Amendment, bussing, affirmative action, sexual permissiveness, and such things as the secular curriculum in public schools. Militant anti-communism is the third set of new right assumptions. Rooted in the McCarthy era, it postulates a conflict between the West and communism which is a conflict between good and evil.

This ideology has become especially mobilized under the organization called the Moral Majority. Liebman (1983) adds that this ideology is combined, essentially, with American fundamentalism characterized by a large number of small denominations with strong, charismatic leaders. It is relatively successful, however, in its ability to mould disparate local activities into a national movement. The locus of this mobilization is the local church.

How widespread and powerful is the Moral Majority? Does it receive support from all conservative churches and conservative political adherents? Shupe and Stacey (1983) argue that it does not. In a sample of 905 respondents in the Dallas-Fort Worth metropolitan area, they found no basis to Jerry Falwell's (a leader of the Moral Majority) contention that most conservatives support the movement. They also found that Falwell and other leaders of the New Religious Right seriously overestimate the amount of agreement among modest supporters on the issues the leaders hold to be

important. Finally, while Falwell contends that the movement is only political and not religious, these researchers found that the grassroots people
who support the movement are more likely to come from sectarian and fundamentalist Christians and not moderate and conservative Protestants and
Roman Catholics.

Guth (1983) adds further credibility to Schupe and Stacey's conclusions
from data gathered from 453 Southern Baptist ministers drawn from about
40,000 pastors of the denomination. He finds that there is little support for
the Moral Majority's campaign. He argues that the right draws its strength
from those ministers who are less educated and are less professional. The
number of Southern Baptist ministers of this type are becoming rarer and
rarer as the church becomes more and more like other denominations in the
United States. These findings are more significant given that this denomination is not only the largest Protestant church in the world but is also the
most conservative. Thus, even in one of the most conservative churches,
there is not significant support for the movement.

What sociological circumstances have given rise to the New Religious
Right? Wuthnow (1993) offers some answers. He argues that the movement
is similar to the rest of American Protestantism in presenting a "this-
worldly orientation" (from Weber 1978). It is an orientation not toward
some other world but toward an active engagement in moral reform and
social service. In line with the wider conservatism within American culture,
a second circumstance is the new emphasis on values, particularly family
values. In response to Watergate and the *Roe vs. Wade* decision in 1973 on
women's right to abortion, the movement has been engaged in the public
meaning of values. A third circumstance, unique to America, is the willingness of people to financially support their churches and causes like the
New Religious Right. There are also some organizational factors that led to
its growth. Relying on his earlier work on the restructuring of American
religion, Wuthnow (1988a) notes that the declining significance of denominationalism, the rise of special interest groups, leadership networks,
sources of social strain, the growth of higher education, the growth of the
welfare state, and political upheavals have all contributed to the emergence
and the growth of the movement. I shall conclude the discussion on the
New Religious Right by following Wuthnow in his predictions for the
future of the movement.

A study of the movement by the religious studies scholar Walter Capps
(1990:5-14) focuses not so much on the world view or the mythology of the
New Religious Right but, rather, on its instinctual basis that is the social
and psychological source of its motivational power.[4] Elements of that

---

4   Capps acknowledges Thomas O'Dea (1966) for this perspective.

instinct include the reassertion of patriarchy, indulging in nostalgia, a reaction to secularization, an engagement in spiritual warfare that pits "us" and "them" in polar opposites, striving to be intellectually respectable, and using television to create a positive image. This instinctual focus is combined with a certain kind of mythology that is in keeping with a fundamentalist world view. The political message is communicated via biblical symbols that are interpreted in a literalist way. This absolutist dedication to literalism (especially in the biblical text that is apocalyptic in nature) encourages the tendency toward intolerance of others, doctrinal fanaticism, and the reading of symbols and mythologies as facts. It is a mythology that divides the world into good and evil, darkness and light, God and Satan. Capps writes:

> Like Manichaeism[5] of old, it is a disposition that understands the ingredients of the world to be arranged as polar opposites: something is either good or evil, represents light or darkness, embodies truth or error, for there is no middle ground. But it is also a reading of the world in which no great allowances are made for distinctions between the image and its referent, the symbol and that to which the symbol may refer, or even between empirical and imaginative portrayals. (1990:14)

293

Capps continues his study of the movement by presenting biographical accounts of four prominent leaders: Jerry Falwell, Francis Schaeffer (a philosopher-theologian), Jim and Tammy Bakker, and Pat Robertson, who went as far as to become a serious presidential candidate in 1988.

In analyzing these figures, Capps (1990:186ff) posits the following observations. First, they all agree that the nation is suffering because its spiritual vitality is weak. This suffering takes the name of a rampant drug culture, the prevalence of sexual promiscuity,[6] the frequency of teenage abortions, and deviant behaviour both in communities and schools. Second, the reasons for this malaise is a secularism that is manifested through liberalism,

---

5   The term refers to a religious world view common in the first centuries of Christianity. The religion comes from Persia and posits a belief that creation is a dual product of an all powerful "Good Being" and an equally all powerful "Evil Being." Anything that is spiritual or of the soul is good but anything of a material nature is evil. This is a classic case of extreme dualism.

6   Contrary to this opinion, Michael, Gagnon, Lauman and Kolata (1994) provide evidence from an American national sample of adults that the sexual promiscuity image has no empirical basis. In fact, most Americans stay faithful to their spouses, have few sexual partners, do not enjoy "kinky sex," and are heterosexual.

secular humanism, ecumenical Christianity, and all the human potential movements. According to these leaders, this kind of secularism has reduced human dependence upon God and has failed to offer a satisfactory vision of human transcendence.

The theme that has the most far reaching implication is the response to the secularization processes of modern America. Its roots, according to the New Religious Right, go back to the Enlightenment that substituted a theism for a humanism. This needs to be replaced with a new theism that focuses on an apocalyptic image of America and the world. In this view, the world is coming to its end. The Messiah (Jesus Christ) is to return to bring judgement on a disobedient world. In this coming, America has been given a special role to serve the Kingdom of God.

A study of New Right leaders continues with the work of Micheal Lienesch (1993). In this text, the author provides evidence that the movement is not as monolithic as previous accounts would assert. He argues that rather than providing a single world view, it was beset with the inability to go beyond a collection of single-issue reactions to the secular enemy. His research focuses on values and indicates how important the Born-Again experience is, how central the family is for maintaining spirituality, how laissez-faire capitalism is necessary for the success of America, and the attempt by the leaders of the movement to give back to America her place as the "New Jerusalem" of the modern world.

In contrast to these studies, Moen (1992) is struck by a new accommodation within the New Religious Right. His main thesis is that it has gradually become more politically sophisticated and, as a consequence, has shed much of its sectarian mode to become more accommodating to the political realities of the 1990s (some of this may be due to the demise of Moral Majority as an organization in 1989). In addition, rather than choosing to fly under the banner of an organization like the Moral Majority, it has now aligned itself more with the Republican Party. From this grass roots approach, its membership within the party has increased substantially. A critique offered by Guth (1992) is useful, however. Moen's data do not use "grass roots" information but, rather, information from interviews with leaders who are limited in number (33). Kenneth Wald (1987) does not so much speak of accommodation but states that, for the most part, the New Religious Right has not succeeded in achieving its goals.

What future does the New Right have? In his book on the future of Christianity in the twenty-first century, Wuthnow (1993) attempts to answer this question. He sets his argument as a dialectic between social forces which would present a positive future for the movement against those which could herald its demise. The movement has several resources that could be mobilized for future success. First of all, there appear to be more sympathizers on New Right issues than actual committed members. He acknowledges studies that show that there is a strong and wide interest in pro-family issues, concern about sexual infidelity, and a commitment to traditional standards of honesty and integrity. A second reason for optimism is that conservative clergy are becoming increasingly more educated and have the ability to muster support for a cause at the grass roots level.

A third reason is that the lack of political success of clergy like Falwell and Robertson may indicate a change in strategy, i.e., not having clergy leaders who are handicapped because of their commitment to their own denomination. Wuthnow (1993:162), relying on Hadden's (1987a) work on TV evangelists and the New Right, suggests that the new leaders should come from writers, counsellors, lobbyists, and business people. A fourth reason follows. Wuthnow considers that the high profile of the TV evangelists did give a lot of momentum to the movement, but it also made them very vulnerable as in the cases of the Bakkers and Jimmy Swaggart. For a movement to be successful, some form of environmental, powerful support is important. Ronald Reagan, in the 1980s, gave much support to the movement. Without this support, however, will the movement grow?

Wuthnow also outlines some of the reasons for a potential decline of the movement. Another necessary resource is time and labour. With the educational achievement of many conservative Christians, women are much more likely to be in the labour market. The downside of this for the church is that these women are no longer available as voluntary agents for the movement. He adds an interesting note on the potential consequences of the New Right achieving its objectives. If it did (for example, reversing the Roe vs. Wade decision and re-introducing prayer in the public schools) what would motivate its continued existence? And, if it lost, would it not lose its enthusiasm? A final reason is that although there is widespread support for many of the issues in the movement, there is still much disagreement. For example, Falwell (a fundamentalist evangelical) did not join forces with Robertson (a charismatic evangelical) because of internal division within the evangelical community. Catholics would join with fundamentalists on issues of abortion and sexual codes but would be significantly divided on many others.

What of the future then? Wuthnow predicts that there will continue to be a strong segment of the American people firmly committed to their churches and who respect moral values. These Americans will more likely be middle-class suburbanites who are well educated and have talents for mobilization. Furthermore, the majority of these conservative Christians will participate in politics because they consider it their entitlement. In the end, Wuthnow does some wishful thinking that the New Right "will be less concerned with achieving its ends through politics alone but be more devoted to service, caring for the poor and disadvantaged, promoting community, reconciliation, and the transmission of values through teaching and training the young" (1993:167).

The Division Paradigm

This paradigm is a third response to secularization that is common in the modern world, especially in the United States. Marty (1959) considers that the French Revolution of 1789 marked the turning point in another kind of linkage between religion and the state. Although Napoleon tried to turn the tide, the virtual crossing of the Rubicon had happened. In Marty's words,

> With all exceptions in mind, however, we can safely generalize that the modern trend has been toward the disestablishing of papal religion, removing from it political sanction, and forcing it to make its way on a voluntary principle among the other denominations and religions. (1959:281)

Marty adds that Protestantism faced a similar fate. From about 1650 to the present, there has been a gradual decrease of official influence of Protestants in the political sphere. Frederick the Great of Prussia (who reigned from 1713-40) was intent on imposing Enlightenment on Protestantism. In England, after the Great Rebellion of 1642-49, the Church of England as the established church lost more and more of its official status. It was in the United States, however, that the doctrine of separation of the church and the state reached its apex. Even though the Constitution did not explicitly propose the separation (Article One of the Amendments states: "Congress shall make no law respecting an establishment of religion, or prohibiting the free exchange thereof"[7]) a virtual pattern of division was institutionalized.[8] However, the division is not as profound as one might think, as the research on civil religion testifies. This will be the topic of our next discussion.

Civil Religion

Civil religion does not fit into any of the three paradigms above but is a complex union of several elements of the three. Bellah (1970) introduces the

---

7   The Constitution of the United States 1952.

8   Wuthnow (1996) terms this the second restructuring of American religion. See Chapter Three of this text.

term into the sociology of religion by arguing that there exists a religion in the United States that is inclusive enough to include all Christian denominations and exclusive enough to exclude atheism, agnosticism, and polytheism. He builds on the idea from the writings of the eighteenth-century political philosopher Jean-Jacques Rousseau's *Social Contract*, noting that the philosopher includes the following as central to religion: the existence of God, the life to come, the reward for virtue and punishment for vice, and the exclusion of religious intolerance (1970:172).

He continues his analysis and reviews literature on the American Revolution, the American Civil War, presidential speeches, and sociological studies (by de Tocqueville [1945] and Lipset [1964]) to give the following as a summary definition of civil religion:

> a religion that includes the doctrines of belief in God (albeit, unitarian) and religious liberty; biblical archetypes such as Exodus (movement from Europe), Chosen People (Americans are called to spread the message of democracy throughout the world), Promised Land and New Jerusalem (America the free and the beautiful), Sacrificial Death (the death of Lincoln) and Rebirth (emancipation of the nineteenth century and the civil rights of the twentieth); and rituals such as the celebration of Memorial Day and feast days, Thanksgiving Day on November 26, the Fourth of July, and presidential inaugural days. (1970:168-86)

297

Bellah, with his colleague Hammond (1980), reflect further on the topic. They use the republican political tradition to argue that civil religion is necessary for the maintenance of democracy. A communitarian set of values undergirds the very reality of a democracy, and a religion is a necessary ingredient of this set of values. He adds that the United States' existence depends upon some sort of "national community" that contributes to the social integration of the state. Roberts, in his introduction to the sociology of religion, notes:

> Regardless of one's personal evaluation of civil religion, the student of religion must keep in mind that it serves functions for the individual and for the society as a whole. American civil religion provides a sense of ultimate meaning to one's citizenship. It causes people to feel good about themselves as participants in the nation. It is not likely to disappear soon from the American scene. Besides simple survival, the particular style and character of American civil religion in the future is important, for civil religion may be influential in shaping the course of the nation. (1995:387)

SOCIETY, SPIRITUALITY, AND THE SACRED

Is there evidence for a Canadian civil religion? Blumstock (1993) thinks not. As noted above, Bellah (1980) theorizes that for American society to survive, there must be a basic consensus. This basic consensus is found in American civil religion. It is different, though, for Canadians. Blumstock lists reasons for there not being a national religion that unites Canadians. Even though some Canadians sing "God Save the Queen," there is little substance to that prayer. The value consensus is different: there is little symbolic power in such Canadian values as peace, order, and good government compared to life, liberty, and the pursuit of happiness in the United States. The United States Loyalists are in sharp contrast to the Sons of Liberty; Canadians have no Lincoln who became a civil and religious hero and who was sacrificed for the sake of the emancipation; and Canadians still do not have a symbol of unity that compares to the flag of the United States. The Quebec Referendum of October 1995 reflects a deep-rooted disunity that no religion, civil or denominational, seems able to solve.

In summary, civil religion is a response to secularization that selects some of the themes from the Judeo-Christian past by expanding the meaning of denominational Christianity to include as much as possible from this tradition. It is an attempt to go beyond the secular, hierocratic and division paradigms of linking religion and politics. Its true effects have not been empirically verified. One might ask the question: has American civil religion brought a sense of national unity to Americans or does there continue to be evidence of deep-rooted divisions, especially in the wake of the re-emergence of racism in the guise of the Nation of Islam's leader Farrakhan and the criminal law verdict of O.J. Simpson? Has it made any difference in unity issues with the 1998 national controversy over President Clinton and his moral leadership?

Summary of the Four Responses to Secularization

As was noted in the section on the privatization of religion, it has become clear that voluntarism is a salient code of behaviour in the modern, secularized world. In regard to the O'Deas' fifth dilemma, it is also quite clear that all four of these responses are not coercive responses. No persons or social groups that reflect privatization, religious political activism, the division of the state and religion, or civil religion, would tend to opt for coercion. The only one that would approximate it would be the New Religious Right in the 1980s with its fundamentalist tendencies. Even this movement, in the 1990s, however, is closer to the voluntaristic model of religious conversion.

| CONCLUSIONS

I have attempted to present a view in this chapter that reviews the literature and the research on the linkages between religion and politics. I have done so by positioning it under the fifth and final religion-society dilemma of the O'Deas. The central thesis is that as a religious movement becomes more accommodated to the social environment, it takes on more of the values and ways of acting of the political and economic spheres. On the other hand, it may react to this accommodation and choose a different path. I argued that in the early Christian church, the response to accommodation was increased accommodation that used coercive power in leadership. This resulted in two forms: Cæsaropapism or the secular paradigm in which the state uses the sacred for its own ends. This continued to be the most common paradigm in Eastern Europe and Russia for many centuries. It was resurrected in the early years of the Reformation where Protestant princes used coercive force to elicit conformity to Protestantism.

The hierocratic paradigm began in the mature years of the medieval era and declined in the later years. I outlined a twentieth-century version of the paradigm in modern day Iran and fundamentalist Islam.

The reformation period witnessed another kind of political response to extreme accommodation: communal withdrawal from politics. The example given here was the Anabaptist Reformation.

The modern era has elicited several kinds of response. After laying the groundwork of the secularization thesis in the modern world, I outlined four kinds of response to secularization: personal privatization, liberal and conservative activism (using the Cooperative Commonwealth Federation of Saskatchewan, the Social Credit party of Alberta, and the New Religious Right of the United States), the division paradigm or the separation of the state and religion, and the civil religion response.

What of the future of the connection between religion and politics? Given the many different kinds of social responses in the past, there will likely be a continuation of these in the future. One thing we can be sure of: even though there is a strong move to personal privatization, I would agree with Wuthnow (1993) that there will likely continue to be a salient linkage between the two institutions.

In his discussion on the future of the linkages between religion and politics, Wuthnow (1993) uses the Religious Right as a case study. Religion will matter to the level that believers have firm convictions in a divine truth in a pluralistic society. He outlines how this conviction will not so much create a religious hegemony but, rather, crystallize "the power of the holy" in things that matter to the majority of Americans. Even though the Religious Right has not changed the abortion law and has not introduced prayers into schools, it has succeeded in bringing more moderate and even liberal thinkers into considering the question of abortion. It has not succeeded in having legislation to ban all violence and sexual innuendo on TV and in the movies, but it has raised consciousness on these matters.

The issue of the religious influence in the public domain is not so much one of ministers and priests in positions of political leadership but one of influencing a shift in values. The legacy of the New Religious Right lies not in fundamentalism and sectarianism but in the creation of a public symbol, a public discourse on morality. The public role of religion is to inform the public on a range of moral issues that affect all Americans (or Canadians), not just the conservative constituency.

The Linkage of Religion to Other Institutions, Secularization, and Religious Responses to Postmodernity

CHAPTER ELEVEN

Religion and the Family: Continued Dilemmas

This chapter begins our investigation of the relationship between religion and other social systems and starts Part Three of the text. The focus of this chapter will be on the tension that exists between religion and the family. I begin with an outline of the relationship and present a comparison between traditional and modern societies as they have negotiated the linkage. I continue with a comparison between the connection in an oriental society and Western societies. Then I discuss the linkage between religion and the family, with examples from nineteenth-century America and recent and current empirical research on the relationship between the two institutions.

From a social scientific point of view (see Chapter One), if we were to compare all the social institutions with religion, we would find that the one that is most closely linked to it is the family. This is so because, in the light of our using Weber's (1978) threefold division of social action into traditional, rational-legal, and affective, we discover that at the heart of both religion and the family is affective social action. As I argued in Chapter One, that action is affective if it satisfies a need for revenge, sensual gratification, devotion, contemplative bliss, or for working off emotional tensions. As I have demonstrated throughout this text, affective action is at the core of religion (Weber 1978:25). It is also at the core of the family.

By implication, Weber (1978:356-358) considers the family as an institution that focuses on affective social action, since the sexual relationship between a man and a woman that results in a child is at the core of the family. A definition of the family that relies, in part, on a cross-cultural survey of 250 societies from the anthropologist Murdock (1949) is "an intimate group of persons who are bound together by procreative, sexual, emotional and economic ties that, typically, result in children who are socialized into being socially competent and who all live in a common residence." It should be noted that procreative, sexual, and emotional ties indicate affective social kinds of relationships.

A second social scientific link between religion and the family in the modern world is established through the work of Berger (1967), who argued that religion and the family are the two remaining "private institutions." His thesis is that as modernity grows, religion tends to lose its once-held public place in the lives of people and is relegated to their private lives. My analysis of his position leads me to conclude that there continues to be evidence for his thesis (see Chapter Nine for the extended discussion). Thus their unity is that, at least in modernity, they are of a private nature.

Another connection between religion and the family comes from the literature that forms the comparative religion background to the text. As we saw in Chapter Two, a second function of mythology is sociological, including social support, social control, and socialization. Campbell (1964, 1987) focuses on the family as the key socialization function of myth. He outlines how important "rites of passage" are for the integration of the individual into the social group, and religion is a vital mechanism for this integration. He goes as far as to say that an unsocialized child is a pain to the social group, but a disobedient adolescent is a threat to the very existence of that same group. The puberty rites of passage are important rituals that link the child from the family to the social group. Thus family and religion are connected substantially in most folk religions as well as in classical and modern religions.

A fourth and final basis of the linkage emerges from sociobiology. Two family scholars, Troost and Filsinger (1993), review a wide range of literature that presents a thesis that the family is the one institution that fully combines nature and nurture. However, one rarely considers that there may be a biological basis to religion. Reynolds and Tanner (1995) offer us some reflections on the relationship.

They start off with a provocative question: how does membership in a religious group affect individuals' chances of survival and reproduction? In response, they acknowledge that cultures (within which religions are subsumed), are largely independent of genetic causal factors. However, they are at the ecological interface; it is cultures that determine how biologically successful, in terms of survival and reproduction, human groups and individuals will be. This is where religion comes in. We saw in Chapter Nine how central ethos was to an understanding of religion. The many moral rules that command and prohibit, allow and disallow, enforce and give freedom have a basis in the success (or lack thereof) of human survival and reproduction. The biological basis of religion, then, is in how well the social construction of culture contributes to the success of the human species.

The affinity of religion to the family clusters about the second most important biological need of any species (including the human): reproduction. Reynolds and Turner note that religions are very concerned about matters that are biological — sex, reproduction, contraception, abortion, birth, and child-rearing. The successful survival of the human species is at stake. As we saw with Campbell's outline of the sociological nature of myth, so it is the case with biology: religions are intricately involved with the human life cycle from conception through to death.

This, then, is the basis of a linkage between religion and the family. What, then, of the dilemma? Selecting the first basis for the linkage between religion and the family, the dilemma consists in affective social action being primarily in a vertical relationship with the divine and a horizontal relationship with others in the case of religion; in the family, only the horizontal relationship is present. Therein lie the tension and the dilemma. Various religions, societies, and cultures respond to that tension and dilemma in different ways. In this chapter, I will outline the various kinds of responses that are framed in historical, cross-cultural, and contemporary literature.

305

| TRADITIONAL AND MODERN SOCIETIES

In this section I will present a thesis that in folk societies[1] (using an anthropological database) and in oriental religions, the linkages between religion and the family are harmonious, and there is little tension between the two. Observers have noted that among native Americans the cosmos, the earth, the clan, the animals, and the plants are seen as one great expression of the *Wakan* (the Great Spirit). Of special interest, however, is that these objects are seen not so much as independent units but rather as part of a holistic relationship, and these relationships are redolent with familial images such as Grand-Mother Earth, Grand-Father Sky, Mother Moon, and Brother Elk. In modern societies, things are different, especially within modern Christianity. As in the case of religion, this unity is significantly reduced and, as we shall see, a tension exists between the two institutions in the modern world.

Folk and Oriental Societies

To form a contrast that may shed light on the dilemma between religion and the family, I shall analyze folk and oriental linkages between religion and society.

RELIGION AND FAMILY IN FOLK SOCIETIES

As we saw in Chapter Two on folk religions, one is struck by the tendency to unity and the reduction of differences and contrasts. A unity of the pro-

---

1   The central source is the studies of Durkheim (1947 and 1965).

fane and the sacred in folk societies may be illustrated by the beliefs of animism. Animism does not recognize transcendental gods or spirits, but does assume that supernatural forces have an impact on human life and recognizes active, animate spirits operating in the world. Although these spirits are not gods and are not worshipped, they are regarded as forces that may be benevolent or evil. People must take these spirits into account and may try to influence them. Animistic religions have been common among tribes of Africa and the Americas.

The example I will use here is the same one referred to in Paper's (1989) study of ritual among aboriginal people. His focus is on the vitality and importance of the Sacred Pipe ceremony. He argues that the Sacred Pipe and the sweat lodge are the most pervasive rituals throughout Native North America and that the Sacred Pipe is as central to these religions as is the Torah to Judaism, the Koran to Islam, and the Bible to Christianity. The sacred pipe is the ritual symbol that connects the self to his/her family, clan, humanity, nature, the cosmos, and to the eternal or spiritual realm (Paper 1989:39ff).

Family images are redolent in this symbol and ritual. Through the smoking of this Sacred Pipe, one becomes integrated with the whole of creation wherein "all are my relations" (1989:53). The bowl (made of stone and symbolizing earth) is female, whereas the stem (made of wood and symbolizing trees and the sky) is male. In unison with the analysis of religion in folk societies, aboriginal peoples hold no absolute distinction between the creator and creation. Spirits dwell in animals, plants, minerals, and the earth. These various forms are termed grandfather, grandmother, mother, and father.

Primary spirits are distant and remote. The Great Spirit, the Creator, is beyond all spirits and is symbolized by the sky, the heavens. This Great Spirit is masculine and is called Father or Grandfather. The Earth is Mother or Grandmother, whereas the moon is Mother, and the Sun is Grandfather. Spirits that are less remote are effective spirits, and it is to them that the Sacred Pipe can be offered. Every animal has one of these spirits; these animals are referred to as brothers or sisters. Originating spirits are special spirits which dwell in some animals, and their function is to create order out of chaos or to restore what has been undone by human malice or natural catastrophe.

Two things stand out. First, there is evidence for a synthesized monism or unity between religion, as manifested in the world of spirits and ritualized by the Sacred Pipe, and the family. This monism keeps tension at a minimum between the family realm and the religious world. Second, the meaning of family far exceeds blood line and the nuclear family. Family includes the self, kin, the clan, humanity, nature, and the cosmos. The reality of family is as extensive as that of religion: including all that there is. Thus, if they are co-extensive and interdependent, there is less potential for tension and dilemma.

THE RELIGION AND FAMILY LINK IN TRADITIONAL CHINA

I chose to reflect on the relationship between religion and the family in an oriental setting by looking at traditional China. Spiro (1984), the anthropologist we met in our study of Buddhism in Burma, makes a very interesting observation of the connection between religion and family in that these two systems are related to one another in a systematic relationship that is unlike the linkage between any two other sociocultural systems (1984:35). His thesis is that people in social relationships within families psychologically construct myths and religious cognitions which, in turn, are transformed and elaborated in the cultural realm to become sociocultural religious systems. He uses data from the Far East to substantiate his thesis.

He makes a distinction between the invariant biological characteristics of the family and the variant sociocultural ones. Of six invariant elements, two are relevant to our discussion. He argues that because of the neotenous nature of human children they become attached to their parents, especially their mothers. This attachment is a consequence of the gratification they experience in having their physical and emotional needs met. However, their emotional needs and wants go beyond parental gratification. Parents not only respond to these emotional needs and wants, but also frustrate them. Children are not only bonded to their parents but experience some hostility toward them as well. This hostility, if manifested, will result in social disintegration. The sociocultural systems provide a wide range of ways to regulate these emotions and to socially control them. De Vos (1984) adds that the religious sociocultural system regulates this hostility and facilitates some levels of harmony and order.

As it is theorized that there is a lack of tension between oriental religions and families, we find only partial evidence for this in Spiro's (1984) analysis but support for it in Wei-Ming's (1984) study of Neo-Confucianism in traditional China.[2] I shall offer some reflections on the contrasting interpretations at the conclusion of this section.

2   Confucianism is very ancient. The founder is Confucius (551-479 BC) whose best known texts are the *Analytics* (Noss and Noss, 1984:269). In the beginning of the twelfth century, a Neo-Confucian revival emerged. In response to a decline in Confucian belief and a dominance of Buddhism, scholars constructed a Confucian metaphysical and ethical system that would eventually rival and then supplant the Buddhists (*Encyclopædia Britannica*, 1987).

In a similar fashion to the overall thesis of this chapter that family and religious life are represented by tension and dilemma, Spiro (1984) argues that tension is endemic to East Asian family life. His thesis is that the theistic conceptions (mythologies) are more or less isomorphic with the conceptions, conscious or unconscious, which family members form of other family members and, more particularly, conceptions which children form of their parents (one is reminded of Freud's theory of religion). He further argues that the presence of the nurturing mother results in belief in a mother-like superhuman being, while the authoritarian father gives rise to an authoritarian male deity. The nurturing mother (and female deity) evokes compassion and love, whereas the authoritarian father evokes fear and anxiety (1984:39).

Ancestor worship reflects this. These ancestors (who become a form of deity) are not only revered (which is an extension of filial piety) but also feared, and represent the authoritarian father. Part of East Asian family ideology is that a good mother cares for the child beyond death. In Japan, the benevolent deity (Kannon) is feminine. She is kind, nurturing, merciful, compassionate, and, especially, omnipotent, and thus has power to care for believers just as a mother cares for her children.

Another example Spiro (1984) presents is from monastic Buddhism. He theorizes that the Buddhist monastery is a family surrogate: a substitution of a biological-kinship family for a voluntary community based on religio-mystical ties. He asks the question: How could a Chinese young man leave his family when doing so would be a gross infraction of filial piety? He contends that the tensions, fears, and resentments engendered by the father and the dependency anxiety that the son feels in relationship to his mother give him a "push"[3] toward monastic and non-familial commitment.

Wei-Ming (1984) presents the contrasting interpretation. Similar to my argument that there are an implicit monism and a lack of tension between the sacred and the secular in oriental religions, Wei-Ming substantiates this position with an investigation of Neo-Confucianism. The focus of this philosophical/religious system is the development of the self. Quoting from an ancient text, he writes:

> When the personal life is cultivated, the family will be regulated; when the family is regulated, the state will be in order; and when the state is in order, there will be peace throughout the world. (1984:114)

---

3 His thesis is given some support through the work of Lancaster (1984). He interviewed Korean Buddhist monks, 70 per cent of whom entered the monastery against the wishes of their parents and carry a lingering guilt that they have abandoned their parents.

Further, he notes that the idea of the family is a complex of ethico-religious as well as social and political implications. The whole of the cosmos is redolent with familial imagery. In an ancient text (c. 11th century) we read: "Heaven is my father and Earth is my mother.... All people are my brothers and sisters and all things are my companions" (Wei-Ming 1984:117).[4] Neo-Confucian ideology and mythology provide the model, the pattern of human relationships according to five fundamental dyads: father-son, parent-child, wife-husband, ruler-subject, and friend-friend. Wei-Ming (1984) considers the wife-husband dyad to be the fundamental dyad of all, for it is through this dyad that all persons are generated. In addition, the ideal is not gender subordination but, rather, mutuality and reciprocity. If there are conflict and dishonour, domestic harmony is disrupted and social stability is jeopardized. Quoting from a source book in Chinese philosophy (Chan 1963), Wei-Ming notes that a scholar by the name of Ch'eng I writes:

> she [his mother] and father treated each other with full respect as guests are treated. Grateful for her help at home, the father is treated with even greater reverence. But mother conducted herself with humility and obedience.... She was humane, altruistic, liberal, and earnest. (1984:121-122)

Therefore, in spite of the society being male-centred, the active participation of the wife in shaping the family is recognized and encouraged. The division of labour is between the inner (domestic) and the outer (public), where the woman assumes a major role in the home.

Why the contrasts between Spiro and Wei-Ming? Why is there an interpretation by Wei-Ming of resolved tensions and continued tensions in families and religious phenomena? I would contend that the contrasts may have something to do between what an anthropologist (Spiro) and an historian and philosopher (Wei-Ming) see. Spiro elicits his data from field studies whereas Wei-Ming investigates religious texts nearly 1,000 years old. These texts say little about the social life of the Chinese people of the twelfth century. They can give us insight into the mythology and ideology of Neo-Confucianism but not the social history of the people. I argue that Spiro's analysis is potentially the stronger empirical one and that Wei-Ming's is the more useful in assisting us in understanding family/religious mythology and ideology of Neo-Confucianism. Thus, the basis for the thesis of reduced tension between religion and the family in ancient China is substantiated primarily from a textual basis. However, the thesis is weakened when one uses Spiro as an anthropological observer.

309

---

4   There is a striking similarity between this teaching and that of aboriginal folk religion.

Nineteenth-Century Mormonism:
A Unique Response to the Religion and Family Tension

To look at an example of occidental religion in Christianity, we discover that there have been tensions and dilemmas between society and Christianity since the foundation of the religion. There are examples of tensions and dilemmas within the New Testament itself. Jesus calls for a kind of discipleship that places God above family commitments in a radical way (Luke 14:25-27). He also says that, in heaven, marriage will be no more (Luke 20:36). However, marriage is still to be revered. Divorce is prohibited (Luke 16:18), marriage is to be honoured (Hebrews 13:4), and even thoughts of adultery are banned (Matthew 5:27-30).

As we saw in Chapter Five, the social-historical situation of early nineteenth-century New York was a setting where these tensions became acute. Foster (1981), cited in Swenson (1996b), documents that the period in American history between the war of 1812 and the Civil War was one of buoyant optimism and expansiveness. The Erie Canal that linked the Great Lakes to New York City had been completed; it was opened on October 25, 1825, by the canal boat *Seneca Chief*. The canal opened western New York state to commercial and industrial enterprises and was, in part, responsible for the expansion of New York City. Economic differentiation began to take men away from home to work, and women assumed the primary role in child care. Geographical mobility improved, resulting in the separation of young people from tight parental and community control, the emergence of free choice in marriage, the growth of individualist romantic love, the erosion of sexual controlling mechanisms, and the first signs of female emancipation.

The region where both the Shakers and the Oneida Perfectionists found a home and where Joseph Smith proclaimed he had a prophetic-religious experience was called the *burned-over district* (see pp. 124-25). The Shakers, Oneida Perfectionists, and the Mormons were some of the many utopian and millennial groups which materialized (Foster 1981). All three groups radicalized Christian interpretations of marriage, sexuality, and family forms. They attempted a unique response to the inherent tension between religion and the family. In short, the Shakers formed communities of celibate men, women, and children (thus opting for no marriage); the Oneida Perfectionists introduced pantogamy or group marriage; and the Mormons opted for celestial marriage[5] and polygyny.

---

5 A teaching and practice in the faith that believes that a marriage on earth blessed by the priesthood (a temple marriage) is eternal and will continue in the heavenly realm. McConkie (1979:18) writes: "Celestial marriage is a holy and eternal ordinance; as an order of the priest-

There were many common features of these seemingly divergent experiments of familial-communal living. Each had its own charismatic original
leader: John Humphrey Noyes (1811-1886) for the Oneida Perfectionists,
Ann Lee (1736-1784) for the Shakers, and Joseph Smith (1805-1844) for the
Mormons. All of them had personal experience of marital tensions. Ann
Lee had a poor marriage and negative sexual experiences, Noyes struggled
with his sexuality and the suffering of his wife with childbirth, and Smith
sensed he had a revelation to have multiple wives. And, lastly, all three
groups recruited members from an Anglo-Saxon-Puritan base and all were
from the same area of western New York state.

The three communities believed in earnest that the world was coming to
an end soon and that their cosmic role was to restore the primitive
Christian church in the midst of a corrupt and decadent society (Foster
1981). It is also interesting that all three groups used a common New
Testament text to construct their marital (or non-marital) patterns. In a
paraphrased form, the conversation between the Sadducees and Jesus (Luke
20:27-36) becomes a setting for teaching. The religious leaders query Jesus
on which man would have a particular woman for his wife in heaven if she
were married to seven men during her lifetime. His answer was that it is on
earth that men and women marry but in heaven, no one marries.

Foster (1981) notes that each of the groups interpreted this passage in a
way that came to be central to their beliefs and practices. Because Ann Lee
(and the Shakers in general) believed that sexual relationships are the central sin and that she was Christ incarnate, the resurrection had already
come, and sexual relationships were to be prohibited. Noyes saw in this passage the prohibition of marriage between one woman and one man and the
provision for each adult man to have sexual relationships with any other
adult woman in the community.

Smith understood that the passage meant that in heaven, there were to
be no marriages performed, but that a marriage sealed on earth through the
Mormon priesthood (a Temple Marriage) was to continue throughout
eternity. Also, because it was very important that the Mormon progeny be
"judged worthy" (from the passage), there would be allowed polygyny (as
with the Hebrew patriarchs) for the men of high status who would produce
many "righteous children."[6] Each of these three groups, then, endeavoured

hood, it has the name of the new and everlasting covenant of marriage.... Its importance in
the plan of salvation and exaltation cannot be overestimated."

6   Joseph Smith married three sets of sisters, Brigham Young married 27 women and had 56 children, and Herber C. Kimball (Young's first counsellor) was reported to have had 45 wives and
68 children (Kephart 1987:232). However, Arrington (1985) noted that Young also had 30 celestial marriages that were not consummated.

to resolve the tensions and dilemmas of marriage, family, and sexuality in relation to their religious mythologies and practices. For the Mormons, I will outline the core mythologies (primarily their images of the divine) as well as the marital and family practices. I hypothesize that the images of the divine are intricately connected both to family structures and practices (see Swenson [1996b] for an expanded version of this hypothesis).

In generic terms, Mormon theology is linked to the trinity of orthodox Christianity. However, there is a significant nuance that distances this theology from the orthodox interpretation. There are three Gods: the Father, the Son, and the Holy Ghost. They are separate in personality but are united in purpose, plan, and all the attributes of perfection. The Father is the ultimate and the one supreme being. However, there is also a plurality of gods beyond these three. Of special note for our purposes is the *Mother in Heaven* teaching. It is understood that there could not be an Eternal Father without an Eternal Mother. Indeed, this Mother is the spouse of the Father (Campbell and Campbell 1988). All people (their souls) are originally born of this union "in the similitude of the universal Father and Mother, and are literally the sons and daughters of Deity" (McConkie 1979:516). Mormons believe that the Father, Son (who became Jesus Christ), and the Holy Ghost are still supreme and that they are the only ones adored and worshipped.

From this imagery flows something of the emphasis within Mormonism on the importance of the family in general, and patriarchy, celestial marriage, and polygyny in particular. The first teaching makes sense of the distribution of the heavenly pantheon. The supreme deity is male, and the Heavenly Mother is his equal spouse. This may account for the practice of patriarchy.[7] Celestial marriage, however, is vital to the teachings of the church and may be a reflection that there is also an *Eternal Mother* — a kind of eternal marriage in the deity. This teaching may also account for so much emphasis being put on family life that forbids divorce (except in unusual circumstances), premarital or extramarital sex, masturbation, birth control, and abortion.

Polygyny does not seem to be directly related to the mythology of the deity. It is argued that because God allowed the Hebrew patriarchs and early Kings (Saul, David, and Solomon) to be polygynous, it is possible, through a specific revelation, for the leaders of the new church to also be polygynous. This occurred through a revelation to Joseph Smith and, in

312

---

7 It should be understood that Mormonism is no more or less patriarchal than other Christian denominations in its image of the divine. Also, "patriarchal" should not be understood as the husband "lording it over" his wife, as research about Mormon marriage shows that while the myth may be considered to be patriarchal, the actual behaviour is quite egalitarian.

about 1841, Smith made public the revelation about polygyny (Bringhurst 1986) that became the practice until 1890. In that year President Woodruff received a second revelation on the matter, and monogamy was re-instituted, and polygyny forbidden (see Chapter Eight).

Unlike the Oneida Perfectionists and the Shakers, the LDS Church is still very vibrant and growing. One of the reasons why this may be so is that the solution to family and religion tension is to focus on the family and to integrate it into the larger family, the ward (local congregation). Another reason may be the continued emphasis on patriarchal control both in the family and in the church. Polygyny is a dead issue now and no longer part of the option. It is to the credit of the Mormons that they seem to successfully unite the individual, the family, and the church into a whole that is functional for all concerned. Current research on the Mormon family substantiates an argument that they, like conservative Christians, opt for traditional morals that impact family: no pre-marital sex, a pronatal stand in regard to abortion, life-long marriage (even eternal marriage), and no divorce (Heaton 1988).

Religion and the Family in the Modern World

To summarize the variety and complexity of family life in the United States and Canada in the contemporary period would take us well beyond our purpose here in this chapter. I will restrict the time frame to between 1970 and 1990, with a special emphasis on the late 1980s. To accomplish this task, I will rely upon family sociologist Arlene Skolnick's (1991) analysis of the current family. Her data are American, and although one cannot extrapolate directly from her work and apply it to Canada, the two nations are very similar on many measures of family structure and processes, and thus extrapolation is reasonably warranted.

Skolnick's central thesis is that the family as an institution has changed as a result of three major factors: economic, demographic, and social. She argues that the shift from an industrial to a post-industrial or service economy, a demographic revolution, and *psychological gentrification* in tandem have all produced major changes in the family (1991:11). The new economy has put new strains on parents (both normally work) and has led to a state of poverty for many. The most important demographic revolution is that men and women live longer, which has implications for marriage and for an extension of cross-generational parenting. The term psychological gentrification refers to a shift in family life from a *positional family* to a *person-centered family*. This has increased a sense of individualism in the family, where men and women seem more committed to their own personal development than to each other and their children.

Religion is to be considered as Skolnick's *third realm* wherein this socio-cultural system is seen as an attempt to reduce the tension and to resolve the dilemmas. However, as we have seen so many times in this text, religion is also experiencing major changes. Similar to Skolnick's "cultural earthquake" is what Marty (1979) calls a "seismic shift" in modern American religion. Modern forms of religion and the family have a common root during the period of what some scholars refer to as late capitalism or postindustrialism. Common in both religion and the family, the individual has become disconnected from others, is loosely connected to kin, prone to precarious relationships as evidenced from high divorce rates (as in the case of family), and finds religious meaning more in personal experiences and less so in communities. The central dilemma present is between the vitality of individualism and the supportive mechanism of community.

314

A modern response to the dilemma of religion and the family, then, is to navigate the "seismic shift" and the "cultural earthquake" with an ever-increasing emphasis on the individual as reflected in personal human rights, choosing one's own god among many, and opting for a variety of familial life styles. Bellah and his colleagues (1985) used the term "Sheilaism"[8] to describe this kind of response in religion, and one could use a common first name "Johnism" to illustrate a similar phenomenon within the family. Linkages between religion and the family are also reflected in Wuthnow's (1988a) work on the creation of religious organization into two new symbolic boundaries: between liberal and conservative Christianity and religious special interest groups.

The liberal special interest groups are indicative that modern Christianity is highly individualistic, concerned with self-fulfilment and human rights for the poor. These interest groups gather like-minded members who are interested in such things as human potential, the ecology, civil rights, social action for the disadvantaged, gender equality, and sexual orientation equality. They tend to be much more isomorphic to the modern ethos of individuality, justice, equality, and the like. In a word, these interest groups tend to opt for the secular-individualist horn of the religious-familial dilemma.

On the other hand, conservative Christianity has another agenda. One part of conservative religion in America is the concern for the family. These interest groups, sometimes referred to as the Religious Right, are pronatal, support an image of the family common in the 1950s (two parents with the

---

8 The term was coined by Bellah and his colleagues (1985) to describe a religious commitment that did not extend beyond the person — a completely individualist interpretation. Here, "Sheila's" religion is unique to her alone.

father the good provider and the mother the caregiver), engage in political action against such organizations as Planned Parenthood, and long for the resurrection of the mythical family of the past. These interest groups opt for the sacred-communitarian horn of the dilemma. In addition, conservative Christians choose another option in response to the dilemma between religion and the family: the construction of a moral community (Bellah *et al.* 1985). Family images tend to be common, and fellow members become fictive-kin. It is here that these churches endeavour to provide a "safe" environment for families that are perceived to be threatened by secularism, familial fragmentation, public and family violence, and the erosion of Judeo-Christian familial values.

In light of these observations, one may argue that the most fundamental dilemma both for religion and family is that of the individual and community. The tradition of both institutions is heavily accented toward community. Nisbet depicts community as having "a high degree of personal intimacy, emotional depth, moral commitment, social cohesion and continuity over time." Furthermore "its archetype, both historically and symbolically, is the family, and in almost every type of genuine community the nomenclature of family is prominent" (1966:47-48).

A strong tradition in the sociology of religion also highlights the perspective that religion is intricately connected to community. This tradition, discussed in the third chapter on social boundaries, is especially reflective of Durkheim. For Durkheim (1965:62), in his definition of religion, we have seen that religion includes myth, ethos, and rituals. These beliefs and corresponding rituals are of a particular kind — they pertain to the sacred (not the mundane or the secular). Again, to mention only a few of the functions of ritual that I outlined in Chapter Nine, rituals function to unite believers into a single moral community — in other words, into a socially cohesive group. This community is both a source of support and an agent of control.

I have already argued that the focus on the individual is common in both modern religion and family. The positive result of this focus is that both these institutions have not had the power to control people socially. However, the proverbial baby seems to have been thrown out with the bath water. This new individualism has resulted in a lack of social support both within the family and religion and between the two institutions. Community construction has become difficult. The communitarian basis of religion and the family are challenged by the state, the economy, and the media. It is not a viable option to go back to the "good old days" (which were not really "good") to lose the sense of the individual but, rather, to construct those kinds of human relations within religious and familial settings that balance the tensions of the individual and the community.

CURRENT RESEARCH ON THE RELIGION AND FAMILY CONNECTION

I begin our investigation here by reviewing some of the findings and reflections from two edited books and one chapter in a handbook on the family. The first one is edited by Joan Aldous and William D'Antonio (D'Antonio and Aldous 1983). The second, another edited text by Darwin Thomas (1988). The third source is an article by Teresa Donati Marciano (1987).

All three works portray a central dilemma for families and religions of the twentieth century: the dilemma of modernity. I begin here to look at some of the issues of this dilemma.

The Dilemmas of Modernity

316

The main theme of the edited text by D'Antonio and Aldous reflects tension and change in the interchange between the two institutions. The opening chapter illustrates how modernization has been disruptive to both religion and the family by eroding their authority to maintain control over their members. Further, demography has had an effect on both religion and the family. Their thesis is that contemporary family behaviours — especially divorce, contraception, abortion, premarital sexuality, and women's greater equality — arise from changed demographics and have an impact upon corporate bodies like religion. Another insight illustrates how the relationship has become problematic: in the not too distant past, family members looked to religion for comfort and support in times of crises like death. Today, there are additional crises such as divorce and abortion. Modern religious leaders appear ill-equipped to meet these crises and to respond in a creative way to the increased emancipation of women. Additional perceptions show how the dominant economic and political structures have resulted in the dominance of individualism which has, in turn, led to more liberal values both in religion and the family. Some religious bodies (the Religious Right, the hierarchy of the Roman Catholic Church, the Mormons, and the Unification Church) have opted for the past where traditional values were predominant. The challenge is not to return to the past but to encourage religious groups to be supportive of families and not dictators of behaviours.

The second section of the text focuses on specific religious denominations and how they have responded to familial values and behaviours. A chapter of the text argues that the mainline Protestant Churches have moved away from traditional values on divorce, abortion, and premarital and extramarital sexuality[9] to emphasize support for family members. In

---

9 See Chapter Nine in the discussion on the crystallization of liberal values about Liberal Christianity.

regard to Roman Catholicism, there is an indication that there is a growing gap between the official teaching of the Church and the actual behaviour of many American Catholics. Issues for the Jewish population of
America are different from others and centre around survival. As Jews have
increasingly adopted to modern values in regard to the family, many more
Jews are intermarrying and are having fertility rates below the rates of
replacement. African American Christians and their families are discussed
in another chapter. They still tend to adhere to traditional teachings on
issues of sex, abortion, and divorce. However, African American churches
have allowed for adaptability in these areas and are more concerned with
providing support to members and their families. The final chapter in this
section is on Hispanic Americans (most of whom are Roman Catholic),
who currently face problems that every new immigrant group has faced in
the past. They come from a cultural past that reflected strong familial and
community ties and now are in a tense, conflictual relationship with an
American culture that has long challenged these values. The problem with
the Catholic Church is that most Hispanic people are loosely linked to the
institution and do not look there for a way to resolve the dilemmas of accul-
turation.

317

The last section of the text by D'Antonio and Aldous is a reflection of
negotiating dilemmas between the modern world and tradition by choosing tradition. Two religious groups, the Unification Church and the
Mormons, and one religious movement, the New Christian Right, are
analysed. All adhere to a code of ethics that stresses the patriarchal role of
the husband-father and the caregiving role of women. In addition to viewing the family in this form, these religious groups emphasize concern and
care for their members. I would contend that the reason why such a family
form can exist in today's world of gender equality is because of this community support. According to the authors of this section, they all try to gain
new members to justify their adherence to these traditional family forms.

In the beginning of the Thomas text, it is argued that even though it is
usually thought that changes to religion and the family are effects of larger
political and economic changes, it is also important to realize that the
family institution influences other institutions. Another chapter focuses on
the Jewish family and posits a similar thesis found in the D'Antonio and
Aldous text of survival as a people. An analysis of a central dilemma of the
Catholic family is outlined. It is noted that the negative effect of the church
not modifying its teaching on contraception and abortion may lead to
delegitimization of the institution and loss of members. Building on early
research on Middletown USA, a study reprinted in the text theorizes that
there has been little change in this mid-western city for the past 50 years.

An interesting chapter on the Amish is included. Even though the Amish have been quite successful in maintaining a traditional family, family members need to make a living in the modern world, and when they work outside of the community, they are affected by that. Two chapters are devoted to gender. In both cases, it becomes evident that it is within religion and the family that the changes in gender roles become a salient issue. Another chapter compares the social-psychological commitment to public institutions in contrast to religious and familial institutions, noting that particularly in religion and the family the focus is on personal well-being. Another study in the text indicates that the more integrated a person is into family and religion, the less likely that person will be to commit suicide.[10] Thomas concludes his introduction by saying that familial and religious institutions need to be studied simultaneously. They are at the core of the human collectivity — still the most universal of all human social institutions.

Marciano's (1987) analysis of the dilemma of modernity concludes this section of the chapter. She reflects on the family and cults,[11] TV evangelism, and feminism. Her thesis is that one way in which families navigate the modern dilemma is not to revert to the past but to create their own personal religion through processes of synthesis and syncretism. To synthesize one's religion is to bring together elements from one's own personal biography as they fit with religious beliefs and practices. For families this means that one chooses from a variety of religious beliefs and practices to suit one's own familial lifestyle. Examples she uses are choices of fertility, socialization of children, divorce, and abortion. In short, the dilemma of modernity is met by personal choice: selecting from the religious repertoire what is most suited to a person's familial choices. This is similar to what the "new voluntarism," selective Catholicism, and fragmented gods concepts mean: syncretism refers to religious organizations' attempt to blend various beliefs and practices from a variety of religious sources. The New Age Movement would be a good example of this process.

The Tenuous Connection between Religion and the Family

In light of what I have argued in this section of this chapter, we observe that religion and family are in somewhat of a tenuous relationship insofar as both have been significantly affected by individualism. In fact, as one

---

10 This is exactly what Durkheim (1951) found in his study on suicide.

11 Marciano's use of this term is similar to Paloutzian's (1996) notion of "destructive cults" (see Chapter Eight).

reviews the linkage through current empirical research, the relationship appears to be a weak one. One may argue that individuals who are involved in familial and religious relationships resolve the inherent tension by creating two social spheres of life, the familial and the religious, and do little to construct a vital interface between them. For example, in a review of the literature on marital quality and religion, Booth *et al.* (1995) indicate that contemporary religion is only modestly related to marital quality. Their own study, using data from a 12-year longitudinal study of 2,033 married persons and drawing from the two last waves (1988 and 1992), investigates the linkage. They find little support that there is a significant correlation between various measures of religiosity and marital quality. It is only on two of the five dimensions of religions that there is a modest correlation. This is substantiated by a review done by Larson (1991), who calls the linkage between religion and family phenomena a "tenuous connection."

A similar result comes from Swenson (1996a), who, using a large American study of human sexual behaviour (Laumann *et al.* 1994), tests a model that posits a link between religion and sexual satisfaction. Of four predictors (church attendance, being born again, believing that extramarital sex is wrong, and religious beliefs guiding sexual behaviour), only the latter was significant in a logistic regression model. This is not the whole story, however. Greeley (1991), using data from two probability samples (Gallup 1989-1990 and two General Social Surveys of 1985 and 1989), saw several ways that religion was correlated to various kinds of familial behaviour and attitudes. His focus was on sexual satisfaction. Of twelve predictor variables, two religious ones were significant predictors in the national samples: spouses praying together and the partner having "god-like" characteristics.

Also, Swenson (1995), in a Canadian national sample of evangelical clergy and spouses, found that religion did matter. Of six different measures of religion (personal meditation, spouses praying together, the nature of one's spiritual life, frequency of personal prayer, how long one prayed [measured in minutes per day], and viewing God as a protector), three were significant for ministers and two were significant for spouses. For ministers, personal meditation, praying with ones's spouse, and the nature of one's spiritual life were significant factors. For spouses (mostly wives), personal meditation and praying together were significant.

Conclusions

Recent and current research on the relationship between religion and the family reveals two main themes: the dilemma of modernity (particularly individualism and communitarianism) and the tenuous linkage between religion and the family. The former will continue to be a dilemma as modern Canadians and Americans strive to reduce the tension of modernity by choosing among several possibilities. In regard to the tenuous linkage between religion and the family, I would contend that for many religious adherents, the impact of the secular world is so strong that religion matters less in the familial lives of individuals.

| SUMMARY AND CONCLUSIONS

As with the whole text, this chapter has focused on dilemmas and tensions between religion and other social phenomena. Although religion and the family have much in common, there is continued evidence for tension. This tension has been negotiated and responded to in a wide variety of ways: from reducing the tension because of myth (as in the case of folk and oriental religions), to choosing individualism (as in the case of some modern options) and communitarianism (as in the nineteenth-century Mormons and modern conservative religions). There appears to be conflicting evidence for the linkage: some national studies indicate a significant link (as in the case of Greeley and Swenson in Canada) while others imply a tenuous nexus (from Booth *et al.*, Swenson, and Larson).

■ CHAPTER TWELVE ■

Religion, the Economy, and Social Stratification

This chapter has a dual focus: how religion is linked to the economy and how it is connected to social stratification systems. The first major section will present theories and evidence that religion has influenced economies and has been an agent of social change in the development of modernity, yet has also inhibited change. The first thesis may be termed the Weberian and the latter, the Marxian. The second major part of the chapter investigates the relationship of religion with social strata and social mobility. This chapter reviews literature that is central to a sociology and a social psychology of religion. Some relevant questions asked are: How does religion influence the economy and stratification systems? How is religion influenced by the economy and social stratification systems? This chapter continues a central theme of the text, that of tension and dilemma.

A frequent leitmotif discovered in the history of the link between religion and stratification systems is that the initial appeal of religion is to the marginalized and the middle class. This has been documented, in the case of Christianity, by Troeltsch (1931) and Stark (1996). What frequently happens, however, as we shall see, is that as these non-elite and marginalized experienced economic and social benefits, a routinization of charisma process occurs. Routinization processes tend to accommodate religious adherents to the world of money, business, success, and social mobility. Therein is a dilemma. To be religious is to be in contact with economic and stratified systems. However, in this contact, there is a tendency to engage in and adhere to economic values which may erode the sacred. I will illustrate how this pattern is explicated by research.

The section on stratification reviews a thesis that as the modern world has matured, there is a less obvious correlation between various dimensions of religion and stratification variation. Evidence will be provided that in pre-modern societies, there was a stronger link between various dimensions of religion and types of religious organizations and socio-economic strata.

The last section of the chapter will be devoted to the discussion of social mobility and religion.

RELIGION AS AN AGENT OF CHANGE AND AS A FACTOR IN THE GENESIS OF MODERNITY

The thesis in this section on the linkage between religion and the economy is that religion is defined as an independent variable and the economy as a dependent one. Further, it is argued that religion is seen to be an agent of change — particularly in the creation of the modern world. I first look at the original thesis as found in Weber and then consider the subsequent empirical research on the thesis.

322

Weber's Original Thesis

As it should be understood now, Weber's work is central to the perspective of this text. To recall, Weber places a lot of emphasis on understanding social actors by interpreting the meaning that they attach to their social action.[1] This process is called *verstehen*, which Giddens (1976b) acknowledges as essential to the interpretation of human action. This framework is at the heart of how Weber links religion and the modern world, particularly Protestantism and capitalism.

Weber's (1976) focus is not on capitalism as an economic system but on one, albeit central, part: the *spirit* of capitalism. He distinguishes capitalism from previous economic systems that also focused on a desire for gain or a desire for wealth. Capitalistic activity is associated with the "rational organization of formally free labour" (Giddens 1976b:3). This implies two things: a disciplined labour force and the regulated investment of capital. It is the regular reproduction of capital through investments that distinguishes this economic activity from traditional versions. In addition, it is the accumulation of wealth for its own sake and not for the sake of conspicuous consumption that distinguishes capitalism from traditional entrepreneurship.

Further characteristics of capitalism include the systematic utilization of goods or personal services as means of acquisition, rational book-keeping, the separation of business from home, and the place of law and bureaucratic administration (Weber 1958a:18-20). The spirit of capitalism includes such elements from the work of Benjamin Franklin as: time and credit are

---

1   It should be noted, however, that the sociological theorist Jeffrey Alexander argues that Weber kept too close to this perspective in his early writings but later focused primarily on structural factors of the higher collective order (Alexander 1983, Vol III: 76-127).

money, the good paymaster is lord of another's purse, the duty of the individual toward the increase of capital, and honesty. However, the *summum bonum*[2] of the spirit of capitalism is the earning of more and more money combined with a strict avoidance of all spontaneous enjoyment of life. The capitalistic entrepreneur avoids ostentation and unnecessary expenditure, a conscious enjoyment of his power, and is embarrassed by the outward signs of the social recognition which he receives (Weber 1958a:48, 71).

The central link to a religious root (the Protestant ethic) of this kind of entrepreneurship proceeds in two directions: the notion of calling and the quest for assurance of salvation. The notion of calling was a focus of Martin Luther (1483-1546), who argued that a supreme purpose of the Christian was a divine call to work very hard in this world. The quest for assurance of salvation emerges from the theological scholarship of John Calvin (1509-1564). Calvin argued that men and women are predestined for eternal salvation or eternal damnation, a doctrine known as double predestination. God's grace for salvation remains central, but it is up to the individual to seek assurance that he or she is predestined for salvation. As acknowledged by Calvinism, the believer cannot rely on the church to be an intermediary in the process. The believer is without the priest, Mary, the saints or the hierarchy as a channel of salvation. The believer is alone with his or her transcendent God. Weber writes:

> In what was for the man of the age of the Reformation the most important thing in life, his eternal salvation, he was forced to follow his path alone to meet a destiny which had been decreed for him from eternity. No one could help him. No priest, for the chosen one can understand the work of God only in his own heart. No sacraments, for though the sacrament had been ordained by God for the increase of His glory, and must hence be scrupulously observed, they are not a means to the attainment of grace. (1958a:104)

How, then, is this assurance to be achieved? It is in the daily struggle of life that involves intense worldly activity for the glory of God. A sign of this assurance is wealth or personal success and is a blessing from God. In summary, it is the notion of calling that entails hard work and the quest for assurance of salvation that links the ethic of Protestantism to the spirit of capitalism. Weber explains:

---

2 Literally, "*the chief good.*"

In conformity with the Old Testament and in analogy to the ethical valuation of good works, asceticism looked upon the pursuit of wealth as an end in itself as highly reprehensible; but the attainment of it as a fruit of labour in a calling was a sign of God's blessing. And even more important: the religious valuation of restless, continuous, systematic work in a worldly calling, as the highest means to asceticism, and at the same time the surest and most evident proof of rebirth and genuine faith, must have been the most powerful conceivable lever for the expansion of that attitude toward life which we have here called the spirit of capitalism. (1958a:172)

This is an illustration of what Weber calls *inner-worldly asceticism* (see Chapter Three). To recall, this means that one attains salvation by denying oneself pleasures, working hard, and, in doing so, glorifying God. Schluchter, an interpreter of Weber, writes that "the unique character of Occidental asceticism derives from the fact that it is basically an asceticism of work — by contrast with Indian asceticism" (1987:110).

Weber's analysis has not been without criticism. Giddens (1976b:12) summarizes these criticisms into three domains. First, the distinctiveness of the notion of a calling in Lutheranism is questioned. Second, the presumed lack of affinity between traditional Catholicism and regularized entrepreneurial activity is challenged with social historical evidence. Third, the degree to which Calvinistic ethics served to dignify the amassing of wealth is critiqued. In light of these criticisms, is there current empirical proof of the thesis?

Empirical Research and the Weberian Thesis

In response to the question of empirical verification of Weber's thesis, the evidence is inconsistent. Some data provide credibility for the thesis while other data question it. A review article by Bouma (1977) presents us with an overview of the evidence and counter-evidence.

Bouma (1977) refers to several studies before 1960 that said, in effect, that there was little or no empirical evidence to substantiate the Weberian position (for example, Mack, Murphy and Yellin 1956, and Lipset and Bendix 1959). However, the well-known study of religion in Detroit in the late 1950s by Gerhard Lenski (1961) provided some evidence for the thesis. Using several items that measured the Protestant ethic, Lenski concluded that Protestants have identified themselves with more individualistic and competitive patterns than Catholics. In addition, Catholics were more likely to have collectivistic values and security-orientated thinking than

Protestants (from Lenski 1961, and quoted in Roberts 1990). Lenski argues, then, that the Protestant ethic remains linked to a capitalistic spirit.

Bouma (1977), furthermore, presents two theses: ascetic Protestant beliefs and norms produce achievement motivation among Protestants that is higher than among Roman Catholics, and ascetic Protestant beliefs and norms predispose Protestants to make more effectual use of educational opportunities than do Roman Catholics. Regarding the first thesis, he writes that there is no reliable indication of a relationship between religion and achievement orientation. Relevant to the second thesis, the empirical evidence is inconsistent and there is neither confirmation nor support. Bouma concludes here that one of the reasons why there are no appreciable differences between the two Christian religions is that there is too much variation within Catholicism and Protestantism. Seeing this, Schlenker (1991) investigates the Baptist denomination in Canada to see if there is validity to the Weberian thesis.

His approach is on the level of organization: the bureaucracy of the Baptist Convention of Ontario and Quebec. The data consist of an analysis of social concern resolutions passed at the General Assemblies from 1900 to 1987. Contrary to the Bouma review, he finds evidence for the linkage between the Protestant ethic and capitalistic values. He limited his research to the Baptists, for it is the Baptists that Weber (1958a) recognized as especially embodying the ethic and the spirit. Schlenker's results indicate that during periods of relative social and economic calm, the linkage between the Protestant ethic and the capitalistic spirit is salient, while during periods of social and economic upheaval (for example, during the two world wars) it is the weakest. He concludes by saying that it is not the time to abandon the search for evidence for the linkage but rather a time to move to a different level of analysis — on the organizational level of various denominations.

Given that there is inconsistency in the research, one is unable to establish a valid correlation between Protestantism and capitalism. A conclusion one may take is that the most important legacy is that religion is seen to be an independent factor in social change. This is a similar observation to one made by Coleman. He acknowledges that

> It is in the more abstract and general form that the Protestant ethic has any relevancy for an understanding of twentieth-century economic change. It is Weber's heuristic intent and not his specific hypothesis which can serve to provide continuity of thought in sociology of religion. (1968:57)

Two empirical examples will be excerpted here to suggest this heuristic intent. One is from the special place of Christianity in Canada, and the other is from the relationship of early Christianity to Greco-Roman society.

O'Toole (1996), citing various sources, argues that the vitality of Victorian Christianity has profoundly shaped the character and the identity of the Canadian nation. He argues that many features of modern Canadian life — like the political party system, the welfare state, foreign policy, and a Canadian version of "law and order" — have been shaped, in part, by religious myths, attitudes, and structures of nineteenth-century Christian religion.

Stark (1996), in his study of the rise of Christianity, contrasts the mythological systems of Greco-Roman religion and Christianity. His focus is on what was unique and new in Christian mythology compared with the religious culture of late Roman Antiquity. Several tenets are central: the belief that God loved all of humanity was radically new; in addition, not only was this love combined with unearned mercy, it was required that all Christians imitate God and show mercy, kindness, compassion, and forgiveness to others. Stark writes:

> Perhaps even more revolutionary was the principle that Christian love and charity must extend beyond the boundaries of family and tribe, that it must extend to "all those who in every place call on the name of our Lord Jesus Christ" (I Cor. 1:2). Indeed, love and charity must extend beyond the Christian community. ... This was revolutionary stuff. Indeed, it was the cultural basis for the revitalization of a Roman world groaning under a host of miseries. (1996:212)

Chief among these revitalizing elements was the fact that Christianity was "entirely stripped of ethnicity" (1996:213). Earlier in his study, Stark shows that the new faith grew most rapidly in cities that were a hub of ethnic differences. The God of Christ was a god who transcended ethnic and racial diversities. In addition to transcending these variations, Christianity offered, both within the church community and the family, liberation to women who suffered discrimination in the Greco-Roman society, and also brought people together of radically different social class positions, in that a patrician would embrace a plebeian or a slave as a brother or a sister.

A second major contrast was the radically different world views of humanity. The Greco-Roman world was "saturated with capricious cruelty and the vicarious love of death" (Barton 1993, cited by Stark). Christians condemned both the cruelties and the spectators[3] because the command-

---

3 Constantine (emperor from 272-337 AD) made these games illegal.

ment, "You shall not kill," was central to the faith. Stark brings his study to a conclusion thus: "Christians effectively promulgated a moral vision utterly incompatible with the casual cruelty of pagan custom. Finally, what Christianity gave its converts was nothing less than their humanity. In this sense virtue was its own reward" (1996:215).

RELIGION AS AN INHIBITOR OF CHANGE: THE MARXIAN THESIS

The Traditional Marxian Model

We come to Karl Marx and Friedrich Engels' theory of religion as it applies to the linkage to the economic system. Their work on religion is not extensive, but they do provide a classic definition of religion that was presented in Chapter Two:

> The basis of irreligious criticism is: Man makes religion, religion does not make man. In other words, religion is the self-consciousness and self-feeling of man who has either not yet found himself or has already lost himself again. But man is no abstract being squatting outside the world. Man is the world of man, the state, society. This state, this society, produce religion, a reversed world-consciousness because they are a reversed world. Religion is the general theory of that world, its encyclopaedic compendium, its logic in a popular form, its spiritualistic *point d'honneur*, its enthusiasm, its moral sanction, its solemn completion, its universal ground for consolation and justification. It is the fantastic realization of the human essence because the human essence has no true reality. The struggle against religion is therefore immediately the fight against the other world, of which religion is the spiritual aroma.
>
> Religious distress is at the same time the expression of real distress and the protest against real distress. Religion is the sigh of the oppressed creature, the heart of a heartless world, just as it the spirit of a spiritless situation. It is the opium of the people. (Marx and Engels, 1964:41-42)

Before I attempt to interpret this statement, it may be good to recall Marx's theory of society. Figure 12.1 presents us with a visual image of the theory.

Following his view that society is rooted in the economic means of production, Marx argues that social life is a result of the interactions between people in all societies in their worlds of work — their attempt to make a

327

MARXIAN MODEL OF SOCIETIES

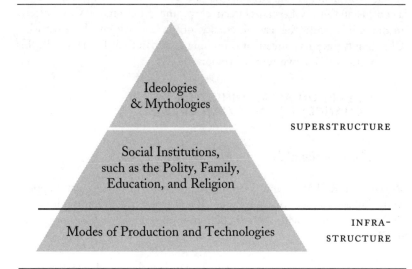

FIGURE 12.1

living and provide for their basic physical needs. This is augmented with technology — from simple tools to complex computers. The infrastructure forms this social base. The social institutions (politics, religion, family, and education) are part of the superstructure built on the economic base. Further, at the pinnacle of the superstructure are the ideas, the culture (that includes the ideologies and mythologies) of a people. This theory is a reductionist theory: reducing religion to social or economic sources.

The place (actually the misplace) of religion is explained in the following way. In an interpretation of Marx and religion, Birnbaum (1973) argues that the negative situation of people is alienation. This alienation is due to class differentials wherein one class (or estate) has nearly all the economic and political power. This class exploits the common people (in capitalistic societies, the proletariat) for its own ends. This is a very difficult position for the proletariat or any other oppressed group. To try to cope, the alienated people seek some way to assuage the pain and suffering by creating religion. For example, African Americans under slavery met their suffering by hoping for a land of freedom after this life had ended. This is what Marx and Engels mean by religion as being the "opium" of the people.

On the other hand, religion serves the powerful as well. Here the experience is not alienation but control. Religion provides an ideology for the rich to control the marginalized people. In summary, the Marxian theory of religion is threefold:

- · Religion is a social construction built on economic relationships.
- · Religion acts as an opium that assuages the pain of alienation of the marginalized.
- · Religion is used by political and economic elites to control the people.

Empirical Studies of the Marxian Model

Is there an empirical legacy to this theory? Yes. Birnbaum (1973) adds, interestingly enough, Weber's work. It should be noted that Weber studied not only Catholicism and Protestantism but also Judaism, Hinduism, Buddhism, Taoism, and Confucianism (Weber, 1951, 1952, 1958b).[4] In these studies, according to Birnbaum, there is significant evidence that the religious organizations and symbolic structures are developments within limits set by material factors such as property and production relations and their political correlates. I shall return to Weber's work when we look at stratification. Birnbaum (1973) further adds that colonialism and imperialism inflict alienation upon cultures and peoples of non-Western societies and that religious control was part of that colonial expansion.

One part of the Marxian heritage is illustrated with the work of Lanternari (1965), who studied religious movements of the oppressed. He looked at millennium movements in Africa, the United States, Central America, South America, Melanesia, Polynesia, Asia, and Indonesia. An example from the native plains peoples of the United States illustrates two theses of Marx and Engels: that religion is a source of alienation of the people and that religion acts as a defence mechanism against this alienation and as an opium. Lanternari outlines this by investigating the Peyote Cult, which cult emerged on the heels of the domination of the plains Aboriginals by the American state. In the midst of oppression and despair, these plains peoples had hope — hope in a future wherein all Aboriginals would be emancipated. This would consist of a collective salvation and collective protection from tribal disintegration. In 1890, a man received visions that created a mythology wherein peyote (a drug from the peyote plant) is the comforter, the Holy Spirit, that enables the believer to achieve supernatural revelations and spiritual and cultural emancipation from the oppression of the white man. The mythology presented a reinterpretation of the

---

4   He also investigated Islam but did not devote large pieces of scholarship to it (see Weber 1978:623-627).

Christian myth: Jesus, along with the Holy Spirit, is the Peyote Spirit; Christian brotherhood is really Pan-Indianism. These beliefs were a synthesis of Aboriginal and Christian myths. Salvation was defined as freedom not from sin but from the domination and exploitation of the white man.

Gary Marx's (1967) important study of the civil rights movement and religion gives credibility to both the Marxian and Weberian perspectives. Using survey data (N = 1,119 and representative of northern and southern cities) of urban African American churches and blacks in predominantly Caucasian middle-class churches, he found that civil rights activism was more likely to be found among blacks in the Caucasian churches and less likely in the African American ones. For African Americans, it appears that religion functioned more as an opium and an inhibitor of change. On the other hand, blacks in middle-class Caucasian churches used their religion as a vehicle of social change.

This was in contrast to a later study by Nelsen, Madron, and Yokley (1975 and cited in Hunt and Hunt 1977), who discovered that if one distinguished between "church-like" religiosity and "sect-like" religiosity, it was the latter that was inversely correlated to civil rights activism, whereas the former was positively correlated to this activism. Hunt and Hunt (1977) see this as a classical research problem and address it by re-analyzing the original Marx (1967) data. They proceeded on several fronts. When there are no controls in the analysis, the re-analysis confirms the original position of Marx. However, when secular controls (like SES, region, type of community, region of birth, age, and sex) are introduced, there are different results. The religious differences are no longer significant, and the differences (some blacks being more activist than others) are accounted for by the secular factors (which were the controls). Where religious factors still matter is among black activists within black churches and not in predominantly Caucasian churches. In addition, confirming Nelsen et al.'s (1975) findings, activism is more likely to occur among African American churches which are more "church-like" in orientation.

These kinds of questions continue to be asked, and two studies are particularly relevant. The first one, by Stark and Christiano (1992), addresses the opiate theory that religion blocks human rights activity; the second by Clayton (1995), continues the investigation of Gary Marx. Previous research by Stark (1964) and Christiano (1988) presented evidence for the opiate thesis and found that because of the salience of religion in the United States, there was relative weakness in American radicalism. Using voting data for the 1920 and 1924 presidential elections, they present a further test of the thesis (Stark and Christiano 1992). They select this period because by 1920 many radical Americans believed that the time was ripe for substantial changes among the electorate toward the Left. This consideration was due, in part, to the fact that women had recently received the right to vote (rat-ification of the Nineteenth Amendment in 1920), and they were thought, in socialist circles, to be more left leaning than men.

Using three measures of radicalism, Stark and Christiano (1992) found that there was a negative correlation between the strength of religion and the manifestation of radicalism. Their search, however, led them further to question the possibility of a spurious correlation. They discovered that the origins of the socialist leaders and the areas of strongest support were among Scandinavians. When tested for a relationship between Scandinavian-born residents and radicalism, the correlation was strong. When the original negative correlation between religion and radicalism was controlled by Scandinavian ethnicity, the correlation drops to insignifi-cance. Thus, we are left with the conclusion that the opiate thesis of Karl Marx is not substantiated by investigating the voting patterns of Americans where socialism was strong.

331

Clayton (1995), in a recent article as part of the journal *Dædalus'* special issue on revising the American dilemma, re-examines the problem. He does not use survey research but rather a combination of demographic data, texts on the religious African experience, and news releases.

From slavery times, through to emancipation, and to the immigration of African Americans to the north, the churches have been sites of belonging, encouragement, and hope. This hope was focused on the Christian belief in the afterlife: that the sufferings of this world would be richly rewarded in heaven. In contrast to the Stark and Christiano study (1992), this is a good illustration of the Marxian image of religion as an opium. The response of Caucasian Christians in the South illustrates another of Marx's theses: that those in political and economic power use religion to further their own ends. Using studies of black histories, Clayton observes:

> Just as American churches tended to identify with the American cul-ture, so Southern churches identified with the Southern culture. Practically speaking, most Southern churchgoers were traditional Southerners, expressing traditional Southern viewpoints, including the support of segregation. (1995:106)

In essence, Clayton argues that the Southern viewpoint is reinforced by the economic and political elite who did not want integration and who even transferred funds to support segregation and removed the tax deduction status to those churches who chose to integrate their congregations.

As this was happening, other major socio-economic changes were occurring. America was becoming an urban society and with this, African Americans from the South moved to the North in search of work. With limited resources that did not meet the needs, some black churches became sites of belonging. However, large numbers of blacks abandoned their churches altogether and sought alternatives to inequality through secular, political means. On the other hand, some churches and religious groups became sources of change. Clayton presents three groups: the Black Methodists for Church Renewal, the Church of God in Christ, and the Nation of Islam. The Church of God in Christ welcomed women as leaders and responded to the spiritual and economic needs of its members. The one that continues to be a strong voice in black activism is the Nation of Islam. Members spoke out against atrocities against African Americans and endeavoured to reach out to the most disenfranchised of black people.

As seen earlier in the text, Gardell's (1996) study of the Nation of Islam presents a clear example of religion not being an opiate but being an agent of change. He notes that the central thesis that the *black-man-is-God* is a cogent religious tenet that has significant consequences for the empowerment of African Americans. Gardell argues that this conviction is an extreme version of positive thinking, a therapy that creates self-esteem. In real life, there is evidence that members of the Nation are, indeed, changing not only their own lives but also the social conditions about them. Gardell quotes Farrakhan: "You say that the buildings are all run down. Yeah, but they weren't always ... whatever's run down, we run 'em up. We got carpenters, brick masons, electricians, we got everything we need in the black community to rebuild the black community" (1996:347).

A final study gives further credibility to the Marxian model, particularly the thesis that religion is a result of economic factors. Liston Pope (1942) conducted a case study of the textile industry in Gason County, North Carolina, in the late 1930s. In this county in 1939, there were 570 plants that produced 80 per cent of the cotton yarn in the United States. The author used observational methods of research and interviews with hundreds of residents. In addition, he utilized historical records of the county to document his study. Even though the relations between religious and economic institutions have been reciprocal, the significant evidence here is that the religious institutions have been formed by economic patterns. However, this was not the case in the early years of the textile industry in Gaston County. Pope recognizes the following evolution. In the 1880s, religious institutions were considerably more active in shaping the economic affairs of the people of the county. He notes that in the time of his research, the churches seldom defined or introduced new social values in the county. Yet, even though they were not initiators of social change, they still retained a measure of uniqueness and separateness.

332

Summary of the Weberian and Marxian Models

The discussion about these two models and the studies that surround them are critical to understanding the link between religion and other social institutions. In this review, there is convincing evidence to suggest that religion functions both as an agent of social change as well as an inhibitor of it. With some qualification, both the Weberian and the Marxian models, along with the studies that have tested them, reveal that under certain temporal, social, and economic conditions, religion can make a difference.

| RELIGION AND SOCIAL STRATIFICATION

In the tradition of linking religion to society, there has continued to be a link between religion, the economy, and social stratification. Some frequent questions are asked when we consider social stratification and religion: Who tend to be more committed to and more active in their religion, the rich or the poor? Are some religions more likely to be concentrated in the lower, middle or upper classes? Does social mobility increase or decrease religious activity? The question I will focus on here is the link between denominational affiliation and social class.

The Linkage between Religion and Social Stratification

To endeavour to understand the relationship between religion and social stratification, the model that will be used is the sociologist Peter Blau's (1977) theory of inequality and heterogeneity. The social theorist Ruth Wallace (1995) presents us with a summary of Blau's theory. I will add to it in applying it to religion and social inequality.

Blau introduces his readers to a term called "parameters," which are those characteristics which differentiate people from one another. These differences have an effect on their social relationships. He further distinguishes two types: nominal and graduated. Nominal parameters are differentiations that have no rank-order between them such as sex ratio in a population, and marriage, divorce or fertility rates of a nation state. A graduated parameter is one wherein there is a rank-order such as income, wealth, education, and power. These parameters result in different kinds of social differentiation. Nominal parameters are those which effect homogeneity or heterogeneity. However, graduated parameters result in inequality. He adds that the greater the heterogeneity and inequality, the more barriers there are to social intercourse and social cohesion.

As I will outline shortly, in the pre-modern and early modern period in the Western world, there is evidence linking certain religions and social class. In Blau's terms this is illustrated by the thesis that social inequality is associated with differentiation in religious organizational affiliation. This has changed. With an increase in heterogeneity, there has been a decrease in the linkage between organizational affiliation and social class. Both historical and empirical studies will illustrate this.

The Correlation between Religion and Social Stratification: Historical Sources

Our discussion begins with Weber's (1978) work on religion and social stratification systems. Weber utilizes historical data from a variety of sources that include Ancient Greece, China, India, the medieval Middle East, and pre-modern Europe. He starts with a reflection on the peasantry. Because the peasantry are so linked to nature and dependent upon natural events and, consequently, not orientated to rational economic systematization, they are also less likely to become carriers of a rationalized religion. In other words, the peasant stratum would be inclined to animism and magic. Similarly, the warrior nobles have very little affinity with the systematic ethical demands of a transcendent god. Concepts such as sin, salvation, and religious humility are foreign to this kind of ruling strata. Their only linkage to religion is to seek protection against evil through magical or ceremonial rites congruent with their sense of status (Weber 1978:472).

A similar story emerges among the merchant classes of the classical and medieval periods. These merchants have a strongly mundane orientation to life and are not likely to develop a religion that is ethical and prophetic in nature. In ancient Greece, the merchants appeared to have no fear of the gods. Together with the merchant classes of China, Rome, and India, religion was not a means of acquiring an ethical or rational way of thinking but, rather, a means of being ritually pure.

With some exceptions (he makes note, for example, of the merchant classes of Zoroasterism), it was not until the pre-modern era (from the Protestant Reformation until the Industrial Revolution) in Europe that there was a direct linkage between the merchant class and an ethical and rational religion. Here Weber duplicates much of what he argued in the *Protestant Ethic and the Spirit of Capitalism* and writes that "the closest connection between ethical religion and rational economic development — particularly capitalism — was affected by all the forms of ascetic Protestantism and sectarianism in both Western and Eastern Europe, viz., Zwingians, Calvinists, Baptists, Mennonites, Quakers, Methodists and Pietists" (1978:479). It is here, then, that there is documentation for a direct link between religious affiliation and social stratification.

For another stratum, the artisans, there appears to be a wider diversity of religious attitudes. For artisans in India, there is a wide variety of caste taboos and magical or mystagogic[5] religions; these parallel animism in China; dervish religion in Islam, and pneumatic-enthusiastic early Christianity.

Finally, among slave and day-labourers (including nineteenth-century proletarians), Weber recognized no linkage to any distinctive type of religion. In ancient Rome, slaves and day-labourers tended to follow the religion of the other strata. Using research from the German economist Sombart (1906), Weber argues that the modern proletariat is characterized by indifference to or a rejection of religion. He notes that any dependence of the proletariat upon magic or providence has been eliminated. We shall see that this interpretation is in contrast to the English proletariat, which does have a connection to a particular religious affiliation, as seen through a social historical analysis.

In Weber's work (1958a) on the religious world views of Protestants, we find that the springboard to his study of the Protestant ethic and the spirit of capitalism was his observation of class differentials between Catholics and Protestants. In the Western Europe of his day, Weber observed that those who were leaders and owners of capital were skilled labourers, and those with technical skills were overwhelmingly Protestant. Even Catholic graduates who were trained technically lagged behind their Protestant counterparts. The pattern, however, was for Catholics to become trained not in the technical areas but rather in the traditional arts of philosophy, law, theology, and literature. This, in turn, was reflected in their lowered class position.

In regard to early Christianity, Ernest Troeltsch (1931), with some reliance on Biblical scholarship, identified Jesus of Nazareth as an artisan and his first followers as fishermen and tax collectors. Representing a tradition that goes back to the famous English historian, Gibbon (1960), Troeltsch adds that the early church had great appeal and support among the deprived strata of the Roman Empire: slaves, the poor, and subjected peoples. Gibbon writes:

> The Christian religion, which addressed itself to the whole human race, must consequently collect a far greater number of proselytes from the lower than the superior ranks of life ... the new sect of Christians was almost entirely composed of the dregs of the populace, of peasants and mechanics, of boys and women, of beggars and slaves, the last of whom might sometimes introduce the missionaries into the rich and noble families to which they belonged. (1960:187)

---

5 From the word "mystagogy," which is the art of explaining or interpreting mysteries of religion.

This is not the whole story, however. Stark (1996) cites several historians who argue that early Christianity thrived more among a middle-class, literate, and relatively well-educated people. He notes that the church grew more within the middle class and then spread to the marginalized. Stark paints a picture of ancient Antioch and Rome that included a minority of Christians. Under the reign of the Emperor Theodosius (378–395 AD), Antioch housed a Christian community of 100,000 believers that included about 3,000 who were supported by the community. In Rome, under the reign of Nero (54–68 AD), Stark (199:184) estimates that there were approximentally 7,000 Christians. The number of persons in need (widows, infirm, and poor) amounted to 1,500. Therefore, the early Church does not seem to have been made up of the marginalized but more likely those of middle-class status who gave aid to the marginalized.

With the conversion of the Roman Emperor Constantine (272–337 AD), things begin to change from a marginalized middle class to an elite. The historian Cahill (1995) notes that once privilege was conferred upon Christians through the edicts of Constantine, middle-class Roman citizens "converted" to Christianity. A major shift in class basis occurred. In the latter period of the Western Roman Empire (c. 300–450 AD) Christians were less likely to be recruited from the marginalized or disinherited and more likely to come from the privileged.

St. Patrick of Ireland (c.389–c.461 AD), however, reversed this. A Briton Celt, he experienced a conversion during his enslavement by Irish lords during the first part of the fifth century. Returning to his home in south England, he decided to come back to Ireland to bring Christianity to the Irish. He had a phenomenal success — especially among the disinherited. This pattern continued for several more centuries in Ireland through the male and female monasteries. Monks constructed monasteries to facilitate their commitment to Christianity. This commitment involved service to the disinherited who came from all over Ireland seeking either faith or fellowship. Under the auspice of a woman, Brigid of Kildare, a daughter of a local king and convert of St. Patrick, a monastery was born and flourished. Her monastery became famous for its hospitality. A table grace is attributed to her:

> I should welcome the poor to my feast,
> For they are God's children.
> I should welcome the sick to my feast,
> For they are God's joy.
> Let the poor sit with Jesus at the highest place,
> And the sick dance with the angels.
> God bless the poor,
> God bless the sick,

And God bless our human race.
(Cahill, 1995:174)

The social historian E.P. Thompson (1980) introduces us to the wide variation in religious affiliation and social class position in the years preceding the Industrial Revolution until the middle of the nineteenth century. In a chapter devoted to religious dissent as an agent of the growth of the working class of England, Thompson observes the linkage between social class and organizational affiliation. The established Church of England was substantially associated with the patricians and the elite. Middle-class entrepreneurs or those devoted to business were more likely to be Baptists linked to the Calvinist Reformation. Intellectuals within the middle class were likely to be members of the more liberal churches such as the Unitarians. The working class, however, were overrepresented in the Methodist Church.

337

It was among the Methodists that working-class people (principally industrial labourers) had a way of defining themselves rather than merely being defined by those in economic and political power. In this way, according to Thompson, organizational affiliation contributed to the unique identity of the working class in early industrial England. In addition, he argues that Methodism was a part of the creation of the English working class in the pre-industrial and industrial periods.

The Correlation between Religion and Social Stratification: Sociological Sources

Although a theologian, H. Richard Niebhur (1957) developed a cogent sociological thesis linking religious affiliation with denominational distinctiveness in Europe and America. He documents his first linkage of the disinherited with the Anabaptists, the Quakers, the Methodists, and the Salvation Army. There is not only a correlation but also a causal relationship. With the religious historian Troeltsch (1931), he argues that creative, church-forming, religious movements are the work of the lower strata. Among those of the lower strata, the desired salvation is not only eternal salvation but a social salvation from being disinherited. Niebhur documents historical data to substantiate this thesis.

His evidence, in part, emerges from the kind of social background from which some of the leaders came. Liburne, a leader and founder of the Levellers,[6] was an apprentice of a London cloth-maker. Gerald

---

6 A member of a radical group organized during the English Civil War of 1642-1649, advocating political equality and religious tolerance.

Winstanley, leader of the Diggers,[7] had been a London tradesman who had been beaten out of estate and trade and was forced to live a country life were he had to labour hard to make a living. George Fox (1624-1691), the founder of the Quakers, was a cobbler and the son of a weaver (Niebhur 1957: 47). The founder of the Shakers, Ann Lee (1736-1784), who is not mentioned by Niebhur but who should be included in this catalogue, was an uneducated daughter of a poor family and worked in a textile factory in England (Morse 1980). Niebhur goes on to say that just as the leaders were of the disinherited, so also were the followers. Rank and file followers of these leaders were "of the dregs of the common people" (Niebhur 1957:48).

These religions were not far-reaching and had few members. Methodism, however, had a wide range of influence. John Wesley (1703-1791), founder and first leader of the church, although an educated Anglican priest, went to the disinherited and working class to proclaim in simplistic terms the Christian gospel. In the early years, Methodism was characterized by small groups and congregations that included members from different social strata, by its emotionalism, by its mechanism of offering an escape from the drudgeries of an unromantic and routine life, by its lay and democratic character, by an unwillingness to hire salaried clergy, and by its philanthropic activity. Later Methodism moved beyond the disinherited to the middle class. I will come back to discuss this when we ask the question if conversion to alternative religious organization results in social mobility.

In his discussion of the middle class, Niebhur expands upon the Weberian analysis of the Puritans. He argues that the religious needs of the middle class are not as well defined as are those of the poor, and that political, cultural, and economic desires have an impact upon these needs. Further, religion among the middle class appears to have the following characteristics: a high development of individual self-consciousness, being affirmative toward life, being educated, the enjoyment of economic security, and an emphasis upon natural and individual rights.

In regard to religious belief and practice, Niebhur notes that the problem of personal salvation is far more important than the problem of social redemption. The idea of God that is common in bourgeois faith is that of a dynamic will who is much more like the Hebrew Bible's teaching of a divine creator and judge than the notion of a redeemer and a saviour. Sin is seen not so much as a state but as a social action; on the other hand, righteousness is a matter of right actions carried out in obedience to commandments. Religious ethics consist of honesty, industry, sobriety, thrift, prudence, and an emphasis upon family life (1957:82-88).

---

7 A group of agrarian communalists who, after the same war, began to live on and cultivate common land. They were harassed by legal actions, and by 1650, were dispersed. Their ideas, however, were supported by others in Kent, Buckinghamshire, and Essex.

Finally, there is a distinct kind of religious organization that frames the bourgeois class. The churches they are affiliated with are typically democratic and are designed to give free scope to the individual, preserve morality, train character, and fulfill in their structure divine ordinances. The leader (minister) is democratically chosen. These organizational characteristics were common in Calvinistic churches of Western Europe, the Presbyterian church of Scotland, the Puritans of England and America, and the far-reaching Baptist churches in both England and the United States.

Empirical research in the United States paints an interesting picture of the linkage between social class and religion. Demerath III (1965) reviewed literature as a precursor to his own study of Protestantism. A selected sample of his review is presented to illustrate some of these studies. He notes that the Lynds (1929), in their study of "Middletown" USA, found that members of the working class show a disposition to believe in their religion more fervently and to cling to values more emotionally than the higher classes. Fukuyama (1961), in his study of Congregationalists, discovers that those of lower social economic status are less likely to attend worship services and know less about their faith than those of middle and upper classes. However, they are more likely to be more devotional than those of the other two classes.

Another early case study of a small urban community — "Yankee City" — was done by Warner and Lunt (1941) in the 1930s. Their research revealed a relationship between affiliation and social class. Thirteen churches of four denominations were present to respond to the religious needs of the people; they varied according to social class. Although there was some class variation between congregations within one denomination, the denominational differences were the most striking. Episcopal, Unitarian, and Presbyterian churches appealed to upper classes; Congregational to middle classes; and most of the members of the Methodist and Baptist churches were from lower classes.

Demerath III (1965) conducted his own research among Baptists, Congregationalists, Disciples of Christ, Lutherans, and Presbyterians (N = 2,371) to extend the discussion on how various measures of religion were related to social class. A unique feature of his study was that he collapsed measures of religion into an ideal-type dichotomy of church-like and sect-like religious organizations. Demerath III used Glock's (1959) four dimensions of religion — behavioural, ideological, experiential, and consequential[8] — to construct the church-like and sect-like dichotomy. His data

---

8   *Behavioural* refers to rites (such as church attendance); *ideological* indicates beliefs and intellectual understanding of doctrine; *experiential* concerns one's emotional responses; and *consequential* illustrates how religion makes a difference or not in one's everyday life (Demerath III 1965:31).

indicated that lower-status adherents were more often sect-like, whereas higher status members were more frequently church-like. Glock and Stark (1965) conducted research on a sample of church-members in the San Francisco Bay area in the 1960s. Results showed that, on the measure of religious participation, there is less participation among the proletariat than among the middle class.

Stark (1972) expands the linkage between religious participation and social class by adding other dimensions of religion in a further analysis of the San Francisco Bay area data. His basic thesis is not that the poor are more religious than the rich, but that they are more religious in some ways and in some circumstances and are less religious in other ways and in other circumstances. Already it is known that on the measure of ritual (religious attendance), the lower classes participate less. In contrast, however, they are more likely to hold traditional and orthodox Christian beliefs than the middle-educated stratum. In addition, those in the lower classes are more likely to believe that religion offers a solution to the questions about such issues as the meaning of life.

Further, even though lower-class people are not as involved in public ritual, they are more likely to participate actively in private ritual such as prayer. This is similar to their involvement in religious organizations within their congregations. Lower-class Christians in the San Francisco Bay area are less likely to be part of these organizations than are the middle and upper classes. Lastly, on a measure of religious experience, the hypothesis that lower classes are more likely to have religious experiences than are the other classes is verified by the data. In Stark's later study on the emergence of early Christianity (1996), he reviews a 1977 Gallup Poll and comments on the social class base of cults. He notes that those who are attracted to and involved in such cults as Transcendental Meditation, Yoga, Zen, New Age, Scientology, Wiccan, Eckankar, and Mormonism are significantly more educated than mainline Christian churches or sects. In effect, then, it is important in searching for the linkages between religion and social stratification to keep in mind that only one dimension of religion is not sufficient to make valid conclusions.

In an introduction to the social psychology of religion, Batson, Schoenrade, and Ventis (1993) offer us some further insight that had not been observed by Stark. In their review of the linkage between religious beliefs and social class, they select educational achievement as the indicator of class. Their observations are consistent with Stark's, but they add a nuance. In a study of college students, it was found that when students were in the college setting they tended to change their traditional beliefs to liberal ones. However, when the students graduated and then married and entered the world of work, they became traditional again in their religious orientation (Feldman and Newcomb 1969). Batson *et al.* argue that the reason for the changes were social in nature. When at college, students networked with others in a reference group that was liberal and secular in values and beliefs. However, when the students graduated, their new work and kin reference group influenced them back to more traditional ideas, values, and beliefs.

Data from Canada also present us with evidence for a linkage between religious affiliation and social class. John Porter (1965), a well-known political economist-sociologist, analyzed the Canadian census of 1951. He constructed a simple denominational categorization between Roman Catholic and Protestant and found that 60 per cent of those with a high income across Canada were Protestant. In addition, he analyzed the economic and political elites of Canada. The elites are a more specific group than the upper class; Porter defined economic elites as those who were directors of large corporations. At the time Porter did his study (1951), they numbered 760. Of them, only 10 per cent were Roman Catholic, 25 per cent Anglican, 11 per cent Presbyterian, and 20 per cent United. The remaining included Baptists, Methodists, Jews, and others. Data from Canada, then, in the 1950s, suggest that there is a link between religious affiliation and social class. Because there is a remarkable difference between Protestants and Catholics, there also appears to be some evidence for the Weberian thesis.

More recent studies reveal a somewhat different picture of the correlation between social class and various dimensions of religion. Roof and McKinney (1987) will be the source of this review. As we saw, the linkage between religion and social class was relatively strong. However, beginning in the 1960s and 1970s, Roof and McKinney (1987) observe that the correlation became weaker. Whereas church attendance was positively related to social class, polls conducted during the recent decades reveal a gradual decline in religious attendance across all the classes, particularly, they note, among the higher educated. In tandem with this, there emerged a more vocal and salient secular "new class" who derived their livelihood from the construction of and dissemination of ideas and information.[9] Roof and McKinney echo earlier observations that the new class represents secularization and a distancing from traditional bourgeois life orientations (Berger 1979 and Gouldner 1978, cited in Schmalzbauer 1993).

Roof and McKinney use this distinction to assist us in understanding the dividing lines between and within religious organizations. The New Religious Right has a strong affiliation with the old bourgeois class. Many

---

9   Another term used to describe the same stratum is "the knowledge class." This has been conceptualized to include professionals, managers, academics, journalists, and educated civil servants.

conservative Christians see themselves as new custodians of bourgeois morality and orthodoxy. They also adhere to the conviction that they are to be vocal in the public life of America whereas members of the new class disagree.

An important question to ask is what of those evangelicals who are working in the new class? Do they tend to retain their traditional values and beliefs or are they liberal like their counterparts? Schmalzbauer (1993) attempts to answer this question from data gathered from General Social Surveys during the years from 1972 to 1989 (N = 20,954). His results reveal a significant verification of three hypotheses: new-class workers are more liberal than the working class on sexuality, abortion, sex roles, and civil rights after controlling for religious measures; evangelicals are more conservative than mainline Protestants on the same attitudes after controlling for class; and evangelical new-class employees resist the liberalizing effects of the new class more than non-evangelicals.

The message is twofold. New-class evangelicals have changed and are more liberal on these attitudes than are working-class evangelicals. This finding is substantially consistent with the literature already reviewed. On the other hand, the evangelical subculture still retains resistance power that does prevent the new class ideologies from changing these workers. A similar story has been told by Hunter (1985), a sociologist who has published research on evangelicals, who argues that the modern world has liberalized evangelical mythologies and ethos but also has met with resistance.

The Correlation between Religion and Social Stratification: a Summary

The sociologists and economists who have investigated the linkage between social class and religion illustrate in generic terms what Blau (1977) modelled about social class in modern Canada and the United States that I presented in the beginning of this section. There is evidence that up until the 1960s, there was a relationship between organizational affiliation and social class. In Blau's terms this is illustrated with the thesis that social inequality is associated with differentiation in religious organizational affiliation. This has changed. With an increase in heterogeneity (measured here with the dramatic increase in different mythologies and ideologies), and a decrease in social inequality among the middle class, there has been a decrease in the linkage between organizational affiliation and social class (the exception to this would be those who are involved in cults who recruit from the upper middle class).

There is also substantial evidence for tension and the experiences of a wide range of dilemmas. We have seen that when religious participants and organizations adapt to the economic realities about them, accommodation occurs. The routinization of charisma is evidenced by middle- and upper-class churches, particularly among mainline Protestants. On the other hand, resistance is also present and the routinization and accommodation processes are delimited, as we have seen with the evangelicals, who tend more and more to be middle class. Again, religion needs to accommodate to the world, but in doing so it may accommodate too far and lose its sacred element. Religion's ties to the economy as well as to the modern social class systems reveal this dilemma.

| RELIGION AND SOCIAL MOBILITY

Niebhur (1957) provides us with an initial insight into the relationship between religion and social mobility. A central thesis of his text is how religious organizations change from being a sect of the disinherited to become a denomination of the inherited or those having experienced social mobility. The example that he gives is Methodism. As argued earlier in the chapter, early Methodism was characterized as a religious movement of the working class or the disinherited. In time, however, a transformation began to occur and the sect began to look increasingly like a church whose members were in the process of social mobility. In a similar vein, Weber quotes Wesley in warning his members of this accommodation and, indeed, predicts this transformation:

> I fear, wherever riches have increased, the essence of religion has decreased in the same proportion. Therefore I do not see how it is possible, in the nature of things, for any revival of true religion to continue long. For religion must necessarily produce both industry and frugality, and these cannot but produce riches. But as riches increase, so will pride, anger and the love of the world in all its branches. How then is it possible that Methodism, that is, a religion of the heart, though it flourishes now as a green bay tree, should continue in this state? For the Methodists in every place grow diligent and frugal; consequently they increase in goods. Hence they proportionately increase in pride, in anger, in the desire of the flesh, the desire of the eyes, and the pride of life. So, although the form of religion remains, the spirit is swiftly vanishing away. Is there no way to prevent this — this continual decay of pure religion? We ought not to prevent people from being diligent and frugal; we must exhort all Christians to gain all they can, and to save all they can; that is, in effect, grow rich. (1958a:175)

Ricco (1979) gives us an update on mobility patterns of Protestants and Catholics in the United States. An initial test of mobility patterns between Catholics and Protestants was presented by Lenski (1963) in his study of Detroit males. His data revealed that more Protestant men than Catholic men rose into upper middle-class status or retained their status. For African American Protestants, there was little movement out of the working class. As some examples of the literature on differences between Catholics and Protestants, Ricco cites Mack, Murphy and Yellin (1956), who used a national sample of males and found no differences between Catholics and Protestants both between and within generations. However, another national sample conducted by Jackson, Fox and Crokett Jr. (1970) found that Protestants were more likely to have higher rates of entrance into professional and business occupations than Catholics. Ricco reviews several other studies and finds that it was more common to find no differences based on religious affiliation than differences in regard to achievement.

Ricco goes on to present an extensive review of the literature and finds that inconsistency in the studies is the norm. These inconsistencies may be, in part, explained by researchers using different measures of religion, comparing probability samples with non-probability samples, and lacking controls. However, the final conclusion he comes to is that "religious affiliation does not explain much of the variance in socioeconomic achievement" (Ricco 1979:226).

Roof and McKinney (1987) further update the linkage between religious affiliation and social mobility. In contrast to Ricco, whose review primarily investigated Protestant-Catholic differences, these authors argue that more specific affiliational differences still remain when correlated with social mobility. In fact, Niebhur's original observation of the movement from sect to denomination has been witnessed again and again. Several denominations stand out as having framed the social mobility of their members: the Methodists, Nazarenes, Adventists, Pentecostals, and Holiness.

Roof and McKinney construct a table to illustrate how affiliation members have experienced social mobility over a thirty-year period between the mid-1940s and 1970s. Table 12.1 depicts these changes.

Roof and McKinney offer several observations on the statistics. Consistent with Ricco (1979), over this period of time, the Protestant-Catholic differences vanished, and in the mid 1980s, Catholics more generally resembled moderate Protestants.[10] The denominations which changed the most are the Mormons, evangelicals, and fundamentalists. It is also interesting to note that the religious "nones" also experienced significant changes. Benton Johnson's (1961) observation about holiness groups achiev-

---

10 See Chapter Nine for the meaning of the term "moderate Protestants."

SOCIAL MOBILITY AND RELIGIOUS DENOMINATIONS

(from Roof and McKinney 1987:110)

	1945-1946	1980s
TOP RANK	Christian Science Episcopal Congregationalist Presbyterian Jewish	Unitarian Jewish Episcopal Presbyterian United Church of Christ
MIDDLE RANK	Reformed Church Methodists Lutherans Disciples of Christ	Mormons *Nones* Christian Science Methodists Roman Catholics Lutherans Disciples of Christ White Southern Baptists Seventh Day Adventists
BOTTOM RANK	Protestant Sects Roman Catholics Baptists Mormons *Nones*	Pentecostal Assemblies of God Jehovah's Witnesses Black Northern Baptists Black Methodists Black Methodist Pentecostals

TABLE 12.1

ing higher socioeconomic status seems to be extended beyond their frontiers to include Mormons, evangelicals, and Pentecostals.

Roof and McKinney's reflections are consistent with Poloma's case study of the Pentecostal Assemblies of God Denomination. She writes: "Demographics indicate, however, that the Assemblies of God is no longer the 'disinherited' of American society. As storefronts were replaced by handsome new churches, the Assemblies attracted other adherents of similar class status" (1989:160). Their research is also consistent with a period of time in the evolution of the Nation of Islam. According to the research by Gardell (1996), when the Nation was under the leadership of Wallace

Muhammad (Imam Warith Deen Muhammad), original members who came from marginalized classes experienced significant social mobility and moved from lower classes to middle classes. This, in turn, led them to want to assimilate with mainstream America causing them to change some of the original mythological tenets (see Chapter Two). This gives further evidence to Wuthnow's (1988a) thesis that with increased wealth and more education, there tends to be a liberalization of beliefs and values.

RELIGION, ECONOMY, AND SOCIAL CLASS: A SUMMARY

What we have found out about the relationships between religion and economy and between religion and social stratification is a dynamic and varied correlation. Evidence shows that in some situations, religion is an agent of social change as revealed by the initial study by Weber and by subsequent research. On the other hand, Marx's theory of religion being an opium, founded on economic interest, and used by the elite in the control of the marginalized also has an empirical basis. Further, we find that in certain times and places, religion does serve the needs of the marginalized. It is more common, however, that it disassociates itself from the marginalized and creates links with the privileged. In terms of charisma and the routinization of charisma, when religion tends to serve the needs of the marginalized, it seems to be charismatic. On the other hand, however, as it becomes more routinized, it tends to forge connections to the elite, the privileged, and the educated.

■ CHAPTER THIRTEEN ■

The Encounter with Culture: Secularization and Postmodernism

The final linkage I make in this text is that between religion and culture. This is to be accomplished on two fronts. I shall first discuss a much-debated linkage between religion and culture known as secularization. Second, what has been named a major cultural position of the late twentieth century is postmodernism. Here an attempt will be made to understand what postmodernism is and then to present several religious responses to it.

It is a fundamental thesis of this text that as the sacred is manifested in the secular, there is a basic tension that emerges between the two phenomena. Two concepts capture this tension: secularization and sacralization. Secularization consists in the erosion of the sacred by the secular; sacralization is the ascendancy of the sacred over the secular. In the real world, neither pole exists in a pure form. For this reason, both are ideal types in the Weberian sense of the term. In human societies, this polarity is the basis of the dilemma between opposites. There is a constant tension between the two. An important sociological question relevant to this tension is: Which will be ascendant?

Two models will form the discussion: the cultural analytical and the rational choice paradigms. As Warner (1993) notes, the theory of secularization cannot be adequately explained by using the cultural analytical (the *first* in Warner's language) paradigm (see Chapter One). I shall address some of the controversy in interpreting secularization in the modern Western world by utilizing the two paradigms.

I shall begin this chapter by outlining what secularization is.[1] This will be followed by presenting the cultural analytic paradigm that attempt to explain and understand the process. The chapter will continue by explaining the rational choice model that addresses some of the lacunae and inconsistencies of the first paradigm. In conclusion to the first two sections, an

---

1   This is an extension of my discussion of secularization begun in Chapter Ten.

attempt will be made to reconcile the differences between the two paradigms in our understanding of secularization and sacralization. The chapter will close by first presenting what the postmodern and postmodernism
are, and, second, viewing various religious responses to them.

THE CONCEPTS OF SECULARIZATION AND SACRALIZATION

To recall from Chapter Ten, Berger (1969) offers a definition of secularization that is both objective and subjective. Objective secularization refers to
the process by which social institutions and culture shed the domination of
religious institutions and symbols. Subjective secularization indicates the
marginalization of myths and ethos within human consciousness (Berger
1969:107-108). A nuance to this definition is presented by Demerath III and
Williams (1992), who see the process not so much as creating another
enclave where religion can survive but, rather, in their terms, an abridging
of faith or the diminishment of the sacred in the arms of the secular: "the
process by which the sacred gives way to the secular" (1992:190). A synthetic
definition of secularization is:

> a process wherein the sacred and its institutional extensions is either
> marginalised, in sociological or psychological ways, or diminished by
> the secular.

The concept of sacralization connotes the opposite. In the spirit of what
Jeffrey Hadden (1987b) addresses about the secularization thesis, one may
describe sacralization as the process of the social institutions becoming
more and more influenced by both sacred symbols and institutions as well
as the movement of the sacred from the periphery of people's consciousness
to the centre.

The "Received Tradition of Secularization": Wilson and Martin

Two well-known British sociologists of religion, Bryan Wilson and David
Martin, give us what may be termed "the received tradition of secularization." By this is meant a baseline tradition that has resulted in a significant
amount of theory and research concerning the future of religion. In a
propositional form, as modernity advances, religion recedes. I begin with
Wilson.

In setting the baseline for a series of articles organized by the Society for
the Scientific Study of Religion to reflect on the status of the scientific

study of religion from 1965 to 1985, Wilson (1985) makes the following observations about secularization:

· religion is no longer a dominant institution in the economic and political sphere;

· the education systems of the Western world are removed from significant influence of the churches;

· religion moves from the centre of people's consciousness to the periphery.

In an earlier work, Wilson (1982) argues that secularization is understood not only as a change occurring *in* society but also a change *of* society. It is but one of a number of concomitant processes (such as industrialization, modernization, rationalization, bureaucratization, and urbanization) that have contributed to fundamental changes in Western societies. He notes the following indicators of these changes:

> Secularization relates to the diminution in the social significance of religion. Its application covers such things as the sequestration by political powers of the property and facilities of religious agencies; the shift from religious to secular control of various of the erstwhile activities and functions of religion; the decline in the proportion of their time, energy, and resources which men devote to super-empirical concerns; the decay of religious institutions; the supplanting, in matters of behaviour, of religious precepts by demands that accord with strictly technical criteria; and the gradual replacement of a specifically religious consciousness (which might range from dependence on charms, rites, spells, or prayers, to a broadly spiritually-inspired ethical concern) by an empirical, rational, instrumental orientation; the abandonment of mythical, poetic, and artistic interpretations of nature and society in favour of matter-of-fact description and, with it, the rigorous separation of evaluative and emotive dispositions from cognitive and positivistic orientations. (1982:149)

Like Wilson, Martin sees that secularization is part of the larger process of modernization. He uses the theories of Comte, Tonnies, Durkheim, and Spencer to note the evolutionary path of modernity — from *Gemeinschaft* to *Gesellschaft*. Secularization is not so much a process of changes in consciousness (as with Weber) as it is a decline in secular institutional supports of religious systems. Martin notes that with the advent of the first industrial revolution and the maturity of urbanization and mobility, there emerge personal anonymity and depersonalization processes. It is the horizontal sphere of relationships that is undermined, eventually leading to the demise of religion. The second revolution is referred to as the communication revolution. This process, of wide appeal, homogenizes individuals into separate spheres — again without any social basis to give credibility to the religious institution.

In sum, the received tradition of secularization is linear in nature and evolves as the modern world matures. Religion will eventually evaporate into non-significance. The anthropologist Wallace puts it well:

> the answer must be that the evolutionary future of religion is extinction. Belief in supernatural beings and in supernatural forces that affect nature without obeying nature's laws will erode and become only an interesting historical memory. (1966:264)

INTERPRETATION I: THE CULTURAL ANALYTIC APPROACH

We were introduced to what Warner (1993) calls the new and old paradigms in the sociology of religion in Chapter One. Because the characteristics of the old paradigm approximate an approach in sociology termed the cultural analytic one, I name it accordingly and present its meaning. The new paradigm was entitled the rational choice model. A sample of several authors will be selected who theorize about secularization from a cultural analytical point of view: Peter Berger, Will Herberg, Phillip Hammond, Jeffrey Hadden, Robert Wuthnow, and Penny Long Marler.

Cultural Analysis

Cultural analysis has been present in the sociology of religion from its inception. Durkheim and Weber are the classical representatives of the model. In the post-war period, Peter Berger is the most important figure to interpret religion through its lens. Recently, Robert Wuthnow and his colleagues have summarized and presented insights that have shed light on religion in the modern world. Wuthnow, Hunter, Bergesen and Kurzweil (1984), Wuthnow (1987), and Wuthnow and Witten (1988) document the central features of the approach. A focal concept is the vitality of the human symbol within cultures. Not only do human subjects give meaning to their lives through symbols, but they also construct patterns and rules of these symbols (Wuthnow et al. 1984). Using the symbol as the starting point, Wuthnow (1987:4) defines culture as "the symbolic-expressive aspect of human behaviour." It will be in this sense that culture will be used in this section.

Wuthnow (1987), in part, provides us with a valuable outline for this investigation. His concern is to understand moral order in a society and how it is constructed. He divides his book into four approaches: the subjective, the structural, the dramaturgic, and the institutional nature of culture. This approach is very close to the overall orientation of this text. However, it is not the same. In my approach to religion there is also the social and individual experience of the sacred. My approach considers the religious person (*the sacred person*) to be one who experiences the sacred.

On all other fronts, however, there is a strong similarity. The subjective and structural aspects of the cultural analytic approach are those parts of religion known as mythology (Chapter Two) and religious ethos (Chapter Nine). The dramaturgical characteristic is the acting out of mythology that we discussed under ritual in Chapter Seven. Finally, the institutional dimension of religion is subsumed under questions of religious leadership (Chapter Six) and religious organization (Chapter Eight).

Peter Berger: Plausibility Structures and Responses to Secularization

Hammond (1986) presents Berger's theory of secularization, both subjectively and institutionally. Subjective secularization is reflected by the rationalization of beliefs. In this way, Berger resurrects an earlier theme developed by Max Weber. A second source of secularization is in the pluralization of world views within institutions. The effect is the relativization of myths, a crisis of credibility, and even social homelessness. A third way that secularization manifests itself is with what Berger (1969)[2] calls "the problem of plausibility." As pluralism advances and the economic and political systems become increasingly divorced from religious institutions, there is produced what he calls a "liberated territory" with respect to religion (1969:129). The overall effect of these processes, these polarizations between the political and economic spheres and religion, is that religion manifests itself as a public rhetoric and private virtue, or what he terms the "privatization of religion."

This does not necessarily leave religion totally ineffective, however. Berger objects to the linear theory of secularization presented by Wilson, Martin and Wallace. In a text entitled *The Heretical Imperative* (1979b), he offers contemporary possibilities of religious affirmation: the deductive, reductive, and inductive possibilities.

The deductive option to secularization is both a reaction and a resistance. It is the reaffirmation of the religious tradition that has been challenged by non-religious processes. The example he uses is neo-orthodoxy,

---

2   See Chapter Two.

JOHN PAUL II: THE DEDUCTIVE LEADER

POPE JOHN PAUL II: TIME MAGAZINE'S CHOICE FOR MAN OF THE YEAR, 1994

For 16 years now, Karol Wojtyla, once actor, then priest, then Archbishop and Cardinal – has been Pope John Paul II, the Supreme Pontiff, bishop of Rome, leader of a church of nearly 1 billion souls.... Some dissident liberal Catholics ... see him as the product of a conservative patriarchal church, which helps explain his increasingly autocratic and negative pronouncements on such subjects as the ordination of women and artificial birth control.... The testimony is universal that prayer, more than food or liquid, is the sustaining force of this Pope's life. He makes decisions 'on his knees' says Monsignor Diarmuid Martin, secretary of the Vatican's Justice and Peace Commission. ... His goal is nothing less than the establishment of a completely Christian alternative to the humanistic philosophies of the twentieth century. ... He once told TIME's Wilton Wynn "It is a mistake to apply American democratic procedures to the faith and the truth. You cannot vote on the truth. You must not confuse the *sensus fidei* (sense of faith) with 'consensus.'"

SOURCE: *Time*, January 2, 1995, p. 21-39.

BOX 13.1

defined as "the reaffirmation of the objective authority of a religious tradition after a period during which that authority had been relativized and weakened" (179:79). In addition, neo-orthodox adherents claim that the destination is the starting point and are determined to remain faithful to their own religious experiences even in the face of contrary evidence. The New Religious Right would be a more contemporary example of this option. In Roman Catholicism, referred to in Box 13.1, Pope John Paul II reflects this.

A second option is what Berger entitles the reductive possibility or the modernization tradition. In essence, this possibility accepts modern science in general, and psychology and philosophy in particular, as the authority to challenge and to change religious world views or mythologies. Adherents accomplish this in two ways: cognitive bargaining and translating. By cognitive bargaining, Berger means the attempt by Christian theologians to adapt the sacred world view to the secular world view in the hope of salvaging the necessary and important parts of the sacred world view (the mythology) and eliminating that which is offensive to the modern mind. Miracles are one such offence. A process termed "demythologization"

THE REDUCTIVE OPTION AS APPLIED TO THE CHRISTIAN BELIEF IN THE RESURRECTION OF JESUS

SCHOLARS DENY THE RESURRECTION OF JESUS

German New Testament scholar Gerd Ludemann, a visiting professor at the Vanderbilt Divinity School ... [notes] the Resurrection is 'an empty formula' that must be rejected by anyone holding a 'scientific world view.' Ludemann argues that Jesus' body 'rotted away' in the tomb. The Risen Christ that appeared to the Apostle Peter ... was a subjective 'vision' produced by Peter's overwhelming grief and 'guilt' for having denied Jesus when he was arrested. ... In short, modern psychology reduces the Risen Christ to a series of interpsychic experiences that produced in the disciples a renewed sense of missionary zeal and spiritual self-confidence. ... According to this elaborate and academic protocol, the Resurrection is ruled *a priori* out of court because it transcends time and place.

SOURCE: *Newsweek*, April 8, 1996, p. 60-70.

BOX 13.2

interprets certain aspects of a religious tradition as not necessary for faith (for example, the resurrection of Jesus or the virgin birth of Christ in Christianity).

A second part of this option is translation. Berger defines this process as follows: "Terms of transcendent reference in the tradition must be either eliminated [in the case of those deemed marginal] or translated into terms of immanent reference [in the case of those deemed part of the core to be preserved]" (1979:112). This is illustrated in terms of ethics. Religion is not so much a relationship with the sacred as it is striving for justice, being compassionate, having a concern for the marginalized, and striving for world peace. Box 13.2 illustrates the reductive option.

Berger's final response to secularization is the inductive possibility or the movement from tradition to experience. His mentor here is the nineteenth-century German theologian, Friedrich Schleiermacher.[3] Schleiermacher takes human experience as the starting point of religious reflection and sees that revelation is understood to be every new or original disclosure of the cosmos to the innermost consciousness of the person. One begins with the widest variety of these kinds of experiences and induces from them what is common and most important. This is what he considers Liberal

---

3 See Chapter Four.

Protestantism does. Once this induction is completed (however, it is never really completed) it results in the essence of religion.

Where does Berger stand in presenting these options? The first option is too doctrinaire and reverses time to a place were traditional beliefs and practices were relevant to that time but are no longer pertinent to the late twentieth century. The second option is too reductionistic and the sacred element is next to being eliminated. The last option serves the modern world the best. It still attempts to retain the essential nature of the sacred (that has roots in the past) but is flexible enough to adapt to changing circumstances as societies evolve. In short, Berger argues, religion will not evaporate but will change to be meaningful to a succession of future generations.

As a final note on Berger, he continues the reflection on the third option by expanding the importance of human-religious experience (Berger 1992). The solitary individual, one who can exist only in the modern world, is at an advantage in that she or he is able to make an independent decision without being coerced by a monopolistic religious system. This individual is able to have an experience of reality that exists regardless of desires and wishes. The reality Berger refers to is the sacred, as described in Chapter Four. It is this kind of experience that carries one through the uncertainties of a modern, secularized world. Yet this cannot be done alone. There still needs to be some institutionalization of the experience. In what he wrote about 25 years before this publication, religious institutions are necessary to provide a plausibility structure for these experiences. Something similar is still needed today.

Will Herberg: The Problem of America Being Both Secular and Sacred

Will Herberg's (1960) publication had a significant effect on the thinking on secularization. Principally, his understanding is that the process of religious growth is concomitant with the secularization process. His often quoted phrase is that "America is at once the most religious and most secular society of the world" (1960:3). This puzzled him and presented him with a classic research question. Indeed, there was abundant evidence that, from 1925 to 1955, the membership rate of the churches outstripped the birth rate in the United States. A national survey done in the 1950s revealed that in the previous twelve weeks, 82 per cent of Roman Catholics, 68 per cent of Protestants, and 44 per cent of Jews had attended religious services.

Yet there was also a strong sense of the secular in these same people. He noted in a study of relevant surveys that although the vast majority of

Americans belonged to Protestant, Catholic, or Jewish institutions, their knowledge of their particular faith was superficial. Also, people were less interested in eternal life, heaven, hell or sin and more in worldly comfort and ease. In fact, he found evidence to show that people were religious because they wanted to be more successful in their work, make more money, and be accepted by others.

His interpretation of this led him to posit that people were religious in their external lives and secular in their internal lives. In Berger's understanding of secularization, religious institutions were central to people's location in social life, but religious values and ideas were pushed to the periphery of their consciousness. It was not faith in God that motivated people but "faith in faith." By this Herberg means positive thinking and a confidence in oneself and one's activities. He theorized that it was people's desire to be part of a congregation in order to be more American that was the most significant motivation. A theocentrism was substituted for an anthropocentricism, where people tend to be religious in form and secular in content.

Philip Hammond and the Distinction Between the Sacred and Religion

A third way to try to understand the inconsistent story of the modern world that is both secular and sacred at the same time (especially in Canada and the United States) is to make a simple distinction that Hammond (1986) makes in his introduction to the reader in *The Sacred in a Secular Age*. He acknowledges scholarship that reveals both secularization and sacralization processes occurring concomitantly. One way to interpret this problem is to use the distinction that Simmel made between the sacred (which Simmel calls "piety") and religion. The sacred is the purer reality that is "religiosity in a quasi-fluid state." Religion, on the other hand, is "objectivised sacredness" or "the objectivised world of faith" (Simmel 1959:11 and cited by Hammond 1985:3-4).

Hammond observes that religion appears to be diminishing as an institution but that the sacred is being retained. The past has transformed the sacred into religion (in Weber's terms, routinization of charisma), but as religion declines, this does not necessarily mean the experience of the sacred will erode as well.

Hammond's insights are given some empirical verification through a study of the baby boomer generation by Roof (1993). He found that even though this generation was increasingly leaving institutional religion, many were still seeking a meaningful spirituality, the sacred.

Jeffrey Hadden and the Processes of Sacralization

The basic position of Hadden (1987b) is that secularization should be viewed as a theory and that it has become sacred itself. By this he means that secularization is an ideological characterization of the modern world and not a theory that has an empirical base. He flatly denies secularization.

He presents five indicators of the persistence of religion in the United States:

1 From 1935-1985, there has never been a lower proportion than 94 per cent of Americans who have believed in God.

2 In 1937, 73 per cent of all Americans were church members in comparison to 68 per cent in 1984.

3 Essentially the same proportion reported attending church in 1984 as in 1939.

4 In relationship to personal religious practices, in 1985, 87 per cent of people said they prayed on a daily basis in comparison to 90 per cent in 1948.

5 On a per capita basis, Americans gave almost 20 per cent more to their churches in 1982 than they did in 1962.

He cites other sources of evidence to challenge the secularization thesis. New religious movements have attracted many Americans. The young are the most likely to become involved in such movements, and they, in turn, are least likely to continue involvement in mainline Christianity. This can be interpreted as a sacralization process in the lives of youth at the expense of their involvement in more established churches.

A further source of evidence that he presents is the relation between religion and political authority in a global perspective. In the American case, he cites the Civil Rights Movement and the Moral Majority (since Hadden's observation, this has been replaced by the New Religious Right in the 1990s). However, outside of America, there is ample evidence to substantiate the claim of sacralization: the establishment of Israel as a religious state; Gandhi's non-violent civil disobedience as a political strategy rooted in religious convictions; the religious in modern-day India with its factions of Hindus, Muslims, and Sikhs; the overthrow of the Shah of Iran by fundamentalist Muslims; the Roman Catholic "factor" in the overthrow of Marcos in the Philippines and Duvalier in Haiti; the explicit presence of the Anglican Church in South African politics in the person of Bishop Tutu; and the rise of liberation theology as a religious-political movement in Latin America.

356

Beyond Hadden's observations, one could make a strong case for the resurgence of religious conviction in the socialist bloc of Eastern Europe and Russia.[4] As we saw in Chapter Ten, the present-day New Democratic Party in Canada has primary roots in the social gospel movement of Western Canada under the leadership of Thomas Douglas, a former Baptist minister who founded the CCF party. Further west in Alberta, the Social Credit party was begun on an explicit evangelical platform that was later led by an evangelical minister (Ernest Manning) who acted as premier while still retaining his ministerial credentials.

A Mannheimian Attempt to Reconcile Secularization and Sacralization

In a study of secularization on the community level in a New England city, Demerath III and Williams (1992) make the observation that most sociologists of religion see the phenomenon as a continuous one. This they can say in spite of it being delimited and being reversed with sacralization processes as well. Long Marler (1989) presents us with another way to interpret these two processes. She returns to Weber and Durkheim. Weber predicts the gradual decline of religion, whereas Durkheim argues for its persistence in spite of the modern world's enlightenment campaign against it. She uses the sociologist Karl Mannheim to present a theory that accounts for both processes.

Long Marler sees Weber's thinking on secularization in much the same way as Berger thinks of subjective secularization. She summarizes Weber's question as: "What role does religious ethos and action play in the rational structure of society?" Long Marler adds that Weber was concerned specifically with the sources and effects of rationality in modern life. Weber used the term disenchantment in a similar way that subsequent sociologists use secularization.

Things were different for Durkheim. As the modern world moved from mechanical solidarity to organic, religion did not disappear but, rather, was transformed.[5] The direction of this transformation was away from the *cult of the social* to the *cult of the individual;* from the religion of the tribe, to the religion of the nation. It is a religion but not a religion of sacred, transcen-

---

4 In a national survey in 1991 in Russia, Greeley (1994) estimated that 20 per cent of the Russian people have moved from atheism to theism and from having no affiliation to the Orthodox Church. Prosaically, Greeley concludes the article by saying that St. Vladimir has routed Karl Marx.

5 For a discussion on this, see Chapter Three and Chapter Eight.

dent deities but sacred individuals and humanity. For Durkheim, the important thing to remember is that religion persists, but does change.

Long Marler concludes her analysis of Weber and Durkheim by noting that because they begin with different questions, they end up with dichotomous conclusions. Researchers who use Weber and Durkheim in their interpretation of secularization will also end up in a dichotomous way: either the end of religion or its continuity. She then moves on to using Mannheim as a means of reconciliation.

Using Mannheim's (1936) book *Ideology and Utopia*, as well as others, she presents a theory of secularization that takes into account the problems of both the persistence and decline of religion. Both an ideology and a utopia are world views in a constant, relational dialectic with a particular time and place. An ideology is a system of ideas that are immanent and essentially part of a socio-historical context. A utopia is a situationally transcendent system of ideas "which succeeds … in transforming existing historical reality into [another historical reality] … in accord with its own conception" (Mannheim 1936:176, and cited by Long Marler 1989:28). Utopias are defined by their potential to motivate revolutionary action and produce social change.

Religion is a utopian world view that can challenge and change the status quo. However, as utopias (sacred world views or mythologies) are transformed into ideologies (a secular world view), they lose this potential. Nonetheless, the ascendancy of new utopian idea systems is never ruled out. Neither the secularization nor the sacralization ends in an inevitable outcome. The key to which has ascendancy is largely dependent on the power and dynamism of the social actors and the institutions of which they are a part.

The Restructuring of American Religion: Robert Wuthnow

As Will Herberg's study of American Christianity presented an image of America structured according to Roman Catholic, Protestant, and Jewish affiliations in the 1950s, Robert Wuthnow's (1988a) reading of Christianity in America from the end of World War II until the late 1980s sees a restructuring according to criteria other than denominational.

As we saw in Chapter Three, the restructuring crosses denominational lines to result in two cultural structures: liberal and conservative. To better illustrate this religious realignment, Table 13.1 assists us in understanding the process. The liberal alignment is reflective of secularization and the conservative, sacralization. Wuthnow's observation of Christianity in America is a concomitant view of sacralization and secularization — both are happening together. But why? Why is secularization so common in the

THE RESTRUCTURING OF AMERICAN RELIGION

(adapted from Wuthnow, 1988:13ff)

ELEMENTS OF RESTRUCTURING	CONSERVATIVE	LIBERAL
MYTHOLOGY	Evangelical Fundamentalist Focus on a special knowledge of the Bible Strong sense of orthodoxy	Liberal theology Minimal Knowledge of the Bible Tend to be heterodox
ETHOS	Intolerant Morally rigid Abortion is always wrong	Tolerant Morally flexible Abortion is optional; Women's reproductive rights are emphasized
POLITICAL	Contra state control Critical of the welfare state Some New Right involvement For defense spending	For state influence For the welfare state Critical of the New Right Critical of defense spending

TABLE 13.1

liberal alignment? Several sources are working in tandem: the protest against the Vietnam War; denominational mergers that resulted in dissent and controversy; the rise of new religions; and, especially, the phenomenal increase in higher education.

Wuthnow notes that from 1960 to 1970, the percentage of youth who went on to college after high school increased from 22 per cent to 35 per cent while the budget increased from $2 billion to $23 billion in 1970 to $51 in 1980 (1988a:155,167). A correlation with this increase was the liberalization of a wide range of values, attitudes, and behaviours. He writes, "So powerful, in fact, were the effects of higher education on a wide range of values and beliefs that speculation began to emerge in the 1970s as to whether a new class had come into being" (1988a:157). This observation is reinforced with survey data. Relying on a Gallup (1982) study, he observes that the education gap in social attitudes and in religion has become more evident if one is either conservative or liberal. Again, he writes: "of all the social background questions in the study, education was the factor that most clearly discriminated between religious liberals and religious conservatives" (1988a:169).

Wuthnow's observation of the data gives credibility to Weber's understanding of secularization. What is presented here is a version of disenchantment or the rationalization of religious social actors. And the reason for that is the ascendancy of the rational mode of higher education with its emphasis on empiricism and reason as the mode of thinking.

Summary of Interpretation I

All of the interpreters of secularization outlined here fit well into the cultural analytic perspective. Berger's insights inform us of the subjective, structural, and institutional dimensions of secularization. The subjective and structural elements are illustrated in his discussion on rationalization and pluralization of life worlds. The institutional aspect is revealed in his discussion of the problem of plausibility structures. He adds to this approach by emphasizing the need for the experience of the sacred.

Herberg's contribution to the debate focuses on the subjective, the dramaturgical, and the institutional dimensions of religion. He argues that subjectively, secularity is alive and well, but, dramaturgically and institutionally, religion is still ascendant. In looking at the sacred as a core of religion, Hammond contends that it is possible for the sacred to continue even though institutionally the sacred objectivized continues to be subject to secularization. Hadden's statement that secularization is not substantiated by data emerges from subjective, dramaturgical, structural, and institutional dimensions of religion. In his discussion on the vitality of religious belief, public and private ritual, vibrant faith systems or myths, and the institutional linkage between religion and politics in nations outside of America, he gives evidence for the cultural analytic.

Finally, Long Marler, in her discussion of Mannheim, reveals the structural dimension of religion and secularization in the dialectical relationship between ideology (reflective of the secular) and utopia (indicative of the sacred). In summary, all authors referred to illustrate the cultural analytic view and, in their interpretation of secularization, both it and sacralization processes continue through the modern world.

INTERPRETATION II:
THE RATIONAL CHOICE MODEL

In setting a framework for a new paradigm in the study of religion in the United States, Warner (1993) argues that in interpreting secularization, the fact that the "reigning theory [the old paradigm] does not seem to work has become an open secret" (1993:1048). Citing several authors who represent the cultural analytic paradigm (again, my term for the old paradigm), Warner notes that the anomalies of the paradigm in disclaiming secularization consist of the resurgence of fundamentalism, the persistence of evangelicalism, and the continuity of liberal Protestantism. The rest of the article is devoted to those who are opponents of the secularization theory and who have created the new paradigm. According to Warner, then, the new paradigm has evolved because of anomalies in attempts to explain secularization using the old paradigm.

I shall present several authors who have forged new ways to address the secularization debate in light of the rational choice model. Stark (1985) and Stark and Bainbridge (1987) develop a theory of sect and cult formation seeing secularization as a delimiting process. Bibby (1987, 1993a, 1993b) uses the term "fragmentation of the gods" as a response to secularization in the light of survey data in Canada. Stark and Iannaccone (1994) address the phenomenon in Europe. This section will conclude with a review of the Warner (1993) article, which is a comprehensive view of the new paradigm, with secularization as the central question.

Secularization as a "Delimiting Process": Stark and Bainbridge

Stark (1985) frames his discussion within the church-sect dichotomy, which should not be considered to be a theory but rather a typology. While acknowledging that Niebhur (1957) used it as a theory, most church-sect researchers have indeed used it as a typology. Yet Stark, with his colleague Bainbridge, has moved the typology to the level of a theory using a rational choice model.

Stark begins his theory with the concept of a religious economy that is defined as "consisting of all the religious activity going on in any society. Religious economies are like commercial economies in that they consist of a market of current and potential customers, a set of firms seeking to serve the market, and the religious 'product lines' offered by the various firms" (Stark and Iannaccone 1994:232). An important consideration is the extent to which a market is regulated. In a society where a religious economy is unregulated, pluralism will grow. In Stark's words, "the 'natural' state of religious economies is one in which a variety of firms successfully cater to the special religious interests of limited market segments" (1985:143). The more dominant a religious firm is, the more church-like it will be and the more it will be in low tension with the social environment. This is the process of secularization.

However, as this happens it does not necessarily lead to the demise of religion that Martin, Wilson, and Wallace would predict. It does suggest, on the other hand, the eventual failure of a specific religious organization if it becomes too secularized and divorced from the sacred. So from where do the continuity or resurrection of the sacred and the growth of other kinds of religious organizations emerge? They emerge because secularization is a self-limiting process. As the church-like organization becomes too secularized, various forms of protest occur. A sect emerges from the dust of a church; it is high in tension with the social environment, and it revives the lost sense of the sacred, the charisma. If this revival is a renewal, a revival of the old faith, we have a sect. If, in contrast, a new sense of the sacred, a religious innovation is constructed that varies with the old faith, a cult is the result.[6]

Bibby in Canada: Fragmentation as a Response to Secularization

With Stark, Bibby (1987, 1993a, 1993b) frames his discussion of religion in Canada in terms of a religious economy or the market model that includes a firm, products, and consumers (1987:118ff). The four main "firms" are the Roman Catholic, Anglican, United, and Conservative churches. Each is competing for limited resources — particularly, members as consumers of religious products. And the competition is getting keener as affiliation remains stable but active participation grows weaker. Evidence for the latter comes from a more recent book by Bibby (1993b) which indicates about a 25 per cent active participation rate.

Bibby's interpretation of secularization begins with the same religious organization type as Stark and Bainbridge: the church. Unlike them, however, he does not follow their theory of sect and cult formation. Rather, religious organizations in Canada appear to adapt themselves to Canadian culture and "give the consumers what they want." In addition, consumers tend to select from these organizations "consumer items" which fit their own lifestyles and life orientations. In other words, both the organizations

---

6 Although not part of Stark's discussion, the theory could be used to explain the formation of movements of renewal that I outlined in Chapter Eight. As a church becomes too secularized, a protest may emerge which visions itself as renewing the church from within. I used the monastic movement and the modern day charismatic movement as historical examples.

(in Berger's term, objective) and the members have distanced themselves from the sacred (again, to use Berger, subjective) and have become increasingly secularized. Fragmentation, then, is a response to these processes. Indeed, fragments are powerful because they work. Bibby says it in the following way:

> Modern women and men continue to identify with established religious traditions, selectively adopt certain beliefs, practices and teaching, and occasionally turn to groups for specialized professional services — a baptism, a wedding, a funeral. Consumer-oriented as they are, many supplement the items available from their core religious traditions with fragments from other systems. They read their horoscopes, give credibility to psychic phenomena, think they might be reincarnated, don't rule out the existence of a spirit world. They are into fragments, not systems, into consumption, rather than commitment. (1993a:76-77)

It should be emphasized, however, that secularization is not the end product. Canadians do not say no to the sacred, but they do select and choose what appeals to them about the sacred. Bibby (1993b) adds that Canadians are still intrigued with mystery, search for explanations of the unknown, and seek meaning to their secular lives. Religion has not eroded in Canada, but it definitely has changed.

Secularization in Europe, England, and the United States: Stark, Finke, Guest, and Iannaccone

Not all researchers and theorists of secularization are in agreement within the new paradigm. Warner (1993:1048) states that in Europe secularization is an historical fact as well as a theory. Stark and Iannaccone (1994) disagree. In fact, they set out to agree with Hadden and argue that "we think the time has come for the notion of secularization per se to be returned to whence it came, to Comte's unscientific philosophizing on the brave new world to come" (1994:250). They are not saying that there is no evidence for the secular but rather that secularization as a process from pre-modern times to the present post-industrial world has no empirical basis not only in the United States but in Europe as well. In fact, they set out to test a series of propositions that Europe is not as secular in the present as it was in pre-modern times.

For times when religion is weak in Europe, they focus not so much on the demand side of the religious economic scale but on the supply side — the side of the religious firms. Their overall thesis is that religion has been

363

SOCIETY, SPIRITUALITY, AND THE SACRED

weak in Europe, the churches have not created a demand for their religious products. For example, in Scandinavia, does the low level of religious mobilization illustrate weak demand or a soft supply? They set out to provide evidence that the soft supply of the firms is the primary ingredient for secular phenomena to emerge and grow.

The authors' data and evidence for these positions are impressive. They use not only national comparative databases but also social historical sources to present their case. The propositions of most interest to us here are that religious firms offered little in the way of piety to attract members, and that modern Europe, as a whole, is more religious today than it was in pre-modern or medieval times.

Social historians of medieval Europe reveal the following. Outside of the cities where most people lived, churches were very small and could not accommodate more than a handful of members. Anglican clergy in the late medieval period were bereft of knowledge of their faith. Similarly, Roman Catholic priests in southern Italy could hardly read and could understand even less. Moreover, many Catholic clergy kept concubines and fathered many children. Memories of sexual improprieties on the part of the priests were common. In addition to this laxity, the Roman Catholic leaders exhibited a disdain for the peasants, were hostile toward them, and made accusations of bestiality, violence, and avarice against them. Most of the people were peasants, and their religion approximated animism in catholic form. When they did enter the church buildings, as indicated by a British historian, they jostled for seats, nudged their neighbours, hawked and spat, knitted and slept.

Church participation rates are more revealing. Estimates show that, for example, in the district of Oxfordshire in England, in 1738, 5 per cent of the population attended the major Christian feasts. In the late eighteenth century, about 11 per cent of the population were participants, and in 1850, about 16 per cent. This latest figure is comparable to a 1980 number of 15 per cent. A similar story is told in Ireland, when in 1840 about 33 per cent of the population were active Roman Catholics.

In further extending the study of secularization in England and adding historical data from the United States, Stark, Finke and Iannaccone (1995) and Finke, Guest and Stark (1996) review literature and provide new evidence that challenges the Durkheimian view that pluralism threatens religion and makes it weaker because people choose their gods rather than the gods choosing them.

In contrast, the British sociologist of religion Steve Bruce (1992), in analyzing an 1851 religious census of England and Wales, found evidence to the contrary. Stark, Finke and Iannaccone (1995) subject Bruce's findings to more statistical and historical analysis and conclude that the proposition is challenged by evidence from these data as well. The primary statistical tool they used that was not used by Bruce was to control for other social factors. In doing so, they did discover that the relationship between pluralism and participation was still present, with one qualification. In the case where competition is constrained by social forces (for example, workers may not participate just because they are poor and not because they do not want to), the correlation between pluralism and participation is not as strong.

Finke, Guest and Stark (1996) indicate that in the pre-revolutionary era of the United States, religion was not salient (for example in 1776 only 17 per cent of the colonists were affiliated with a church). However, since the disestablishment of religion in early America, and in spite of industrialization, urbanization, and rationalization, religion, on a variety of measures, has increased. They write: "An immense body has demonstrated [that] American religion has been more vigorous than ever and seems entirely immune to secularization" (1996:203).

In a quest to present further verification of the correlation between pluralism and religious salience, Finke, Guest and Stark (1996) tested the thesis that religious pluralism is positively correlated with religious participation using census data from New York state from 1855 and 1865. By using data from two time periods, they were able to see if there were changes in church participation. As predicted, attendance increased between 1855 and 1865. In addition, the time from the revolution to 1855 and 1865 witnessed an increase in population density and urbanization. Contrary to the traditional secularization thesis, church participation rates increased rather than declined.

What is this saying? Essentially, in pre-modern times and early periods of industrialization and urbanization, secularization was alive and well. In fact, as far as these authors can estimate, Europe, England, and the United States have experienced a process of sacralization rather than of secularization.

Secularization and the Social Scientific Study of Religion: Stephen Warner

Warner's view of the new paradigm is that the need for a new one arises because the old paradigm does not adequately address the problem of secularization. He elaborates and presents a significant volume of research to substantiate the thesis. I presented an overview of this in Chapter One; my focus here will be on the specifics of interpreting the problems with secularization as a linear process in the United States.

According to Warner (1993), during Colonial America, church involvement and participation rates were quite low. After the disestablishment of religion in post-revolutionary times, the number of people enrolled in churches grew throughout the nineteenth and into the twentieth century. This trend has continued through to the present even though there were fluctuations. The reasons for this support the rational choice paradigm: with increased pluralism and competition, sacralization is the outcome. Because no single religious group has a monopoly, a large social market place is created for a variety of religious groups to mobilize in order to provide a more attractive "firm" to encourage church participation. They mobilize to increase the marketability of their religious product.

Some examples of such organizations include churches (synagogues, mosques, and temples as well) responding to the needs of immigrant groups, as in the case of nineteenth-century Irish and twentieth-century Muslim and oriental peoples. In addition, many Christian denominations and Jews have opened their ordination rites of passage to women. Even gays and lesbians find some sacred social space in a denomination called the Metropolitan Community Church. For African Americans, churches were frequently empowerment centres for civil rights.[7]

Taking the demand side of the market model, Warner challenges the view that the new voluntarism[8] of the modern religious believer is not necessarily a signal of secularization. However, the new voluntarism can be an instrument of change and vitality in religion. For example, when people switch denominational affiliations, there is evidence that this is a serious commitment to participate more religiously than before the switch.

Summary of Interpretation II

All these authors offer us some answers to the problems, anomalies, and questions of the linear thesis of secularization. Stark and Bainbridge inform us that both processes of secularization and sacralization occur at different times and in different organizational configurations. Bibby's interpretation assists us in seeing that fragmentation is a response to the religious firms not doing well on their supply side of the market equation. Stark and Iannaccone address a similar concern to Bibby's — secularization is a result of religious firms not marketing their religious products well. They should be especially remembered, however, for their radical position that modern Europe is more religious than during pre-modern times. This is especially important because of the centrality of the secularization theory in sociological discourse. Finally, Warner's review of the evidence for the new para-

---

7   On the other hand, see the research on religion as an opium in Chapter Twelve.

8   See Chapter Three.

digm presents evidence that America is more religious today than it was in colonial times (which is consistent with Finke, Guest and Stark). All authors in the rational choice model are united in giving us cogent evidence that the linear model of secularization has significant flaws.

ATTEMPTS TO RECONCILE
THE TWO INTERPRETATIONS

The first interpretation of secularization and sacralization presents a thesis that the sacred culture is in tension with the secular culture. The ascendancy of the sacred over the secular depends upon changes within either the sacred or the secular culture. No other sources of change are considered. A problem with this model for understanding secularization is that of not locating sources of change outside the sacred or secular culture. In contrast, the significant strength of the rational choice model is searching for and discovering sources of change in the social system — namely in the economic and political systems. Also, rational choice models offer powerful explanatory strength to the data.

367

A possible reconciliation of the two models may be in the making. One way is to use an ecological model of nesting the sacred cultural system in the centre of a system that includes, in the following order, the secular culture and the social system. The market model argues that, for example, pluralism in the social system encourages changes within the sacred and secular cultural systems. Where there are elevated levels of pluralism, the sacred culture will be in ascendancy (sacralization). On the other hand, with low levels of pluralism, the secular cultural system will be dominant.

To add to the strength of this reconciliation interpretation, there are already some established linkages. Hammond (1986) observed that Berger uses the market model to understand four features of modern religion: growth of the ecumenical movement, pressure to compete with better religious products, appealing to people's desires, and marketing youth to become active. However, as Warner (1993) implies, Berger's market framework does not become a central feature of his work.

Wuthnow (1988b) also includes market model language in his sociology of religion. In his discussion of the relationship between religion and the social environment, he sees the importance of social resources in understanding religion when religious systems often engage in competition with one another for scarce resources. In addition, he views the institutional nature of religion (the fourth level of the cultural analytic approach) as represented by organizations which extract resources from the environment, then coordinate them, and finally direct them toward accomplishing a goal. He then goes on to interpret the church-sect dichotomy using these concepts.

A final note. Neither model addresses the importance of religious experience.[9] A way to include the relevancy of the phenomenon is that in light of a pluralistic social system, there is more likelihood for the personal religious experience of the sacred to emerge. All things being equal, this experience may lead to the formation of a social group, the growth of a sect or a cult, or a movement of renewal. One practical way to test this is to see if there is a correlation between the number of founders or reformers of religion within a pluralistic society compared to a non-pluralistic one.

POSTMODERN SOCIETY
AND POSTMODERNISM

The conclusion to this chapter addresses the question of a more advanced stage of Western society. Although there is vibrant debate as to how this late development is typified, there is a substantial agreement that the latter part of the twentieth century has either moved into or is defined as being postmodern.[10] Two sections will capture the discussion here. First of all, the terms postmodern and postmodernism will be defined. Thereafter, I will summarize two religious responses to the condition of the postmodern and postmodernism.

Definitions of the Postmodern and Postmodernism

Although these terms have been and continue to be used interchangeably, they do describe two different sets of phenomena. Postmodern refers to the social, economic, and political conditions of late second millennial societies. Postmodernism refers to the culture of the postmodern period.

In the years just preceding the accelerated Vietnam War, the well-known critical sociologist C.W. Mills reflected that the modern age is being succeeded by a postmodern period (cited in Borgata and Borgata 1992). Shortly after Mills, Amitai Etzioni (1968 and cited in Bell, 1976) uses the term postmodern to describe a society that has experienced unprecedented transformation of the technologies of communication. Etzioni puts the date of the beginning of this period in 1945 — much earlier than most observers.

To what these terms mean, I turn, in part, to Featherstone (1988), who introduced a dedicated journal issue to the topic. He presents us with a

---

9   The exception would be Berger.

10 Giddens (1993) objects to the use of postmodernism and prefers to use the term "radicalized modernity." He takes the position that there has not been a break in modernity but, rather, that modernity has moved to a more radical stage.

POSTMODERN RELIGION – INTERNET STYLE

RELIGION ONLINE

The signs of online religious activity are everywhere. If you instruct AltaVista, a powerful Internet search engine, to scour the Web for references to Microsoft's Bill Gates, the program turns up an impressive 25,000 references. But ask it to look for Web pages that mention God, and you'll get 410,000 hits. Look for Christ on the Web and you'll find him – some 146,000 times. ... The harvest is even more bountiful on the Web, where everyone from Lutherans to Tibetan Buddhists now has a home page, many crammed with technological bells and whistles. Mormon sites offer links to vast genealogical databases, while YaaleVe'Yavo, an Orthodox Jewish site, forwards e-mailed prayers to Jerusalem, where they are affixed to the Western Wall. Two websites are devoted to Cai Daiism, the tiny Vietnamese sect that worships French novelist Victor Hugo as a saint, and a handful probe the mysteries of Jainism, an Indian religion in which the truly beautiful sweep the ground with a small broom to avoid accidentally stepping on insects or other hapless creatures. Even the famously technophobic Amish are represented online by a website run by Ohio State University. ... Even holy texts have begun to be adapted to the new technology. The interconnection of religious documents through so-called hyperlinks has produced a new form of scholarship called "hyper-theology."

SOURCE: *Time,* December 16, 1996, p. 52-58.

BOX 13.3

369

sense of the meaning of the terms through a contrast and comparison with their antonyms.

THE MEANING OF POSTMODERN

Modern indicates a kind of society and social organization that emerged after the Reformation, Enlightenment, and industrial and political revolutions (the Civil War of England from 1640-1650, the American Revolution of 1776, and the French Revolution of 1789). This period was set off from the medieval era, termed "traditional society." Special features include the creation and continuation of nation states, political systems founded on democracy and socialism, and a general challenge to monarchal systems; in the twentieth century, the creation of welfare capitalism; a geometric increase in the production of material goods through capitalist or socialist

PRE-INDUSTRIAL, INDUSTRIAL, AND POST-INDUSTRIAL SOCIETIES

(adapted from Bell 1976:117)

	PRE-INDUSTRIAL	INDUSTRIAL	POST-INDUSTRIAL
CURRENT REGIONS	Parts of Africa and Asia	Eastern Europe	W. Europe, USA, Japan
ECONOMIC SECTORS	Primary	Secondary	Tertiary and Quaternary
OCCUPATIONS	Farming, Mining, and Unskilled Labour	Semi-Skilled Labour	Professional, Skilled, and Educated
TECHNOLOGY	Raw Materials	Energy and Industrial Machinary	Information, Advanced Technology, esp. Computers, and Human Service
RELATIONSHIP WITH NATURE AND PEOPLE	Against Nature	Against Fabricated Nature	Between Persons
METHODOLOGY	Common Sense	Empiricism	Abstract Models and Post-Empiricism
TIME	Orientation to the Past	*ad hoc* Adaptiveness	Future Orientation
AXIAL PRINCIPLE	Traditionalism and Land/ Resource Limitation	Economic Growth: State or Private Control	Centrality and Codification of Theoretical Knowledge

TABLE 13.2

industrialism; learning and knowledge expanding on the philosophic-scientific traditions of Galileo, Copernicus, Newton, Descartes, Kant, and Locke that all converged into positivism; great hope for the future that was typed as progressive; and a goal that would offer emancipation to all peoples including all marginalized races, ethnic groups, and religions. In addition, Weber (cited in Whimster and Lash 1987 and Roth 1987) focuses upon two central tenets of modernity: the increase in rationalization processes (represented by science and positivism) and bureaucratization of both secular and religious organizations.

The postmodern world is quite different. The social conditions of this world are reflected in the work of Bell (1976) and Jameson (1984, and cited in Kellner 1988). Jameson does not discuss the postmodern (the social, economic, and political phenomena) but, rather, postmodernism, which I will discuss shortly. He is the one, however, who links it to late capitalism through the work of Mandel (1975). I shall use Bell (1976) and Mandel (1975) to outline the postmodern society. Bell uses the term post-industrial[11] and Mandel, late capitalist.

Bell (1976) considers the post-industrial to be a new axial principle of social organization that is intricately tied to new technologies. His focus is not on culture but on social structure. As the crucial problem of the industrial period has been that of capital or how to institutionalize a process of creating sufficient savings and the conversion of these savings into investment areas, the problem of the post-industrial period has been the organization of science and the primary institution, the university, where this research has been carried out. From Bell (1976:117), Table 13.2 was constructed.

We might add to this that post-industrialism also indicates the growth of the new class, the geometric increase in information technology that was referred to by Etizioni, the decline of the welfare state as nation states are intent on reducing their debts by cutting social programs, the globalization of the economy wherein nation states increasingly have little control over their national economies, and the strong potential for the shrinkage of the middle class. The British sociologist Bauman (1997) adds to this list: the advanced erosion of the global structure of domination of the West over all the world; the global market system seducing national populations into external dependency; and the market supplying societal members not only with material goods but with symbolic ones as well. And it will be through the electronic media (particularly the Internet) that the market will sell both durable and symbolic goods (such as advanced education).

---

11   I am using the term post-industrial to mean postmodern.

Mandel (1975) uses the classical form of Marxist political economy to describe the global economy of capitalism. Classic Marxist political economy was an analysis of nation-state capitalism. Mandel considers three eras of capitalism: market (nineteenth century), monopoly (late nineteenth and most of the twentieth century), and late. His main description of late capitalism consists of the bourgeois quest for further profits by engaging in two main strategies: replacing human labour with technology and increasing surplus value (profits) not by reducing salaries and wages (welfare capitalism provided increases of wages in western societies during most of the twentieth century), but by relocating industries to third-world countries and paying workers significantly less than workers in the welfare capitalist nations.[12] Other features of late capitalism include third-generation technologies (information and computers), permanent arms production, the internationalization and centralization of capital, neo-colonialism, and permanent inflation.

An important thing to remember in this analysis is that we live in an increasingly "borderless" world of nation states, and the economic structure is a capitalist, international one. This is even more evident in the 1990s with the collapse of socialism in Russia and Eastern Europe and the continued exodus of industrial jobs from the first world to the third world.

THE MEANING OF POSTMODERNISM

The cultural term that corresponds to the modern world is modernity. Its emphasis is on master narratives, positivism, the recognition of human rights, and conformity through law rather than power. Featherstone (1988) adds that modernity is a quality of modern life with a break from tradition: "Modern man is the man who constantly lives to invent himself" (1988:199). The down side of modernity is a sense of homelessness (Berger), alienation of workers (Marx), a feeling of anomie (Durkheim), being dominated by an objective culture (Simmel), and a sense of being locked in the cage of capitalist or socialist state bureaucracies (Weber).

As the postmodern is the social structural system, postmodernism is the culture of the same social structure. Featherstone (1988) observes that postmodernism has been used for a longer time than the term postmodern. He traces it to the 1930s when it was first used to indicate a minor reaction to modernity. It became popular in 1960s New York among artists and writ-

---

12 As can be seen, Mandel is quite prophetic. Political economic sociologists have observed that there has been a significant increase in the transfer of industrial businesses from Canada and the northeastern United States to the southern United States, Mexico, Central America, and southeast Asia (see Magdoff and Sweezy 1989).

ers. During the 1970s and 1980s, it was illustrated in avant-garde art, architecture, and the performing arts. Academically, attempts have been made at creating theories by Foucault (1993), Marcuse (1993), and Derrida (1993). Featherstone gives us a definition:

> [It is] ... an æsthetic self consciousness and reflexiveness; a rejection of narratives in favour of simultaneity and montage; an exploration of the paradoxical, ambiguous and uncertain open-ended nature of reality and a rejection of the notion of an integrated personality in favour of an emphasis upon the restructured, dehumanized subject. (1988:209)

The term reveals a quest not for certainty or for objective truth but for a situation that is never closed, ever open-ended, and incomplete. In postmodernism, there is never a finished project (scientific or otherwise); no hope for the continued perfection of the human person and human species; and no desire to join others in the quest for wholeness, social bonding, and connectedness. The modernist agenda of major narratives (for example, Christianity, progressivism, Marxism, or socialism) is defunct. The only acceptable narratives are the narratives of each person or social group and each is as valid as the other.

Bauman (1997) adds to the discussion and paints further portraits of postmodernism, including a lack of commitment, a constant search for new experiences, the frequent adopting and shedding of identities, political institutions competing in dismantling all collective interference into individual fate by deregulation and privatization, the decline of neighbourhoods and families, and a radical uncertainty about the material and social worlds we inhabit.

This is not the whole story, however. Griffin (1990), a philosopher of religion, and Smith (1989), a scholar of religion, add that there are two major types of postmodernism: destructive and constructive or revisionary. Destructive postmodernism refers to an anti-world view that deconstructs the elements necessary for a world view, such as God, self, purpose, meaning, a real world, and truth. It ends up in nihilism. Constructive or revisionary postmodernism involves not a wholesale denial of modernity but a revision of some of its elements, including a new approach to scientific, ethical, aesthetic, and religious institutions. It rejects scientism (where science is considered to be the answer to everything) but not science. Moreover, it is not a simple extension of modernity, for it breaks with a modern world locked in individualism, anthropocentricism, patriarchy, mechanization, consumerism, nationalism, and militarianism.

Religious Responses to the Postmodern World and Postmodernism

Flanagan (1996), in an introduction to conference proceedings on post-modernism, religion, and sociology, identifies two major responses to post-modernism: fundamentalism and the New Age Movement. I shall follow this direction in this final section of the chapter. The nuance to Flanagan's distinction is to go beyond the restrictions of fundamentalism to include a conservative response. I have discussed fundamentalism (both Islamic and Christian) under the title of religion and politics. Here I will focus on a conservative response and the New Age Movement.

BELL AND CONSERVATISM

O'Neill (1988), a Canadian sociologist, presents a conservative response to postmodernism in the work of Daniel Bell. O'Neill observes that for Bell, the world of today is not only a post-industrial one that involves a crisis of capitalism but also a crisis of religion, for postmodernism denies the need for meaning. Bell (1980, cited in O'Neill) believes that the post-industrial society is threatened by postmodern hedonism and self-gratification. Early capitalism was more healthy because of its connection to religion, namely, the Protestant ethic. Later capitalism has lost its linkage to religion and values in general. In the spirit of Weber, capitalism has left the cage of Protestantism and has created its own that bears no ethical meaning. Therein we find its danger and crisis. Bell (1980) offers three positive responses: a new moralistic religion typified by evangelicalism, a redemptive religion wherein religious institutions become mediating institutions of care, and kinds of mystical religions which accent sacred experiences.

THE NEW AGE MOVEMENT

New Age can be seen as a viable candidate to be a response to postmodernism.[13] Kurtz (1989 and cited in Chalfant et al. 1992) considers it to be a protest movement that exhibits a distrust of science and seeks to develop new levels of spiritual awareness. Marilyn Ferguson (1980), a reporter by profession, was one of the first to document the movement and presents several characteristics of its mythology.

---

13 There is debate in seeing the New Age Movement as a response to postmodernism. One dissenting voice is Heelos (1996), who presents five theses arguing that the link between the two is erroneous.

A central tenet of the movement is that it really has no tenets. What Ferguson terms "New Age Spirituality" (1980:369) is a diminution of doctrine, an exchange of faith for experiential knowledge, and a transformation from compartmentalized cognition to unitary thinking. This direct knowledge is considered to be a glimpse of the true nature of reality, a disassociation from the ego or the individual self, a connection with the source of all that generates the world of appearances, and a reunion with all living beings. In addition, one may add more elements of the movement by categorizing the literature into the experiential, mythological, ritual, ethical, and collective dimensions of religion.

Experience of the Sacred, Myth, Ritual, and Ethos

The Christian theologian John Newport (1998) groups the movement into two schools. The mainstream aspect enters into the cultural landscape through the domains of health, psychology, art, education, and work. The focus is on such themes as getting in touch with one's potential, personal spirituality, acknowledging that human growth and potential are unlimited, and a major shift in world consciousness as the twenty-first century approaches. The second school, which he terms *occult*, embraces a wide variety of myths, rituals, and behaviour that include channelling (or receiving messages from spiritual masters who have been transformed and live in heavenly realms), meditation, astrology, Tarot card reading, reincarnation, out-of-body experiences, and dream analysis.

375

The range of beliefs, however, is so diverse that it is hard to reduce them to a set of tenets, as is common in more traditional religions. In fact, the notion of beliefs is secondary to the focus on the transformation of the human condition in terms of healing and wholeness with self, others, nature, and the whole cosmos (Bibby 1993). Yet according to Newport (1998), in spite of this diversity, there is a remarkable unity. He presents five central tenets of the mythology: monism, pantheism, "God is within you," reincarnation and karma, and changing one's consciousness or transformation.

In monism[14] (*All is One*), the cosmos is seen as a pure, undifferentiated, universal, energy-interconnected phenomenon. This can be seen as a *theory of correspondence*, which refers to the belief that the external world is a reflection of internal consciousness. There is one basic reality: energy. In addition, God is beyond personality and is an impersonal energy force or consciousness. This supreme God or ultimate reality manifests itself as a dynamic polarity of light/dark, male/female, good/evil. This version of

---

14 Monism is any doctrine based on the assumption of a single underlying principle or, all is one and one is all, or the cosmos equals the self which in turn equals the divine.

mythology is similar to Lévi-Strauss' binary structures that we investigated in Chapter Two. Furthermore, the God who is ultimate is within the person, and people may be viewed as *gods and goddesses in exile*. New Age adherents report a sense of self-affirmation, a release from guilt, and an acceptance of life as it is. Evil is described as linked to ignorance and as a lack of enlightenment.

Reincarnation and karma are an integral part of New Age mythology. Becoming aware of one's own divinity and being transformed from ignorance to spiritual knowledge take more than a lifetime. Several incarnations are necessary. What I do in this life determines my karma for the next: if I accumulate good fruit in my life, positive benefits will come in my next life. The ultimate goal is the realization of unity with the divine, a merging with the cosmos when I shall become fully enlightened. The last central tenet of the mythology is transformation. Transformation consists of the movement from ignorance to enlightenment. This transformation is all-inclusive: personal, social, societal, and cosmological. The power to bring about this transformation is through tapping into the universal energy referred to above.

Sources of New Age mythology are wide ranging. Ferguson (1980), Naisbett and Aberdene (1993 cited by Bibby 1993), and Newport (1998) outline several. In order to discover people's first-hand experience, Ferguson (1980) conducted a non-probability sample of people (N=185) and targeted those she considered as being "social transformers." Their spiritual sources were predominantly Eastern in origin: Zen, Yoga, Christian mysticism, psychosynthesis, Jungian therapy, Tibetan Buddhism, transcendental meditation, Sufism,[15] and transactional analysis. According to Ferguson, most (ranging from 57 per cent to 96 per cent) believed in and practised telepathy, psychic healing, precognition, clairvoyance, cosmic intelligence, postdeath survival, and reincarnation.

Naisbett and Aberdene (1993) consider that the roots of New Age mythology are in the human potential movement, which include encounter groups, gestalt awareness training, transactional analysis, sensory awareness, primal therapy, bioenergetics,[16] massage, psycho synthesis, humanistic psychology, and psychic healing (see also Westley 1983).

Newport's (1998) search for seeds is much more extensive. He begins with the Hellenistic eras in Western society and traces influences up to the latter part of the twentieth century. He identifies the first source in *gnosti-*

---

15 Psychosynthesis: a theoretical effort to reconcile components of the unconscious with the rest of the personality. Sufism: Islamic mysticism.

16 The study of energy transformation in living systems.

cism, which co-existed with Judaism and early Christianity and was, essentially, an adaptation of these faiths to Greek dualistic and Platonic philosophy. It accents *gnosis* or knowledge as the way to liberation or salvation. He adds many: Neoplatonism, Hermeticism, alchemy, Celtic religion, the Renaissance, Freemasonry, Swedenborgianism, Mesmerism, spiritualism, Hinduism, Transcendentalism, theosophy, New Thought,[17] and positive thinking. The denomination called Christian Science is also considered by Newport to prepare the way for the New Age. Through the mind, one can overcome sickness and death. The problem with human life is not sin (as in orthodox Christianity) but a profound error in thinking. If you think properly, you will live well.

Hargrove (1989), an American sociologist, adds that it is seen as a response to the perception that modern society has reached its limits in some aspects. In other words, modernity has not been successful in fulfilling its promises of equality and progress. New Age predicts that there are new and important realities to be explored that have been ignored by the "single vision" of modern science. Spiritualistic (and mythical) systems include retracing presumed earlier lives, making contact with spiritual powers through the use of crystals, and the like. Roberts (1995) augments this interpretation by noting that the movement is very mystical (intuitive)

377

---

17 *Neoplatonism*: a philosophical-religious movement during the early centuries of the Christian era marked by the fact that the ultimate idea is the One who is superior to the Nous or the Mind. The World Soul is co-extensive with the material world. *Hermeticism*: this religious philosophy synthesized Gnosticism, neoplatonism, astrology, and various other spiritual leaders from Greece. *Alchemy*: elementary science with spiritual overtones. The practitioners tried to discover a way to change material objects into gold and to discover the divine spark identified as the Self. *Celtic religion*: pre-Christian religion of the Irish and English. *Freemasonry*: an alternative gnostic spirituality adapted to the modern world. *Swedenborgianism*: named after its founder, Emanuel Swedenborg (1688-1772), who argued that everything in the visible material world corresponds to something in the spiritual world (the theory of correspondence). The Divine and the natural exist in both God and Man. *Mesmerism*: from a Viennese physician, Mesmer (1733-1815), who taught that everything was connected to everything else, and the source of this nexus is the universal magnetic fluid. *Spiritualism*: movement during the eighteenth and nineteenth centuries in the United States that sought truth by hearing the spirits of the dead. *Transcendentalism*: in nineteenth-century America, the sacred books of Hinduism were introduced, leading to the development of this movement; it combined nature religion with Hindu nuances. It was unique to America in that it united cultural themes such as individualism, success, and self-actualization to Hindu monism. *Theosophy*: the first nineteenth-century movement which spoke of a new era and a new beginning and combined this with Hindu mysticism. *New Thought*: a nineteenth-century movement whose founder, P. Quimby (1802-1866), defined God as the divine mind.

AMERICANS IN SEARCH FOR MEANING

THE SEARCH FOR THE SACRED:
AMERICA'S QUEST FOR SPIRITUAL MEANING

Check out the barometers in the cultural marketplace. Bookstores are lined with spiritual missives. Music stores feature best-selling Gregorian chants. Hollywood salts its scripts with divine references and afterlife experiences. Want to give that special seeker on your winter-solstice list a crystal? ... For entrepreneurs with a keen sense of the Zeitgeist, this is an obvious opportunity. Déjà Vu tours, based in Berkeley, California, specializes in "spiritual adventure" travel. It boasts that its clients have "seen the sun rise at Stonehenge, visited the 'Room of the Spirits' at the Dalai Lama's monastery, participated in rituals led by a shaman at Machu Picchu, sung a greeting to the Kumari, the Living Goddess of Nepal, and received baptisms in the Jordan." Inevitably there's a high-tech component to this phenomenon, too. On the internet, devotees can find Bible study groups, meditation instruction, and screens of New Age Philosophy ... A lot has changed in the last century, says Nuckolls, an anthropologist at Emory University who studies religion and healing: "We've stripped away what our ancestors saw essential – the importance of religion and the family ... people feel they want something they've lost, and they don't remember what they've lost."

SOURCE: *Newsweek*, November 28, 1994, p. 53-55.

BOX 13.4

---

in its source of knowledge, combining human potential psychology, holistic medicine, and a process philosophy. It is an attempt to combine diverse orientations into a single whole. In addition, the proponents of the movement argue for a global theology that would unite all people. They present an agenda that is democratic, where all people are members of a single, egalitarian, global network.

Meredith McGuire (1992) has researched religious groups in suburban America and presents data that would include these kinds of groups in New Age spirituality. One such group, called the Meditation Circle, is highly eclectic in beliefs and practices. The group selected beliefs and rituals such as yoga and meditation, Arica,[18] Tibetan Buddhism, and Reiki. In this group, members had tried a wide variety of New Age elements such as rebirthing, crystal healing, and transcendental meditation.

---

18 A New Religious movement that has borrowed from the human potential movement.

No single path was considered to be the right way, since there are as many paths as there are members. Interestingly, McGuire notes, there is little or no focus on fixed moral norms, guilt or sin. The goal of life, the journey, is continual growth of the self that is informed by having a greater knowledge of one's self, of others, and of one's body, as well as a greater balance between the inner self and others, and with the whole cosmos. Although the sacred was considered greater than oneself, it was met by going within oneself. The sacred, then, is defined as relatively imminent, subjective, not anchored to one place, a system of belief, or external religious object. Religious rituals were present, but they were intended to free the self from any external restraints and negative results of guilt. A focus was on energizing religious experiences without a commitment.

Further insights into the belief system of the New Age is presented by another sociologist of religion, Thomas Luckmann (1995). He argues that the movement stresses the development of the individual and is syncretistic in nature. It sometimes revives elements of an older tradition (Hinduism, Christianity or Buddhism, for example) and frequently interprets them in unorthodox ways. From a wide variety of sources, members of the movement collect psychological, therapeutic, magic, marginally scientific, and older esoteric traditions. Then they repackage them and offer them for use and added private syncretism. A further goal is to offer integration and a holistic approach to life.

Chalfant *et al.* (1992) summarize several authors in painting a picture of New Age. O'Hara (1989) argues that scientific materialism has eroded mainstream religion's ability to meet the needs of people. New Agers embark into a world of ancient religious myths, pseudopriests, and pseudoscientists. A special feature of the movement that gives it a unique belief and ritual is *channelling*. Alcock describes it as "what supposedly occurs when an individual serves as a conduit for some other-worldly entity to communicate with people of this world. It can take many forms: the channeler might be wide awake, in a trance, or even asleep" (1989:380 and cited in Chalfant *et al.*, 1992:277). Reed (1989:387 and cited in Chalfant *et al.*, 1992) finds that people channel because it is functional and serves the needs of these individuals. Among these needs are:

· EGO-ENHANCEMENTS: these produce attention, respect, gratitude, and affection.

· COMPENSATION: this affects excitement in a routine life. The channeller is given a higher status as seer, oracle, and spiritual advisor.

· MATERIAL REWARDS: the one who channels can receive money for relatively simple training and capital investment.

From these sources, one may now be in a position to outline the central elements of the mythology of the New Age Movement:

- there is an emphasis on human potential, personal spirituality, movement towards a higher spiritual self; growth is a personal thing and individualistic. This captures the meaning of transformation, which includes changes in one's environment, one's society, the globe, and the whole cosmos.

- personal transformation takes a long time and cannot happen in one lifetime. There is a need to include the Hindu and Buddhist belief in reincarnation and karma.

- although the sacred may exist beyond the person, to be in touch with the sacred is to search within the individual person. Some would claim that each person is God or divine. In addition, adherents are more likely to be monists rather than theists.

- elements come from a long history of spiritualism present in the United States for many years. Recent influences emerge from the psychological human potential movement and the counter culture of the 1960s.

- many New Agers become channellers who achieve a status similar to religious leaders in more mainstream religions.

- there is a global and future perspective that hopes that through communication and using the positive forces within people, a world harmony will be possible.

- the concrete beliefs tend to be eclectic and syncretic, allowing for many paths to be followed to truth.

- in relationship to the body, there is hope to be in touch with one's body and, sometimes, to seek out-of-body experiences.

- the theory of correspondence: all that is visible and material corresponds to something that is spiritual and transcendent.

- lastly, there is a strong emphasis on mysticism and intuition, in contrast to science and reason.

A final word on the social and individual experience of the sacred, mythologies, and ritual of the New Age: as Westley (1983) observed that New Religious Movements are illustrations of Durkheim's *cult of man*, the New Age Movement stresses the validity of his claim even more. The sacred within the person (or the *sacred within*) is at the core of the mythology of the movement.

Organization

Unlike most religions, which have become institutionalized into religious collectives or organizations, the New Age Movement is what is called a "decentralized mega-network" (Christensen 1993 and cited in Bibby 1993) or networks (Newport 1998). There is no equivalent to Christian churches, Islamic mosques, or Sikh temples.[19] However, this does not mean it is without institutional substance. It is expressed in a wide variety of seminars, books, training centres (for example, Vision Mountain Leadership Training Centre in Nelson, BC) and a multitude of New Age related businesses. Newport says it well:

> churches are developing less frequently now than are groups of people who gather around institutes, study centers, seminars, trance channellers, psychics, teachers, healers, and expositions. All of these interrelate, or "network," with one another. (1998:15)

Its greatest impact seems to be with those who have another religious affiliation. Bibby, using 1990 and 1995 Canadian national survey data, notes the following (1993:51 and 1995:130):

· about 30 per cent of Canadians say they are familiar with New Age ideas (1990 data)

· 11 per cent indicate they are either "somewhat interested" (8 per cent, in 1990) or "highly interested" (3 per cent, both in 1990 and 1995)

· 3 per cent say they are involved in New Age activities, 2 per cent have joined groups, and 2 per cent are in networks (1990)

· in 1995, 3 per cent were involved in activities, 2 per cent part of groups, and less than 1 per cent in networks (note an actual decline over the five-year period).

· those most interested in New Age thought in Canada are Christians (81 per cent) — 53 per cent Roman Catholic and 28 per cent Protestant (1990 data).

---

19 It should be recognized that there are some churches. Newport (1998:15) writes that they have names such as Church of Spiritual Healing, the Church of Ageless Wisdom, Radiant Light Interfaith Church, the Church of the Earth Nation, and the Church of Truth.

- · 5 per cent actually identify with some other kind of religion (unspecified) which could be New Age (1990 data)

- · finally, 75 per cent of this core of adherents indicate that they have no intention of abandoning their traditional affiliations (1990 data).

Internationally, the numbers may be quite significant. Robertson (1995:408) estimates (from a World Almanac and Book of Facts) that their numbers would be included in the larger category, New Religious Movements, which constitute about 2.6 per cent of the world's population.

McGuire (1992), in her research on a suburban meditation group, saw that the group members were very loosely committed. The practices (rituals, belief and normative systems), changed continuously, and this resulted in little long-term commitment. Individuals did care for individuals as individuals but there was no focus on the solidarity and cohesiveness of the group. For many, this was only one commitment out of a host of others, and some belonged to traditional mainline Christian churches while being members of the group. Luckmann (1995) agrees with the lack of official organization of the movement, which seems to prefer social networks rather than social groups or institutions. He writes,

> It has no stable organization, canonized dogmas, recruitment system, or disciplining apparatus. This may be a structural precondition for the successful maintenance of its vague holistic approach, which meets — among other things — the rising demand for an overall hierarchy of meaning that overcomes the specialization of those cultural domains, such as science, religion, art and the like that had found reasonably firm institutional bases. (1995:243)

In summary, the New Age Movement is a religious response to the kind of world we live in today. It challenges modernity on two fronts: a reaction against rationalization with a focus on religious experience and bureaucratization, resulting in a concerted effort to be organizationally fluid. It should be seen not so much as a cult or a sect (it lacks the organizational dimension to be considered so) but more of an amorphous movement of relatively disconnected adherents with a syncretic mythology that approximates what Durkheim has called the "Cult of Man." It has much more in common with oriental mythology than with occidental (see Chapter Two). Finally, the focus is much less on mythology, ethos, and collectivity, and more on religious experience (being in touch with the sacred both within and without) and ritual (particularly channelling).

An established thesis of sociology is that there is a reciprocal relationship between social structure and culture. In this section, I have outlined the social structural basis of the postmodern world. To that, postmodernism was shown to be a culture consistent with the kind of social structure that is common in the Western world toward the end of the twentieth century. Finally, there were considered two sacred responses to the postmodern world with its culture of postmodernism that tend to "fit" with this kind of world: conservatism and New Age spirituality.

| SUMMARY

I have reviewed a range of literature in this chapter to assist us in understanding religion in Canada and the United States from the point of view of social change. Two questions frequently asked by many sociologists and lay people are: Is religion dead or dying? As the modern world moves from a traditional period through to a postmodern one, is the destiny of the sacred to disappear? To these questions, the central response of these authors has been twofold. Those who represent the cultural analytic position argue that both secularization and sacralization continue through to the present. For those authors who represent the rational choice or market model, evidence continues to mount that it is not the sacred world that is in demise but, rather, the secular. A sacred response to postmodernism is illustrated in that it is religion that offers meaning to a central tenet of postmodernism: meaninglessness.

CHAPTER FOURTEEN

Synthesis and Conclusions

This final chapter will be less of a summation and more of a synthesis of the text. A feature of this project has been to provide the reader with an approach to the social scientific study of religion that is sociologically multidimensional, focussing upon social action, social structure, and culture.

A central thesis has been to consider religion in the following way. Religion's genesis is with the personal and social experience of the sacred. The sacred is at the very heart of religion and gives it its most essential feature. The sacred is seen to be a binary phenomenon that inspires awe and fear as well as desire and attraction. The personal experience of the sacred, in Weber's sociology of religion, was seen to be the genesis of religions that began with a founder, such as in Buddhism, Judaism, Christianity, and Islam. Weber's insights assist us in understanding that, after the charismatic dimension of the personal experience of the sacred wanes, there frequently emerges various routinization processes. This dynamic and dilemma enable us to cover a wide range of religious expressions in these particular traditions.

It was further argued that the "charisma and routinization of charisma" dilemma was at the core of both the dynamism and the ossification of religion. Through the eyes of O'Dea, this was further specified through five dilemmas: mixed motivation, symbol, administrative order, delimitation, and power.

All of these dilemmas fare well in synthesizing religious phenomena. Religion (that which emerges from a founder, reformer, renewer, and revolutionary prophet) begins with the personal experience of the sacred that becomes manifested in myth, ritual, ethos, and institutions. The dilemmas of mixed motivation and administrative order have structured organizational features of religion that include leadership and institutional dimensions. The symbolic dilemma structures ritual, and the dilemma of delimitation, ethos. The dilemma of power became the framework for researching linkages between religion and politics.

FACTORS AND EFFECTS OF THE NUMEN

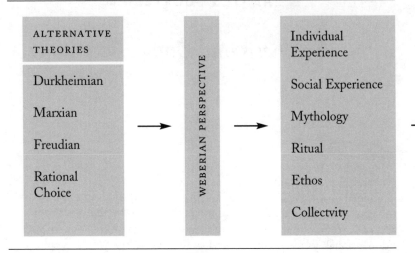

FIGURE 14.1

The personal experience of the sacred as the genesis of religion is useful in understanding the religious traditions mentioned above. However, it is not useful in interpreting Hinduism, the religions of the ancient world (such as the Egyptian, Babylonian, and Greco-Roman), and the many religions of aboriginal peoples. This is where Durkheim's sociology of religion becomes very useful, focusing as it does on the social experience of the sacred. The evidence stems from the anthropological literature of aboriginal peoples' religion wherein ritual is the beginning point. It is through ritual that the social experience of the sacred emerges and from which come myth, ethos, and institutions.

The social science which has expanded our understanding of the personal experience of the sacred in the arms of believers is psychology. This discipline has developed a wide range of research literature that was reviewed in this text and that enables us to interpret religious experience, spirituality, types of spirituality, mysticism, psychic experiences, and conversion. It was noted that a specific model of spirituality, attribution theory, fits well with the Weberian perspective that is another feature that synthesizes the text.

A central aspect of the Weberian perspective is interpretive sociology. This kind of sociology assists us in outlining the importance of world views in general, and myth in particular. Myths are central features of religion that assist religious people in interpreting their worlds. A whole chapter was devoted to this phenomenon to illustrate how focal it is in understanding religion.

FACTORS AND EFFECTS OF THE NUMEN (CONT'D)

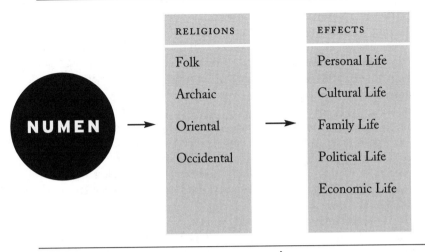

	RELIGIONS	EFFECTS
	Folk	Personal Life
	Archaic	Cultural Life
NUMEN →	Oriental →	Family Life
	Occidental	Political Life
		Economic Life

387

FIGURE 14.1 CONT'D

A further feature of this project expanded on what has come to be known as substantive and functional definitions of religion. Comparative religious studies and the social science of religion revealed that there was also a distinction between substantive and functional dimensions of myth, ritual, ethos, and organizations. A review of relevant literature illustrated these two dimensions.

Another feature of the text was the discovery of binary structures in religious phenomena. Various authors revealed this structure present in the sacred (Otto and Durkheim), mythology (Lévi-Strauss), and two types of spirituality (Allport and Spilka and his colleagues). This binary nature was expanded to include all the dilemmas of religion which are accretions of the central dilemma, "charisma and the routinization of charisma."

The text was also structured around three different aspects of the sacred: the *sacred within, between, and among*. The sacred *within* pertains to the study of the experience of the sacred (spirituality) that has been the speciality of psychology; the sacred *between* focusses on numinous manifestations in ritual; and the sacred *among* lies in mythology, ethos, and organizations.

The links between religion and the family, the economy, social stratification, the secular, and postmodernism are also framed within these various foci. The link between the sacred and the family illustrates the dilemmas inherent in various kinds of mythologies, and how families experience tensions in sacred versus secular options. The most critical question in the relationship between the sacred and the economy is this: how does the sacred influence the economy from the heritage of Weber? In contrast, how does the economy have an impact upon the sacred from Marx's legacy? A further ramification of this relationship is: how much of the charismatic dimension of the sacred is lost or retained?

The question of secularization also reveals dilemmas. Although some of the authorities reviewed here argue for the gradual continuation of secularization, there is evidence that as soon as this position is set in place, counter-evidence emerges for processes of sacralization. Evidence reveals that these processes vary throughout modern and postmodern history. Under what social conditions is one in ascendency? The postmodern society and postmodernism represent new problems and issues in the negotiation of believers through their maze. Binary expressions were also revealed as responses to this interface: conservative religion as tending toward an exclusive commitment to the sacred and the New Age Movement representing an inclusive alternative.

Figure 14.1 is an attempt to visually represent the structure of the text. As can be seen from this figure, the core of religion is the *numen* or the sacred. The model shows that various theories have been used to interpret the multidimensional phenomenon. It is the Weberian perspective, however, which is here the central theoretical framework. The third column is intended to show the multidimensionality of religion and its link to the *numen*. The individual and social experience of the sacred that is manifested in mythology, ritual, ethos, and collectivities is expressed in four kinds of religions in the human experience: folk, archaic, oriental, and occidental. Finally, the social scientific study of religion is especially useful in classifying and interpreting the effects this phenomenon has on the personal, cultural, family, political, and economic life of people.

A final point should be made about the Weberian perspective of this project. This is a perspective that includes most of the major dimensions and various phenomena of religion. In being bonded to the cultural analytic framework and Durkheim's sociology of religion, it has structured my review of the literature. This perspective provides a framework for studying the personal and social experience of the sacred, the emergence of myths, the expression of the sacred through ritual, the living out of myths through ethos, and the social structuring of the sacred in organizations. Indeed, this text has outlined what is defined as religion:

> the individual and social experience of the sacred that is manifested in mythologies, rituals, and ethos, and integrated into a collective such as a community or an organization.

Glossary

AFFECTIVE SOCIAL ACTION · an action is affective if it satisfies a need for revenge, sensual gratification, devotion, contemplative bliss, or for working off emotional tensions.

ALCHEMY · elementary science with spiritual overtones; the practitioners tried to discover a way to change material objects into gold and to discover the divine spark identified as the Self.

APOTROPAIC BUDDHISM · from the Greek, a ritual designed to avert evil; is concerned with what happens in this world, in the everyday, the mundane; both morality and ritual are designed to ward off evil and to protect the faithful against calamity and illness.

ASCETICISM · the practice of self-denial and self-mortification for religious reasons.

BIOENERGETICS · the study of energy transformation in living systems.

BORN AGAIN · a term that has emerged from evangelical Christianity which means an experience of God's salvation through Jesus.

BOUNDARY · defines the system (understood as an institution) and represents the interface or point of contact between the system and other systems, between the system and its subsystems and supra systems or the environment.

CÆSAROPAPISM · the monarchial control over ecclesiastical affairs; particularly, it connotes the intrusion of a civil officer into the sanctuary, the crossing of the line from the imperial to the priestly.

CELTIC RELIGION · pre-Christian religion of the Irish and English Celts.

CHURCH · leaders are priests or ministers who are professionally trained and hold not a personal charisma but a charisma of office. Authority is "top-down" in a series of hierarchical rankings. There tends to be a liaison between the religious and the secular leaders. The religious leaders seem to be concerned about the welfare of the larger society. These leaders tend to be conservative in doctrine, especially in traditional societies, but move toward liberalism in the modern world.

Members are mostly members from birth and have an ascriptive status. The people appear to be socially controlled by the leaders, large in numbers, and there is a relatively high level of organizational stability. Ritual is more important than spontaneity and the fellowships lean toward impersonality and a kind of collectivity. Church members tend to be ascetic in religious practices in traditional societies but are much more relativistic in the modern setting.

The church accommodates itself to the external environment and thus may become overly secularized. It has a level of low tension with this environment and because of its bureaucratic "weight" tends to break down.

CIVIL RELIGION · a religion that includes the doctrines of belief in God (albeit, unitarian) and religious liberty; biblical archetypes such as Exodus (movement from Europe), Chosen People (Americans are called to spread the message of democracy throughout the world), Promised Land and New Jerusalem (America the free and the beautiful), Sacrificial Death (the death of Lincoln) and Rebirth (emancipation of the nineteenth century and the civil rights of the twentieth); and rituals such as the celebration of Memorial Day and feast days, Thanksgiving Day on November 26, the Fourth of July, and presidential inaugural days.

COLLECTIVE CONSCIENCE · a set of beliefs and sentiments common to average citizens of the same society and which forms a determinate system with its own life.

COMMITTED SPIRITUALITY · described as the kind of faith that is open, candid, personally relevant, abstract, relational, discerning, and differentiated.

COMPENSATOR · the belief that a reward will be obtained in the distant future or in some other context which cannot be immediately verified.

CONSENSUAL SPIRITUALITY · tends to lack a knowledge base, is restrictive, detached, irrelevant to everyday life, concrete, vague, and simplistic.

CONVERSION · a change from one aim in life to another; a journey from a divided self to a united self; a new perception of life; an emotional transformation; the experience of someone whose religious ideas, peripheral in his consciousness, now take a central place, and that religious aims form the habitual centre of his energy; an organized set of beliefs that provide a superordinate framework for the individual's life; changes involving cognitive, emotional, and belief dimensions.

CUIUS REGIO, EIUS RELIGIO · whatever is the religion of the monarch or prince, all members under his rule are to have the same religion.

CULT · a belief system which is deviant from the traditional religious doctrines of the host society. Members tend to blend non-traditional with traditional tenets that make it syncretic. There is a special focus on the individual who becomes almost sacred. This emphasis on the individual leaves the association thus formed in a loose, informal, organizational structure. Finally, the cult stands in a high-tension relationship with the external environment.

CULT OF MAN OR THE INDIVIDUAL · a mixture of the late stages of the human potential movement, the positive-thought movement, and the occult traditions. The point of agreement of all these is that it is the human individual who is seen as sacred, as all powerful. This sacred power is seen as located deep within the individual personality. Actions in the outer world become significant, not in themselves, but only in terms of their impact on this inner self.

CULTURAL BOUNDARIES · see symbolic boundaries.

CULTURAL EARTHQUAKE · changes in the family due to increased individualism.

DEMYTHOLOGIZATION · the attempt by Christian theologians to adapt the sacred world view to the secular world view in the hope of salvaging the necessary and important parts of the sacred world view (the mythology) and eliminating that which is offensive to the modern mind; miracles are one such offence.

DENOMINATION · a religious organization common in pluralist societies which generally supports the social order and is tolerant of other similar types; its attitude to organization and to liturgy tends to be pragmatic and instrumental, while its sacramental conceptions are subjective and individualistic; it is traditional in eschatology; and in moral theory, its conception of the relation of faith and works is dynamic but balanced.

DEVOTIONALISM · as measured by personal communication to God through prayer and meditation.

DIGGERS · a group of agrarian communalists who, after the English Civil War, began to live on and cultivate common land. They were harassed by legal actions and by 1650, were dispersed. Their ideas, however, were supported by others in Kent, Buckinghamshire, and Essex.

ELEMENTARY SOCIAL ACTION · social behaviour is elementary in the sense that the two social actors are in face-to-face contact, and each is rewarding the other directly and immediately; each is able to do his/her work better here and now.

EMPIRICAL SELF · the observable self.

ENLIGHTENMENT · the dominant philosophy during the seventeenth and eighteenth centuries that focused on science, rationalism, secularism, and an optimism of progress; another term used in the history of philosophy is the age of rationalism.

ESCHATOLOGY · teachings in any religion that outline the end of the world.

ESOTERIC BUDDHISM · a cult in Buddhism that it is a syncretism of traditional beliefs, local animistic practices, and quasi-secretive sects; also called chiliastic.

ETHOS · a cluster of behavioural codes including values, norms, morals, and laws.

391

EXTRAORDINARY RELIGION · encourages a special language that also distinguishes it from the rest of culture, and its sense of going beyond the boundaries often finds expression in universal statements, intended to apply to all peoples; its special language maps a landscape that people have not clearly seen; it gives people names for the unknown and then provides access to a world beyond; it assures people that the "other" world does touch this one but is never merely the same as it; its counterpart is "ordinary religion."

EXTRINSIC SPIRITUALITY · is utilitarian and is sought after for external reasons such as social status and safety from a hostile world.

FOUNDING PROPHET · a person who begins a new religion.

FREEMASONRY · an alternative gnostic spirituality adapted to the modern world.

FUNCTIONAL DEFINITION OF ETHOS · what religious ethos does or what its social effects are.

FUNCTIONAL DEFINITION OF RITUAL · the effects and consequences of ritual to people and to societies.

FUNCTIONAL DEFINITION OF MYTH · what myth does in people's lives and how it affects institutions and whole societies.

FUNCTIONAL DEFINITION OF RELIGION · what the effects of religion are.

FUNCTIONAL DEFINITION OF A RELIGIOUS ORGANIZATION · embodies a religious organization that serves to provide social solidarity, integration, global well-being, and meaning.

GEMEINSCHAFT · in the tradition of sociologists like Comte, Tonnies, Durkheim, Spencer, and Parsons, the term refers to the kind of society that is based on personal relationships, the importance of ascribed social status, the vitality of kin, a link to nature, the centrality of religion, and traditional social action; it is the ideal type opposite to Gesellschaft.

GESELLSCHAFT · in the same tradition of sociologists like Comte, Tonnies, Durkheim, Spencer, and Parsons, the term refers to the kind of society that is based on impersonal relationships, the importance of achieved social status, the marginalization of the centrality of kin, a break with nature, the pivotal importance of the secular, and rational instrumental social action; it is the ideal type opposite to Gemeinschaft.

GNOSTICISM · from the Greek gnosis, a word that simply means "knowledge," knowledge that leads to salvation. The mythology that extends the meaning of the term is Gnosticism. Its origins go back to Egyptian religion which had a central tenet, "He who knows himself, knows the All." Other important features include the teaching of the Divine Man (a man who was both human and divine); Sophia or the feminine manifestation of the divine essence, similar to the Divine Mother; having special knowledge available only to a few; a strong distinction between the spiritual and the material; and a symbolic reading of canonical texts from Judaism, Christianity, and Islam.

HERMETICISM · this religious philosophy synthesized Gnosticism, neoplatonism, astrology, and various other spiritual leaders from Greece.

HIEROCRATIC · the term refers to the rule or government by priests or religious leaders.

HINAYANA BUDDHISM · the earlier of the two major schools of Buddhism, still prevalent in Sri Lanka, Burma, Thailand, and Cambodia, emphasizing personal salvation through one's own efforts; also called Theravada; compare with Mahayana Buddhism.

HOMOOUSIOS · of one essence; the Christian doctrine that Jesus is one person but he has two natures, human and divine.

IDEAL TYPE · an analytical construct that serves as a measuring rod to determine similarities, and differences in concrete cases; it does not exist in its pure form, but it is of heuristic value for discussing the real world.

INSTITUTION · specific areas of human social life that have become broadly organized into discernible patterns. Institution refers to the organized means whereby the essential tasks of a society are organized, directed, and carried out. In short, it denotes the system or norms that organize human behaviour into stable patterns of activity.

INTRINSIC SPIRITUALITY · refers to viewing faith as supreme, orientated toward a unification of existence, honouring universal brotherhood (and, by implication, sisterhood), and striving to overcome self-centredness.

KAMMATIC BUDDHISM · a type of Buddhism in Burma wherein believers follow the customs and norms of the religion in order to achieve a better karma; this means that in the next reincarnation, if they follow the rules diligently, they will be reincarnated into a better life.

LEVANTINE · refers to the cultures bordering the eastern Mediterranean that gave rise to Judaism, Islam, and Christianity.

LEVELLERS · members of a radical group organized during the English Civil War of 1642-1649, advocating political equality and religious tolerance.

393

MAHAYANA BUDDHISM · one of the two major schools of Buddhism, characterized by a belief in a common search for salvation; compare with Theravada or Hinayana.

MAINLINE CHRISTIANITY · in general, it refers to the large and established denominations that constitute the majority of organized American and Canadian Christianity; in Canada, the term refers to the Anglican, Roman Catholic, and United Church churches; in the United States, it covers the Episcopalians, Congregationalists, Presbyterians, Roman Catholics, Methodists, and Lutherans.

MANICHÆISM · the term refers to a religious world view common in the first centuries of Christianity; the religion comes from Persia and posits a belief that creation is a dual product of an all powerful "Good Being" and an equally all powerful "Evil Being"; anything that is spiritual or of the soul is good but anything of a material nature is evil; this is a classic case of extreme dualism.

MANYNESS OF RELIGIONS · religious pluralism.

MECHANICAL SOCIAL SOLIDARITY · the kind of society wherein persons act like parts of a machine, indicating little individuality; persons are bonded to each other because they resemble one another and share what Durkheim termed a "collective conscience."

MESMERISM · from a Viennese physician, Mesmer (1733-1815), who taught that everything was connected to everything else, and the source of this nexus is the universal magnetic fluid.

MILLENNIALISM · literally, of or pertaining to 1000 years; in religious terminology it refers to the future, the coming age; see eschatology.

MONISM · a myth based on the assumption of a single underlying principle; a belief that all is one and one is all, or the cosmos equals the self which in turn equals the divine.

MORAL CASUISTRY · refers to a minute analysis of human acts to see if they accord to a rigid rule of behaviour.

MOVEMENT OF RENEWAL · stays within the original church organization; the leaders (and members) endeavour to renew the collectivity by invoking something of the tradition as a source of this renewal.

MYSTAGOGY · the art of explaining or interpreting mysteries of religion.

MYSTERIUM TREMENDUM · from the work of the philosopher of religion, Otto, who uses it to describe that part of the sacred which reflects awe and distance of the believer to the holy.

MYSTICISM · an oceanic experience; cosmic emotion; union with the divine; sudden raptures of the divine presence; doctrine that special mental states or events allow an understanding of ultimate truths; noetic (a valid source of knowledge); ineffable, holy, having a positive affect, and paradoxical in that it defies logic.

MYTHOLOGY · a system of beliefs; a system of myths that describe breakthroughs of the sacred or the holy into the world; it is this sudden breakthrough of the sacred that really establishes the world and makes it what it is today; it is a result of the intervention of the holy that humans make themselves what they are.

NEOPLATONISM · a philosophical-religious movement during the early centuries of the Christian era marked by the fact that the ultimate idea is the One who is superior to the Nous or the Mind. The World Soul is co-extensive with the material world.

NEW THOUGHT · a nineteenth-century movement whose founder, P. Quimby (1802-1866), defined God as the divine mind.

NIBBANIC BUDDHISM · from nibbana, or nirvana; this kind of Buddhism is the closest version approximating the path of the Gautama; it is the Buddhism of the monks who obey the five or eight precepts as a means to achieve nirvana; this kind of Buddhism has a morality that is primarily a form of spiritual discipline; it is a means to the attainment of a certain psychological state which is the first condition for the achievement of nirvana.

NONES · those who do not have any religious affiliation.

ONENESS OF RELIGION · the religious unity among societies; it refers to the dominant public cluster of organizations, ideas, and moral values that have characterized a society.

ORDINARY RELIGION · the religion that is more or less synonymous with culture; it shows people how to live well within boundaries; it is a taken-for-granted world view; its counterpart is "extraordinary religion."

OTHER-WORLDLY · Weber's term for the kind of religion that focuses upon the other world or heaven; its counterpart is "this-worldly."

PLAUSIBILITY STRUCTURES · social interactions within a group which serve to sacralize the shared meanings of the group; they make the religious world view "plausible" or believable.

PNEUMATOLOGY · the doctrine or study of spiritual beings.

POST-STRUCTURALISM · the theory that there is no structure in language, myths, and communication.

PRIEST · a leader of a religion who is the most routinized and has the most mixed motivation; its counterpart is the prophet.

PROPHET · a leader of a religion who is the least routinized and is the most single-minded; its counterpart is the priest.

PSYCHOLOGICAL GENTRIFICATION · refers to a shift in family life from a positional family to a person-centred family.

PSYCHOSYNTHESIS · a theoretical effort to reconcile components of the unconscious with the rest of the personality.

RATIONAL SOCIAL ACTION · legal or instrumental rational action is determined by the expected responses of others as "conditions" or "means" for the actor's own rationally pursued and calculated ends.

REAFFILIATES · those who switch from one church or denomination which is very similar to the original affiliation.

REFORM PROPHET · a prophet who accepts the main tenets of a religious tradition but tries to reform it because so much of the tradition has become routinized.

RELIGION · the individual and social experience of the sacred that is manifested in mythologies, rituals, and ethos, and integrated into a collective such as a community or organization.

RELIGIOUS HUMAN CAPITAL · the skills, talents, and training necessary to produce religious products that include familiarity with religious doctrine, rituals, traditions, and members.

RELIGIOUS ORGANIZATION · a cluster or a complex of ranked roles that are, in turn, a cluster or a complex of norms that are routinized elements of charismatic or affective social action focused on creating relationships of an individual to the sacred, the cosmos, nature, others, and oneself.

RELIGIOUS PRODUCTION · the production of such products as Sunday clothes, sacrificial offerings, time, and labour.

RESTRUCTURING OF AMERICAN RELIGION · a restructuring that crosses denominational lines and is marked by a new alignment of liberalism and conservatism.

REVOLUTIONARY PROPHET · a prophet who begins with an established religious tradition and changes it radically according to a new revelation that he or she claims to have received.

REWARD · religious activity that results in tangible rewards such as social status, earning a living, leisure, and human companionship.

SACRED · also called the holy; the term from Durkheim and Otto that specifies the religious object as separate from and removed from the profane; see mysterium tremendum.

SECT · a religious organization that includes members who are considered to be converted, who follow stringent rules of behaviour, who form a small, primary and intimate group, who opt for spontaneity rather than for formalized ritual, and form an egalitarian moral community. The leaders of the organization protest against the "over-accommodative" nature of the church type and tend to be lay, charismatic, non-professional, and adhere to clear doctrinal statements. As a whole, the organization stands in a high-tension relationship to the environment and is organizationally precarious in that it endeavours to maintain the pristine message while providing a sense of social order. As an organization, it tends not to accommodate to the external environment and may take a stance of indifference, intolerance or hostility towards that environment.

SECULARIZATION · the process by which sectors of society and culture are removed from the domination of religious institutions and symbols.

SEISMIC SHIFT · changes in North American religion due to individualism.

SHEILAISM · the term was coined by Bellah and his colleagues (1985) to describe a religious commitment that did not extend beyond the person—a completely individualist interpretation. Here, "Sheila's" religion is unique to her alone.

SHI'ITE ISLAM · the faithful believe that proper interpretation lies in those who are in the lineage of Muhammad's son-in-law.

SOCIAL ACTION · human action that assumes that persons are free agents who, in their relationships with others, attach a subjective meaning to their behaviour and take into account the behaviour of others.

SOCIAL CONSCIENCE · Durkheim's counterpart to collective conscience; the term indicates a conscience of a group of people within a larger society like a religious group, a labour organization, or a voluntary organization.

SOCIAL ORGANIZATION OR SOCIAL INSTITUTION · a complex or cluster of ranked roles which in turn are a complex or a cluster of expectations of behaviours within a social interaction setting. In addition, it is focused by a common goal or a function to fulfil.

SOLA FIDE · faith alone for salvation (from Luther).

SOLA GRATIA · only by grace is salvation given and not by good works (from Luther).

SOLA SCRIPTURA · only the Bible is to be the rule of the Christian life and not tradition (Luther).

SPIRITUALISM · movement during the eighteenth and nineteenth centuries in the United States that sought truth by hearing the spirits of the dead.

SPIRITUALITY · a quality of a person whose internal life is orientated toward God, the supernatural or the sacred; those aspects of religion and religiosity or religiousness that have an internal presence to the individual that includes such elements as feelings, moods, attitudes, beliefs, attributions, and the like.

SUNNI ISLAM · mainstream Islam that believes the proper interpretation of the Koran is a careful, reasoned reading of the text and tradition by those who are the most learned, the "ulama."

STRUCTURALISM · the term tries to capture the "grammar of social life," the order present in what appears to be chaos, and the common features of social organization that are quite variant.

SUBSTANTIVE DEFINITION OF ETHOS · what ethos is; the living out in everyday life the experience of the holy or the sacred.

SUBSTANTIVE DEFINITION OF MYTH · what myth is; the stories of the sacred being manifested in human conditions and various situations.

SUBSTANTIVE DEFINITION OF RELIGION · what religion is in itself; the core of religion is the experience of the sacred, both personally and socially.

SUBSTANTIVE DEFINITION OF A RELIGIOUS ORGANIZATION · of a religious organization that facilitates both the individual and collective experience of the sacred.

SUBSTANTIVE DEFINITION OF RITUAL · what ritual is; the reliving of the experience of the holy or the sacred.

SUFI ISLAM · ascetic, mystical Islam.

SWEDENBORGIANISM · named after its founder, Emanuel Swedenborg (1688-1772) who argued that everything in the spiritual visible material world corresponds to something of the spiritual world (the theory of correspondence); the Divine and the natural exist in both God and Man.

SYMBOLIC BOUNDARIES · a boundary between two symbolic domains such as Hispanic and Asian cultures in the United States or between anglophone and francophone cultures in Canada; the term "cultural boundaries" is used in this text.

SYNCRETISM · refers to religious organizations' attempt to blend various beliefs and practices from a variety of religious sources.

SYNTHESIS · to synthesize one's religion is to bring together elements from one's own personal biography as they fit with religious beliefs and practices; similar to new voluntarism, selective Catholicism, and fragmented gods.

397

THEODICY · a religious legitimation of anomic phenomena such as suffering, death, or tragedy.

THEORY OF CORRESPONDENCE · refers to the belief that the external world is a reflection of internal consciousness.

THEOSOPHY · the first nineteenth-century movement which spoke of a new era and a new beginning, and combined this with Hindu mysticism.

THIS-WORLDLY · the kind of religion that focuses upon this world or the secular; its counterpart is "other-worldly."

TRADITIONAL SOCIAL ACTION · guided by set patterns that have developed over time together with a sense that things must "always be that way."

TRANSCENDENTALISM · in nineteenth-century America, the sacred books of Hinduism were introduced, leading to the development of this movement; it combined nature religion with Hindu nuances; it was unique to America in that it united cultural themes such as individualism, success, and self-actualization to Hindu monism.

TRUE SELF · a responsible and harmonious self.

UNIT OF EXALTATION · in Mormonism it means that one not only needs to be a baptized Mormon but must continue to be a faithful follower in order to be exalted or raised up to eternal life.

References

Abbott, Walter, S.J. (1966). *The Documents of Vatican II.* New York: Guild Press.

Albanese, Catherine (1981). *American Religion and Religions.* Belmount, CA: Wadsworth.

Albanese, Catherine (1990). *Nature Religion in America: From the Algonkian Indians to the New Age.* Chicago: University of Chicago Press.

Albanese, Catherine (1992, second ed.). *American Religion and Religions.* Belmount, CA: Wadsworth.

Alexander, Jeffrey (1982). *Theoretical Logic in Sociology: Volume Two: The Antinomies of Classical Thought: Marx and Durkheim.* Berkeley: University of California Press.

Alexander, Jeffrey (1983). *Theoretical Logic in Sociology: Volume Three: The Classical Attempt at Theoretical Synthesis: Max Weber.* Berkeley: University of California Press.

Alexander, Jeffrey (1987). "The Centrality of the Classics." In Anthony Giddens and Jonathan Turner (eds.), *Social Theory Today.* Stanford, CA: Stanford University Press.

Allen, Richard (1973). *The Social Passion: Religion and Social Reform in Canada 1914-1928.* Toronto: University of Toronto Press.

Allen, R.O., and Bernard Spilka (1967). "Committed and Consensual Religion: A Specification of Religion-Prejudice Relationships." *Journal for the Scientific Study of Religion* 6:191-206.

Allport, Gordon (1960). *Personality and Social Encounter.* Boston: Beacon Press.

Allport, Gordon (1966). "The Religious Context of Prejudice." *Journal for the Scientific Study of Religion* 5:447-457.

Arjomand, Said Amir (1988). *The Turban for the Crown: The Islamic Revolution in Iran.* New York: Oxford University Press.

Armstrong, William (1971). "Demos Shakarian — A Man and his Message." *Logos* 39.4:14-15.

Aron, Raymond. (1970). *Main Currents in Sociological Thought II.* Garden City, NY: Anchor Books.

Arrington, Leonard. (1985). *Brigham Young: American Moses.* New York: Alfred A. Knopf.

Athanasius, St. (1976). In the Divine Office. *The Liturgy of the Hours. Volume II.* New York: Catholic Book Publishing Co.

Augustine, St. (1952). *The City of God.* Vol 18, *The Great Books of the Western World.* Chicago: Encyclopaedia Britannica, Inc.

399

Bach, Kurt W. (1973). *Beyond Words.* Baltimore: Penguin Books.

Baer, Hans A., and Merrill Singer (1992). *African-American Religion in the Twentieth Century.* Knoxville: University of Tennessee Press.

Bailey, Edward (1998). "Sacred." In William Swatos, Jr. (ed.). *Encyclopedia of Religion and Society* (pp. 443-444). Walnut Creek, CA: Altamira Press.

Bainbridge, William Sims, and Rodney Stark (1980). "Sectarian Tension." *Review of Religious Research* 22:105-124.

Bainton, Roland (1958). *The Travail of Religious Liberty.* New York: Harper and Brothers Publishers.

Batson, C. Daniel, and W. Larry Ventis (1982). *The Religious Experience.* New York: Oxford University Press.

Batson, C. Daniel, Patricia Schoenrade, and W. Larry Ventis (1993). *Religion and the Individual.* New York: Oxford University Press.

Bauman, Zygmunt (1997). *Postmodernity and Its Discontents.* Cambridge: Polity Press.

Becker, Howard (1932). *Systematic Sociology on the Basis of the Beziehungslehre and Gebildelehre of Leopold Van Wiese.* New York: Wiley.

Bell, Daniel (1976). *The Coming of Post-Industrial Society: A Venture in Social Forecasting.* New York: Basic Books.

Bell, Daniel (1980). *The Winding Passage: Essays and Sociological Journeys: 1960-1980.* Cambridge: ABT Books.

Bell, Edward (1993). *Social Class and Social Credit in Alberta.* Montreal: McGill-Queen's University Press.

Bellah, Robert (1970). *Beyond Belief: Essays on Religion in a Post-Traditional World.* New York: Harper and Row.

Bellah, Robert (1973). *Emile Durkheim. On Morality and Society.* Chicago: University of Chicago Press.

Bellah, Robert, and Phil Hammond (1980). *Varieties of Civil Religion.* San Francisco: Harper and Row.

Bellah, Robert, Richard Madsen, William M. Sullivan, Ann Swidler, and Steven M. Tipton. (1985). *Habits of the Heart.* New York: Harper and Row.

Bendix, Reinhard (1962). *Max Weber: An Intellectual Portrait.* Garden City, NY: Anchor Books.

Bennent, Dennis, and Rita Bennent (1971). *The Holy Spirit and You.* Plainfield, NJ: Logos International.

Bennent, John C. (1955). *The Christian as Citizen.* New York: Association Press.

Berger, Peter (1961). *The Noise of Solemn Assemblies: Christian Commitment and the Religious Establishment.* Garden City, NY: Doubleday.

Berger, Peter (1963). *Invitation to Sociology: A Humanistic Perspective.* Garden City, NY: Doubleday.

Berger, Peter (1967). "Religious Institutions." In Neil Smelser (ed.). *Sociology* (pp. 329-379). New York: Wiley.

Berger, Peter (1969). *The Sacred Canopy.* New York: Doubleday.

Berger, Peter (1979a). "Religion and the American Future." In Seymour Lipset (ed). *The Third Century* (pp. 65-78). Chicago: University of Chicago Press.

Berger, Peter (1979b). *The Heretical Imperative.* Garden City, NY: Anchor Press of Doubleday.

Berger, Peter (1992). *A Far Glory: The Quest for Faith in an Age of Credulity.* New York: Free Press.

Berger, Peter (1995) [1954]. "The Sociological Study of Sectarianism." In Steve Bruce (ed.). *The Sociology of Religion. Volume II* (pp. 3-21). Aldershot: Edward Elgar Publishing.

Berger, Peter, and Thomas Luckmann (1966). *The Social Construction of Reality.* Garden City, NY: Doubleday.

Bibby, Reginald (1987). *Fragmented Gods: The Poverty and Potential of Religion in Canada.* Toronto: Irwin.

Bibby, Reginald (1990). *Mosaic Madness.* Toronto: Stoddart.

Bibby, Reginald (1993a). "Secularization and Change." In W. E. Hewitt. (ed.). *The Sociology of Religion: A Canadian Focus* (pp. 65-81). Toronto: Butterworths.

Bibby Reginald (1993b). *Unknown Gods: The Ongoing Story of Religion in Canada.* Toronto: Stoddart.

Bibby, Reginald (1995). *The Bibby Report: Social Trends Canadian Style.* Toronto: Stoddart.

Bibby, Reginald, and Merlin B. Brinkerhoff (1973). "The Circulation of the Saints: A Study of People Who Join Conservative Churches." *Journal for the Scientific Study of Religion* 12:273-83.

Bibby, Reginald, and Merlin B. Brinkerhoff (1983). "Circulation of the Saints Revisited: A Longitudinal Look at the Conservative Church Growth." *Journal for the Scientific Study of Religion* 22:253-62.

Bibby, Reginald, and Merlin B. Brinkerhoff (1994). "Circulation of the Saints 1966-1990: New Data, New Reflections." *Journal for the Scientific Study of Religion* 33:273-280.

Birnbaum, Norman (1973). "Beyond Marx in the Sociology of Religion?" In Charles Glock and Phillip E. Hammond (eds.). *Beyond The Classics: Essays in the Scientific Study of Religion* (pp. 3-70). New York: Harper and Row.

Blasi, Anthony (1998). "Definition of Religion." In William Swatos, Jr. (ed.). *Encyclopedia of Religion and Society* (pp. 129-133). Walnut Creek, CA: Altamira Press.

Blau, Peter M. (1977). *Inequality and Heterogeneity. A Primitive Theory of Social Structure.* New York: The Free Press.

Blizzard, Samuel (1956). "The Minister's Dilemma." *Christian Century* 73:508-509.

Blizzard, Samuel (1958). "The Protestant Parish Minister's Integrating Roles." *Religious Education* 53:374-380.

Blumer, Herbert (1966) [1962]. "Society as Symbolic Interaction." In James Farganis (ed.) *Readings in Social Theory: The Classical Tradition to Post-Modernism* (pp. 350-366). New York: McGraw-Hill.

Blumstock, Robert (1993). "Canadian Civil Religion." In W. E. Hewitt (ed.) *The Sociology of Religion: A Canadian Focus* (pp. 173-194). Toronto: Butterworths.

Boas, Franz (1938) [1911]. *The Mind of Primitive Man.* New York: MacMillan.

Booth, Alan, David Johnson, Ann Branahan, and Alan Sica (1995). "Belief and Behavior: Does Religion Matter in Today's Marriage?" *Journal of Marriage and the Family* 57: 661-671.

Borgatta, Edgar, and Marie Borgatta (1992). *Encyclopedia of Sociology.* New York: MacMillan.

Bouma, Gary (1977). "Beyond Lenski: A Critical Review of Recent 'Protestant Ethic' Research." *Journal for the Scientific Study of Religion* 11:141-153.

Bringhurst, Newell (1986). *Brigham Young and the Expanding Frontier.* Boston: Little, Brain and Company.

Bruce, Steve (1992). "Pluralism and Religious Vitality." In Steve Bruce (ed.). *Religion and Modernization* (pp. 170-194). Oxford: Clarendon Press.

Bruce, Steve (1995a). "Religion and Rational Choice: A Critique of Economic Explanations of Religious Behaviour." In Steve Bruce (ed.). *The Sociology of Religion. Volume I* (pp. 342-354). Aldershot: Edward Elgar Publishing.

Bruce, Steve (ed.) (1995b). *The Sociology of Religion. Volumes I and II.* Aldershot, UK: Edward Elgar Publishing.

Brunner, F. D. (1970). *A Theology of the Holy Spirit.* Grand Rapids, MI: William Eerdmans Publishing.

Buckland, R. (1993). *Buckland's Complete Book of Witchcraft.* St. Paul, MN: Llewellyn Publications.

Byrne, James (1971) "Charismatic leadership." In Kevin Ranaghan and Dorothy Ranaghan (eds.). *As the Spirit Leads Us* (pp. 187-210). Paramus, NJ: Paulist Press.

Cable News Network (1995). "On the March." October 16, 1995.

Cahill, Thomas (1995). *How the Irish Saved Civilization.* New York: Doubleday.

Cahill, Thomas (1998). *The Gifts of the Jews.* New York: Doubleday.

Campbell, Bruce, and Eugene Campbell (1988). "The Mormon Family." in Charles Mindel, Robert Habenstein, and Roosevelt Wright, Jr. (eds.). *Ethnic Families in America* (pp. 456-494). New York: Elsevier.

Campbell, Colin (1998). "Cult." In William Swatos, Jr. (ed.). *Encyclopedia of Religion and Society* (pp. 122-123). Walnut Creek, CA: Altamira Press.

Campbell, Joseph (1962). *The Masks of God: Oriental Mythology.* New York: Viking Press.

Campbell, Joseph (1964). *The Masks of God: Occidental Mythology.* New York: Viking Press.

Campbell, Joseph (1968a). *The Masks of God: Creative Mythology.* New York: Viking Press.

Campbell, Joseph. (1968b). *The Hero With a Thousand Faces.* Princeton, NJ: Princeton University Press.

Campbell, Joseph (1987). *The Masks of God: Primitive Mythology.* New York: Penguin Books.

Capps, Walter (1990). *The New Religious Right: Piety, Patriotism, and Politics.* Columbia: University of South Carolina Press.

Carroll, Jackson (1992). "The 1991 H. Paul Douglas Lecture. Toward 2000: Some Futures for Religious Leadership." *Review of Religious Research* 33:289-304.

Chalfant, H. Paul, Robert E. Beckley, and C. Eddie Palmer (1984, second ed.). *Religion in Contemporary Society.* Palo Alto, CA: Mayfield.

Chalfant, H. Paul, Robert E. Beckley, and C. Eddie Palmer (1994, third ed.). *Religion in Contemporary Society.* Itasca, IL: F. E. Peacock.

Chan, Wing-tsit (1963). A Source Book in Chinese Philosophy. Princeton, NJ: Princeton University Press.

Chang, Patricia (1997a). "Introduction to Symposium: Female Clergy in the Contemporary Protestant Church: A Current Assessment." *Journal for the Scientific Study of Religion* 36:565-573.

Chang, Patricia (1997b). "In Search of Pulpit: Sex Differences in the Transition from Seminary Training to the First Parish Job." *Journal for the Scientific Study of Religion* 36:614-627.

Chang, Patricia (1998). "Introduction: The Crisis is About Control: Consequences of Priestly Decline in the US Catholic Church." *Sociology of Religion* 59:1-5.

Charlton, Joy. (1978). "Women entering the Ordained Ministry: Contradictions and Dilemmas of Status." Paper presented at the meeting of the Society for the Scientific Study of Religion. Hartford, CT, October 26-29.

Charlton, Joy. (1997). "Clergywomen of the Pioneer Generation: A Longitudinal Study." *Journal for the Scientific Study of Religion* 36:599-613.

Charon, Joel M. (1992). *Symbolic Interactionism: An Introduction, an Interpretation, an Integration.* Englewood Cliffs, NJ: Prentice Hall.

Chaves, Mark (1996). "Ordaining Women: The Diffusion of an Organizational Innovation." *American Journal of Sociology* 101:840-873.

Chaves, Mark, and James Cavendish (1997). "Recent Changes in Women's Ordination Conflicts: The Effect of a Social Movement on Intraorganizational Controversy." *Journal for the Scientific Study of Religion* 36:574-584.

Christensen, L. (1993). "Beyond Belief: Understanding the New Age Experience." Paper presented at the annual meeting of the Pacific Sociological Association, Portland, OR, April.

Christiano, Kevin (1988). "Religion and Radical Labor Unionism: American States in the 1920s."*Journal for the Scientific Study of Religion* 27:378-388.

Clark, Samuel Delbert (1948). *Church and Sect in Canada.* Toronto: University of Toronto Press.

Clark, Stephen (1971). "Charismatic Renewal in the Church." In Kevin Ranaghan and Dorothy Ranaghan (eds.). *As The Spirit Leads Us* (pp. 17-37). Paramus, NJ: Paulist Press.

Clark, Stephen (1976). *Unordained Elders and Renewal Communities.* New York: Paulist Press.

Clayton, Obie, Jr. (1995). "The Churches and Social Change: Accommodation, Moderation, or Protest." *Daedelaus* 124: 101-117.

Clouse, Robert (1979). "Flowering: The Western Church." In Tim Dowley (ed.). Eerdman's *Handbook to the History of Christianity* (pp. 252-299). Grand Rapids, MI: Wm. B. Eerdmans.

Coleman, John S.J. (1968). "Church-Sect Typology and Organizational Precariousness." *Sociological Analysis* 29:55-66.

Collins, Randall, and Scott Coltrane (1991, third ed.). *Sociology of Marriage and the Family.* Chicago: Nelson Hall.

Constitution of the United States of America (1952 [1787]). *American State Papers. The Great Books of the Western World.* Volume 43. Chicago: Encyclopaedia Brittanica.

Coot, Nancy (1977). *The Bonds of Womanhood: "Women's Sphere" in New England, 1780-1935.* New Haven, CT: Yale University Press.

Cory, Stephen (1989). *The 7 Habits of Highly Effective People.* New York: Simon & Schuster.

Coser, Lewis A. (1956). *The Functions of Social Conflict.* New York: Free Press.

Coser, Lewis A. (1967). *Continuities in the Study of Social Conflict.* New York: Free Press.

Coser, Lewis A. (1977, second ed.). *Masters of Sociological Thought.* New York: Harcourt Brace Jovanovich College.

Cross, Whitney R. (1950). *The Burned-over District: The Social and Intellectual History of Enthusiastic Religion in Western New York, 1800-1850.* Ithaca, NY: Cornell University Press.

D'Antonio, William, and Joan Aldous (eds.) (1983). *Families and Religion: Conflict and Change in Modern Society.* Beverly Hills: Sage.

Dahrendorf, Ralf (1959). *Class and Class Conflict in Industrial Society.* Stanford: Stanford University.

Davis, Kingsley (1948-49). *Human Society.* New York: MacMillan.

de Tocqueville, Alexis (1945) [1835]. *Democracy in America.* New York: Vantage Books.

De Vos, George (1984). "Religion and Family: Structural and Motivational Relationships." In George A. De Vos and Takao Sofue (eds.). *Religion and the Family in East Asia* (pp. 3-33). Berkeley: University of California.

Demerath, Nicholas Jay III (1965). *Social Class in American Protestantism.* Chicago: Rand McNally.

403

Demerath, Nicholas Jay III, and Rhys Williams (1992). "Secularization in a Community Context: Tensions of Religion and Politics in a New England City." *Journal for the Scientific Study of Religion* 31:189-206.

Derrida, Jacques (1993). "The Decentering Event in Social Thought." In Charles Lemert (ed.). *Social Theory: The Multicultural and Classical Readings* (pp. 447-451). Boulder: Westview Press.

Dittes, James (1969, second ed.). "Psychology of Religion." In Gardiner Lindzey and Elliot Aronson (eds.). *The Handbook of Social Psychology* (pp. 602-659). Volume Five. Reading: Addison-Wesley.

Divine Office (1975). *The Liturgy of the Hours. Vol. IV.* New York: Catholic Book Publishing.

Dolan, Jay (1985). *The American Catholic Experience, 1830-1900.* Notre Dame, IN: University of Notre Dame.

Douglas, Tommy (1973). "The Highlights of the Dirty Thirties." In Douglas Francis and Herman Ganzeevoort (eds.). *The Dirty Thirties in Prairie Canada* (pp. 163-173). Vancouver: Tantalus Research.

Dowley, Tim (ed.) (1977). *Eerdman's Handbook to The History of Christianity.* Grand Rapids, MI: Wm. B. Eerdmans Publishing.

Durkheim, Emile (1933) [1911]. *The Division of Labour In Society.* New York: Free Press.

Durkheim, Emile (1938) [1895]. *The Rules of Sociological Method.* New York: Free Press.

Durkheim, Emile (1951) [1897]. *Suicide: A Study of Sociology.* Glencoe, IL: Free Press.

Durkheim, Emile (1965) [1915]. *The Elementary Forms of The Religious Life.* Trans. Joseph Ward Swain. New York: Free Press.

Durkheim, Emile (1969) [1898]. "Individualism and the Intellectuals." Translation of 1898 article by Steven Lukes with note. *Political Studies XVII:* 14-30.

Durkheim, Emile (1973) [1914]. "The Dualism of Human Nature and Its Social Conditions." In Robert Bellah (ed.). *Emile Durkheim on Morality and Society* (pp. 149-163). Columbus: Ohio State University Press.

Durkheim, Emile (1974) [1906]. *Sociology and Philosophy.* New York: Basic Books.

Dworkin, Andrea (1974). *Women Hating.* New York: E.P. Dutton.

Eisenstadt, Shmuel Noah (1968). "Charisma and Institution Building: Max Weber and Modern Sociology." In S.N. Eisenstadt (ed.). *Max Weber on Charisma and Institution Building* (pp. ix-lvi). Chicago: University of Chicago Press.

Eister, Allan (1967). "Toward a Radical Critique of the Church-Sect Typologizing: Comments and some Critical Observations on the Church-Sect Dimension." *Journal for the Scientific Study of Religion* 6:85-90.

Eliade, Mircea (1959). *The Sacred and the Profane: The Nature of Religion.* New York: Harcourt, Brace & World.

Eliade, Mircea. (1973). "Myth." In Thomas O'Dea and Janet O'Dea (eds.). *Readings on the Sociology of Religion* (pp. 70-78). Englewood Cliffs, NJ: Prentice Hall.

Eliade, Mircea (ed.) (1995). *The Encyclopedia of Religion.* Volume Five. New York: Simon and Schuster Macmillan.

Ellwood, Robert (1973). *Religious and Spiritual Groups in Modern America.* Englewood Cliffs, NJ: Prentice-Hall.

Encyclopaedia Britannica (1987). "Confucius and Confucianism." *The New Encyclopaedia Britannica* Vol. 16 (pp. 691-700). Chicago: Encyclopaedia Britannica.

Epstein, Barbara (1981). *The Politics of Domesticity: Women, Evangelism, and Temperance in Nineteeth-Century America.* Middletown, CT: Wesleyan University Press.

Eshleman, J. Ross (1994, seventh ed.). *The Family.* Boston: Allyn and Bacon.

Estep, William (1963). *The Anabaptist Story.* Nashville: Broadman Press.

Etzioni, Amitai (1968). *The Active Society.* New York: Free Press.

Evans-Pritchard, Edward Evan (1965). *Theories of Primitive Religion.* Oxford: Clarendon Press.

Featherstone, Mike. (1988). "In Pursuit of the Postmodern." *Theory, Culture and Society* 5:195-215.

Feldman, K.A., and T.M. Newcomb (1969). *The Impact of College Education on Students.* San Francisco: Jossey-Bass.

Ferguson, Everett (ed.) (1990). *Encyclopaedia of Early Christianity.* New York: Garlund Publishing.

Ferguson, Marilyn (1980). *The Aquarian Conspiracy.* Los Angeles: J.P. Tarcher.

Fichter, Joseph H. (1972). *The Catholic Cult of the Paraclete.* New York: Sheed and Ward.

Finke, Roger, Avery Guest, and Rodney Stark (1996). "Mobilizing Local Religious Markets: Religious Pluralism in the Empire State, 1855-1865." *American Sociological Review* 61:203-218.

Flanagan, Kieran (1996). "Introduction." In Kieran Flanagan and Peter Japp (eds.). *Postmodernity, Sociology and Religion* (pp. 1-13). New York: St. Martin's Press.

Florida, Robert (1994). "Buddhist Ethics." *Religious Humanism* 28:107-114.

Ford, J. Massingberd (1971). "Tongues-Leadership-Women." *Spiritual Life* 17:19-23.

Foster, Lawrence (1981). *Religion and Sexuality: Three American Communal Experiments of the Nineteenth Century.* New York: Oxford University Press.

Foucault, Michel (1993). "Discourse on the West." In Charles Lemert (ed.). *Social Theory: The Multicultural and Classical Readings* (pp. 451-455). Boulder: Westview Press.

Freud, Sigmund (1914). *The Future of an Illusion.* In James Strachey (ed.) *The Standard Edition of the Complete Psychological Works of Sigmund Freud.* London: Hogarth Press and the Institute of Psycho-Analysis.

Freud, Sigmund (1952) [1930]. *Civilization and its Discontents. Great Books of the Western World.* Volume 54. Chicago: Encyclopaedia Britannica, Inc.

Fukuyama, Yoshio (1961). "The Major Dimensions of Church Membership." *Review of Religious Research* 2: 154-161.

Fuller, Andrew R. (1986). *Psychology and Religion: Eight Points of View.* Lanham, MD: University Press of America.

Gallup, George (1982). *Religion in America, 1982.* Princeton, NJ: Princeton Religious Research Centre.

Gallup, George Jr., and Sarah Jones (1989). *100 Questions and Answers: Religion in America.* Princeton, NJ: Princeton Religious Research Centre.

Gardell, Mattias (1996). *In the Name of Elijah Muhammad, Louis Farrakhan and the Nation of Islam.* Durham: Duke University Press.

Gaustad, Edwin S. (1974). *A Religious History of America.* New York: Harper and Row.

Geertz, Clifford (1966). "Religion as a Cultural System." In Michael Banton (ed.). *Anthropological Approaches to the Study of Religion* (pp. 1-46). London: Tavistock Publications.

Geertz, Clifford (1968). *Islam Observed: Religious Development in Morroco and Indonesia.* Chicago: University of Chicago Press.

Geertz, Clifford (1973). *The Interpretation of Cultures.* New York: Basic Books.

Gerlach, Luther, and Virginia Hine (1970). *People, Power, Change Movements of Social Transformation.* Indianapolis: Bobbs-Merril.

Gibbon, Edward (1960) [1776]. *The Decline and Fall of the Roman Empire.* Abridged version by D. W. Low. New York: Harcourt, Brace and Company.

Giddens, Anthony. (1976a). *New Rules of Sociological Method.* London: Hutchinson of London.

Giddens, Anthony (1976b). "Introduction." In Max Weber, *The Protestant Ethic and the Spirit of Capitalism* (pp. 1-12[b]). New York: George Allen & Unwin.

Giddens, Anthony (1977). *Studies in Social and Political Theory.* London: Hutchinson and Co.

Giddens, Anthony (1981). "Agency, Institution, and Time-Space Analysis." In Karen Knorr-Centina and Aaron Cicourel (eds.). *Advances in Social Theory and Methodology* (pp. 161-174). Boston: Routledge and Kegan Paul.

Giddens, Anthony (1991). *Modernity and Self-Identity.* Cambridge: Polity Press.

Giddens, Anthony (1993). "Post-Modernity or Radicalized Modernity?" In Charles Lemert (ed.). *Social Theory: The Multicultural and Classical Readings* (pp. 531-538). Boulder: Westview Press.

Glenn, Norval D., and Kathryn B. Kramer (1987). "The marriages and divorces of the children of divorce." *Journal of Marriage and the Family* 49:811-825.

Globe and Mail (1995). "Crowds heed call to blacks." October 17, 1995.

Glock, Charles, and Rodney Stark (1965). *Religion and Society in Tension.* Chicago: Rand McNally.

Gloudner, Alvin (1978). "The New Class Project." *Theory and Society* 6:153-204.

Goode, William (1951). *Religion Among the Primitives.* New York: Free Press.

Gottwald, Norman (1979). *The Tribes of Yahweh: A Sociology of the Religion of Liberated Isreal, 1250-1050 B.C. E.* Maryknoll, NY: Orbis Books.

Grant, John W. (1967). *The Canadian Experience of Church Union.* Richmond: John Knox Press.

Grant, John W., Steven Chambers, Dianne Forrest, Bonnie Greene, Sang Chul Lee, and Peter G. White (1990). *Voices and Visions: 65 Years of the United Church of Canada.* Toronto: The United Church of Canada Publishing House.

Greeley, Andrew (1974). *Ecstasy. A Way of Knowing.* Englewood Cliffs, NJ: Prentice-Hall.

Greeley, Andrew (1975). *The Sociology of the Paranormal: A Reconnaissance.* Newbury CA: Sage Publications.

Greeley, Andrew (1977). *The American Catholic: A Social Portrait.* New York: Basic Books.

Greeley, Andrew (1991). *Faithful Attractions: Discovering Intimacy, Love, and Fidelity in American Marriage.* New York: Tom Doherty.

Greeley, Andrew (1994). "A Religious Revival in Russia?" *Journal for the Scientific Study of Religion* 33:253-272.

Greeley, Andrew (ed.) (1995). *Sociology and Religion: A Collection of Readings.* New York: Harper Collins.

Griffin, David (1989). "Introduction to SUNY Series in Constructive Postmodern Thought." In David Griffin and Huston Smith (eds.). *Primordial Truth and Postmodern Theology* (pp. xi-xiv). Albany: State University of New York.

Guth, James (1983). "Southern Baptist Clergy: Vanguard of the Christian Right?" In Robert Liebman and Robert Wuthnow (eds.). *The New Christian Right* (pp. 117-130). New York: Aldine Publishing.

Guth, James (1992). Book Review of Matthew Moen's *The Transformation of the Christian Right. Journal for the Scientific Study of Religion* 32:186.

Hadaway, Christopher (1978). "Denominational Switching and Membership Growth: In Search of A Relationship." *Sociological Analysis* 39:321-337.

Hadaway, Christopher (1980). "Denominational Switching and Religiosity." *Review of Religious Research* 21:451-461.

Hadaway, Christopher, and Penny Long Marler (1993). "All in the Family: Religious Mobility in America." *Review of Religious Research* 35:97-116.

Hadaway, Christopher, and Penny Long Marler (1996). "The Problem with Father as Proxy: Denominational Switching and Religious Change, 1965-1988." *Journal for the Scientific Study of Religion* 35:156-164.

Hadden, Jeffrey (1969). *The Gathering Storm in the Churches*. Garden City, NY: Doubleday.

Hadden, Jeffrey (1987a). "Religious Broadcasting and the Mobilization of the New Christian Right." *Journal for the Scientific Study of Religion* 26:1-24.

Hadden, Jeffrey (1987b). "Toward Desacralizing Secularization Theory." *Social Forces* 65: 587-611.

Hammond, Philip (1985). "Introduction." In Phillip Hammond (ed.). *The Sacred in a Secular Age* (pp. 1-6). Berkeley: University of California Press.

Hammond, Philip (1986). "Religion in the Modern World." In James Davison Hunter and Stephen C. Ainlay (eds.). *Making Sense of Modern Times* (pp. 143-158). New York: Routledge & Kegan Paul.

Hardy, A.C. (1970). "A Scientist Looks at Religion." *Proceedings of the Royal Institute of Great Britain* 43:201.

Hargrove, Barbara (1989). *The Sociology of Religion*. Arlington Heights, IL: Harland Davidson.

Harris, James H. (1987). *Black Ministers and Laity in the Urban Church: An Analysis of Political Social Expectations*. New York: University Press of America.

Heaton, Tim (1988). "Four C's of the Mormon Family: Chastity, Conjugality, Children and Chauvinism." In Darwin Thomas (ed.). *The Religion and the Family Connection* (pp. 107-124). Provo, UT: Brigham Young University.

Heelos, Paul (1996). "De-Traditionalism of Religion and Self: The New Age and Post-Modernity." In Kieran Flanagan (ed.). *Post-Modernity, Sociology, and Religion* (pp. 64-82). New York: St. Martin's Press.

Hennis, Wilhelm. (1987). " Personality and Life Orders: Max Weber's Theme." In S. Whimster and Scott Lash (eds.). *Max Weber, Rationality, and Modernity* (pp. 52-74). Boston: Allen and Unwin.

Herberg, Will (1960). *Protestant, Catholic and Jew*. New York: Anchor Books.

Hershberger, Guy (ed.) (1957). *The Recovery of the Anabaptist Vision*. Scottdale, PA: Herald Press.

Hill, Martin (1973). *The Religious Order*. London: Heinemann Educational Books.

Himmelstein, Jerome (1983). "The New Right." In Robert Liebman and Robert Wuthnow (eds.). *The New Christian Right* (pp. 13-30). New York: Aldine Publishing.

Hoge, Dean (1976). *Division in the Protestant House: The Basic Reasons Behind Intra-Church Conflict.* Philadelphia: Westminister Press.

Hoge, Dean (1987). *The Future of Catholic Leadership: Responses to the Priest Shortage.* Kansas City, MO: Sheed and Ward.

Hoge, Dean, Benton Johnson, and Donald Luidens. (1994). *Vanishing Boundaries: The Religion of Mainline Protestant Baby Boomers.* Louisville: Westminister/John Knox Press.

Hoge, Dean, Benton Johnson, and Donald Luidens. (1995). "Research Note: Types of Denominational Switching among Protestant Young Adults." *Journal for the Scientific Study of Religion* 34: 253-258.

Hoge, Dean, and David Roozen (eds.) (1979). *Understanding Church Growth and Decline: 1950-1978.* New York: Pilgrim Press.

Hole, Judith, and Ellen Levine (1971). *Rebirth of Feminism.* New York: Quadrangle Books.

Homans, George (1961). *Social Behaviour: Its Elementary Forms.* New York: Harcourt, Brace and World.

Homans, George (1964). "Bringing Men Back In." *American Sociological Review* 29: 809-818.

Hood, Ralph (1970). "Religious Orientation and the Report of Religious Experience." *Journal for the Scientific Study of Religion* 9:285-291.

Hood, Ralph (1975). "The Construction and Preliminary Validation of a Measure of Reported Mystical Experience." *Journal for the Scientific Study of Religion* 14:29-41.

Hood, Ralph (1998). "Psychology of Religion." In William Swatos, Jr. (ed.). *Encyclopedia of Religion and Society* (pp. 388-391). Walnut Creek, CA: Altamira Press.

Hozeski, Bruce (1994). *Hildegard of Bingen: The Book of the Rewards of Life.* New York: Oxford University Press.

Hughes, Pennethorne (1971). *Witchcraft.* Harmondsworth, England: Penguin Books.

Hunt, Larry, and Janet Hunt (1977). "Black Religion as Both Opiate and Inspiration of Civil Rights Militance: Putting Marx's Data to the Test." *Social Forces* 56:1-14.

Hunt, Richard, and Morton B. King (1971). "The Intrinsic-Extrinsic Concept: A Review and Evaluation." *Journal for the Scientific Study of Religion* 10:339-365.

Hutchison, William R. (ed.) (1989). *Between the Times: The Travail of the Protestant Establishment in America: 1900-1960.* Cambridge: Cambridge University Press.

Iannaccone, Laurence (1990). "Religious Practice: A Human Capital Approach." *Journal for the Scientific Study of Religion* 29:297-314.

Ice, Martha Long (1987). *Clergy Women and their Worldviews.* New York: Praeger.

Jackson, Elton, Willam Fox, and Harry Crockett, Jr. (1970). "Religion and Occupational Achievement." *American Sociological Review* 35:48-63.

Jacquet, Constant H. (ed.) (1988). *Yearbook of American and Canadian Churches.* Nashville: Abingdon.

James, William (1902) [1920]. *The Varieties of Religious Experience.* New York: Longmans, Green, and Company.

Jameson, Fredric (1984). "Postmoderism, or the Culture of Late Capitalism." *New Left Review* 146:53-93.

Jensen, Jerry (ed.) (1963). *Presbyterians and the Baptism in the Holy Spirit.* Los Angeles, CA: Full Gospel Businessmen's Fellowship International.

Johnson, Benton (1961). "Do Holiness Sects Socialize in Dominant Values?" *Social Forces* 39:309-16.

Johnson, Paul (1976). *A History of Christianity.* New York: Atheneum.

Johnstone, Ronald L. (1992, fourth ed.). *Religion in Society. A Sociology of Religion.* Englewood Cliffs, NJ: Prentice Hall.

Jones, Alexander (ed.) (1966). *The Jerusalem Bible.* Garden City, NY: Doubleday.

Kant, Immanuel (1929) [1781]. *Critique of Pure Reason.* Trans. N. Kemp Smith. London: Macmillan.

Kellner, Douglas (1988). "Postmodernism as a Social Theory: Some Challenges and Problems." *Theory, Culture and Society* 5:239-269.

Kelly, Dean (1972). *Why Conservative Churches are Growing: A Study in the Sociology of Religion.* New York: Harper and Row.

Kelsey, Morton (1964). *Tongue Speaking.* Garden City, NY: Doubleday.

Kelsey, Morton T. (1983). *Companions on the Inner Way.* New York: Crossroad.

Kephart, William (1987, third ed.). *Extraordinary Groups.* New York: St. Martin's Press.

Kertzer, David (1988). *Ritual, Politics and Power.* New Haven: Yale University Press.

Kligman, Gail (1988). *The Wedding of the Dead: Ritual, Poetics, and Popular Culture in Transylvania.* Berkeley, CA: University of California Press.

Kluckhohn, Clyde (1972). "Myths and Rituals: A General Theory." In William Lessa and Evon Vogt (eds.). *Reader in Comparative Religion: An Anthropological Approach* (pp. 76-105). New York: Praeger.

Koran (1974). Translated with Notes by N.J. Dawood. New York: Penguin Books.

Kox, Willem, Wim Meeus, and Harm 't Hart (1991). "Religious Conversion of Adolescents: Testing the Lofland and Stark Model of Religious Conversion." *Sociological Analysis* 52:227-240.

Kurtz, Paul (1989). "The New Age in Perspective." *Skeptical Inquirer* 13:365-367.

Lancaster, Lewis (1984). "Elite and Folk: Comments on the Two-Tiered Theory." In George A. De Vos and Takao Sofue (eds.). *Religion and the Family in East Asia* (pp. 87-95). Berkeley: The University of California Press.

Lanternari, Vittorio (1965). *The Religions of the Oppressed.* New York: Mentor.

Larson, Lyle. (1991). "Religiosity and the family: A tenuous connection." Paper presented in the Religion and Family Section at the annual meeting of the National Council of Family Relations, Denver, November 20.

Larson, Lyle, Walter Goltz, Don Swenson, Irwin Barker, Melanie Driedger, Terry LeBlanc, and Bryan Rennisck (1994). *Clergy Families in Canada: An Initial Report.* Markham, ON: Evangelical Fellowship of Canada.

Latourette, Kenneth (1975). *A History of Christianity.* Vol II. New York: Harper and Row.

Lawless, Elaine (1988). *Handmaidens of the Lord: The Power of Women Preachers and Traditional Religion.* Philadelphia: University of Pennsylvania Press.

Lee, Cameron (1988). "Toward a social ecology of the minister's family." *Pastoral Psychology* 36:249-259.

Lee, Cameron, and Jack Balswick (1989). *Life in a Glass House: The Minister's Family in its Unique Social Context.* Grand Rapids, MI: Zondervan.

Lee, Richard Wayne (1992). "Christianity and the Other Religions: Interreligious Relations in a Shrinking World." *Sociological Analysis* 53:125-139.

Lehman, Edward Jr. (1985). *Women Clergy: Breaking through Gender Barriers.* New Brunswick, NJ: Transaction Books.

Lehman, Edward Jr. (1987). *Women Clergy in England: Sexism, Modern Consciousness and Church Viability.* Lewiston, NY: Edwin Mellen Press.

Lenski, Gerhard (1963). *The Religious Factor.* Garden City, NY: Doubleday.

Lévi-Strauss, Claude (1978). *Myth and Meaning.* New York: Schocken Books.

Lévi-Strauss, Claude (1987). *Anthropology and Myth.* New York: Basil Blackwell.

Lévi-Strauss, Claude (1993) [1963]. "Structural Study of Myth." In Charles Lemert (ed.). *Social Theory: The Multicultural & Classic Readings* (pp. 335-339). Boulder: Westview Press.

Levine, David (1984). "Production, Reproduction, and The Proletarian Family in England 1500-1851." In David Levine (ed.). *Proletarianization and Family History* (pp. 87-127). Toronto: Academic Press.

Libreria Editrice Vaticana (1993). *Veritatis Splendour.* Vatican City: Libreria Editrice Vaticana.

Liebman, Robert (1983). "Mobilizing the Moral Majority." In Robert Liebman and Robert Wuthnow (eds.). *The New Christian Right* (pp. 49-73). New York: Aldine Publishing.

Liebman, Robert, and Robert Wuthnow (eds.) (1983). *The New Christian Right.* New York: Aldine Publishing.

Lienesch, Micheal (1993). *Redeeming America: Piety and Politics in The New Christian Right.* Chapel Hill: University of North Carolina Press.

Limieux, Raymond (1990). "Le catholicisme québécois: une question de culture." *Sociologie et Sociétés* 22:145-164.

Lincoln, C. Eric (1961). *The Black Muslims in America.* Boston: Beacon Press.

Lincoln, C. Eric, and Lawrence H. Mamiya (1990). *The Black Church in the African American Experience.* Durham: Duke University Press.

Linder, Robert (1979). "Rome Responds." In Tim Dowley (ed.). *Eerdman's Handbook to the History of Christianity* (pp. 404-422). Grand Rapids, MI: Wm. B. Eerdmans.

Lipset, Seymour (1959). *Agrarian Socialism: The Cooperative Commonwealth Federation in Saskatchewan.* Berkeley: University of California Press.

Lipset, Seymour (1964). *The First New Nation.* New York: Basic Books.

Lipset, Seymour, and Rienhard Bendix (1959). *Social Mobility in Industrial Society.* Berkeley: University of California Press.

Lofland, John, and Rodney Stark (1965). "Becoming a World-Saver: A Theory of Conversion to a Deviant Perspective." *American Sociological Review* 30:862-875.

London, Harlan, and Katherine R. Allen (1985-86). "Family versus career responsibilities." *Marriage and Family Review* 9: 199-208.

Long Marler, Penny (1989). "Of Apples and Butterfiles: Revising the Secularization Thesis." Paper presented at the Society for the Scientific Study of Religion annual meetings, Salt Lake City, Utah, October.

Luckmann, Thomas (1995). "The New and the Old in Religion." In Andrew Greeley (ed.). *Sociology and Religion* (pp. 232-248). New York: Harper and Collins.

Lynd, Robert, and Helen Lynd (1929). *Middletown.* New York: Harcourt, Brace and Company.

Lyon, David (1996). "Religion and Postmodernity." In Kieran Flanagan and Peter C. Jupp (eds.). *Postmodernity, Sociology and Religion* (pp. 14-29). New York: St. Martin's Press.

Mace, D. and V. Mace (1980). *What's Happening to Clergy Marriages?* Nashville: Abingdon.

MacIver, Robert Morrison, and Charles H. Page (1957). In J. Milton Yinger (ed.). *Religion, Society and the Individual* (pp. 318-329). New York: MacMillan Company.

Mack, Phyllis (1987). "Feminine Symbolism and Feminine Behaviour in Radical Religious Movements: Franciscans, Quakers and the followers of Gandhi." In Jim Obelkevich, Lyndal Roper, and Raphael Samuel (eds.). *Disciplines of Faith: Studies in Religion, Politics and Patriarchy* (pp. 115-130). London: Routledge and Kegan Paul.

Mack, Raymond, Raymond Murphy, and Seymor Yellin (1956). "The Protestant Ethic, Level of Aspiration and Social Mobility." *American Sociological Review* 21:295-300.

Macleans (1993). "God is Alive: Canada is a Nation of Believers." April 12, pp. 32-42.

Macleans (1998). "Phipps, Word for Word." December 15:43.

MacLennan, Hugh (1978) [1945]. *Two Solitudes*. Toronto: MacMillan.

Magdoff, Harry, and Paul Sweezy (1989). "A New Stage of Capitalism Ahead." *Monthly Review.* May. Cited in Peter Li and B. Singh Bolaria (1994) (eds.). *Essentials of Contemporary Sociology* (p. 130). Toronto: Copp Clark Longman Ltd.

Mahoney, John (1987). *The Making of Moral Theology: A Study of the Roman Catholic Tradition.* Oxford: Clarendon Press.

Malinowski, Bronislaw (1932). *Argonauts of the Western Pacific.* London: George Routledge and Sons.

Malinowski, Bronislaw (1954). *Magic, Science, and Religion and Other Essays.* Garden City, NY: Doubleday Anchor Books.

Mandel, Ernest (1975). *Late Capitalism.* London: New Left Books.

Mann, W. Edward (1955). *Sect, Cult, and Church in Alberta.* Toronto: University of Toronto Press.

Mannheim, Karl (1936). *Ideology and Utopia.* London: Routledge and Kegan Paul.

Marciano, Teresa Donati (1987)."Families and Religion." In Marvin Sussman and Suzanne Steinmetz (eds.). *Handbook of Marriage and the Family* (pp. 285-315). New York and London: Plenum Press.

Marciano, Teresa Donati (1990). "Corporate church, ministry, and ministerial family: embedded employment and measures of success." *Marriage and Family Review* 15: 171-193.

Marcuse, Herbert (1993). "Repressive Desublimation." In Charles Lemert (ed.). *Social Theory: The Multicultural and Classical Readings* (pp. 471-474). Boulder: Westview Press.

Martin, David (1962). "The Denomination." *The British Journal of Sociology* 13:1-14.

Martin, David (1978). *A General Theory of Secularization.* New York: Harper and Row.

Martin, Ralph (1971). "Life in community." In Kevin Ranaghan and Dorothy Ranaghan (eds.). *As The Spirit Lead Us* (pp. 145-163). Paramus, NJ: Paulist Press.

Marty, Martin (1959). *A Short History of Christianity.* Cleveland: William Collins and World.

Marty, Martin (1979). "Introduction." In Dean Hoge and David Roozen (eds.). *Understanding Church Growth and Decline* (pp. 9-15). New York: The Pilgrim Press.

Marx, Gary (1967). "Religion: Opiate or Inspiration of Civil Rights Militancy Among Negroes." *American Sociological Review* 32:64-72.

Marx, Karl (1967) [1867]. *Capital. Volume I: A Critical Analysis of Capitalist Production.* New York: International Publishers.

Marx, Karl, and Friedrich Engels (1964). *Marx and Engels on Religion.* New York: Schocken Books.

Maslow, Abraham (1970) [1964]. *Religions, Values, and Peak-Experiences.* New York: Viking.

Mauro, James (1992). "Bright Lights, Big Mystery: Near-death experiences have become a cottage industry." *Psychology Today* (July/August): 54-57, 80-82.

Maxwell, Leslie (1971). *The Pentecostal Baptism.* Three Hills, AB: Prairie Press.

May, Rollo (1991). *The Cry for Myth.* New York: Bantam Doubleday Bell.

McCann, Joseph (1993). *Church and Organization: A Sociological and Theological Enquiry.* Cranbury, NJ: University of Scranton Press.

McClenon, James (1998a). "Psychic Phenomena (psi)." In William Swatos, Jr. (ed.). *Encyclopedia of Religion and Society* (p. 388). Walnut Creek, CA: Altamira Press.

McClenon, James (1998b). "Mysticism." In William Swatos, Jr. (ed.). *Encyclopedia of Religion and Society* (p. 316). Walnut Creek, CA: Altamira Press.

McConkie, Bruce (1979). *Mormon Doctrine.* Salt Lake City: Bookcraft.

McDonnell, Kilian (1970). *Catholic Pentecostalism: Problems in Evaluation.* Pecos, NM: Dove Publications.

McGuire, Meredith (1982). *Catholic Pentecostals: Power, Charisma, and Order in a Religious Movement.* Philadelphia: Temple University Press.

McGuire, Meredith (1988). *Ritual Healing in Suburban America.* New Brunswick, NJ: Rutgers University Press.

McGuire, Meredith (1992, third ed.). *Religion: The Social Context.* Belmont, CA: Wadsworth.

McKinney, William, and Wade Clark Roof (1990). "Liberal Protestanism's Struggle to Recapture the Heartland." In Thomas Robbins and Dick Anthony (eds.). *In Gods We Trust: New Patterns of Religious Pluralism in America* (pp. 167-183). New Brunswick, NJ: Transaction.

Mensching, Gustav (1959). "Religion and the Holy." In Louis Schneider (ed.). *Religion and Culture: A Reader in the Sociology of Religion* (p. 36). New York: John Wiley & Sons.

Menzies, William W. (1971). *Anointed to Serve: The Story of the Assemblies of God.* Springfield, MO: Gospel Publishing House.

Merton, Robert (1957, rev. ed.). *Social Theory and Social Structure.* Glencoe, IL: Free Press.

Meyer, John, John Boli, and George Thomas (1994). "Ontology and Rationalization in the Western Cultural Account." In W. Richard Scott, John Meyer, and Associates (eds.). *Institutional Environments and Organizations: Structural Complexity and Individualism* (pp. 1-27). Thousand Oaks, CA: Sage.

Meyer, John W. (1980). "The world polity and the authority of the nation-state." In Albert Bergesen (ed.). *Studies of the Modern World-System* (pp. 109-37). New York: Academic Press.

Meyer, Katherine, Helen Rizzo, and Yousef Ali. (1998). "Islam and the Extension of Citizenship Rights to Women in Kuwait." *Journal for the Scientific Study of Religion* 37:131-144.

REFERENCES

Miller, I. (1977). "Aberhart." In Thomas, Lewis (ed.). *William Aberhart and Social Credit in Alberta* (pp. 18-19). Vancouver: Copp Clark Publishers.

Miner, Horace (1939). *St. Denis: A French-Canadian Parish.* Chicago: University of Chicago Press.

Moaddel, Mansoor. (1998). "Religion and Women: Islamic Modernism versus Fundamentalism." *Journal for the Scientific Study of Religion* 37:108-130.

Moberg, David (1964). "Social Differentiation in the Netherlands." In Louis Schneider (ed.). *Religion, Culture & Society: A Reader in the Sociology of Religion* (pp. 542-548). New York: John Wiley & Sons.

Moen, Matthew (1992). *The Transformation of the Right.* Tuscaloosa: The University of Alabama Press.

Mol, Hans (1976). "Correlates of Churchgoing in Canada." In Stewart Crysdale and Les Wheatcroft (eds.). *Religion in Canadian Society* (pp. 241-254). Toronto: MacMillan of Canada.

Monter, W. William (1977). "The Pedestal and the Stake: Courtly Love and Witchcraft." In Renate Bridenthal and Claudia Koonz (eds.). *Becoming Visible: Women in European History* (pp. 119-136). Boston: Houghton-Muffin.

Morgan, S. Philip (1983). "A Research Note on Religion and Morality: Are Religious People Nice People?" *Social Forces* 61:683-693.

Morioka, Kiyomi, and William H. Hewell (1968). *The Sociology of Japanese Religion. International Studies in Sociology and Social Anthropology 6.* Leiden, Netherlands: Brill.

Morrow, E. Lloyd (1923). *Church Union in Canada.* Toronto: Thomas Allen.

Morse, Flo (1980). *The Shakers and the World's People.* New York: Dodd, Mead and Company.

Mott, Paul (1965). *The Organization of Society.* Englewood Cliffs, NJ: Prentice-Hall.

Murdock, George P. (1949). *Social Structure.* New York: MacMillan.

Murion, P. J. (1992). *New Parish Ministers: Laity and Religious on Parish Staffs.* New York: National Pastoral Life Centre.

Musick, Marc, and John Wilson (1995). "Religious Switching for Marriage Reasons." *Sociology of Religion* 56:257-270.

Naisbitt, John, and Patricia Aburdene (1990). *Megatrends 2000.* New York: Warner Books.

Nason-Clark, Nancy (1993). "Gender Relations in Contemporary Christian Organization." In William E. Hewitt (ed.). *The Sociology of Religion: A Canadian Focus* (pp. 215-234). Toronto: Butterworths.

Neitz, Mary Jo (1987). *Charisma and Community: A Study of Religious Commitment within the Charismatic Renewal.* New Brunswick, NJ: Transaction Books.

Neitz, Mary Jo (1998). "Feminist Research and Theory." In William Swatos, Jr. (ed.). *Encyclopedia of Religion and Society* (pp. 194-186). Walnut Creek, CA: Altamira Press.

Nelsen, Hart, Thomas Madron, and Raytha Yokley (1975). "Black Religion's Promethean Motif: Orthodoxy and Militancy." *American Journal of Sociology* 81:139-146.

Nesbitt, Paula (1997). "Clergy Feminization: Controlled Labor or Transformative Change." *Journal for the Scientific Study of Religion* 36:585-598.

Newport, Frank (1979). "The Religious Switcher in the United States." *American Sociological Review* 44:528-552.

Newport, John (1998). *The New Age Movement and the Biblical Worldview.* Grand Rapids, MI: William B. Eerdmans Publishing Company.

Newsweek (1993). "Playing a different tune." June 28:30-31.

Newsweek (1994). "The Search for the Sacred: America's Quest for Spiritual Meaning." November 18:52-62.

Niebhur, H. Richard. (1957) [1929]. *The Social Sources of Denominationalism.* New York: World Publishing.

Nisbet, Robert (1966). *The Sociological Tradition.* New York: Basic Books.

Noll, William (1992). "A Welcome in the Ministry: The 1920 and 1924 General Conferences Debate Clergy Rights for Women." *Methodist History* 30:91-99.

Norbeck, Edward (1961). *Religion in Primitive Society.* New York: Harper and Row.

Norrell, J. Elizabeth (1989). "Clergy family satisfaction." *Family Science Review* 2: 337-346.

Noss, John, and David Noss (1984, seventh ed.). *Man's Religions.* New York: MacMillan.

Nottingham, Elizabeth (1971). *Religion: A Sociological View.* New York: Random House.

O'Connor, Edward (1971). *The Pentecostal Movement in the Catholic Church.* Notre Dame: Ave Maria Press.

O'Dea, Thomas F. (1957). *The Mormons.* Chicago: The University of Chicago Press.

O'Dea, Thomas F. (1966). *The Sociology of Religion.* Englewood Cliffs, NJ: Prentice Hall.

O'Dea, Thomas F. (1970). *Sociology and the Study of Religion.* New York: Basic Books.

O'Dea, Thomas, and Janet O'Dea (1983, second ed.). *The Sociology of Religion.* Englewood Cliffs, NJ: Prentice Hall.

O'Hara, Maureen (1989). "A New Age Reflection in the Magic Mirror of Science." *Skeptical Inquirer* 13:368-374.

O'Neill, John (1988). "Religion and Postmodernism: The Durkheimian Bond in Bell and Jameson." *Theory, Culture and Society* 5:493-508.

Orsi, Robert (1991). "'He Keeps Me Going': Women's Devotion to Saint Jude Taddeus and the Dialectics of Gender in American Catholicism, 1929-1965." In Thomas Kselman (ed.). *Brief in History: Innovative Approaches to European and American Religion* (pp. 137-169). Notre Dame, IN: University of Notre Dame.

Orthner, Dennis K. (1986). *Pastoral Counselling: Caring and Caregivers in the United Methodist Church.* A Report to the Board of Higher Education and Ministry.

Osis, Karlis, and Erlendur Haraldsson (1977). *At the Hour of Death.* New York: Avon Books.

O'Toole, Roger (1996). "Religion in Canada: Its Development and Contemporary Situation." *Social Compass* 43:119-134.

Otto, Rudolph (1958) [1923]. *The Idea of the Holy.* New York: Oxford University Press.

Paloutzian, Raymond (1996, second ed.). *Invitation to the Psychology of Religion.* Boston: Allyn and Bacon.

Paper, Jordon (1989). *Offering Smoke: The Sacred Pipe and Native American Religion.* Edmonton: University of Alberta Press.

Parsons, Talcott (1951). *Religious Perspectives of College Teaching in Sociology and Social Psychology.* New Haven: Hazen Foundation.

Parsons, Talcott (1964). "Christianity and Modern Industrial Society." In Louis Schneider (ed.). *Religion, Culture & Society: A Reader in the Sociology of Religion* (pp. 273-298). New York: John Wiley & Sons.

Parsons, Talcott (1968) [1937]. *The Structure of Social Action. Volume I: Marshall, Pareto, and Durkheim.* New York: The Free Press.

Pettigrew, Thomas, and Ernest Q. Campbell (1958-59). "Racial and Moral Crisis: The Role of the Little Rock Ministers." *American Journal of Sociology* 64:509-516.

Piazza, Thomas, and Charles Glock (1979). "Images of God and Their Social Meanings." In Robert Wuthnow (ed.). *The Religious Dimension: New Directions in Quantitative Research* (pp. 69-91). New York: Academic Press.

Pinkares, Servais (1995). "The Use of Scripture and the Renewal of Moral Theology: The Catechism and *Veritatis Splendour*." *Thomist* 59:1-19.

Polanyi, Michael (1949). "The Nature of Scientific Convictions." In Fred Schwartz (ed.). *Scientific Thought and Social Reality* (pp. 49-66). New York: International Universities Press.

Poloma, Margaret M. (1982). "Toward a Christian Sociological Perspective: Religious Values, Theory and Methodology." *Sociological Analysis* 43, 2:95-108.

Poloma, Margaret M. (1983). *The Charismatic Movement: Is There a New Pentecost?* Boston, MA: Twayne Publishers.

Poloma, Margaret M. (1989). *The Assemblies of God at the Crossroads: Charisma and Institutional Dilemmas.* Knoxville: University of Tennessee Press.

Poloma, Margaret M. (1995). "The Sociological Context of Religious Experience." In Ralph W. Hood (ed.). *Handbook of Religious Experience* (pp. 161-182). Birmingham, AL: Religious Education Press.

Poloma, Margaret M. (1997). "The 'Toronto Blessing': Charisma, Institutionalization, and Revival." *Journal for the Scientific Study of Religion* 36:257-271.

Poloma, Margaret, and George Gallup, Jr. (1991). *Varieties of Prayer: A Survey Report.* Philadelphia: Trinity Press, International.

Poloma, Margaret, and Lynette Hoelter (1998). "The 'Toronto Blessing': A Holistic Model of Healing." *Journal for the Scientific Study of Religion* 37:257-272.

Poloma, Margaret M., and Brian F. Pendleton (1991). *Exploring Neglected Dimensions of Religion in Quality of Life Research.* Lewiston, NY: Edwin Mellen Press.

Poloma, Margaret M., and Brian F. Pendleton (1992). "Mysticism and Subjective Perceptions of Well-Being." Paper presented at the Annual Meetings of the Association for the Sociology of Religion, Pittsburgh, PA.

Pope, Liston (1942). *Millhands and Preachers.* New Haven: Yale University Press.

Porter, John (1965). *The Vertical Mosaic: An Analysis of Social Class and Power in Canada.* Toronto: University of Toronto Press.

Powell, Walter, and Paul DiMaggio (eds.) (1991). *The New Institutionalism in Organizational Analysis.* Chicago: University of Chicago Press.

Prell, Riv-Ellen (1989). *Prayer and Community: The Havurah in American Judaism.* Detroit: Wayne State University Press.

Presnell, W.B. (1977). "The Minister's own marriage." *Pastoral Psychology* 25:272-281.

415

Proudfoot, Wayne (1985). "Attribution Theory and the Psychology of Religion." *Journal for the Scientific Study of Religion* 14, 4:317-330.

Raglan, Lord (1949). *The Origins of Religion.* London: Watts.

Raglan, Lord (1956) [1936]. *The Hero: A Study in Tradition, Myth, and Drama.* New York: Vintage Books.

Ranaghan, Kevin, and Dorothy Ranaghan (1969). *Catholic Pentecostals.* Paramus, NJ: Paulist Press.

Reed, Graham (1989). "The Psychology of Channeling." *Skeptical Inquirer* 13:385-390.

Reilly, Mary Ellen (1975). "Perceptions of the Priest Role." *Sociological Analysis* 36:347-356.

Reynolds, Vernon, and Ralph Tanner (1995). *The Social Ecology of Religion.* New York: Oxford University Press.

Richardson, James (1998). "Conversion." In William Swatos, Jr. (ed.). *Encyclopedia of Religion and Society* (pp. 119-121). Walnut Creek, CA: Altamira Press.

Ricco, James A. (1979). "Religious Affiliation and Socioeconomic Achievement." In Robert Wuthnow (ed.). *The Religious Dimension: New Directions in Quantitative Research* (pp. 199-228). New York: Academic Press.

Ritzer, George (1996, fourth ed.). *Sociological Theory.* New York: McGraw Hill.

Rivers, William Halse (1968). "The Socio-logical Significance of Myth." In G.H. Georg (ed.). *Studies in Mythology* (pp. 27-45). Homeward, IL: Dorsey Press.

Roberts, Keith (1991, second ed.). *Religion in Sociological Perspective.* Belmont, CA: Wadsworth Publishing.

Roberts, Keith (1995, third ed.). *Religion in Sociological Perspective.* Belmont, CA: Wadsworth Publishing.

Roof, Wade Clark (1979). "Denominational Switching." *Journal for the Scientific Study of Religion* 18:363-379.

Roof, Wade Clark (1989). "Multiple Religious Switching: A Research Note." *Journal for the Scientific Study of Religion* 28:530-535.

Roof, Wade Clark (1993). *A Generation of Seekers.* San Francisco: Harper.

Roof, Wade Clark, and William McKinney. (1987). *American Mainline Religion.* New Brunswick, NJ: Rutgers University Press.

Roof, Wade Clark, and Sarah McFarland Taylor (1995). "The Force of Emotion: James's Reorientation of Religion and the Contemporary Rediscovery of the Body, Spirituality, and the 'Feeling Self'." In Donald Capps and Janet Jacobs (eds.). *The Struggle for Life: A Companion to William James's The Varieties of Religious Experience* (pp. 197-208). West Lafayette, IN: Society for the Scientific Study of Religion and Princeton Theological Seminary.

Rose, Herbert Jennings (1959). *Religion in Greece and Rome.* New York: Harper and Row.

Roth, Guenther (1987). "Rationalization in Max Weber's Developmental History." In Sam Whimster and Scott Lash (eds.). *Max Weber, Rationality, and Modernity* (pp. 75-91). Boston: Allen and Unwin.

Ryan, Mary (1981). *Cradle of the Middle Class: The Family in Oneida County, New York, 1790-1865.* Cambridge: Cambridge University Press.

Sapir, Edward (1960). *Culture, Language and Personality.* Berkeley: University of California.

Sawatsky, Rodney (1992). "The One and the Many: The Recovery of Mennonite Pluralism." In Walter Klassen (ed.). *Anabaptism Revisited* (pp. 141-154). Waterloo, ON: Herald Press.

Schleiermacher, Friedrich (1988) [1799]. *On Religion: Speeches to its Cultured Despisers.* Trans. Richard Crouter. New York: Cambridge University Press.

Schlenker, Dale (1991). "Pursuing a Phantom? The Protestant Ethic and the Spirit of Capitalism in Twentieth Century Canadian History." Paper presented at the Canadian Sociology and Anthropology Association Annual Meetings, Kingston, Ontario, June.

Schluchter, Wolfgang. (1987). "Weber's Sociology of Rationalism and Typology of Religious Rejections of the World." In Sam Whimster and Scott Lash (eds.). *Max Weber, Rationality, and Modernity* (pp. 92-115). Boston: Allen and Unwin.

Schmalzbauer, John (1993). "Evangelicals in the New Class: Class versus Subcultural Predictors of Ideology." *Journal for the Scientific Study of Religion* 32:330-342.

Schoenfeld, Eugen, and Stjepan Mestrovic (1991). "From the Sacred Collectivity to the Sacred Individual: The Misunderstood Durkheimian Legacy." *Sociological Focus* 24:83-92.

Schoenherr, Richard, and Lawrence Young (1993). *Full Pews and Empty Altars.* Madison: University of Wisconsin Press.

Segel, Robert A. (1989). *Religion and the Social Sciences. Essays on the Confrontation.* Atlanta, GA: Scholars Press.

Shepherd, Gordon, and Gary Shepherd (1984). *A Kingdom Transformed: Themes in the Development of Mormonism.* Salt Lake City: University of Utah Press.

Sherkat, Darren (1991). "Leaving the Faith: Testing Theories of Religious Switching Using Survival Models." *Social Science Research* 20:171-187.

Sherkat, Darren, and John Wilson (1995). "Preferences, Constraints, and Choices in Religious Markets: An Examination of Religious Switching and Apostasy." *Social Forces* 73:993-1026.

Sherrill, John (1964). *They Speak with Other Tongues.* Old Tuppan, NJ: Pyramid Publications.

Shipps, Jan (1985). *Mormonism: The Story of A New Religious Tradition.* Chicago: University of Chicago Press.

Shupe, Anson, and William Stacey (1983). "The Moral Majority Constituency." In Robert Liebman, and Robert Wuthnow (eds.). *The New Christian Right* (pp. 104-116). New York: Aldine Publishing.

Simmel, Georg (1959) [1906]. *Sociology of Religion.* Trans. C. Rosenthal. New York: Philosophical Library.

Sinnott, Jeremy (1995). *Thursday pastors Meeting: Worship.* Audiotape. Toronto Airport Vineyard.

Skolnick, Arlene (1991). *Embattled Paradise: The American Family in an Age of Uncertainty.* New York: Basic Books.

Smith, Joseph (1957). *The Pearl of Great Price.* Salt Lake City, UT: The Church of Jesus Christ of Latter-day Saints.

Smith, W. Robertson (1956) [1989]. *The Religion of the Semites.* New York: The Meridian Library.

Smith-Rosenberg, Carroll (1985). *Disorderly Conduct: Visions of Gender in Victorian America.* New York: Knopf.

Spilka, Bernard, Ralph W. Hood, Jr., and Richard L. Gorsuch (1985). *The Psychology of Religion: An Empirical Approach.* Englewood Cliffs, NJ: Prentice-Hall.

Spiro, Melford (1982). *Buddhism and Society: A Great Tradition and Its Burmese Vicissitudes.* Berkeley: The University of California Press.

Spiro, Melford (1984). "Some Reflections on Family and Religion in East Asia." In George A. De Vos and Takao Sofue (eds.). Religion and the Family in East Asia (pp. 35-54). Berkeley: University of California Press.

417

Stace, Walter (1960). *Mysticism and Philosophy*. New York: Macmillan.

Starhawk (no first name) (1988, second ed.). *Dreaming the Dark: Magic, Sex and Politics*. Boston: Beacon Press.

Stark, Rodney (1964). "Class, Radicalism, and Religious Involvement in Great Britain." *American Sociological Review* 29:698-706.

Stark, Rodney (1972). "The Economics of Piety: Religious Commitment and Social Class." In Gerald Thielbar and Saul Feldman (eds). *Issues in Social Inequality* (pp. 483-503). Boston: Little, Brown and Company.

Stark, Rodney (1985). "Church and Sect." In Phillip Hammond (ed.). *The Sacred in a Secular Age* (pp. 139-149). Berkeley: University of California.

Stark, Rodney (1992, fourth ed.). *Sociology*. Belmont, CA: Wadsworth Publishing.

Stark, Rodney (1996). *The Rise of Christianity: A Sociologist Reconsiders History*. Princeton, NJ: Princeton University Press.

Stark, Rodney, and William Bainbridge (1979) "Of Churches, Sects, and Cults: Preliminary Concepts for a Theory of Religious Movements." *Journal for the Scientific Study of Religion* 18:117-131.

Stark, Rodney, and William Bainbridge (1985). *The Future of Religion*. Berkeley: University of California Press.

Stark, Rodney, and William Sims Bainbridge (1987). *A Theory of Religion*. New York: Berne.

Stark, Rodney, and Kevin Christiano (1992). "Support for the American Left, 1920-1924: The Opiate Thesis Reconsidered." *Journal for the Scientific Study of Religion* 31:62-75.

Stark, Rodney, Roger Finke, and Laurence Iannaccone (1995). "Pluralism and Piety: England and Wales, 1851." *Journal for the Scientific Study of Religion* 34:431-444.

Stark, Rodney, and Charles Glock (1968). *American Piety: The Nature of Religious Commitment*. Berkeley: University of California Press.

Stark, Rodney, and James Mauss (1993). "Market Forces and Catholic Commitment: Exploring the New Paradigm." *Journal for the Scientific Study of Religion* 32:111-124.

Stark, Werner (1965). "The Routinization of Charisma: A Consideration of Catholicism." *Sociological Analysis* 26: 203-211.

Steeves, Paul (1979). "The Orthodox Church in Eastern Europe and Russia." In Tim Dowley (ed.). *Eerdman's Handbook of the History of Christianity* (pp. 310-313). Grand Rapids, MI: Wm. B. Eerdmans Publishing.

Stein, Stephen (1992). *The Shaker Experience in America: A History of the United Society of Believers*. New Haven: Yale University Press.

Stone, D. (1976). "The Human Potential Movement." In Charles Glock and Robert Bellah (eds.). *The New Religious Consciousness* (pp. 93-115). Berkeley: The University of California Press.

Sumner, William G. (1906). *Folkways*. New York: Mentor Books.

Swanson, Guy (1960). *The Birth of the Gods*. Ann Arbor, MI: University of Michigan Press.

Swatos, William H., Jr. (ed.). (1987). *Religious Sociology*. New York: Greenwood Press.

Swatos, William H., Jr. (1998). "Religiosity." In William H. Swatos, Jr. (ed.). *Encyclopedia of Religion and Society* (pp. 406). Walnut Creek, CA: Altamira Press.

Swenson, Don (1972). "The Charismatic Movement within Denominational Christianity." Unpublished MA Thesis. Calgary: The University of Calgary.

Swenson, Don (1989). *Cultural and Structural Factors of Family Attitudes in Roman Catholic Parochial Environments.* Ph.D. Dissertation. Notre Dame, IN: The Department of Sociology, Notre Dame University.

Swenson, Don (1990). "A Charismatic Church: A Cultural Analysis." Annual meeting of the Canadian Sociology and Anthropology Association, Victoria, May.

Swenson. Don (1995). "The Religious Bases of Marital Quality: A Study of Ministers and their Spouses." Paper presented in the Religion and Family Section at the annual meeting of the National Council of Family Relations, Portland, Oregon, November.

Swenson, Don (1996a). "Religion and Sex: An Intimate Connection?" Paper presented in the Religion and Family Section at the annual meeting of the National Council of Family Relations, Kansas City, Kansas, November.

Swenson, Don (1996b). "A Theory of the Religion and Family Connection." *Family Science Review* 9:133-151.

Swenson, Don (1997). "Religion and Family Linkages from a Model Definition of Religion." Paper presented in the Religion and Family Section at the annual meeting of the National Council of Family Relations, Crystal City, Virginia, November.

Swenson, Don (1998). "Religious Differences Between Married and Celibate Clergy: Does Celibacy make a Difference?" *Sociology of Religion* 59:37-43.

Swenson, Don and John Thompson (1986). "*Locus theologicus* and constructing a sacred past: Charismatic Renewal among Catholics as a movement of renewal." Paper presented at the Annual Meeting of the Canadian Association of Sociology and Anthropology, Winnipeg, Manitoba, June.

Swenson, Don, Lyle Larson, Walter Goltz, Irwin Barker, Melanie Driedger, Terry LeBlanc, and Brian Rennick (1994). *Roman Catholic Priests, Evangelical Clergy, and Clergy Families in Canada.* Markham, ON: Evangelical Fellowship of Canada.

Thomas, Darwin (1988). *The Religion and the Family Connection.* Provo, UT: Brigham Young University.

Thomas, Lewis (1977). *William Aberhart and Social Credit in Alberta.* Vancouver: Copp Clark Publishers.

Thomas, William I. (1923). *The Unadjusted Girl.* Boston: Little and Brown.

Thompson, Edward P. (1980). *The Making of the English Working Class.* New York: Penguin.

Thompson, John (1976). "Social Processes Related to Revivifying Religious Forms Within an Institutional Context: A Case Study of Charismatic Renewal among Roman Catholics in Southern California." Unpublished Ph.D. Dissertation. Santa Barbara: The University of California.

Tilley, Terrence. (1994). "The Institutional Element in Religious Experience." *Modern Theology* 10:185-212.

Time (1995). "The Message of Miracles." April 10:38-45.

Tipton, Steven (1982). *Getting Saved From the Sixties.* Berkeley: University of California Press.

Todd, Richard (1979). "The Fall of the Roman Empire." In Tim Dowley (ed.). *Eerdman's Handbook of the History of Christianity* (pp. 179-203). Grand Rapids, MI: Wm. B. Eerdmans.

Troeltsch, Ernest (1931). *The Social Teachings of the Christian Churches.* Vols I and II. New York: Harper and Row.

419

Troost, Kay, and Erik Filsinger (1993). "Emerging Biosocial Perspectives on the Family." In Pauline Boss, William J. Doherty, Ralph LaRossa, Walter R. Schuum, and Suzanne Steinmetz (eds.). *Sourcebook of Family Theories and Methods* (pp. 677-710). New York: Plenum.

Turner, Victor (1967). *The Forest of Symbols: Aspects of Ndembu Ritual.* Ithaca, NY: Cornell University Press.

Tyler, Edward (1929). *Primitive Culture.* New York: Brentano.

United States Catholic Conference (1994). *Catechism of the Catholic Church.* Washington, DC: United States Catholic Conference.

Van der Leeuw, Gerundus (1938). *Religion in Essence and Manifestation.* London: Allen & Unwin.

Van Doren, Charles (1991). *A History of Knowledge: Past, Present, and Future.* New York: Ballantine Books.

Van Gennep, Arnold (1960) [1908]. *The Rites of Passage.* Chicago: University of Chicago Press.

Vilarino, Jose, and Jose Sequeiros Tizon (1998). "The Demographic Transition of the Catholic Priesthood and the End of Clericalism in Spain." *Sociology of Religion* 59:25-35.

Wach, Joachim (1967) [1944]. *Sociology of Religion.* Chicago: University of Chicago Press.

Wald, Kenneth (1987). *Religion and Politics in the United States.* New York: St. Martin's Press.

Wallace, Anthony (1966). *Religion: An Anthropological View.* New York: Random House.

Wallace, Ruth (1991). "Women Administrators of Priestless Parishes: Constraints and Opportunities." *Review of Religious Research* 32:289-304.

Wallace, Ruth (1992). *They Call her Pastor: A New Role for Catholic Women.* Albany, NY: State University of New York Press.

Wallace, Ruth, and Alison Wolf (1995, fourth ed.). *Contemporary Sociological Theory: Continuing the Classical Tradition.* Englewood Cliffs, NJ: Prentice-Hall.

Warner, R. Stephen (1993). "Work in Progress toward a New Paradigm for the Sociological Study of Religion in the United States." *American Journal of Sociology* 98:1044-1093.

Warner, W. Lloyd, and Paul Lunt (1941). *The Social Life of a Modern Community.* New Haven: Yale University Press.

Watts, Allan W. (1954). *Myth and Ritual in Christianity.* New York: Thomas and Hudson.

Waugh, Earle (1992). "A Muslim Congregation in the Canadian North: The Ummah of Lac La Biche." In James Lewis and James Wind (eds.). *The Congregation in the American Life. Vol 1 of the Congregational History Project.* Chicago: University of Chicago Press.

Weber, Max (1946) [1906]. "Protestant Sects and the Spirit of Capitalism." In Hans H. Garth and C. Wright Mills (eds.). *From Max Weber* (pp. 302-322). New York: Oxford University Press.

Weber, Max (1947). *The Theory of Social and Economic Organization.* New York: Free Press.

Weber, Max (1951) [1916]. *The Religion of China: Confucianism and Taoism.* New York: Free Press.

Weber, Max (1952) [1917-1918]. *Ancient Judaism.* New York: Free Press.

Weber, Max (1958a) [1904-1905]. *The Protestant Ethic and the Spirit of Capitalism.* New York: Charles Scribner and Sons.

Weber, Max (1958b) [1916]. *The Religion of India.* New York: Free Press.

Weber, Max (1963) [1922]. *The Sociology of Religion.* Boston: Beacon Press.

Weber, Max (1976) [1909]. *The Agrarian Sociology of Ancient Civilizations.* London: New Left Books.

Weber, Max (1978). *Max Weber. Selections in Translation*. W. G. Runciman (ed.). Cambridge: Cambridge University Press.

Weber, Max (1978) [1894]. *Economy and Society.* Berkeley: University of California Press.

Weber, Max (1995) [1916]. "The Social Psychology of the World Religions." In Steve Bruce (ed.). *The Sociology of Religion. Volumes I and II. The International Library of Critical Writings in Sociology* (pp. 13-47). Aldeshot, UK: An Angar Reference Collection.

Webster's Illustrated Encyclopaedic Dictionary (1990). Montreal: Tormount Publications.

Wei-Ming, Tu (1984). "On Neo-Confucianism and Human Relatedness." In George A. De Vos and Takao Sofue (eds.). *Religion and the Family in East Asia* (pp. 111-125). Berkeley: The University of California Press.

Weisman, Richard (1984). *Witchcraft, Magic, and Religion in 17th-Century Massachusetts.* Amherst: The University of Massachusetts Press.

Weiss Ozorak, Elizabeth (1996). "The Power, but not the Glory: How Women Empower Themselves through Religion." *Journal for the Scientific Study of Religion* 35:17-29.

Wenger, John (ed.) (1956). *The Complete Writings of Menno Simons.* Scottdale, PA: Herald Press.

Westhues, Kenneth (1976). "The Adaptation of the Roman Catholic Church in Canadian Society." In Stewart Crysdale and Les Wheatcroft (eds.). *Religion in Canadian Society* (pp. 290-306). Toronto: Macmillan of Canada.

Westhues, Kenneth (1982). *First Sociology.* New York: McGraw-Hill.

Westley, Frances (1983). *The Complex Forms of The Religious Life. A Durkheimian View of New Religious Movements.* Chico, CA: Scholars Press.

Whimster, Steven and Scott Lash (1987). "Introduction." In Steven Whimster and Scott Lash (eds.). *Max Weber, Rationality, and Modernity* (pp. 1-31). Boston: Allen and Unwin.

Whitchurch, Gail, and Larry Constantine. (1993). "Systems Theory." In Pauline Boss, William Doherty, Ralph LaRossa, Walter Schumm, and Suzanne Steinmetz (eds.). *Sourcebook of Family Theories and Methods: A Contextual Approach* (pp. 325-352). New York: Plenum Press.

Whitley, Oliver R. (1964). *Religious Behaviour: When Sociology and Religion Meet.* Englewood Cliffs, NJ: Prentice Hall.

Williams, George. (1962). *The Radical Reformation.* Philadelphia: Westminister Press.

Willits, Fern, and Donald Crider (1989). "Church Attendance and Traditional Religious Beliefs in Adolescence and Young Adulthood." *Review of Religious Research* 31:68-81.

Wilson, Bryan (1970). *Religious Sects.* Engelwood Cliffs, NJ: McGraw-Hill.

Wilson, Bryan (1976). *Contemporary Transformations of Religion.* London: Oxford University Press.

Wilson, Bryan. (1982). *Religion in Sociological Perspective.* New York: Oxford University Press.

Wilson, Bryan (1985). "Secularization: The Inherited Model." In Phil Hammond (ed.). *The Sacred in a Secular Age* (pp. 9-20). Berkeley: University of California Press.

Woodward, Kenneth L. (1976) "There is Life After Death." *McCall's* (August):97-98, 136-39.

Wuthnow, Robert (1976). "Recent Problem of Secularization: A Problem of Generations?" *American Sociological Review* 41:850-867.

421

Wuthnow, Robert (1987). *Meaning and Moral Order: Explorations in Cultural Analysis*. Berkeley: The University of California Press.

Wuthnow, Robert (1988a). *The Restructuring of American Religion*. Princeton, NJ: Princeton University Press.

Wuthnow, Robert (1988b). "Sociology of Religion." In Neil Smelser (ed.). *Handbook of Sociology* (pp. 473-509). Newbury Park: Sage Publications.

Wuthnow, Robert (1989). *Communities of Discourse, Ideology, and Social Structure in the Reformation, the Enlightenment, and European Socialism*. Cambridge, MA: Harvard University Press.

Wuthnow, Robert (1993). *Christianity in the 21ˢᵗ Century: Reflections on the Challenges Ahead*. New York: Oxford University Press.

Wuthnow, Robert (1996). *Sharing the Journey: Support Groups and America's New Quest for Community*. New York: Free Press.

Wuthnow, Robert, James Davison Hunter, Albert Bergesen, and Edith Kurzweil (1984). *Cultural Analysis: The Work of Peter Berger, Mary Douglas, Michel Foucault, and Jurgen Habermas*. London: Routledge and Kegan Paul.

Wuthnow, Robert, and Marsha Witten. (1988). "New Directions in the Study of Culture." *Annual Review of Sociology* 14: 49-67.

Yamane, David (1998a). "Experience." In William Swatos, Jr. (ed.). *Encyclopedia of Religion and Society* (pp. 179-182). Walnut Creek, CA: Altamira Press.

Yamane, David (1998b). "Spirituality." In William Swatos, Jr. (ed.). *Encyclopedia of Religion and Society* (p. 492). Walnut Creek, CA: Altamira Press.

Yamane, David, and Megan Polzer. (1992). "Ecstasy and Religious Organization: A Cultural-Linguistic View." Paper presented at the Annual Meetings of the Association for the Sociology of Religion. Pittsburgh, PA.

Yinger, Milton (1959). *Religion, Society and the Individual*. New York: Macmillan.

Yinger, Milton (1970). *The Scientific Study of Religion*. New York: Macmillan.

Yoder, John, and Alan Kreider (1979). "Anabaptism." In Tim Dowley (ed.). *Eerdman's Handbook of the History of Christianity* (pp. 399-403). Grand Rapids, MI: Wm. B. Eerdmans.

Zinnbauer, Brian, Kenneth Pargament, Brenda Cole, Mark Rye, Eric Butter, Timothy Belavich, Kathleen Hipp, Allie Scott, and Jill Kadar (1997). "Religion and Spirituality: Unfuzzying the Fuzzy." *Journal for the Scientific Study of Religion* 36:549-564.

Index

430